DRUCKER'S LOST ART
OF
MANAGEMENT

PETER DRUCKER'S TIMELESS VISION
FOR BUILDING EFFECTIVE ORGANIZATIONS

JOSEPH A. MACIARIELLO
KAREN E. LINKLETTER

New York Chicago San Francisco Lisbon London Madrid Mexico City
Milan New Delhi San Juan Seoul Singapore Sydney Toronto

Copyright © 2011 by Joseph A. Maciariello and Karen E. Linkletter. All rights reserved. Printed in the United States of America. Except as permitted under the United States Copyright Act of 1976, no part of this publication may be reproduced or distributed in any form or by any means, or stored in a data base or retrieval system, without the prior written permission of the publisher.

1 2 3 4 5 6 7 8 9 0   QFR/QFR   1 6 5 4 3 2 1

ISBN   978-0-07-176581-7   (print book)
MHID   0-07-176581-6

ISBN   978-0-07-176748-4   (e-book)
MHID   0-07-176748-7

This publication is designed to provide accurate and authoritative information in regard to the subject matter covered. It is sold with the understanding that neither the author nor the publisher is engaged in rendering legal, accounting, securities trading, or other professional services. If legal advice or other expert assistance is required, the services of a competent professional person should be sought.
    —*From a Declaration of Principles Jointly Adopted by a Committee of the American Bar Association and a Committee of Publishers and Associations*

Library of Congress Cataloging-in-Publication Data

Maciariello, Joseph A.
    Drucker's lost art of management : Peter Drucker's timeless vision for building effective organizations / by Joseph A. Maciariello, Karen E. Linkletter.
        p.   cm.
    Includes bibliographical references and index.
    ISBN 978-0-07-176581-7 (alk. paper)
    1. Management.   2. Social ecology.   3. Leadership.   4. Drucker, Peter F. (Peter Ferdinand), 1909-2005.   I. Linkletter, Karen E.   II. Title.

    HD31.M28134   2011
    658—dc22   2010047473

McGraw-Hill books are available at special quantity discounts to use as premiums and sales promotions or for use in corporate training programs. To contact a representative, please e-mail us at bulksales@mcgraw-hill.com.

This book is printed on acid-free paper.

CONTENTS

PREFACE

This book represents the union of two very different approaches to the study of management. One author is a professor of management, with expertise in management systems, cost management, and project management. The other is a historian. What the authors have in common, however, is that both personally knew Peter Drucker, and have studied his work intensively.

This shared interest in Drucker's work was the origin of this book. As we conducted our research independently, it became clear that Drucker's vision of management required a deep understanding of the humanities and its goals. Drucker himself called management a "liberal art," linking it directly to the humanities disciplines. What we have attempted to do in this book is to discern what Drucker meant by "management as a liberal art," and to ground that concept in historical context and practice. It is our belief that, practiced in keeping with Drucker's vision, management as a liberal art may offer hope for a more humanitarian, moral society.

Chapters 1 through 3 define the discipline of management as a liberal art. Chapter 1 focuses on the ways in which various disciplines in the liberal arts influenced Drucker's management ideas. Drucker envisioned a moral society of functioning institutions, and his studies in theology, philosophy, political theory, and economics informed his management writings. In Chapter 2, we discuss the historical connection between management education and the liberal arts, and the price that has been paid for cutting that tie. Chapter 3 contains a discussion of management as a liberal art's contributions to both the liberal arts and management. Because Drucker's management philosophy was so driven by ethics and the idea of virtue, we address the questions of values, character, and ethics that are raised by management as a liberal art. Just as a liberal arts education historically emphasized creating people of virtue, management as a liberal art must also deal with these concepts.

The remaining chapters deal with four major topics for putting management as a liberal art into practice—federalism (Chapter 4), the human dimension (Chapter 5), leadership (Chapter 6), and social ecology (Chapters 7 and 8). The book does not address specific functional areas of management such as marketing, operations, accounting, finance, and information technology. Nor does it contain a detailed study of the disciplines that comprise the liberal arts. Instead, it presents new ways of thinking about both the liberal arts and the practice of management by weaving the two together in these four major topics. In the chapter on federalism, we show how political philosophy can have applications to modern organizations. In Chapter 5, we draw on religious and Enlightenment theories to discuss the need for a framework for conceptualizing the nature of human existence. Drawing on American history, we use Abraham Lincoln as a case study to illustrate Drucker's notion of effective leadership in Chapter 6. Finally, we include discussions of sociology, economics, and management theorists to evaluate the function of the social ecologist in Chapters 7 and 8.

Drucker identified the Federalist Papers, and by inference federalism, as a "lasting contribution America has made to Western thought" (Drucker, 1954, p. 280). The arguments made by Federalists and Anti-Federalists during the process of ratifying the Constitution of the United States dealt with difficulties and trade-offs involved in the design of structure and policies for all human organizations. These difficulties, trade-offs, and solutions to ongoing challenges posed by questions of the appropriate distribution of power and design of organization structures are topics considered in Chapter 4.

Organizations are made up of human beings who, while capable of behaving like angels, often insist on behaving perversely. The primary task of management as a liberal art is to provide leadership for human beings to help them fulfill the mission of the organization. The characteristics of human beings at work are topics taken up in Chapter 5. The closely related topic of providing executive leadership to achieve the mission of an organization is the topic of Chapter 6.

Finally, Drucker called himself a social ecologist. The work of a social ecologist is to create and maintain a society of functioning organizations. Doing so requires the social ecologist to anticipate discontinuities in society and to manage them through processes that provide for both continuity and change. The practice of social ecology is, in essence, the practice of management as a liberal art for producing a society of organizations that perform according to their missions.

ACKNOWLEDGMENTS

We are indebted to The Peter F. Drucker Literary Trust for their permission to use the "Peter F. Drucker" trademark in this publication. C. William Pollard, Chairman Emeritus, The ServiceMaster Company, provided the vision and financial support to carry out this project from its inception. We thank Rick Wartzman, Executive Director of The Drucker Institute, for his oversight of this Drucker Institute research project leading to the publication of the book. Zach First, Director of the Drucker Institute, helped us to organize the professional activity associated with advancing the ideas contained in this book. John Peters, Chief Executive of Emerald Group

Publishing Ltd., formulated policies for Emerald authors that permitted adaptation of our previously published work in an Emerald journal associated with the Drucker Symposium in Vienna, Austria, on November 19–20, 2009.

Steve Hanselman, founder and President of LevelFiveMedia, LLC, helped us to position this book. Knox Huston, our editor at McGraw-Hill, supported us at every step of the way during the publication process. It was a pleasure to work with Pattie Amoroso, Senior Editing Supervisor at McGraw-Hill, along with the entire production staff associated with this book. In addition, we are grateful to Professor Jenny Darroch of the Peter F. Drucker and Masatoshi Ito Graduate School of Management at Claremont Graduate University for her encouraging feedback on an early draft of this book. Bernadette Lambeth of The Drucker School assisted both of us during this project and we are very grateful to her. Emily Trent helped us organize a "Drucker knowledge base" that proved useful to us during the past two years. Emily has our thanks.

Karen would like to thank her husband, George, for his patience. And she would like to thank her surgeons, oncologist, and many friends for supporting her through a difficult time while simultaneously working with Joe on this labor of love.

Joe would like to thank Bob Buford and Shao Ming Lo for supporting his research program during these past two years. He also would like to thank his fellowship group at the Claremont Colleges for their friendship and prayers during this time. Finally, he would like to express his love and appreciation to his wife, Judy, who absorbed all family responsibilities as he worked with Karen on this project.

INTRODUCTION

We do not know yet precisely how to link the liberal arts and management. We do not know yet what impact this linkage will have on either party—and marriages, even bad ones, always change both partners.

—*Drucker, "Teaching the Work of Management"*

In the wake of the global financial crisis that began in late 2008, corporate governance has come under substantial fire in the media and public square. Government bailouts of corporations, exorbitant CEO salaries in the midst of high unemployment and outsourcing of jobs, allegations of unethical or illegal business practices—it seems clear to the American public that corporate leaders have lost any sense of moral values or ethics that they once may have had.

What has gone wrong with America's managerial class? A host of books and articles have been published recently that have offered various answers, from Jim Wallis's *Rediscovering Values: On Wall Street, Main Street, and Your Street* (2010) to Jonathan Tasini's *The*

Audacity of Greed: Free Markets, Corporate Thieves and the Looting of America (2009).

Have we trained our managers incorrectly? Or, as Wallis argues, have we as a society lost our sense of right and wrong? Is Tasini correct in blaming America's worship of the free market system? There is certainly no shortage of explanations for what ails the economy and the state of organizational leadership.

Peter Drucker devoted his life to providing managers with guidance so that they could be as effective as possible. He had much to say about the role of power in organizations, as well as the selection and training of effective executives. But his most pressing concern was that organizations concern themselves with people; organizations must provide human beings with status, function, and a sense of community and purpose. Viewed in this context, the management of people within organizations involves an understanding of human nature and cultural or communal values and morals—in Drucker's words, with questions of "Good and Evil" (Drucker, 1988, p. 5).

Although most businesses have some sort of ethics code in their mission statements, matters of "good and evil" are perceived as best left to the realm of theology or philosophy—not the boardroom. Yet Drucker insisted on the need for values in organizations. Given the state of the image of business in the public's eyes, perhaps it would help to at least raise a question: what do managers and executives value, and why? If organizations are about human beings, from where do those human beings derive their values?

One way to begin to address this subject is to take seriously Drucker's statement that management is a liberal art. Although he never fully defined this concept, it is clear that he envisioned a linkage between the liberal arts tradition inherited from Greek and Roman civilizations and the pragmatic, day-to-day operations of an organization.

One crucial element that links the liberal arts and management is the fostering and maintenance of cultural values. Historically, liberal arts training emphasized the cultivation of beliefs, behaviors, and opinions thought to be of high moral quality (good or right) in a given civilization. If management is, as Drucker said, a liberal art, then it must similarly involve the development of shared codes of conduct and beliefs within an organization. The practical implications of management as a liberal art for today's organizations are far-reaching, and may indeed provide a new blueprint for redeeming corporate America's reputation.

THE LIBERAL ARTS: AN HISTORIC TRADITION

The term "liberal art" stems from the concept of the "liberal arts," which has a long history. Although the Latin term *artes liberales* was derived from the Greeks, the Romans, notably Cicero, used it beginning around the first century BCE. The definition of a liberal art was a skill or craft practiced by a free citizen with time and means for study, a member of the elite, ruling classes of society. Liberal arts training, then, meant training citizens to be society's leaders. As such, the ideals of an *artes liberales* education were to instill standards of conduct and character, knowledge and mastery of a body of texts, a respect for societal values and standards, and an appreciation for knowledge and truth.

The content of a liberal arts education changed along with the times, as first the Christian Church and then secular universities adapted the curriculum to meet their needs. However, the emphasis on the values of antiquity and transmission of moral values in order to refine the human being remained at the core of the liberal arts ideal.

In the United States, religious liberal arts colleges, and later large research universities modeled after their European predecessors, again modified their programs, but even the earliest professional business schools assumed that their students would have received some form of liberal arts training in order to foster "character development" or instill moral values.

Therefore, while there certainly has never been one single liberal arts curriculum, what *is* constant is the attempt to inculcate a set of agreed-upon values or cultural beliefs. The values and beliefs change over time, but the overarching goal does not. Ultimately, the *artes liberales* and its various iterations strive to define what is good, right, and just in a given society or culture. As the tradition has shifted its context from pagan to Christian to today's secular society, the ideal of instilling shared values remains, but has become increasingly complex. In a diverse society, what constitutes "right" and "good"? Who or what defines it? Where one locates these values is an important question. To wrestle with this question is to wrestle with the legitimacy and universality of certain values. Ultimately, it involves addressing larger theological or philosophical issues: Drucker's concern with "Good and Evil."

Such big-picture questions are not confined to the ivory tower; the overwhelming success of Rick Warren's book *The Purpose Driven Life* (2002) indicates there is a global search for answers to some of life's most important questions, such as "why am I here?" and "what is my purpose?" Instilling a liberal arts mentality, then, involves an ever-shifting search for the best way to foster values based on tradition, even though that tradition may morph through time. It is to take seriously the counsel of Socrates to examine one's life, for "the unexamined life is not worth living."

Today, the *artes liberales* are widely proclaimed as irrelevant to American society and education. The past goals of liberal arts training seem elitist, culturally insensitive, and totally impractical for today's cadre of up-and-coming executives and professionals, not to mention mid-level managers or entrepreneurs. Liberal arts colleges have radically revamped their curriculum, entrance requirements, and attitude to try to survive, economically as much as culturally. Yet there is much evidence to support the view that the erosion of the liberal arts is in part responsible for our current climate of greed and profit at any cost.

In his book *From Higher Aims to Hired Hands*, Rakesh Khurana argues that the business schools' recent emphasis on maximization of shareholder value as the sole measure of organizational success has demoted professional managers to nothing more than "hired hands." With no responsibilities to anything other than themselves, these hired guns lack any sense of a greater moral, social, or ethical obligation to society or the organizations that employ them.

In the revised edition of *Management,* Peter Drucker, a thinker always ahead of his time, called management a liberal art:

> Management is thus what tradition used to call a liberal art: "liberal" because it deals with the fundamentals of knowledge, self knowledge, wisdom, and leadership; "art" because it is practice and application. Managers [should] draw on all the knowledge and insights of the humanities and the social sciences—on psychology and philosophy, on economics and history, on ethics as well as on the physical sciences. But they have to focus this knowledge on effectiveness and results—on healing a sick patient, teaching a student, building a bridge, designing and selling a "user friendly" software program. (Drucker, 2008, p. 25)

Drucker believed that management would be the key to keeping the liberal arts sentiment alive in today's society. He saw an important relationship between the two forms of training. The liberal arts can bring wisdom and self-knowledge to the practice of management, while management can "be the discipline and the practice through and in which the 'humanities' will again acquire recognition, impact, and relevance" (Drucker, 2008, p. 25). And practicing management as a liberal art might, in fact, return management to its original, intended professional status.

APPLYING MANAGEMENT AS A LIBERAL ART FOR TODAY'S EXECUTIVES

If Peter Drucker was right about management being a liberal art, management must return to the original ideals of liberal arts education that were fundamental to the concept of professionalism in business, and to Drucker's concept of "The Educated Person." The difficulty in implementing management as a liberal art lies in the perceived dichotomy between the "ivory tower" of academia and the "real world" of business. The history of the liberal arts tradition involved training for the "real world" of politics, law, medicine, and religious leadership. Reconciling the classical *artes liberales* with the everyday world has a long tradition in America, from the Puritan colonists' use of Harvard to train community leaders through the founding fathers' desire for republican virtue in those chosen to govern.

One of the keys is to reconnect the liberal arts and management, restoring a union that once existed. *The connection between the goals of the liberal arts and practicing professionals may have been lost, but it can be restored.* In Drucker's view, it was the liberal arts' responsibility to "demonstrate and to embody values, to create vision . . . [and] to lead" (Drucker, 1994, p. 63). Management as a liberal art would require practitioners to do the same.

In Chapters 1 to 3 of this book, we lay out the intellectual framework for Drucker's idea of management as a liberal art, followed by a discussion of how management and the liberal arts were once connected but have become divided. We complete this section with an overview of the potential contributions of management as a liberal art, as well as some caveats regarding what management as a liberal art is not.

In the second part of the text, we illustrate management as a liberal art in practice, concentrating on five primary issues confronting practitioners: the use and abuse of power within organizations (and by organizations in society); the nature of human existence and its implications for management; leadership; "social ecology," or the process of observing various external and internal factors for potential threats and opportunities; and the role of innovation and technology. In each chapter dealing with these topics, we show how a specific discipline in the liberal arts can enhance the performance of management practitioners through providing a different perspective, a new prism through which to view problems, or an enriched sense of the responsibilities of managers.

Why management as a liberal art now? There are many examples within these pages, but four specific instances of management failure provide substantial evidence of the need for management as a liberal art at this crucial moment in time. These four examples show, basically, how management as a liberal art in action has very real consequences for today's world.

Lessons of Power: Goldman Sachs as "Too Big to Fail"

Andrew Ross Sorkin's book *Too Big to Fail: The Inside Story of How Wall Street and Washington Fought to Save the Financial System—and Themselves* (2009) describes the global financial crisis that materialized in September 2008 in terms of concentration of power. As Sorkin argues, executives running a handful of America's financial institutions wielded sufficient power to derail the entire global financial system, and the federal government has done nothing to diffuse or curb that power. Nowhere is the role of concentrated, unchecked power more apparent than in the case of Goldman Sachs' role in the global financial crisis.

Goldman Sachs is one of the firms that received government aid under the Troubled Asset Relief Program (TARP) of 2008. The firm paid back the $10 billion in government loans in April 2009, and reported unexpectedly high profits of over $3 billion in the second quarter of the same year. Goldman Sachs' far-reaching power in the global financial markets was well known on Wall Street, but the TARP bailouts, along with a series of highly publicized articles by *Rolling Stone* investigative reporter Matthew Taibbi, put the investment bank's activities in the public limelight. In April 2010, U.S. federal prosecutors opened an inquiry into potential fraudulent activities at the firm. Specifically, the Securities and Exchange Commission (SEC) accused Goldman Sachs of selling investors mortgage derivatives that were selected and packaged with the help of a major hedge fund that was simultaneously betting on those securities failing. Goldman settled with the SEC in July 2010 by agreeing to pay a fine of $550 million without admitting wrongdoing (CNNMoney .com, 2010).

Goldman Sachs' record profits on both sides were in part due to its ability to leverage its extensive power. The firm reaped profits on both sides of the collateralized debt obligation (the mortgage derivative package known as Abacus). The firm capitalized on its retail and institutional relationships to play a role as both advocate and saboteur of an investment, reaping rewards in both positions. What is more worrisome, Goldman Sachs used its remarkable influence to assemble numerous complex deals involving derivative products, many of which have had significant effects on the global financial crisis. The firm's involvement in the Greek debt meltdown of 2010, which we discuss in this book, is only one example of how Goldman Sachs' behavior is a lesson in the need for recognizing the problem of unchecked power in organizations (Carney, February 15, 2010).

Drucker was keenly aware of this problem, and he saw political theory (specifically the concept of federalism) as a way of controlling power within organizations. Political science and theory, in the domain of the liberal arts, offer a host of opportunities for exploring the nature of power within organizations. The human propensity toward seeking and abusing power is the subject of much literature in the liberal arts, particularly those writings aimed at analyzing governmental institutions. Anyone who remembers reading Niccolo Machiavelli's *The Prince* knows that this 1513 work dealt with the subject of power (although most people probably think only in terms of the negative connotations of Machiavelli's argument: his justification of heavy-handed authoritarianism). An understanding of the liberal arts, specifically political theory, can add much to managers' understanding of contemporary problems related to the question of power. In this book, we focus on the concept of federalism as espoused by the proponents of the U.S. Constitution during the eighteenth century. Drucker identified federalism as an important concept that could be applied to modern industrial organizations; his illustration is an example of how one area of the liberal arts can help today's firms recognize the problem of unchecked power exemplified by Goldman Sachs and the global financial crisis.

Lessons of the Human Dimension: British Petroleum's Misplaced Values

On April 20, 2010, the Deepwater Horizon drilling rig of British Petroleum (BP), located in the Gulf of Mexico, exploded, killing 11 workers and unleashing the worst oil spill in U.S. history. By late May, several British Petroleum efforts to stop the leak from the wellhead had failed. Although the company began to recover the leaking oil in June, it was clear that the environmental devastation was substantial. News stories featured heartbreaking shots of oil-covered birds and ruined wildlife sanctuaries. The related economic and human costs mounted as well; fishermen in Louisiana lost their earnings potential, and southern coastal communities already hard hit by the recession faced a drastic decline in tourism. After months of effort to stop the leak, BP finally killed the well on September 19, 2010 (BP.com, 2010).

The environmental tragedy would have been difficult for any company to deal with, but BP's response to the event, as well as information that came to light as the disaster unfolded, signaled that the company's values were misplaced. BP estimates of the number of gallons being spilled per day proved to be significantly lower than what was actually leaking out of the wellhead; company officials stated that about 200,000 gallons per day were leaked, whereas independent scientists calculated the spill was closer to 500,000 to 1 million gallons per day. Early on, BP used a chemical dispersant to break up the oil; this dispersant has been shown to be toxic to shellfish, and there are concerns that the chemical caused adverse reactions among workers hired to assist in cleanup efforts (Cruz and Cart, 2010).

Perhaps most upsetting, however, was BP CEO Tony Hayward's reaction to the events. Hayward discounted the environmental impact of the spill as "very, very modest," remarked that the cleanup workers' illness was likely due to food poisoning rather than the chemical dispersant, and developed an advertisement in which he lamented that "I'd like my life back." These are hardly the reactions of a remorseful individual whose company was responsible for the worst environmental disaster in American history, and Hayward was subsequently fired as BP's CEO. What was worse than BP's response in the immediate aftermath of the spill was the fact that the company had reason to suspect there could be problems with the Deepwater Horizon rig. The company told congressional investigators that there were a number of "crucial mistakes" involved in the explosion and subsequent leak, including the decision to continue drilling in spite of the appearance of abnormalities in the well shortly before the debacle occurred (Power, 2010). BP appears to have a track record of ignoring the potential human and overall environmental costs of its activities; according to the Occupational Safety and Health Administration (OSHA), the firm has a "serious, systemic safety problem" (Morris and Pell, 2010).

The full extent of the BP mess remains to be seen, and there are many lessons to be gleaned from this terrible event. But it is clear that the oil spill illustrates the consequences of a lack of values. The pursuit of profits, in this case the extraction of resources from the earth, overrode any concern for the risks that activity posed for the natural environment. The price paid by human and other beings will be enormous—all because of the misplaced values of one organization.

Of all of the aspects of management as a liberal art, the human component was most important to Peter Drucker. This was in large part because of the strong Judeo-Christian underpinnings to Drucker's overall concept of management as a way to achieve a *moral* society comprised of institutions. For Drucker, management was a moral force, not merely a tool at the service of the amoral market. As a result, we emphasize the Judeo-Christian origins of Drucker's management ideas, drawing on the liberal arts disciplines of religious and moral philosophy. Other traditions in these liberal arts disciplines can help managers address questions related to human dignity, understand the broader implications of the operational decisions they make, and consider their obligations to something other than their own personal desires or the worldly demands of their organizations.

Drucker found in Confucian ethics fundamental guidelines for moral behavior that are appropriate for all stakeholders in an organization. These guidelines are

—clear definitions of the fundamental relationships [among all stakeholders];

—universal and general rules of conduct—that is, rules that are binding on any one person or organization, according to its rules, function and relationships;

And finally,
—an effective organization ethic, indeed an organization
ethic that deserves to be seriously considered as ethics, will
have to define right behavior as the behavior which opti-
mizes each party's benefits and thus makes the relationships harmonious, constructive, and mutually beneficial.
(Drucker, 1993, p. 213)

Clearly, Drucker's concept of management as a liberal art invokes
the historical emphasis on the search for the "good" and "right" in
life; it requires a definition of "right behavior." Incorporating the
wisdom of the discipline of philosophy into the practice of management may help to avoid future disasters such as the BP Deepwater
Horizon nightmare.

Lessons of Leadership: Toyota's Lack of Accountability

In October 2009, Toyota Motor Corporation issued a safety recall
of several of its cars following a wave of reports of "runaway vehicles," or cars that suddenly accelerated without warning. One outside
safety consulting firm documented 2,000 cases of unintended acceleration, which resulted in 16 deaths and 243 injuries. The problem
was not confined to a single model, but affected the company's popular Camry, Prius, Tacoma, and Tundra models, as well as several
vehicles in the Lexus line. News outlets carried harrowing stories of
those who had experienced the sudden acceleration problem (Rhee,
2009). Such news coverage tarnished the once-sterling reputation of
the auto manufacturer.

Toyota was renowned for producing quality cars, so the recall
was unusual in that it involved a company whose name was associated with reliability. Yet it was Toyota management's handling of the
recall and sudden acceleration problem that exacerbated the event
into a public relations nightmare for the company. The firm's execu-

tives failed to demonstrate effective leadership on a number of levels, from their initial reactions to the reports of acceleration problems to their handling of customer inquiries and needs.

Toyota's first response to the complaints about sudden acceleration in its vehicles was to tell customers to remove floor mats from their cars, claiming that the accelerator pedal could get stuck under drivers' side mats. In October 2009 the company recalled several car models to replace the floor mats, stating that this would solve the problem. But cars without floor mats continued to unexpectedly accelerate, and the government expressed its concern that the company had not addressed the problem. In January 2010 Toyota issued another recall, this time to replace the gas pedals, not just the floor mats. In this recall, the company acknowledged a separate problem related to the acceleration pedal itself: the gas pedal in many Toyota models had a tendency to stick and thus send the car speeding out of control.

In spite of the recalls, there were more cases of runaway Toyotas, leading some to speculate that the problem had to do with the automobiles' software-driven braking system. Toyota finally suspended all sales of the affected car models in January. According to the National Highway Traffic Safety Administration (NHTSA), there were more than 6,200 complaints related to sudden acceleration in Toyota cars from the year 2000 to mid-May 2010; these reports included 89 deaths, well more than previously reported (CBSNews.com, 2010).

In February 2010, the National Highway Traffic Safety Administration launched an investigation into the timing of Toyota's recall efforts to solve the runaway car problem. Based on that investigation, the U.S. Department of Transportation (DOT) found Toyota in violation of federal laws that protect consumers. Specifically, the NHTSA investigation revealed that Toyota was well aware of problems with the accelerator pedal on its cars long before it issued the recall. Furthermore, the company failed to notify the NHTSA of the problem within five days as required by federal law. The department levied the maximum financial penalties against Toyota for its violations, the largest civil penalty ever assessed by the NHTSA against a car company (U.S. Department of Transportation, 2010).

Toyota's management failed to exhibit leadership effectiveness and integrity on many levels. First of all, their failure to acknowledge the sticking accelerator problem in a timely and public manner (and notify federal authorities as required) gave the impression that they intended to hide a very real safety hazard. Leadership integrity involves not only taking responsibility for problems when they arise but also doing all one can to minimize any negative impacts of an organization's operations. As the government investigation showed, Toyota's executives were well aware of the sticking accelerator problem, yet they chose to delay action, placing the blame on floor mats and consumer behavior instead.

Secondly, customers often had no idea as to what to do to make their cars safe. Given the various explanations for the sudden acceleration problem provided by Toyota, dealers were often frustrated as to how to answer consumer questions. Once it acknowledged the gas pedal problem and issued the wider recall, Toyota had to fix its cars, but in fact it did not have a plan in place to repair the vehicles (Bunkley and Maynard, 2010).

Finally, because the sudden acceleration problem involved death and injury to human beings, the lackadaisical response of Toyota's leadership sent a message of indifference to the American public; whereas Toyota was once revered as a brand of quality, it now seemed just another greedy corporation bent on taking advantage of American consumers. Profits and growth clearly were more important to these leaders than a safe product and good service.

Akio Toyoda, grandson of Toyota's founder, appeared before the U.S. House of Representatives' Energy and Commerce Committee in February 2010. During this meeting, he stated that "quite frankly, I fear the pace at which we have grown may have been too quick," leading to sacrifices in quality (*MSNBC.com,* 2010).

Drucker believed that leadership required integrity and values, a focus on developing people, and emphasis on performance and results (although not just financial measures of performance). One of the best ways to study effective leadership is to analyze the qualities and actions of leaders themselves. The discipline of history can help practitioners to better understand leadership in action. Whether one analyzes the decisions of presidents, leaders of social protest movements, or effective executives of the past, historical research into leaders can provide a wealth of information for today's managers facing difficult decisions under trying circumstances. In Toyota's case, a passing understanding of the history of America's progressive movement, and how its leadership spawned significant government reforms of early twentieth-century industrial organizations, would have provided ample evidence for the need to address the runaway car problem early and transparently. Toyoda's remark indicates that the company's leaders lost focus on the important qualities inherent to effective leadership.

Lessons of Social Ecology/Innovation: Massey Coal's Failure to Adapt

On April 5, 2010, the Upper Big Branch coal mine in Montcoal, West Virginia, operated by Massey Energy Company, exploded. Early reports were that 25 men were killed, and rescue efforts targeted four missing workers. As anxious relatives and townspeople waited to hear news of the missing men, four days later, the rescue effort turned into a recovery operation, as there was no hope of finding the workers alive. The 29 deaths from the methane gas explosion made the Upper Big Branch mine disaster the worst U.S. coal accident in 40 years.

Coal mining is by nature a risk-filled endeavor. Much of the work of managing such an enterprise must involve an awareness of changes in the work environment, new technologies that might reduce risk, changes in industry trends that relate to worker safety, and other external or internal sources of opportunity, including changes in public perception. Drucker coined the term "social ecology" to describe the systematic evaluation of these factors. Along with failures in several other areas, Massey Energy lacked the insights of social ecology to see the warning signs leading up to the Upper Big Branch explosion.

Following the West Virginia tragedy, news sources reported that in the year before the explosion, Massey's Upper Branch mine had been cited numerous times for safety violations, including 38 ventilation violations and 37 complaints about flammable materials on the site. The Federal Bureau of Investigation (FBI) launched a criminal investigation of the company, addressing charges of negligence and rumors that Massey representatives had bribed federal mining agency inspection officials. Public outcry was strong when an October 19, 2005, memo penned by Massey CEO Don Blankenship revealed that the executive warned his mining supervisors to ignore any objective other than to "run coal" because "coal pays the bills" (Hamburger and Zajac, 2010).

Massey's safety record caused it problems before the Upper Branch mine disaster. In December 2008, a group of institutional shareholders filed a suit against Massey's board of directors, claiming that they had violated their fiduciary responsibility in part because they had overlooked safety problems that resulted in injury and death to workers. Although the suit was dismissed, it made public a great deal of information on the company, including the management philosophy and style of Blankenship. According to a number of sources, under Blankenship's direction, Massey Energy placed profitability above all else, including safety. In addition, Blankenship was well known for his extravagant personal lifestyle, supported by a lavish compensation package ("Coal Boss Don Blankenship Cast as Cavalier About Worker Safety in Lawsuits," 2010). With this "bottom-line" mentality permeating the company from the top down, Massey Energy was so focused on one aspect of its business—profits—that it failed to recognize a number of factors impacting its rather old-fashioned approach to its operations.

The most obvious oversight was Massey's emphasis on "running coal" at the expense of worker safety. The company's refusal to see the extent of the problems at the Upper Branch mine, in spite of the many violations and citations, is clear evidence of its inability to see a trend within its own operations: a dangerous work environment just waiting for a tragedy to occur. Massey's management also discounted mounting evidence of the environmental impacts of coal production and carbon emissions. At a 2008 mining industry meeting, Blankenship referred to reporters covering global climate change as "communists" and "atheists," and on several occasions he has referred to environmentalists as "greeniacs" (Boselovic, 2010). And, of course, Blankenship's extravagant CEO lifestyle and bloated compensation package could only draw the public's ire following the financial crisis of 2008 and the anger over the TARP bailouts; flaunting corporate wealth is not a good idea during a time of high unemployment, particularly when your company has just been involved in an accident that cost the lives of 29 of its workers. In December 2010, Blankenship announced his plans to retire at the end of the year (Maher and Chon, 2010).

Drucker's practice of social ecology requires that managers recognize that change is a constant; managers must always look out for discontinuities that serve as threats to or opportunities for their organization's activities. The social sciences are enormously helpful in identifying and understanding the nature of large-scale external changes that can potentially impact an organization. Economics can aid managers enormously, but not just in terms of understanding the financial aspects of an operation. The 2009 winners of the Nobel Prize in Economics illustrate how an understanding of contemporary (as well as classic) economics can serve today's managers. The 2009 Nobel Prize winners were Elinor Ostrom (Indiana University and Arizona State University) and Oliver Williamson (University of California, Berkeley). Ostrom and Williamson were recognized for their contributions to our understanding of relationships between firms and their external environments. Ostrom investigated the role of local entities in managing property, showing that there are options other than privatization and governmental control for managing natural resources. Williamson's work involved showing when organizations should leave decisions to market forces versus when managers should exercise control. Much modern economic theory involves the role of human decision making, and thus enables managers to assess their place within a larger socioeconomic and political context.

One wonders what might have happened had Massey's leadership brought an understanding of economics or another related liberal arts discipline to bear on its coal mining operations. Blankenship and others failed to realize that their business was not just "running coal"; it was also about managing the environmental and human costs of their operations, particularly in light of changing attitudes about energy production and use, and corporate responsibility.

Ironically, Massey Energy's tragedy at its West Virginia mine may itself serve as an impetus of change for the industry as a whole. Some have predicted that the disaster will result in new safety regulations, increased environmental restrictions, and more public scrutiny for the entire mining industry (Mulkern and Reis, 2010). If Massey had practiced a little social ecology, looking into its own operations as well as larger trends outside of itself, it might have eased the disruption of change that will likely affect this industry.

CONCLUSION

Drucker left it to others to define the implications of management as a liberal art. Given the historical context of the origins of the liberal arts, as well as the role of liberal arts and professional education in America, Drucker's idea of management as a liberal art involves rethinking not just how we educate managers but also how we approach management as a profession. By preparing students and managers in management as a liberal art, our society will expand the capacity of men and women to assume executive responsibility in a morally and socially constructive manner.

Peter Drucker was well known as an observer who tried to "see the future that has already happened." In a conversation with Bob Buford on August 10, 1993, he reflected on the condition of American civilization:

> I'm going to make myself very unpopular in two weeks in Aspen at the seminar where I am the keynote speaker, by saying we have no economic problems. We have only social problems. But, we have those in spades. This morning when I woke up at three in the morning, you have no idea, I had to pray very hard to get over that despair, and I haven't gotten over it yet. Yes, I know, and yet the very fact that we are conscious of it is probably the only optimistic thing. (Buford, 1993, p. 3)

In *Landmarks of Tomorrow* Drucker argues for human beings' need of spiritual values in order to shape culture. In Chapter 10, "The Human Situation Today," Drucker explores the question of where the human being fits in the postmodern world: "Man has achieved the knowledge to destroy himself both physically and morally" (Drucker, 1959/1996, p. 257). Specifically Drucker refers to advances in knowledge from the behavioral sciences that can "turn man into a biological machine run by manipulation of fears and emotions, a being without beliefs, without values, without principles, without compassion, without pride, without humanity altogether"

(Drucker, 1959/1996, p. 258). Drucker's solution is a return to spiritual values in order to guide the use of the power, created by new knowledge, to serve the highest interests of the human being.

Drucker was strongly influenced by his own liberal arts education, which led him to see these moral and spiritual dimensions of management and society. But is there corroborating empirical and historical evidence for his views? We believe there is. Robert W. Fogel, economic historian and 1993 winner of the Nobel Prize in Economics, believes the most pressing problem in the United States to be the acquisition and egalitarian distribution of *spiritual assets*, not material assets:

> Although the consolidation of past gains cannot be ignored, the future of egalitarianism in America turns on the nation's ability to combine continued economic growth with an entirely new set of egalitarian reforms that address the urgent spiritual needs of our age, secular as well as sacred. Spiritual (or immaterial) inequity is now as great a problem as material inequity, perhaps even greater. (Fogel, 2000, p. 1)

In *The Soul of Capitalism: Opening Paths to a Moral Economy*, journalist William Greider argues that American capitalism can be modified to "conform more faithfully to society's broad values," (Greider, 2004, p. 48), essentially tying the engine of economic growth to the goals of the liberal arts.

Sociologist Robert Wuthnow traces America's long history of attempting to reconcile religious values with economic growth, and points out that in today's society, "our problems as a nation are spiritual as well as material" (Wuthnow, 1994, p. 36). Drucker is not alone in his assessment of our need to consider moral and spiritual issues when operating in the world of management and business.

Ironically, a return to the ideals of the liberal arts may in fact make management once again valuable to the "real world." Fueled by corporate scandal and the behavior of out-of-touch executives who seem to have no moral compass, popular sentiment has turned against management as a profession; as evidenced by the four brief examples in this introduction, as well as the numerous other references in this book, it is clear that there is a call for change. Perhaps the only hope for redemption for management as a true profession is to practice management as a liberal art: to ground it in an understanding of shared cultural values that are inculcated through education and modeled through executive behavior.

CHAPTER 1

ORIGINS OF MANAGEMENT
AS A LIBERAL ART
IN PETER DRUCKER'S WRITINGS

The concept of management as a liberal art comes from Peter F. Drucker's writings.

Drucker stated that one of his most important contributions was that he "focused this discipline [management] on People and Power; on Values, Structure, and Constitution, *and above all*, on responsibilities—that is, focused the Discipline of Management on management as a truly liberal art" (Drucker, 2008, p. v). Drucker didn't define management as a liberal art very clearly, however. His earliest reference to management as a liberal art appears in 1988, when he said that "management is by itself a liberal art. It has to be. It cannot be techne [skill] alone. It cannot be concerned solely with results and performance" (Drucker, 1988, p. 5). Next, in his 1989 work *The New Realities,* he offered the following explanation of management as a liberal art:

Management is thus what tradition used to call a liberal art—"liberal" because it deals with the fundamentals of knowledge, self-knowledge, wisdom, and leadership; "art" because it is practice and application. Managers draw on all the knowledges and insights of the humanities and the social sciences—on psychology and philosophy, on economics and history, on the physical sciences and ethics. But they have to focus this knowledge on effectiveness and results—on healing a sick patient, teaching a student, building a bridge, designing and selling a "user-friendly" software program. (Drucker, 1989, p. 231)

In Drucker's view, management as a liberal art draws on a tradition of knowledge and education. This tradition is a form of self-development that is loosely defined as the liberal arts tradition. While this tradition and its history will be explored at length in the next chapter, in essence, a liberal arts education usually emphasizes broad training in the humanities, science, mathematics, and the arts. Although the end goal of studying the liberal arts has varied throughout time and across cultures, there is usually some mention of instilling values, developing character or good citizens, and nurturing broadly applicable skills, such as critical thinking and analysis. In many respects, a liberal arts education defines itself by what it is not: vocational training. Liberal arts colleges often emphasize the fact that their curriculum is aimed at answering higher moral questions of life, not preparing undergraduates for specific careers.[1] Drucker's concept of management as a liberal art echoes this ideal: that knowledge should deliver wisdom and be guided by matters of morality. However, management as a liberal art is also about practice and application, the pragmatic use of knowledge. Management as a liberal art involves applying the wisdom and moral lessons of the liberal arts to everyday questions of work, school, and society.

By its very nature, management as a liberal art involves the synthesis of many disciplines, including theology, political science, sociology and economics, philosophy, management theory, psychology, and what Drucker termed social ecology. Following an overview of

Drucker's life and work on management, we turn to an analysis of several individuals who shaped his vision of management as a liberal art. Such a discussion allows us to begin to understand how specific knowledge in the liberal arts and management can be brought to bear on matters of problem solving and human development.

DRUCKER'S MISSION: A FUNCTIONING SOCIETY OF INSTITUTIONS

The term *management* is all too often associated only with the private sector. Many people think of Peter Drucker as a writer on business management alone, whose sole customer was the corporate executive. In reality, Drucker's mission was much larger, encompassing questions of the nature of humankind, good and evil, and meaningful existence. This philosophical, theological, and moral component of Drucker's work is too often lost in spite of the fact that Drucker himself often noted its existence:

> Management always lives, works, and practices in and for an institution, which is a human community held together by the bond that, next to the tie of family, is the most powerful human bond: the work bond. And precisely because the object of management is a human community held together by the work bond for a common purpose, management always deals with the Nature of Man, and (as all of us with any practical experience learned) with Good and Evil as well. I have learned more theology as a practicing management consultant than I did when I taught religion. (Drucker, 1988, p. 5)

Drucker believed that, because human beings are always the subject of management, the practice of management must aim to create and maintain healthy organizations in which people can find meaningful existence. Because management deals with human beings,

Drucker believed that managers must also be able to address not just questions of efficiency and profitability but also larger, more philosophical questions of morality, spirituality, emotional well-being, and dignity.

Drucker's human-centered view of management derived in part from his own background. Born in Vienna in 1909, Drucker was raised in a middle-class home. His father, Adolph, was a government official and economist. His mother, Caroline, was a talented musician who studied medicine. Regular guests at the Drucker home included composers, economists, philosophers, poets, and other intellectuals.

Drucker moved to Hamburg at age 18, and he later studied international law at Frankfurt University while working as a securities analyst. In 1929, he took a position as a financial writer for the *Frankfurter General-Anzeiger*, where he eventually became an editor covering politics and foreign and economic news. When the Nazis came to power in 1933, Drucker left for London and worked there as an economist with a bank. He landed a job as foreign correspondent for several British newspapers, emigrated to America in 1937, and launched what would become a successful writing career.

In 1939, Drucker published *The End of Economic Man*, in which he attempted to explain the rise of Nazi totalitarianism (as well as Stalinist Russia). Drucker argued that totalitarianism was the result of the failure of both capitalism and Marxism to deliver on their promises of economic equality. Drucker described a situation in which entire societies had placed their faith in the ideologies of capitalism and Marxism and the ability of those ideologies to provide economic equality and freedom. However, high inflation and unemployment in Western Europe after World War I revealed that neither of these "secular creeds," as Drucker refers to them, could solve the terrible problems facing Germany and other countries (Drucker, 1939, p. xix). The idea of "Economic man," the human defined by his worth through the promise of material prosperity (capitalism) or economic equality (Marxism), was no longer relevant. As a result, "in despair the masses turn to the magician who promises to make the impossible possible" (Drucker, 1939, p. 22). When rational systems fail, irrational promises begin to hold out some hope for meaningful existence. Thus, Europe embraced a new faith in dictatorship: Hitler in Germany, Stalin in Russia, and Mussolini in Italy. "Heroic Man" replaced "Economic Man"; this new "man" was characterized by "his preparedness to sacrifice himself, his self-discipline, his self-abnegation, and his 'inner equality'—all independent of his economic status" (Drucker, 1939, p. 137).

Drucker concluded that the only way to avoid irrational solutions such as totalitarianism was to create a functioning society based on freedom and equality, but not solely defined in economic terms:

> The new society which will ultimately arise out of the collapse of the society of Economic Man will again try to realize freedom and equality. Though we do not yet know which sphere will become socially constitutive in the order of the future, we do know that it will not be the economic sphere, which has ceased to be valid. This means that the new order will be able to realize economic equality. For if every European order by virtue of its foundation on the Christian basis seeks to realize freedom and equality, it also seeks this realization in that sphere which it holds to be socially constitutive. Freedom and equality cannot be realized, they can only be promised in that sphere. . . . Economic equality will equally become possible when it has ceased to be socially all-important and when freedom and equality in a new sphere will be the promise of a new order. (Drucker, 1939, p. 240)

Although Drucker described the limitations of defining human existence solely in economic terms, he had yet to identify the new "sphere" that would constitute a valid source of freedom and equality. Gradually, Drucker began to pinpoint the modern industrial corporation as the potential source of individual meaning and status in society. In his 1942 book, *The Future of Industrial Man*, and his later works *The Concept of the Corporation* (1946) and *The New Society* (1950), Drucker developed his argument that employment within the modern industrial corporation could offer people status and meaning that was not based simply on economic worth. The modern corporation could offer a sense of community and citizenship while still providing dignity and respect for the individual. He saw that the mass-production workplace focused around the assembly line was dehumanizing to the employee. Like Charlie Chaplin's factory worker in the film *Modern Times*, the industrial worker was merely "standardized, freely interchangeable, atomic labor without status, without function, without individuality" (Drucker, 1942, p. 84). Such a view of labor would not allow for a functioning society:

No society can function as a society unless it gives the individual member social status and function, and unless the decisive social power is legitimate power. The former establishes the basic frame of social life: the purpose and meaning of society. The latter shapes the space within the frame: it makes society concrete and creates its institutions. If the individual is not given social status and function, there can be no society but only a mass of social atoms flying through space without aim or purpose. And unless power is legitimate there can be no social fabric; there is only social vacuum held together by mere slavery or inertia. (Drucker, 1942, p. 28)

In *The Future of Industrial Man*, Drucker set forth a fundamental principle behind much of his writings: the modern corporation was the representative social institution, and its management was "the decisive and representative power in the industrial system" (Drucker, 1942, p. 60). In doing so, he also established the two primary questions he needed to answer in order to develop a model of a functioning society: How could individuals find noneconomic status and function in such a social institution, and what would legitimize the power behind the modern industrial corporation? In Drucker's eyes, the only alternative to totalitarianism or socialist revolution was a healthy industrial society, and the only country poised to develop such a society in 1942 was the United States.

In *The Concept of the Corporation*, Drucker analyzed General Motors in terms of its role as a social institution, addressing the key questions he raised in his earlier work. He began to specifically detail how industrial organizations could provide noneconomic meaning to individuals, and how managerial power could be made legitimate within American society. Although one part of the book focuses on the internal operations and structure of General Motors, the other two sections emphasize the connections between the corporation and society. Here and in *The New Society*, Drucker argued that organizations needed to reflect the same values that are embraced by American society, particularly the promise of equal opportunity and individual status and fulfillment. If the "American creed" of a middle-class meritocracy is not reflected in the corporation, then that institution will not survive:

> Industrial society itself will not be able to function or even to survive unless it appears to its members as rational—that is, unless the members see the relationship between their own work and purpose and the purpose and pattern of their society. (Drucker, 1950, p. 26)

Drucker saw this as a particular problem at General Motors and other mass-production facilities, where most workers had few opportunities to rise above their assembly-line jobs. One of Drucker's solutions was to bring workers a sense of citizenship in their plant communities by giving them "initiative and responsible participation" in decisions at the factory floor level (Drucker, 1946, p. 197). Drucker's notion of citizenship in the industrial organization emphasized individual autonomy and respect, not economic equality. Essentially, the self-governing plant community involved giving workers the power of decision making over those issues that most directly impacted them, such as health and safety concerns, benefits administration, and training.

Another, perhaps more pressing problem facing Drucker in his quest for a functioning society of industrial organizations was how to legitimize managerial power and authority. While the self-governing plant community provided an avenue for individual participation and status within the organization, it did not eliminate hierarchy:

> Like every other institution which co-ordinates human efforts to a social end, the corporation must be organized on hierarchical lines. But also everybody from the boss to the sweeper must be seen as equally necessary to the success of the common enterprise. At the same time the large corporation must offer equal opportunities for advancement. (Drucker, 1946, p. 141)

The problem with managerial authority lay not in hierarchy, but in its nature. Observers of American corporations before Drucker, including Adolf Berle and Gardiner Means (Berle and Means, 1932), noted that modern corporations transferred power from shareholder owners to nonowner managers. Those who had the power did not share the same vested interest as those who owned the corporation, and thus would perhaps make decisions that conflicted with the owners' best interests. In the 1940s, Drucker saw this problem, and realized that a functioning society of industrial organizations required that society "make the ruling, decisive power of our industrial system a legitimate power" (Drucker, 1942, p. 77). Drucker devised a number of strategies to legitimize managerial power, including decentralization (which is discussed at length in Chapter 4), proper identification of leaders and leadership qualities (see Chapter 6), and channeling the more destructive aspects of human nature into less-harmful activities (see Chapter 5).

By the time Drucker crafted his magnum opus, *Management: Tasks, Responsibilities, Practices* (1973, 1974), he had clearly identified the broader purpose of the function of management. The goal of management was not simply to run organizations effectively but to ensure a functioning society of well-run organizations. Drucker makes this larger goal clear in the preface to this book:

> Our society has become, within an incredibly short fifty years, a society of institutions. It has become a pluralist society in which every major social task has been entrusted to large organizations. . . . If the institutions of our pluralist society of institutions do not perform in responsible autonomy, we will not have individualism and a society in which there is a chance for people to fulfill themselves. We will instead impose on ourselves complete regimentation in which no one will be allowed autonomy. . . . Tyranny is the only alternative to strong, performing autonomous institutions. . . . Performing, responsible management is the alternative to tyranny and our only protection against it. (Drucker, 1973, 1974, pp. ix–x)

For Drucker, the principal goal of management, then, is to protect individual freedom and opportunity. This is quite a goal, but it is a key component to Drucker's vision of a functioning society and management as a liberal art. By the 1980s, Drucker recognized that corporations would not be the sole source of citizenship and noneconomic status in society. Much of his work from 1990 and later emphasized the role of the nonprofit organizations, or the social sector, in providing individuals with status and meaning.

Drucker's belief was that individuals can find meaning and purpose only through membership in large organizations, including those in the nonprofit or social sector. Importantly, Drucker did not define this meaning and purpose in economic terms, but rather in terms of status, acceptance, and contribution. Viewed this way, the individual teaching a class of students, overseeing research into a new drug, designing a transportation system, organizing volunteers at a fundraiser, or developing a museum exhibit is practicing some form of management. Each person is employed by (or volunteering for) a large organization, involved in supervising the activities of others, interacts with organizations or individuals outside of his or her own, and is responsible for understanding the greater goals and objectives of his or her organization and how his or her specific activities contribute to those goals and objectives.

In Drucker's view, management must focus on the human being and his or her need for status and meaning in society. This approach requires that one take into consideration not just results and performance but also questions of human nature; issues of power, authority, morality, and ethics; and even a consideration of spiritual and theological questions.

This chapter presents a discussion of several individuals whose ideas significantly informed Drucker's concept of a moral society of modern institutions: Søren Kierkegaard, Friedrich Julius Stahl, Joseph von Radowitz and Wilhelm von Humboldt, Edmund Burke, Joseph Schumpeter, and Alfred Sloan. Subsequent chapters will integrate the influences of many other individuals on Drucker's work as he addressed specific aspects of managing society's institutions.

MAJOR SOURCES OF INFLUENCE ON DRUCKER'S CONCEPT OF MANAGEMENT AS A LIBERAL ART

Drucker was educated in the liberal arts tradition and thus read broadly in the humanities and social sciences. This background clearly shaped his concept of management as a liberal art. Drucker specifically credited some individuals with influencing him; other people's impact can be found through close analysis of Drucker's work. By evaluating how various figures who were observers of American culture or important contributors in the humanities, social sciences, and management theory affected Drucker's ideas, it becomes clear how management and the liberal arts can effectively unite.

Religious and Moral Influences

Drucker was immensely private regarding his own religious beliefs. He noted that his family was Lutheran, although not at all devout (Drucker, 1993, p. 425). Yet Drucker wrestled with theological and spiritual matters, both personally and in his work. Although he often referred to himself as a "very conventional traditional Christian" ("Management Guru Peter Drucker," 2004), he also saw the difficulties in adhering to the tenets of the Christian theology as he interpreted it:

> Someone said that the basic essence of Christianity is the tension between the command that the kingdom of God is not of this world and the command that charity is the greatest of them all. That is a conflict that cannot be resolved, that the tension is the essence of why nobody can be a Christian. You can only hope to become a Christian. You know, whenever any of you people talk of me as a Christian, I wince. (Buford, 1991, p. 9)

Drucker's religious and moral beliefs underpin his work on management and a functioning society. In order to begin to understand what he meant by management as a liberal art, we must begin to dissect the key influences on his spiritual worldview, and how those influences appear in his work. Presented here and in Chapter 3 are several important religious figures that impacted Drucker's own religious and spiritual outlook. While one can see discrete contributions from each individual, when taken together, the religious and moral influences most significantly informed Drucker's view of human nature. Drucker inherited the Christian notion of the human as fallible, fallen, separated from God, prone to sin, and in need of redemption and moral direction. Such a view directly impacted his blueprint for a functioning society.

The most important of these religious influences was Søren Kierkegaard.

Søren Kierkegaard (1813–1855)

Several times Drucker stated that Kierkegaard had a profound impact on his life (Beatty, 1998, p. 98; Drucker, 1993, p. 425).[2] He discovered the Danish philosopher's writings at the age of 19 while working as a trainee at a Hamburg export firm. Kierkegaard is one of the most important figures in existentialism. That philosophy emphasizes that the subjective, personal individual experiences in life are more important than social or political experiences of life (Raymond, 1991; Edwards, 1999).

Kierkegaard was a critic of Georg Wilhelm Friedrich Hegel (1770–1831), the important German philosopher who sought to resolve the tensions he saw as a natural part of human existence. One of the tensions Hegel believed was universal to human existence was the pull between individual and collective existence. How can a person be a free individual but still live in accordance with the needs of society?

Hegel's answer to the conflict between living as an individual and living as part of society was the *geist*, a term he gave to the collective human spirit or mind. The *geist* is a complex idea, but it involves unifying individual differences through a higher, spiritual entity. Through Hegel's *geist*, human conflict remained but was ultimately resolved because individuals were all pointing toward a higher, rational force that unified all human beings (the *geist*). The *geist* worked in history, over long periods of time, to ensure that human achievement would follow a path toward an end that was good for all.

Kierkegaard didn't like Hegel's philosophy at all (Lowith, 1964). He thought that it invalidated individual human experience by melding everything together in the *geist* concept. If all opposing, individual opinions were somehow reconciled into an absolute consciousness, what was left of the individual's experience and perspective? Kierkegaard wanted to make the individual important again but also retain the guiding force of a higher power. In Kierkegaard's philosophy, that higher power is the Christian God, to which individuals are accountable and personally responsible.

An important element of Kierkegaard's philosophy that seeps into Drucker's work is the relationship between earthly humans and the Christian God. For Kierkegaard, the awareness of the separation between the spiritual and material realms (between God and man) is the source of despair. As a person becomes more aware of the fleeting nature of life on earth and the fact that people can never be perfect, he or she also becomes conscious of the gap between God and humanity. This leads to despair, and the more self-aware one becomes, the more one despairs.

Kierkegaard explores the nature of this despair in *The Sickness Unto Death* (1849, translated by Hannay, 1989). He declares that the cure for this sickness, or despair, is Christian faith: "to be aware of this sickness is the Christian's advantage over natural man; to be cured of this sickness is the Christian's blessedness" (Kierkegaard, 1849/1989, p. 45).

Because he placed such importance on individual experience, Kierkegaard thought that the only way that people can cure their despair over the gap between humans and God is to focus on God in the human form of Jesus. Because people can only understand their own experience, he reasoned, they can know God only through the physical existence of Jesus, through the example of another human being, albeit a divine one.

In spite of this reasoning, Kierkegaard believed that Jesus reinforced humanity's separation from God. Jesus' life and death on the cross represented the essence of despair, the embodiment of human estrangement from God that physical existence entails. The example of Jesus is a reminder of humankind's imperfection, not its oneness with the Creator (Lowith, 1964, p. 47).

To Kierkegaard, the Christian faith resolved the despair of human separation from God. Jesus' life and death served as an example not only of how to understand God but also of how to comprehend that the nature of physical existence is to live apart from the spiritual realm of God.

Kierkegaard's resolution is not completely satisfying to modern-day thinkers who want simple answers or endings. To understand Kierkegaard (and by extension Drucker's larger ideas of management as a liberal art and a functioning society of organizations), one has to be able to tolerate some degree of "dissonance," or unresolved tension. For Kierkegaard and Drucker, life is, by its very nature, a source of unresolved tension: in this case, the tension between living as a physical human being and understanding the limitations of that existence.

There are three primary elements of Kierkegaard's philosophy that manifest themselves in Drucker's understanding of human nature:

1. The importance of the individual who is responsible and accountable to a higher power (Christian God)
2. The gap between the spiritual and material realms
3. Faith as the solution to despair and seemingly insoluble problems.

These topics appear throughout Drucker's work, but they are particularly evident in his 1939 book, *The End of Economic Man,* as well as his essay "The Unfashionable Kierkegaard" (Drucker, 1949).

The Existential Individual. Drucker recognized that while Kierkegaard's faith could alleviate the despair of the existential individual, it would not solve social problems: "Religion could indeed offer an answer to the despair of the individual and to his existential agony. But it could not offer an answer to the despair of the masses" (Drucker, 1939/1969, p. xx). In the face of a dysfunctional society, individuals would search for meaning elsewhere, outside of religion: "Western Man—indeed today Man altogether—is not ready to renounce this world. Indeed he still looks for secular salvation, if he expects salvation at all" (Drucker, 1939/1969, p. xx). If industrial society failed to provide individuals with meaning and status, and treated them with a lack of dignity and respect, they would look to other solutions, including totalitarianism. As industrialization moved America increasingly toward mass production and assembly-line jobs, Drucker feared the future, as Industrial Man replaced the former Economic Man as a model for individual fulfillment.

Religion, Drucker believed, was intensely personal, and would not provide meaning to one's existence in society:

Christianity and the churches have been unable to provide a religious social solution. All they can do today is to give the individual a private haven and refuge in an individual religion. They cannot give a new society and a new community. Personal religious experience may be invaluable to the individual; it may restore his peace, may give him a personal God and a rational understanding of his own function and nature. But it cannot re-create society and cannot make social and community life sensible. Even the most devout Catholic is today in the religious position of an extreme Protestant like Kierkegaard, for whom God was a purely personal, untranslatable, an uncommunicable experience which only emphasizes his own isolation and loneliness, and the utter irrationality of society. (Drucker, 1939/1969, p. 102)

Thirty years later, in his preface to the 1969 edition of *The End of Economic Man*, Drucker reiterated his view of religion as the realm of the individual and not of society: "Religion, the critic of any society, cannot accept any society or even any social program, without abandoning its true Kingdom, that of a Soul alone with its God" (Drucker, 1939/1969, pp. xx–xxi).

A functioning society of well-managed organizations was Drucker's solution to Kierkegaard's existential individual. Drucker's "new society" would provide individuals freedom and equality through citizenship in large organizations.

The Spiritual and Material Realms. Kierkegaard believed that the separation between God and humankind was an inevitable part of human existence. There was no possibility of self-redemption for Kierkegaard, no merit in pursuing a life modeled on that of Jesus or based on good works alone. The material world was hopelessly flawed.

Drucker, too, believed that the nature of human existence was life apart from God. Like Kierkegaard, he disdained those who thought that the Christian life could be based solely on good works (what Drucker termed the "ethical concept"), claiming that such a path leads to either "sugar coating on the pill of totalitarianism" or "pure sentimentalism—the position of those who believe that evil can be abolished and harmony established by good intentions" (Drucker, 1949, p. 598). Humankind is imperfect, and life on earth can never resemble the utopia of heaven. For both Kierkegaard and

Drucker, faith was the only cure for the despair that results from this awareness:

> Faith is the knowledge that man is creature—not autonomous, not the master, not the end, not the center—and yet responsible and free. It is the acceptance of man's essential loneliness to be overcome by the certainty that God is always with man; even "unto the hour of our death." (Drucker, 1949, p. 599)

Drucker's Christian belief in an imperfect world populated by fallible creatures (see also the discussion of Saints Augustine and Paul in Chapter 3) permeated his management ideas and social analysis. Although he has been criticized for being too idealistic and rather naïve in his assessment of people's capabilities (see the discussion of Maslow in Chapter 6, for example), Drucker's prescriptions for organizations and society often involve suggestions for curtailing abuses of power or channeling baser human tendencies into more positive directions. True, he almost universally assumed that the people in the organizations he described would understand themselves to be "responsible and free," understanding and respectful of authority and order. But Drucker clearly recognized the inherent imperfections in any human system. (See the examples in Chapter 4 and in Chapter 5.)

The Nature and Role of Faith. The entire premise of *The End of Economic Man* revolves around the role of faith in modern society, and what happens when that faith is lost. In this book, Drucker analyzed the failures of capitalism and Marxism to deliver economic equality, which paved the way for totalitarian regimes in Europe. For Drucker, totalitarianism was the result of a Kierkegaardian crisis of faith.

In Drucker's words, "Faith is the belief that in God the impossible is possible" (Drucker, 1949, p. 599). Failed by Marxism and capitalism, the people of Europe turned to totalitarian promises of the impossible. According to Drucker's analysis, the error was not that people had faith but that they put their faith in the wrong place. People will turn to even the most irrational creed of "the magician who promises to make the impossible possible" if they are in despair (Drucker, 1939/1969, p. 22).

Ultimately, Drucker's work involved a search for something valid in which the majority of human beings could place their faith. Convinced that religious faith was individual and personal, and that most people desired "secular salvation," Drucker nevertheless believed that faith was still the only way to overcome the despair of life in modern industrial society:

> In faith the individual becomes the universal, ceases to be isolated, becomes meaningful and absolute; hence in faith there is a true ethic. And in faith existence in society becomes meaningful, too, as existence in true charity. (Drucker, 1949, p. 599)

But faith in what? Drucker clearly called for faith in God, but also for fighting totalitarianism "from a basis of faith—a faith in freedom and in the individual" (Drucker, 1966b, p. 21). Drucker's vision of management required him to see human beings as flawed, but he also had a great deal of faith in human potential. In order to have a society of well-managed organizations, people must have faith in the human capacity for self-direction and appropriate behavior.

There is an inherent tension in Drucker's vision; it is not always easy to have faith in people if one believes that humans exist in a fallen state and that organizations need to be designed to prevent inevitable abuses of power. This tension is more understandable in light of Kierkegaard's philosophy. If the nature of existence is to be in tension, the only way to resolve that tension (for Kierkegaard and Drucker) is to have faith. For Kierkegaard, the answer was faith in God; for Drucker, the answer was a more secularized faith in "freedom and the individual."

Political Influences

Second in importance to the religious and theological influences on Drucker's concept of management as a liberal art are the political thinkers who contributed to Drucker's ideas. Drucker was particularly interested in finding a balance between freedom and authority. The political influences discussed here and in Chapter 4 all deal with the desire to strike a balance between individual liberties and the need for social rule and order.

Although Drucker was very private about his own political affiliations, he remained fearful of totalitarianism all his life. In his lifetime, he witnessed the rise of powerful authoritarian governments that eroded human freedom. Nazi Germany, Maoist China, and the Soviet Union represented the worst of human leadership, the "secular creeds" that he found so worrisome in their appeal to a despairing public. Drucker's fear of totalitarianism drove his search for the functioning society of institutions; in fact, for a time, he saw the industrial organization as the source of salvation for society:

> The emergence of the industrial enterprise may herald a basic reversal of the trend that has prevailed in Western history ever since the collapse of the medieval order. The totalitarian State of our days marks the reduction to absurdity—criminal, wicked, insane absurdity—of the trend toward the State as the sole center, the sole focus and the sole power that began in the fifteenth century. Certainly, the enterprise is the first autonomous institution to emerge since then. (Drucker, 1950, p. 37)

For Drucker, the corporation embodied the primary challenge to totalitarian government, to absolute power in the public sector. Having a private business sector independent of government was crucial to his sense of an orderly society. Thus management became key to a functioning society; if the institutions of society are not run properly, then power can be centralized in the hands of one entity, such as big government or big business.

At the same time, Drucker was no fan of direct democracy; he stated that "the majority principle as it is commonly accepted today is a despotic and tyrannical, and unfree principle" (Drucker, 1942b, p. 485). Ever the champion of the individual, he valued the minority opinion and understood the dangers inherent in strict rule of the majority will.

Drucker faced a dilemma, one that political theorists historically have grappled with: how does society balance the need for governance, for rule and order, with the desire to maximize human liberty? The particular individuals that influenced Drucker say much about his conception of management as a liberal art. Decision making under such a system must involve finding a middle ground between authority and freedom, between the values of the past and the dreams of the future, between individual aspirations and the needs of the community. By its very nature, management as a liberal art will be conservative in the traditional sense of that word: seeking to retain the traditions of the past that still have relevance and meaning in the present. Yet, it will also be liberal in that it aims to maximize human freedom and change those things that no longer serve an institution or its greater society.

Friedrich Julius Stahl (1802–1861): The Trio of German Thinkers

Stahl was one of the earliest and most important influences on Drucker. Early in his academic career, Drucker decided to explore three conservative figures instrumental in developing the Prussian constitution in the nineteenth century: Wilhelm von Humboldt,

Joseph von Radowitz, and Friedrich Julius Stahl. Von Humboldt and von Radowitz are discussed below along with Stahl because of the strength of their combined influence upon Drucker, and because of the similarity of their work and ideas during the same era of German history.

What attracted Drucker to the three was that "they tried to balance continuity and change . . . they were neither unabashed liberals nor unabashed reactionaries. They tried to create a stable society and a stable polity that would preserve the traditions of the past and yet make possible change" (Drucker, 1992, p. 58).

Drucker began writing about Stahl first, composing his first published work, *Friedrich Julius Stahl: A Conservative Theory of State*, in 1931. He arranged for its publication in Germany in 1933, just before he left Nazi Germany for London. Drucker intended to write about each member of the "trio of German thinkers" but succeeded in writing only about Stahl (Drucker, 1992, pp. 58–59).

Stahl was an ecclesiastical lawyer, politician, and philosopher. He lived during a time when many countries in Europe experienced violent revolutions. These working-class revolutions were suppressed, but intellectuals and political theorists began to wonder if the old monarchies would survive, or if future revolutions would inevitably change the political landscape.

Stahl sought to answer this question for Prussia by trying to find an alternative to the old monarchies of the past and the violent revolutions threatened by the present. By blending representative institutions with what he saw as the positive attributes of monarchy, Stahl developed a political framework for avoiding either a radical step forward or a reactionary step backward.

He was interested in a political framework that would find a balance between protecting individual rights and preserving the interests of the larger society. He did so through incorporating his own religious philosophy that countered that of Hegel, who was very influential in Stahl's time.

Like Kierkegaard, Stahl disagreed with Hegel's idea of the unifying *geist* force, believing that it did not allow for individual differences. However, Stahl, like Hegel, wanted to find a way to curb individual rights and emphasize the role of the community in human existence.

Stahl countered Hegel's philosophy with his idea of the personal God who actively created each individual. Stahl's personal God has a personal, individualized connection with every human being. Stahl used the term "personality" to describe the differences among people, and he also applied this term to God to describe His creative spiritual power: "personality is not simply the fullest freedom and political entitlement but also the *fullest satisfaction* and *highest spiritual perfection*" (Stahl, 2007, p. 105). Stahl joins the individual to the Creator in his philosophy; each individual is a direct reflection of a personal, creative God.

In Stahl's system, individuals have free will by intentional design of the Creator God. Ideally, there is no conflict between individual interests and society's when people exercise their free will, because all are united under the interests of a creative Christian personal God. But just as Kierkegaard did, Stahl recognized that humans live apart from God in their physical existence on earth. As a result, people's interests are not always directly in line with those of the Creator. Therefore, human beings must submit their will to civil authority: the rule of state and law.

Stahl used the personal Creator God to align the people's individual rights with the larger needs of society. But he had to deal with the problem of coercion, or forced adherence to state authority. Why would people submit to the rule of law when it impeded personal freedom?

Stahl's solution was to argue that submission to state authority was willing submission. Stahl's notion of freedom involves choice bounded by responsibility to a higher authority and an acknowledgment of a greater good than merely one's own personal desires.

He argues not for freedom as license but for freedom as a source of responsibility and accountability, to either civil codes of conduct in the form of laws or, ultimately, to the religious codes of conduct of a Christian God: "Because freedom arises from the law [*aus dem Rechte*] as an ethical order, it is not unrestricted but from the start has a specific content, standard and boundaries" (Stahl, 2007b, p. 6). People would recognize legal authority because they know that they ultimately are responsible not just to themselves but also to a greater good. As Stahl points out, freedom does not equal the freedom to do whatever one feels like, regardless of the impact on others.

Stahl used this idea of "freedom as an ethical order" to legitimize political authority, in his case, monarchical power. Stahl's legitimacy of authority rests on both ruler and ruled acknowledging a larger moral authority above the material sphere: "Legal freedom is bounded *first* by *higher duties* to which persons must subordinate themselves; not, of course, by claims of (subjective) morality, but indeed by ethical ideas of life relations maintained in common life" (Stahl, 2007b, p. 6). If monarch and subjects align their interests in a personal Creator, then submission is an act of free will; one chooses to obey because one recognizes that doing so benefits both the community and the individual. Political authority is thus legitimate because it is grounded in this higher morality that has been internalized by all.

Just as Stahl sought a middle ground between revolution and the older monarchies of his time, Drucker searched for a functioning society that occupied the moderate space between extreme left and right positions. Based on a view of humankind as flawed and imperfect, in need of authority and regulation, Drucker propelled Stahl's exploration of the legitimacy of authority into the twentieth century.

Legitimacy of Authority. In Drucker's work, freedom is not the absence of limitations but instead freedom of action bounded by accountability to laws or values. The governance of free people in

Drucker's society of functioning organizations involves people who willingly submit to authority because they share the same values as those above them in the organization, and agree to be held accountable to shared values and codes of conduct.

Willing submission to internalized authority is particularly visible in Drucker's concept of Management by Objectives (MBO). MBO in an organization requires that all managers set goals for themselves that are used to measure performance. Importantly, these goals are supposed to reflect the larger goals of the organization, not merely the personal desires and achievements of the individual manager (Drucker, 1954, pp. 121–136).

Just as Stahl's system of authority is aligned with a common, unifying higher power, Drucker's functional society involves a union of interests between managers and their organizations. Because the manager develops his or her goals in alignment with the organization's broader goals, the individual objectives are a form of personal expression, yet informed by the authority of the larger entity.

Drucker clearly believed in a hierarchical structure of power within organizations; he did not embrace a strictly egalitarian view of management or government. Nevertheless, he did argue that those at the top of the food chain needed to justify their position through adhering to shared values. In other words, Drucker believed managerial authority was necessary, but, as did Stahl, he attempted to devise a means for making that authority legitimate through shared values. Why would people lower down the organization chart willingly submit to authority from above? They would if they believed that the organization and its leaders shared their same values of human rights and opportunity:

> Like every other institution which co-ordinates human efforts to a social end, the corporation must be organized on hierarchical lines. But also everybody from the boss to the sweeper must be seen as equally necessary to the success of the com-

mon enterprise. At the same time the large corporation must offer equal opportunities for advancement. This is simply the traditional demand for justice, a consequence of the Christian concept of human dignity. (Drucker, 1946, pp. 141–142)

In essence, Drucker attempted to take Stahl's creative, personal Christian God and secularize Him for the industrial workplace. Unifying the organization around the very American values of equal opportunity and recognition for merit, as well as the religiously derived concept of dignity, Drucker translated Stahl's nineteenth-century ideas for the twentieth century. Stahl's creative God remains, albeit in distilled form.

Yet Stahl's argument for legitimacy of authority relied entirely on the presence of a Christian God. Embracing a constitutional monarchy under a Christian framework, he did not develop a system to establish legitimate leadership in the material realm other than divine inspiration.

Legitimizing managerial power remained a problem for Drucker throughout his productive life. As author Jack Tarrant stated: "Drucker never really solved the problem of legitimacy. His compromise rationalization is summed up in his conclusion, 'That the enterprise is not a legitimate government does not mean it is an illegitimate one'" (Tarrant, 1976, p. 139). As his religious and theological viewpoint prevented him from placing too much trust in human managers, Drucker sought ways to curb what he saw as normal human tendencies toward abuse of power. Other influencers provided him with the means to curtail managerial authority or channel power into least harmful paths. But it was clear to Drucker in 1932 that legitimacy of power must rest upon responsibility, which in turn ultimately must rest upon absolute moral values, not manmade values.[3]

Without a personal, creative deity, the problem of legitimacy of power remains. Drucker continued to wrestle with this issue throughout his writings, exploring a range of solutions, including a return to faith and to federalism. The very variety of responses to the subject of power reveals the underlying problem: an ultimate distrust in a human system that nevertheless is designed to maximize human liberty. Retaining Stahl's nineteenth-century philosophy in a secular twenty-first century setting presents such a challenge.[4]

Joseph Maria von Radowitz (1797–1853) and Wilhelm von Humboldt (1767–1835)

Joseph Maria von Radowitz was educated in France. He fought for Napoleon, and later moved to Prussia and married into an established Prussian family. Radowitz was appointed Prussia's military representative to the federal assembly of the German Confederation in 1836. He advanced a moderate plan to unify Germany in 1848. Radowitz hoped to bridge the gap between the established order and the revolutionaries in the German states (Sheehan, 1970, pp. 711–715).

Wilhelm von Humboldt was raised in Berlin. In 1809, he founded the University of Berlin. He believed that political power should be extremely limited so as not to impinge on personal freedoms, and he was particularly concerned with how individuals could express themselves culturally in a state with increasing central authority. Humboldt embraced the German concept of *Bildung*, which is a process of spiritual, individual development through education not unlike the liberal arts ideal; *Bildung* is highly complex, involving the commitment to an ideal of character development and personal virtue as well as knowledge and wisdom. Humboldt's goal was to infuse the German government with the spirit of *Bildung*. He envisioned "using bureaucratic power to realize his cultural idea. As a result, he presided over a marriage of *Staat* (state) and *Bildung* that would have lasting consequences for German politics, culture, and society" (Sheehan, 1970, p. 365).

Stability with Change. Humboldt, like Radowitz, negotiated a path between two political extremes, attempting to unify Germany's various interests around a moderate concept. As noted by one biographer, "Humboldt's program was neither liberal nor conservative, but contained elements of both" (Sweet, 1980, pp. 345–346). Radowitz's and Humboldt's visions for German government effectively modeled political moderation for Drucker, and they also showed the value of developing solutions that would theoretically appease those on opposite ends of the spectrum.

The influence of the trio of Stahl, Radowitz, and Humboldt on achieving continuity and change in the institutions of society led Drucker to the comprehensive study of the practice of entrepreneurship and innovation. That, in turn, ultimately led to his seminal book *Innovation and Entrepreneurship* (Drucker, 1985). In this work, Drucker argued that if the institutions of society are to retain continuity when confronted with environmental turbulence, they must change by adopting entrepreneurial practices. The lack of innovation leads to stagnation and decline. There is no other way to retain continuity, therefore, except to practice systematic entrepreneurship.

Drucker surmised that continuity and change are not opposites in organizations; rather, they are poles, like the North Pole and South Pole. The more an institution is organized for innovation and change, the more it will have to balance change with mechanisms that facilitate continuity. Of utmost importance during times of rapid change are effective communication mechanisms that facilitate common understanding and trust among stakeholders.

The Importance of Inherited Traditions and Limits on the Exercise of Power. Drucker constantly promoted the theme of balance between *continuity* and *change*. Influenced by the trio of German thinkers, he was especially wary of revolution even though Thomas Jefferson, the third president of the United States, thought periodic revolutions were necessary to rid society of its accumulated ills. Drucker preferred continuous innovation to periodic revolutions:

> They [revolutions] cannot be predicted, directed, or con-
> trolled. They bring to power the wrong people. Worst of all,
> their results—predictably—are the exact opposite of their
> promises. (Drucker, 1985, pp. 254–255)

Drucker's interest in continuity and change was also influenced by the work of Edmund Burke.

Edmund Burke (1729–1797)

Born in Ireland when it was part of the British Empire, Edmund Burke was a British parliamentarian and political writer. He argued against persecution of the Catholics, and also he supported the American Revolution against Britain. Drucker credits Burke with writing one of two books that "permanently changed my life." *Reflections on the French Revolution* (1790) was Burke's contemporary analysis of the less-than-two-year-old event. Drucker read the book when he was a teenager, working in Hamburg, and he later remarked on its impact on him:

> That Germany, and indeed all of Continental Europe, had
> been in a revolutionary period ever since World War I and the
> Russian Revolution, every one of us younger people *knew*—
> only people who had grown to adulthood before 1914 thought
> possibly [sic] a return to "pre-war" and actually wanted it.
> And so Burke's main thesis: that to find in such a period the
> balance between *continuity* and *change* is the first task of poli-
> tics and politicians, immediately resonated with this eighteen-
> year-old reader, 140 years after the book had been written. It
> immediately became central to my own politics, to my own
> world-view, and to all my later work. (Drucker, 2003, p. viii)

As did Stahl and the other German thinkers, Burke provided a model for a middle ground between revolution and a divine monarchy. Specifically, Burke warned of the dangers of rejecting inherited traditions, including religious and political foundations of constitutional government.

In his treatise on the French Revolution, Burke delivered a diatribe against revolution, chastising the French for completely turning their backs on their past. In the first part of the book, he defends England's own political system, holding up Britain's history of political development as a model:

> You will observe that from Magna Charta to the Declaration of Right it has been the uniform policy of our constitution to claim and assert our liberties as an *entailed inheritance* derived to us from our forefathers, and to be transmitted to our posterity—as an estate specially belonging to the people of this kingdom, without any reference whatever to any other more general or prior right. . . . We have an inheritable crown, an inheritable peerage, and a House of Commons and a people inheriting privileges, franchises, and liberties from a long line of ancestors. (Burke, 1790/2005, p. 19)

Burke's argument was intended to directly contrast Britain's constitution with France's revolutionary rejection of monarchy; he "concludes that cautious gradualism in politics, which the British have practiced, is preferable to rationalistic destruction and rebuilding on the French model" (Lock, 2006, p. 288).

Burke rooted European civilization in not just monarchical rule but also the "spirit of a gentleman and the spirit of religion," referring to the power of the nobility and Church, respectively. These forces, argued Burke, upheld education and civilization; when France eliminated the inherited traditions of the ruling class and religion, "along with its natural protectors and guardians, learning will be cast into

the mire and trodden down under the hoofs of a swinish multitude"
(Burke, 1790/2005, p. 69).

Such words may upset modern democratic sentiments, but Burke
(and others at the time) believed that the extreme violence of the
French Revolution was indicative of the nature of direct rule by the
people. Without restraining forces, democracy could unleash dangerous appetites:

> We know, and it is our pride to know, that man is by his
> constitution a religious animal; . . . But if, in the moment
> of riot and in a drunken delirium from the hot spirit drawn
> out of the alembic of hell, which in France is now so furi-
> ously boiling, we should uncover our nakedness by throwing
> off that Christian religion which has hitherto been our boast
> and comfort, and one great source of civilization amongst us
> and amongst many other nations, we are apprehensive (being
> well aware that the mind will not endure a void) that some
> uncouth, pernicious, and degrading superstition might take
> place of it. (Burke, 2005, p. 51)

Deeply suspicious of the idea of the "will of the people," Burke
believed that, ultimately, power would be wielded by a few. The
choices seemed clear: either a few qualified individuals guided by
tradition, or a handful of violent revolutionaries lacking any grounding whatsoever.

Stahl, Radowitz, Humboldt, and Burke all showed Drucker the
importance of retaining the valued institutions of the past while
recognizing the need for updating and innovation. This balance
between continuity and discontinuity is a major theme in Drucker's work. It appears in his writings on society, where he deals with
broad issues and trends, as well as his management texts, in which

he acknowledges the unstable nature of modern capitalism and the need to manage change in a positive way. These eighteenth- and nineteenth-century political influences may seem very remote and esoteric, but the ideas of these men permeate Drucker's work. If one is to understand management as a liberal art, it is important to have a passing understanding of these theorists from the distant past.

Socioeconomic Influences

Although he was not an economist, Drucker used principles of economics to support his management theories and his assessments of government and society. As he sought to make leaders of organizations more productive and effective, as "beacons of productivity and innovation," he also desired to create a system that "makes economics a human discipline" (Drucker, 1987, p. 42). Management, the art of getting things accomplished through people, could, in Drucker's eyes, resuscitate economics, making it a moral force: "a productivity based economics might thus become what all the great economists have striven for: both a 'humanity,' a 'moral philosophy,' a *'Geisteswissenschaft'* [social science]; and, rigorous 'science'" (Drucker, 1980, p. 18).

Drucker's emphasis on casting economics in a moral light through an emphasis on productivity and innovation also allows his ideas to apply to virtually any organization. Although he launched an important defense of profits, Drucker also linked profits to innovation and productivity, making them the more important measures of progress. As a result, not only can the businesswoman use management as a liberal art, but so can the hospital administrator, university provost, and the head of a national charitable foundation. With human productivity and innovation as important measures of value, as defined by Drucker's interpretation of economic theory, management as a liberal art is not a strictly commercial endeavor.

With economics focused on the human being, Drucker saw it intrinsically linked to sociology as a discipline. Innovation and productivity take place in human communities, which involve complex interactions among people. To Drucker, economics and sociology were both humanities, disciplines devoted to studying human relations, particularly those in the workplace. Ultimately, the economists and sociologists that most influenced Drucker conveyed the message that institutions, including those generating profits, were social entities and must provide a sense of community.

The most important influence on Drucker from economics as a discipline came from Joseph A. Schumpeter. Although Schumpeter was one of the greatest economists of the twentieth century, he was able to place his discipline within the larger socioeconomic sweep of history (Schumpeter, 1942). Other socioeconomic influences upon Drucker are discussed in Chapter 7, which deals with the practice of social ecology.

Joseph Schumpeter (1883–1950)

Joseph Schumpeter was named as Austria's finance minister after the First World War. Austria's financial situation was terrible; the dire state of affairs, combined with Schumpeter's outspoken political opinions, which offended many of his colleagues, eventually cost him his position. He resigned in October 1919. Following a brief, unsuccessful career in banking, Schumpeter returned to academia, eventually moving to Harvard in 1932, where, in spite of his successful *Capitalism, Socialism and Democracy* (1942), he was overshadowed by the younger economist John Maynard Keynes.

Schumpeter's primary contribution to Drucker's work was his idea that profit was a moral imperative.

Profit as Moral Force. In "Schumpeter vs. Keynes" (Drucker, 1983), Drucker credited Schumpeter with the idea of profit as part of a moral and ethical system. Schumpeter did not explicitly argue this, but from Schumpeter's theory Drucker concluded that profit was moral. Schumpeter links profit to the role of the entrepreneur. As entrepreneurs innovate, they in turn generate a greater profit. Profit is inherent in entrepreneurial activity: "Without development there is not profit, without profit no development" (Schumpeter, 1934, p. 154). As competitors adopt the same innovations, profit levels fall. If there is no new entrepreneurial activity to infuse new innovations, there is no incentive for profits to increase. Schumpeter noted that profits were not a reward for the entrepreneur's risk taking; rather, profit is "the temporary surplus of receipts over cost of production in a new enterprise" (Schumpeter, 1934, p. 137).

Drucker took Schumpeter's concept of temporary profit and modified it, arguing that profit is a cost: "It is the 'risk premium' that covers the costs of staying in business" (Drucker, 1954, p. 77). Profit is a cost of doing business, not merely surplus cash that executives seek to maximize. Once Drucker devised profit as a cost of doing business, he could develop his moral argument:

> Schumpeter's "innovator" with his "creative destruction" is the only theory so far to explain why there is something we call "profit." The classical economists very well knew that their theory did not give any rationale for profit. . . . If profit is, however, a genuine cost, and especially if profit is the only way to maintain jobs and to create new ones, then "capitalism" becomes again a moral system. . . . As soon . . . as one shifts from the axiom of an unchanging, self-contained, closed economy to Schumpeter's dynamic, growing, moving, changing economy, what is called "profit" is no longer immoral. It becomes a moral imperative. (Drucker, 1983, p. 127)

For Schumpeter, capitalism was a dynamic system of growth and development. Economic downturns were normal periods of adjustment following some kind of dramatic change. Events that change the normal flow of the economy lead to periods of growth and profitability. These events occur when entrepreneurial activity results in new technologies, industries, or modes of production. The results of innovation or entrepreneurial activity then create temporary opportunities. Schumpeter refers to this process as "creative destruction" because entrepreneurial ventures not only bring about something new, they also destroy something old in the process.

Inherent in the concept of "creative destruction" is a problem, one that Schumpeter himself realized. Because entrepreneurial activity and its associated profit are so temporary, every business has the potential to be creatively destroyed. This reality led to Drucker's admonition to businesses to practice "systematic abandonment," or to weed out nonproductive activities, products, or business units:

> Every institution—and not only business—must build into its day-to-day management four entrepreneurial activities that run in parallel. One is the organized abandonment of products, services, processes, markets, distribution channels, and so on that are no longer an optimal allocation of resources. . . . Then any institution must organize for systematic, continuing improvement. . . . Then it has to organize for systematic and continuous exploitation, especially of its successes. . . . And, finally, it has to organize systematic innovation, that is, to create the different tomorrow that makes obsolete and, to a large extent, replaces even the most successful products of today. (Drucker, 1998, p. 174)

In order to survive, then, an organization must have profits—not only to reward risk taking but also to fuel the engines of job creation and innovation. In this way, Drucker used Schumpeter to refute the nineteenth-century debates over the morality of profits. The old problem had been that "profit is needed as the incentive for the risk taker. But is this not really a bribe and thus impossible to justify morally?" (Drucker, 1983, p. 127). Through Schumpeter, Drucker found a way to fashion capitalism into a moral system not based on the pursuit of economic gain. His construction of profit using Schumpeter's system of entrepreneurial innovation allowed him to envision profit within a larger, moral framework.

Executive Leadership and Integrity: Alfred Sloan

Drucker's relationship with Alfred Sloan, chairman of General Motors, proved highly influential to his work. Not only did Drucker's study of the company launch his career as a management writer and consultant but his personal dealings with Sloan also molded his ideas of what an executive should be, and how organizations could provide meaning and function within society and for individuals as well.

Alfred Sloan (1875–1966)

Alfred Sloan graduated from Massachusetts Institute of Technology with a degree in electrical engineering. He became president of Hyatt Roller Bearing, which eventually merged with a company that General Motors acquired. Sloan identified a number of organizational problems with General Motors, and he drafted an organizational overhaul of the firm that maintained divisional autonomy but provided more cohesion. His organizational structure based on decentralization became widespread in American business after the Second World War (Gabor, 2000, pp. 275–288).

In January 1943, Donaldson Brown, Sloan's assistant, invited Drucker to study General Motors' organization. Drucker published the results of his 18-month investigation as *Concept of the Corporation*. In this work, and in subsequent writings, Drucker described the lessons learned from Sloan, notably the importance of, but ultimate limitations of, decentralization in business entities. Also in Sloan, Drucker saw a model of executive integrity, a quality he believed was the "touchstone" or essence of management (Drucker, 2008, p. 287).

The Limits of Decentralization and Importance of Integrity. In developing his idea of a functioning society of institutions, Drucker sought to reconcile the tension between individual desires and the needs of the organizations. He saw the potential to do so in the modern corporation, and Sloan's General Motors provided an example of how. The company consisted of several autonomous divisions (for example, Cadillac, Chevrolet, and Pontiac) that needed to be integrated without unnecessarily impinging on each division's authority. Drucker argued that Sloan devised his solution by studying the U.S. Constitution (Drucker, 1990, p. vii). Just as the debate on the Constitution had focused on the issue of states' rights and limits to the federal government's authority, Sloan's plan for General Motors emphasized the autonomy of each division. Corporate decision areas were clearly elucidated and limited; those decisions not specifically reserved for corporate management remained in the hands of the division managers.

Decentralization spread rapidly through American businesses after World War II; as Sloan noted, "the General Motors type of organization—co-ordinated in policy and decentralized in administration—not only has worked well for us, but also has become standard practice in a large part of American industry." However, Sloan also remarked that "it takes more than the structural design of an organization . . . to ensure sound management." Importantly to Sloan, "no organization is sounder than the men who run it and delegate others to run it" (Sloan, 1963, p. xxi). Sloan's primary concern was that the wrong kind of manager would usurp his power, placing too much authority in the hands of corporate management at the expense of the divisions.

For Drucker, the idea of decentralization became an important vehicle for dissipating and controlling power in organizations (see discussion in Chapter 4). But Sloan showed how crucial it was to have the right people running the organization. Drucker took away from his relationship with Sloan the lesson of the importance of integrity:

> The final proof of the sincerity and seriousness of an organization's management is uncompromising emphasis on integrity of character. . . . A man might himself know too little, perform poorly, lack judgment and ability, and yet not do too much damage as a manager. But if he lacks in character and integrity—no matter how knowledgeable, how brilliant, how successful—he destroys. He destroys people, the most valuable resource of the enterprise. He destroys spirit. And he destroys performance. (Drucker, 2008, p. 287)

Drucker and Sloan disagreed on the social nature of business organizations; Sloan never went along with Drucker's edict that "organizations—and that means the 'professionals' who manage them—must surely take responsibility for the common weal" (Drucker, 1978, p. 293). But ultimately, Sloan modeled the critical role of integrity in business executives. In his characterization of Sloan, Drucker remarked on Sloan's insistence on performance, "great kindness to people," fairness, interest in diversity of opinion, and sense of honor (Drucker, 1978, p. 282). Sloan was the ultimate servant leader, viewing the interests of the organization as the sole focus of his decision making. While Drucker believed this to be too narrow a vision, calling for General Motors to see itself in the broader context of its societal functions, he learned from Sloan the importance of professionalism and values in executive leadership.

Drucker never lost the personal example of integrity he found in Sloan. Drucker was a great proponent of focusing on the strengths of an individual when making a placement or promotion decision. Yet, because executives are powerful examples for their subordinates to follow, Drucker insisted that the lack of integrity in a leader "faults everything else" (Drucker, 1966, pp. 86–87) and is therefore a disqualifier to the otherwise valid rule to always focus upon strengths, what a person could do and do exceedingly well.

A MORAL VISION FOR A FUNCTIONING SOCIETY

Drucker's own background in the liberal arts influenced his idea of management as a liberal art. Coming out of Europe between the two world wars, he saw hope in the United States for a functioning society of institutions that could provide status and meaning for people. This larger mission of fashioning a "tolerable" society was molded by the ideas of Kierkegaard; the trio of German political thinkers and Burke; Schumpeter; and Sloan. Representing a wide range of disciplines, from philosophy to the practice of management, these men shaped Drucker's vision of how a society of organizations might be guided by the right values and also provide for individual achievement and fulfillment.

Kierkegaard, the most important religious and philosophical influence on Drucker, led Drucker to hold the view of humans as imperfect, fallen beings who could only be redeemed through faith. This pessimistic view of humankind is crucial to understanding Drucker's concept of management as a liberal art. Although Kierkegaard's influence led to Drucker's dark assessment of human nature, the Danish philosopher also launched Drucker on his search for a way to inject hope, in the form of faith in a "bearable" society.

Stahl, Radowitz, Humboldt, and Burke helped Drucker hammer out ways to manage and curtail the baser tendencies of Kierkegaard's fallen humans. These political philosophers modeled the need to balance continuity and change, as well as authority and freedom. By legitimizing authority and managing change through innovation, Drucker's "tolerable" society of organizations could perhaps maximize individual liberty but still curtail abuses of power, as well as soften some of the negative impacts of economic progress.

Schumpeter provided Drucker with a way to make his capitalist society of industrial organizations moral, as profit could become an imperative for protecting the very organizations that provided meaning and status.

Finally, Sloan the executive not only modeled integrity and servant leadership but also used decentralization to distill and curtail power.

Importantly, all of these men showed Drucker that management must involve an understanding of the human condition and of human nature. Thus these crucial influences provided the foundation for Drucker's work and in so doing provide the foundations for management as a liberal art.

CHAPTER 2

MANAGEMENT AND LIBERAL ARTS TRADITIONS: BRIDGING THE TWO WORLDS

Practicing managers and those engaged in the study of the liberal arts are often disdainful of each other. People concerned with the day-to-day operations of a hospital, software company, or volunteer organization tend to view academics as sheltered, unrealistic, and out of touch with the real world. Scholars typically treat those in the world of work as shallow, unthinking, and narrow-minded. Even on university campuses, schools of humanities, arts, and social sciences often view the business school as a den of iniquity that sullies the otherwise appropriate endeavors of an academic community. Well aware of this attitude, business faculty and students strike back with strident reminders of their status as the university cash cow or purveyor of marketable employees. Although some business and humanities departments are joining forces through combined degree programs and specialized courses, the cultural divide has a long history, resulting in ingrained prejudice and arrogance on both sides of the fence.

In this chapter, we discuss the history of this cultural divide, and how that very history may contain the avenue to bridging the gap between those in management and those in the liberal arts. We first trace the development of the liberal arts tradition over time, from the Greeks to the present, and debate the relevance of the humanities in a modern society. We then turn to the history of management education, noting its changes over time, including contemporary hand-wringing over the state of business school training. We conclude the chapter with an assessment of how these parallel histories show the potential for management as a liberal art to heal old wounds.

HISTORY OF THE LIBERAL ARTS TRADITION[1]

Most people who invoke the tradition of the liberal arts trace its origin to Classical Greek civilization. Although the idea of a liberal arts education certainly seems to have originated with the Greeks, the nature and goal of that education remained very fluid (Kimball, 1986, pp. 17–25). By the fifth century BCE, Greek political life emphasized the democratic participation of free males in assemblies. Such a political system required an educated citizenry that could engage in enlightened discourse and decision making.

In response to the demand for education, various philosophies arose. The Sophists, for example, emphasized training in argumentative skills, in constructing rational explanations and providing evidence for opinions and positions. The weight that the Sophists placed on speaking ability worried other philosophers, who were concerned that merely mastering the art of rhetorical flourish was not true learning; what if one's positions were poorly thought out or, worse yet, based on lies?

As a result, individuals presented contrasting philosophies of education. Plato, and later Aristotle, emphasized the search for truth and the pursuit of knowledge as its own virtuous endeavor. In contrast, Isocrates, although he opposed the Sophists' teachings, believed that it was the obligation of citizens not only to pursue virtue but also to model virtue through actions, particularly through oratory.[2]

Although there was considerable disagreement as to exactly how, and in what and for how long, free men should be educated, the Greeks had a cultural ideal of *enkyklios paideia*, or general education for free citizens. This concept of general education for those blessed with leisure time to pursue it became the germ of our term "liberal arts."

Although Greek, and later Roman, civilizations disagreed as to the exact curriculum for and goal of a liberal arts education, the basic subject matter was agreed upon, and it later became known as the seven liberal arts. The seven liberal arts consisted of three language arts (grammar, rhetoric, and logic) and four mathematical arts (arithmetic, geometry, music, and astronomy).

The Roman philosophers Cicero and Quintilian stated that training in the liberal arts should produce citizens who could lead society, who knew and respected agreed-upon standards of behavior learned from a body of inherited texts that reflected cultural values and morals. Students studied Greek and Latin languages, reading Homer, Plato, Aristotle, and other classical authors. A liberal arts education was intended to build moral character and inculcate societal values; it was for the elite only, for those men with status and time (certainly not benefits enjoyed by slaves or women).

After the fall of the Roman Empire, Christianity and Islam influenced the earlier Greco-Roman idea of the *artes liberales*. Having conquered much of what formerly was the Roman Empire, Muslims possessed valuable manuscripts, including the works of Aristotle. Muslim scholars translated these writings into Arabic; subsequently, Christian and Jewish scholars translated them into Latin. The "discovery" of Aristotle's writings by the Judeo-Christian west led to a remarkable burst of intellectual activity in the twelfth and thirteenth centuries, as religious scholars attempted to reconcile Aristotle's ideas about reason and logic with religious texts and teachings. The injection of Aristotelian philosophy into the medieval Christian world begged the question: could the *artes liberales* ideal be upheld in a culture based on faith? Catholic scholars such as Thomas Aquinas worked to reconcile Aristotelian reason with Christian faith. Others, such as Saint Bonaventure, rejected Aristotle's philosophy as antithetical to what was contained in inherited religious texts.

The Rise of the University

Aristotle's influence coincided with the rise of the European university, which grew out of cathedral schools set up in various cities. The first (and most prestigious) such university was the University of Paris, founded in 1253. These universities began to develop an increasingly structured curriculum, based on the Greco-Roman *artes liberales* ideal; students would begin their studies with the arts faculty, which provided basic education, and then move on to one of the higher faculties in a specialized area, such as law, medicine, or theology. Although each university's requirements were different, all required a student to obtain a degree from the faculty of arts before advancing further in his studies.

The university curriculum was highly influenced by the new translations of Aristotle's works. At the University of Paris, the arts faculty was prohibited from teaching Aristotle's philosophy, although this ban was apparently not very effective. In order to fold Aristotle's writings into the existing curriculum, the university added philosophy as a separate subject, divided into three subcategories. Thus, the new course of study consisted of the *trivium* (logic, grammar, and rhetoric), *quadrivium* (arithmetic, music, geometry, and astronomy), and courses in natural philosophy, moral philosophy, and metaphysics.

As was the case with Greco-Roman centers of learning, individual universities emphasized different elements of the curriculum—some weighting logic, others the *quadrivium* subjects. Regardless, the medieval version of the liberal arts ideal attempted to blend Christian teachings with those inherited traditions from the Greeks and Romans (Kimball, 1986, pp. 62–68).

Renaissance ideals influenced the liberal arts tradition, once again transforming the curriculum. In the fourteenth and fifteenth centuries, some scholars began to doubt the scholastics' solution of reconciling classic and religious texts. The attempt to unite secular and religious texts through logic came under increasing scrutiny, particularly by Renaissance humanists who believed the solution was to return to the values and ideals of Greco-Roman society. Renaissance thinkers sought to dilute the Church's influence on education, emphasizing the study of those subjects that more directly impacted humankind. Humanism advocated exploration of the human condition more widely through a wider range of texts, not just religious texts and selected classic works. Such changes were radical, however, and spread slowly (Axelrod, 2002, pp. 16–18).

The Reformation spurred the development of a more humanist liberal arts curriculum, particularly in England and later in the United States. Oxford and Cambridge in England emphasized a humanist approach to the liberal arts, reducing instruction in scholasticism. Latin, Greek, and Hebrew were added to the curriculum, and students read a wide array of classical literature. This model was exported to the British colonies in America, with the founding of Harvard (by the Puritans) in 1636, William and Mary in 1693, and Yale in 1701 (Kimball, 1986, pp. 100–106). Although these Protestant colleges significantly altered the liberal arts curriculum, they retained the *artes liberales* goal of building character, of creating citizens worthy to lead the community by example (Bok, 1987, p. 13).

Although the impact of Enlightenment thinkers on liberal arts curriculum initially was minimal, there was a noticeable shift in the goals of liberal arts education by the nineteenth century. The liberal arts ideal began to be influenced by the rise of the modern research university in Germany; increasing emphasis on individual freedom and democratic ideals, particularly in the United States; and the growth of more secular, state-sponsored institutions in Europe and

the United States. Increasingly, training in the liberal arts emphasized preparing young men to make their way in a new, modernizing
world.

A Center of Cultivation and Character Development

The German university system profoundly influenced liberal arts
education in Europe and the United States. As mentioned in Chapter 1, Humboldt's vision for the new German institution embraced
the concept of *Bildung*, or character formation through education,
as a crucial part of German culture. Intrinsic to Humboldt's idea
of education was academic freedom and absence of restrictions on
curriculum; what was most important was the method and goals of
education. Each student should be "educated (*gebildet*) to be moral
men and good citizens (*sittlichen Menschen und guten Bürger*). . . .
The following must therefore be achieved; that with the method of
instruction one cares not that this or that be learned; but rather that
in learning memory be exercised, understanding sharpened, judgment rectified, and moral feeling (*sittliche Gefühl*) refined" (Humboldt, 1903–20 vol. X: 205, quoted in Sorkin, 1983, p. 64).

Although the *artes liberales* ideals of antiquity echo in Humboldt's words, what was new was the idea that the university was *the*
place and source of cultivation and development. As historian Fritz
Ringer noted, the German idea of university training was quasi-
mystical, involving a romantic view of the individual's spiritual self-
awakening rather than a specific curriculum of coursework (Ringer,
1969, pp. 90–105).

The *Bildung* ideal of self-development at the highest level was
reflected in the ideal of the "gentleman" in the American and British
college and university. Although clearly informed by Enlightenment
notions of the reasoning individual, the gentleman was "the meeting
ground of the [medieval] knightly ideal, the Renaissance humanist
program, and the Christian ethical standard" (Kimball, 1986, p. 108).

By the late eighteenth century, a liberal arts education was intended to shape men's manners, minds, and morals in order to instill "the principles of piety and justice and a sacred regard for truth, love of their country, humanity and universal benevolence, sobriety, industry and frugality, chastity, moderation and temperance, and those other virtues which are the ornament of human society and the basis upon which a republican constitution is founded" (Massachusetts General Laws, Chapter 71, Section 30, quoted in Bok, 1987, p. 4).

Increasingly, the gentleman ideal emphasized an education that would prepare one for service in a free society based on some form of representative government, morphing into what Bruce Kimball referred to as the "liberal-free ideal," which emphasized freedom, human intellect and rationality, volition rather than obligation, and an increasing egalitarianism (Kimball, 1986, pp. 119–122). Included in Thomas Jefferson's list of ends for University of Virginia graduates was "to expound the principles and structure of government, the laws which regulate the intercourse of nations, those formed municipally for our own government, and a sound spirit of legislation, which, banishing all arbitrary and unnecessary restraint on individual action, shall leave us free to do whatever does not violate the equal rights of another" (Jefferson, 1818, pp. 459–460). The growing importance of individual freedom and choice, influenced by Enlightenment attitudes about humankind's capacity for rational thought, changed the view of the purpose of liberal education.

An increasing emphasis on freedom and choice necessarily led to a modified curriculum as well, spurred on by the maturation of the modern university in the later nineteenth century. These changes coincided with the philosophical and scientific developments traced throughout this book, notably the retreat from a belief in a world guided by a benevolent God.

Intellectual discourse in the mid-to-late nineteenth century was dominated by the belief in positivism, a philosophy espoused by

Auguste Comte. Positivism entailed an orderly, progressive advance of society and the human condition that could be understood through scientific inquiry and research. Supported by the development of new areas of inquiry, including anthropology and sociology, academics in the nineteenth century believed that truth could be found through specialized research in increasingly narrow areas of specialized knowledge. Led by the German universities, higher education curriculum began to be organized departmentally, as each field and subspecialty sought to establish itself in the hierarchy of academic institutions. The ever-expanding array of offerings available to undergraduates transformed the liberal arts curriculum, and as the "liberal-free ideal" encouraged students to pursue their disciplines of choice, the traditional liberal arts coursework became highly flexible. In the 1870s, Harvard introduced the elective system, allowing undergraduates to select from a wide range of courses rather than complete a fixed path of studies.

Challenges to Learning

By the turn of the century, Humboldt's idealized academia—a place where academic freedom and independent research thrived—had become a research-oriented institution that barely resembled the liberal arts ideal of antiquity. Intellectuals in Europe and the United States retreated from positivism in the face of massive socioeconomic change that challenged the very notion of human progress and rationality. Industrialization and the associated creation of mass societies, the rise of socialism, nationalistic movements, democratic uprisings, and the expansion of suffrage were but a few of the forces at work. New fields of psychology, as well as the philosophies of Henri Bergson and others who espoused direct experience and intuition as being more important than rationalism, challenged old notions of rational, scientific inquiry. That, in turn, created intellectual disorder in universities reflective of the social and cultural disorder that existed outside the ivory tower.

In America, industrial expansion following the Civil War led to calls for a more pragmatic bent to higher education. That fueled the attitude that a liberal arts curriculum was hopelessly outdated and ill suited to the needs of modern Americans.

In the German universities, Fritz Ringer's "German mandarins" decried the modernizing influences of more pragmatic course offerings and an increasingly democratic approach to learning.

The famous debate between Thomas Huxley and Matthew Arnold, two English writers who presented opposing views of a university education in the 1880s, illustrated the core nature of the turmoil within academe. In his address called "Science and Culture," Huxley argued that liberal education should include not just the study of classical literature of antiquity but also scientific inquiry. Arnold later defended the values contained in Greco-Roman texts, arguing that the ideals of the *artes liberales* led to greater understanding of the human condition (Kimball, 1986, pp. 171–174).

There were various responses to the questioning of a liberal arts education's relevance. Some defended the traditional curriculum as being a way to train the mind or develop general intellectual faculties. Others emphasized the importance of counterbalancing the growing emphasis on technical specialization, pointing out the role of the liberal arts in creating "well-rounded" human beings.

One result of this growing debate was the creation of general education courses, a movement influenced by the thinking of John Dewey. In 1920, Columbia University English professor John Erskine devised a core humanities course devoted to the study of classic texts. This two-year honors program centered on student discussions of "great books" designed to pique a life-long interest in reading and intellectual development (Cross, 1995). Another was the "Great Books" program developed by Robert M. Hutchins, president of the

University of Chicago during the 1930s. Hutchins advocated the use of a core canon of texts, or "Great Books," at Chicago; in the 1950s he marketed these texts to businessmen in a special series called *Great Books of the Western World*. During the 1920s and 1930s, there were several such attempts to establish some kind of structure and order in liberal arts curricula, but, as Kimball remarked, such efforts actually led to more diversity rather than less (Kimball, 1986, pp. 186–200). Many new liberal arts colleges were founded in this era, including Bennington College (1932), an independent college for women employing a loosely structured curriculum that emphasized individual creative exploration.

After World War II, enrollment on college campuses skyrocketed, as the civil rights movement paved the way for more access for women and people of color. Student activism and demands for expanded rights dramatically changed the culture on college campuses as university students engaged in the larger issues of their day. Increasing numbers of women and minority students attending colleges led to the appearance of ethnic and women's studies departments in the 1980s and 1990s. These changes led to renewed outcry regarding the fragmentation of higher education, this time over the "balkanization" of the curriculum. Author Allan Bloom published *The Closing of the American Mind*, in which he argued that the liberal arts tradition had become hopelessly tainted by moral relativism and the loss of its earlier ideals (Bloom, 1988).

The idea of a liberal arts education has also come under pressure from the changing role of education in society. Beginning in the 1980s, students started to demand that they receive marketable skills from their university training. Higher education has become a product to be purchased in the marketplace, and thus consumers seek the highest return for their dollar. As the goal of education has shifted from creating an educated human being to providing specific employment-related training that can be leveraged in the job market, the entire concept of a liberal arts education has come under fire (Readings, 1996).

The debate over the status and relevance of the liberal arts continues. Many of the contemporary defenses of a liberal arts education echo the "liberal-free ideal," such as "Respecting Freedom of Inquiry and the Pursuit of Truth," or the appeals to general education ("Developing Critical Thinking and Discernment") or the earlier moral ends of antiquity ("Grounding Education in Values") (Stancil, 2003, pp. 250–251). Others have attempted to reformulate and update the liberal arts ideal for a modern, diverse society; University of Chicago professor Andrew Chrucky has stated that "the aim of liberal education is to create persons who have the ability and the disposition to try to reach agreements on matters of fact, theory, and actions through rational discussions" (Chrucky, 2003, p. 3). Phi Beta Kappa Secretary John Churchill downplayed the role of agreement, instead highlighting the need for the counterbalancing influence of liberal arts training: "If deliberative culture is lost to us—or lost *by* us—it will be because we will lack adequate, publicly accessible processes for the *critical comparison of ideas and the actions to which those ideas lead.* That lack will be traceable to our worship of the specialized and technical to the neglect of the general and the humane. And that, unfortunately, is our trend. The work to counteract this trend must be done in confused and muddy terrain, contentious terrain, where necessary argumentation is obscured by uncertainty and ambiguity" (Churchill, 2006, p. 2).

HISTORY OF MANAGEMENT TRAINING AND PROFESSIONAL BUSINESS SCHOOLS

The rise of the professional business school began in the nineteenth century. As noted, higher education became increasingly specialized, and Americans in particular demanded more pragmatic courses of study in response to the industrialization of the United States. Concurrent with this development was the origin of several professional organizations, as the new, educated middle class sought to distinguish itself from the lower laboring class. The American Medical Association, American Bar Association, and American Economic Association represented the concern in the late nineteenth century and early twentieth century with structure and order; establishing standards for practicing professionals became a way of signaling legitimacy in a complex society (Wiebe, 1967, pp. 111–112).

As the modern corporation provided more and more white-collar job opportunities, individuals in newly created positions also sought professional status and its associated respect and prestige. The history of the business school is thus intrinsically linked to the larger trend toward specialization and professionalization that permeated the American middle class.

In spite of its nineteenth-century context, the history of the business school shares common ground with the longer history of the liberal arts ideal. The idea that one educational path was rooted in pragmatic matters while the other always aimed for more lofty ideals of human development is incorrect. In every era, liberal arts education has involved the nurturing of qualities and abilities that can be put into use in day-to-day life. For example, Greco-Roman societies intended the *artes liberales* education to prepare an elite corps of leaders. Although there were disagreements regarding which elements of the curriculum to emphasize, such as rhetoric or logic, the overarching goal was to produce model citizens who would be prepared to lead society. Also, not all of the medieval students of the liberal arts were monks; many were elites who were expected to become leaders in society following their education (Kimball, 1986, p. 53).

The earliest American liberal arts colleges did not simply educate "deep thinkers"; Yale's founding document states that "youth may be instructed in the Arts & Sciences who through the blessing of Almighty God may be fitted for Public employment both in church and Civil State" ("Act for Liberty to Erect a Collegiate School," 1701, p. 21). Indeed, the Puritans actively sought to reconcile the tension between their religious beliefs and their prosperity; financial gain, honestly earned, was in fact considered a sign of God's favor. The concept of the calling, in which Puritans worshiped God through work, also illustrates this blending of the pragmatic and the holy: "A true believing Christian, a justified person, he lives in his vocation by his faith. Not only my spiritual life but even my civil life in this world, all the life I live, is by the faith of the Son of God" (Cotton, 1956, p. 173).

Once the colonies became the United States, the values of the *artes liberales* were placed in service of the new republic. As Gordon Wood has argued, the founders believed that the success of the new nation depended on its adherence to classical ideals of virtue, ideals that they gleaned from Greco-Roman texts they themselves had read (in translation). And, of course, the only way to instill those ideals was through education.

Benjamin Rush and others noted that the American public would not naturally embrace the spirit of republicanism, or the willingness to consider the needs of the larger nation over individual desires and prejudices. Rather, "the republican pupil must 'be taught that he does not belong to himself, but that he is public property'" (Wood, 1998, p. 427). Thomas Jefferson's University of Virginia was founded not just to "develop the reasoning faculties of our youth," but also "to harmonize and promote the interest of agriculture, manufactures and commerce" (Jefferson, 1818, p. 480).

Ushered in by Jacksonian democracy, universal white male suffrage increased the need for an educated populace; while higher education remained the domain of the elite, the burgeoning public school movement of the nineteenth century spread not only literacy to the general population but also the idea that an educated citizenry would make virtuous and wise voting decisions (Sellers, 1991, pp. 364–369). This connection between the liberal arts and the pragmatic affairs of government and business remains today, as evidenced by the role of general education course requirements at most college campuses. Many institutions have revised or are in the process of revamping their general education requirements to make them more relevant to the needs of today's society, yet the driving philosophy behind the liberal arts ideal remains: to turn out well-rounded students who are grounded in agreed-upon values.[3]

Divisions between Management and the Liberal Arts

If education, particularly in America, has always emphasized the importance of both instilling cultural values and developing the ability to function in society, then what is the source of the current divide between management and the liberal arts? When did the liberal arts become irrelevant to the training of managers? And when did the business of organizations and the concern with a functioning society become divorced from the interests of those engaged in the liberal arts? To understand the origin of this split between management and the liberal arts is to begin to understand how to repair it.

The disruptions associated with the rise of the modern corporation in the United States have been well documented. Beginning with the railroads in the 1860s and 1870s and continuing with entities such as Standard Oil and Carnegie Steel, modern capitalism was met with growing trepidation and suspicion on the part of the American public, as increasingly larger and larger companies wielded more and more power. Labor unrest, such as the Great Railroad Strike of 1877 and the Haymarket Riot of 1884, coupled with a growing urban population of immigrants, added to public concern that the price of progress was perhaps too steep. Progressive reformers sought solutions to poverty, corruption, crime, and other urban ills, while government did little to curb the power of the trusts; in fact, a great merger boom in the late 1890s created even larger organizations with even more economic and political power.

Amid these disruptions of late nineteenth-century society, the leaders of the burgeoning private sector sought to legitimize their authority. As Rakesh Khurana has argued, managers saw that affiliating themselves with the modern research universities would validate business as a profession. Just as higher education had dedicated itself to a tradition inherited from the liberal arts ideal, management, too, could embrace "its own rationality, disinterestedness, and commitment to commonly held values" (Khurana, 2007, p. 87). Through its retention of the liberal arts curriculum, albeit modified through the elective system and acceptance of the "liberal-free ideal," the American university continued the traditional emphasis on character formation and human development through the tumultuous late nineteenth century. Any group of practitioners wishing to consider themselves "professionals" would be well served by having some attachment to that moral and ethical tradition.

It is not surprising, then, that the first business school sought to capitalize on the trend toward scientific specialization while retaining elements of the liberal arts tradition. The University of Pennsylvania's Wharton School of Business, established in 1881, was the first university-based business school; by 1893, there were more than 500 commercial business colleges in the United States (Khurana, 2007, p. 89). As did Penn, Dartmouth and Harvard responded to the growing call for management training and founded their own schools of business: Tuck School of Administration and Finance (1900) and Harvard Business School (1908), respectively.

The curriculum at each school reflected the interest in science that permeated university debates at the turn of the century. Scientific management, notably Taylorism, the scientific study and analysis of work to improve productivity, dominated the coursework at business schools, as managers sought to put themselves on the same level as other professionals by emphasizing the rational nature of their discipline. Yet, Harvard, Dartmouth, and Penn all came from the liberal arts tradition, and thus valued the inherited ideals of character formation and the development of well-rounded citizens and leaders.

There was, therefore, a concern that the new business schools needed to be differentiated from the existing commercial schools. Key to this process of differentiation was the linkage with the liberal arts tradition inherent in each school. Wharton's mission was to educate America's upper crust who had inherited family money and needed to develop the "social consciousness and moral character" behind a life of service to the community, whether through business or government employment. Tuck mandated a "3 + 2" curriculum, in which students were required to complete three years of liberal arts study before they enrolled in the graduate business program; the idea behind this structure was to develop graduates who were broadly educated, not just interested in making money. Similarly, Harvard's business program required incoming students to have a liberal arts education. Referencing Harvard's founding document, which stated that the institution's mission was "to advance Learning, and perpetuate it to posterity, dreading to leave an illiterate Ministery to the Churches, when our present Ministers shall lie in the Dust," Owen Young said in his dedication speech for Harvard Business School that "the Harvard Graduate School of Business Administration will do its utmost to guard against an illiterate ministry of business when our present ministers shall lie in the dust." Linking the new business school with the liberal arts college's founding ensured that the values of old would be inscribed on the new institution (Khurana, 2007, pp. 105–121).

Just as the university-based management programs gained a foothold, government began to scrutinize the private sector more closely. Progressive literature, such as Frank Norris's *The Octopus* (1901), which indicted the railroad monopoly in the west, and Ida M. Tarbell's *The History of the Standard Oil Company* (1904), exposed some of the more questionable practices of American capitalists. President Theodore Roosevelt instigated actions to reign in big business, including the Expedition Act of 1903, which ordered circuit courts to give antitrust suits priority. Roosevelt also created the departments of Commerce and Labor, recognizing the need for government intervention in business affairs. The Panic of 1907, which seized the nation's financial system, precipitated a series of reforms; the Pujo Committee hearings on banking policy and practices would eventually lead to financial reforms under the administration of Woodrow Wilson, such as the creation of the Federal Reserve System.

The new university-based business schools responded to this changing environment. In order to promote the professionalism of businessmen, the new business schools emphasized scientific management and rationalism in their curriculum in the early twentieth century. Much of the disorder of late nineteenth- and early twentieth-century society involved labor disputes. Frederick Winslow Taylor devised scientific management to improve the economic welfare of labor and to reduce labor-management conflict. Taylor's approach to management stemmed from his belief in the common interest between the worker and management. If by the use of scientific management Taylor and his followers could increase the productivity of both labor and capital, the result would be lower unit cost, higher wages, and higher profits. Taylor thus saw congruence between the interests of labor and management.

Taylor's influence on the business school curriculum increased after World War I, when management training was in high demand. After the United States entered the war in 1918, the needs of war production placed unprecedented demands on businesses, and the obsession with efficiency and planning reached new heights. President Woodrow Wilson created the War Industries Board to oversee the production of war materiel. Headed by Bernard Baruch, a successful investor on Wall Street, the War Industries Board exercised broad authority over the public sector. Herbert Hoover headed the Food Administration, using propaganda campaigns to entice the public to regulate its food consumption through such gimmicks as

"Meatless Tuesdays." The War Industries Board served as the model for a new concept of capitalism involving cooperation between government and business.

By 1920, big business was no longer seen as the source of disruption. Instead, business, and its managerial professionals, held the answers to regulating the ups and downs of society. Most Americans believed that management, planning, and efficiency were the key to social order and prosperity.

Scientific management and efficiency were not the only subjects stressed in business school courses, however. As discussed earlier, the belief in science and rational forward progress faced challenges in the late nineteenth and early twentieth centuries. Political upheaval, social disorder, and the technological realities of World War I, which included mustard gas and mechanized warfare, indicated that science and technology did not necessarily promise improvements to the human condition. In the new business schools as well as the research universities, the liberal arts remained the source of moral grounding for students in light of the seemingly immoral face of modern technological developments. In American colleges and universities, faculty sought to reinstate the primacy of the humanities through such vehicles as the core course and canons of "great books." Business schools wrestled with how to incorporate the ideals of the liberal arts into their curriculum. In graduate programs, students were expected to come armed with undergraduate training in the humanities before they began graduate study in business; however, that did not answer the question of how to instill professionalism and a social conscience in the curriculum itself or how to sow those values in undergraduate business programs. The result was a rather shotgun approach to curriculum development, with each school creating its own course structure haphazardly. Some schools organized their courses to train managers for specific jobs, while others sought to link management closely to economics or to restructure traditional liberal arts courses (math, English, and history) to make them relevant to businessmen (accounting, business correspondence, and business history). It was not until the Great Depression that business school curriculum became more standardized, as more and more university deans expressed concern about the quality and goals of programs (Khurana, 2007, pp. 154–170).

During the Great Depression, American capitalism came under scrutiny by those in academe as well as practicing managers and executives. In the early years following the stock market crash of 1929, most Americans continued to embrace corporatism, the cooperative relationship between business and government that reigned during the presidency of Herbert Hoover. However, as economic conditions deteriorated, and as the business experts seemed not to have the answers to the nation's woes after all, management as a profession came under fire. Trained business professionals, the trustees of commerce, clearly could not solve the economic malaise that plagued the country. With the election of Franklin Delano Roosevelt in 1932, Americans rejected the model of the business elite as expert and replaced it with a new emphasis on planning and bureaucracy in the public sector (Kennedy, 2009).

Faced with this new attitude, managers and the business schools that trained them sought to shore up the image of both corporations in general and management as a profession. Two Columbia University professors, Gardiner Means and Adolf Berle, published *The Modern Corporation and Private Property* (1932, 1933), in which they argued that American businesses were no longer run by owner-managers with a vested interest in the company. Instead, ownership in companies had become diffused among many people through profit sharing and pension plans. Corporate managers thus had a passive role and were only interested in the company's profitability, not its day-to-day operations. The modern corporation, Berle and Means concluded, created a new form of property ownership in which the shareholders were subjected to the priorities of powerful managers. *The Modern Corporation and Private Property* presented the case for managers to consider their obligations to society, not just their own interests. In a time when corporate management was blamed for causing the Great Depression, Berle and Means called on managers to understand their responsibilities for serving a much broader, diverse group of shareholders: the general public itself (Berle and Means, 1933).

Business school curriculum also reflected the public's new attitude. Academics criticized the increasingly specialized and technical bent to business school coursework, arguing that managers were no longer inculcated with a sense of social and ethical responsibility. Some called for more liberal arts courses in business schools, stating that a return to the earlier ideals of education would restore a sense of morality in graduates. Many schools created new courses designed to demonstrate the relationship between business and society. Others incorporated new elements into existing classes; for example, Harvard professors began to discuss the importance of government regulation of the private sector. In an effort to respond to the drastic changes taking place during the 1930s, business schools entered a period of "introspection that helped set the stage for a renewal of purpose" (Khurana, 2007, pp. 180–192).

Postwar Challenges

This renewed sense of purpose was short lived, however. After World War II, most business schools returned to their former hodgepodge approach to curriculum "unified by little but the frayed idea of management as a distinct subject of study" (Khurana, 2007, p. 197). In spite of this, the demand for professionally trained managers boomed as America's corporate sector expanded. During the war, government and business adopted the corporatist model of cooperation that dominated the period after World War I. After the bombing of Pearl Harbor brought the United States into World War II, Roosevelt established the War Production Board, which, like the earlier War Industries Board, oversaw production for military operations. Under the command of Don Nelson, Sears's top executive, and other "dollar-a-year" men who agreed to work for no salary, the War Production Board imprinted the influence of corporate executives on the conduct of the war. Marketing campaigns aimed at the public sought to promote conservation, and advertising techniques were used to instill brand loyalty among the troops. Managerial training in productivity paid off in spades, as the private sector produced armaments and supplies on a massive scale to support the war effort.

Following the war, firms faced challenges associated with idle production capacity; factories that had churned out planes and tanks now needed to make something else that people would buy—and buy in large quantities—or sit idle. In many cases, firms diversified in order to use their manufacturing facilities. General Electric and Westinghouse expanded into consumer appliances, and DuPont embarked on an aggressive research and development program to replace its explosives business with other products. As firms diversified, they became more complex, restructuring along divisional lines in order to manage these new enterprises (Chandler, 1977, pp. 299–303).

As corporations became more complex, so did issues involving management. The massive expansion of America's private sector in the post–World War II era drove a heavy demand for trained, professional managers to help run the newly restructured firms as well as the up-and-coming businesses in budding industries such as consumer credit. The GI Bill, or the Servicemen's Readjustment Act of 1944, which provided unprecedented access to higher education for most white American men, resulted in a flood of new students in the nation's colleges and universities. Many of these incoming students opted for degrees in business (Khurana, 2007, pp. 211–212).[4]

The growing demand for and supply of trained managers threw the business schools in the spotlight, and as had occurred in the

1930s, questions of quality and mission surfaced. Despite reform efforts during the Depression, business schools lacked academic credibility well into the 1950s. University faculty in other departments viewed the business department or school as little more than a place for vocational training; business courses were seen as lacking in academic rigor, and department faculty's research was considered second rate at best.

In the 1950s, two research entities, the Ford and Carnegie foundations, reported on the quality of American management programs. Both foundations had substantial impact on higher education, as they gave generous endowments to fund academic research. In 1959, the Ford and Carnegie foundations presented their respective reports; Ford's report, titled *Higher Education for Business*, garnered most of the attention. The tone and content of the Ford document shattered the image and confidence of the business school community. Both studies concluded that business education in America lacked any cohesive curriculum, failed to instill any sense of professionalism and accountability to society, and suffered from a serious absence of academic quality and content. Management curriculum, the authors argued, should reflect the knowledge that management was a science involving methodologies that could be taught in a systematic way. Reflecting the idea that business education should mirror the modern research university, the Ford report posited that business faculty needed to engage in state-of-the-art research to ensure that students were kept abreast of the latest developments in management science.

In part, the Ford report was indicative of broader changes in the American economy and economic inquiry. By the fifties, the American corporation and its representative, the white-collar manager, were ingrained in popular culture. In 1954 approximately 27 percent of the workforce was employed in occupations classified as white collar (Solomon, 1954).[5] C. Wright Mills' *White Collar: The American Middle Class* (1951) and William Whyte's sociological study *The*

Organization Man (1956) characterized the corporate manager as a conformist bureaucrat, exposing fears of the controlling power of modern business. Dramas such as Rod Serling's award-winning film *Patterns* (1956) and *The Man in the Gray Flannel Suit* (1957) captured many of the concerns Americans had about the impact of corporate life on men and their families. The nature of managerial work and the corporate environment came into question: were these new white-collar workers turning into soulless "yes men," willing to sacrifice their individuality and moral fiber for pecuniary gain? If so, a drastic change was needed both to reform the way this work was done and to change the attitude of the workers themselves.

Simultaneously, literature on management began to proliferate. Drucker's *The Practice of Management* (1954) put management on the map as a discipline worthy of study, while Abraham Maslow and others were applying behavioral psychology to the world of work. In economics, John Maynard Keynes's ideas continued to rule the day, but increasingly the field was dominated by those using mathematical models and quantitative methods to evaluate human decisions and behavior. Kenneth Arrow's work on general equilibrium and social choice theory involved innovative use of mathematical models to influence public policy decisions. Thus, as popular culture reflected a corporate world lacking in human dignity and integrity, economists and management theorists countered with a portrait of a cool, calm world based on rational decisions made by trained professionals.

The Ford and Carnegie foundation reports transformed the American business schools. Business faculty, like their peers in other fields, pursued increasingly specialized areas of research, establishing their scholarly credibility. The curriculum at most major schools (except for Harvard, which retained its famous case study method) fell into a prescribed model of coursework; by 1970, one could describe a "typical" MBA program. But, as Khurana argued, the attempt to turn out professional managers via such standardized, academically oriented programs had a cost. By focusing on rational decision making, the business schools lost their original concept of professionalism, which "had always rested on combining mastery of specific knowledge with adherence to certain formal or informal codes of conduct and, even more fundamental, to an ideal of service" (Khurana, 2007, p. 291). In other words, the emphasis on quantitative methods and management science eradicated the ideals of the liberal arts. The human component of management was lost.

This became apparent in the structure and management of many American companies. As firms expanded and diversified in the postwar environment, they experimented with varying degrees of centralization and decentralization. The larger and more diverse firms became, the more their managers relied on financial statistics and information systems to control daily operations. In fact, many of the large conglomerates created during the 1950s and 1960s defied conventional management wisdom, and could only be justified on financial bases. Seeking new investments in a postwar boom environment, companies began to look outside of their areas of expertise to identity acquisition possibilities. Textron, the first such conglomerate, was made up of defense manufacturers, a golf cart company, a financial services wing, and a consumer products division. Whereas the mergers during the late nineteenth century had emphasized developing supply networks, refining distribution systems, or reducing competition, the new merger wave created companies with unrelated businesses in different markets with different customers. Such investment decisions were based on financial projections, as companies looked for new opportunities to invest funds thrown off from their "cash cows." Management theorists emphasized decision models, systems theories, and strategic planning. Robert McNamara and his "whiz kids" brought rationalization and statistical analysis to a new level of importance at Ford. Thus, in spite of work by Drucker and others emphasizing the human component of management, the fifties and sixties were decades in which analytical managers were king.

Social and Economic Upheavals

The shift toward analytical skills and increasing specialization in the business schools went unchallenged until the social and economic upheavals of the late 1960s and 1970s. The civil rights movement spawned a new culture in which tradition and inherited values were questioned, leading to student activism and protest around such issues as the war in Viet Nam, women's and gay rights, and the role of the military-industrial complex. Watergate caused a serious crisis of faith in government, and the financial shenanigans of conglomerate LTV Corporation, which resulted in its bankruptcy, tarnished the image of the private sector. The American economy, too, experienced profound change. Gone were the growth years of the postwar era. Instead, war in the Middle East caused hyperinflation of oil prices, and stagflation defied all explanation from conventional economic theories. American manufacturing jobs began to disappear, a trend that would accelerate into the 1980s. President Jimmy Carter reflected the nation's mood in his July 15, 1979, "malaise" speech, in which he stated, "We are confronted with a moral and spiritual crisis" (PBS.org, n.d.).

Politicians and economists searched for answers to the nation's woes. Milton Friedman and the Chicago School of Economics preached nongovernment interference in markets, arguing against Keynesian policies of public spending to stimulate the economy. Washington blamed the Organization of the Petroleum Exporting Countries (OPEC) for not only gas shortages but also widespread inflation. Management literature reflected the fallen status of business leaders. Henry Mintzberg's 1973/1980 study of managers, *The Nature of Managerial Work*, revealed the dehumanizing nature of managerial activity (Mintzberg, 1973/1980). Like Taylor's shovelers,

Mintzberg's white-collar managers were slaves to the moment, alienated from their work and governed by tasks imposed from above. In their article titled "Managing Our Way to Economic Decline," Harvard Business School professors Robert Hayes and William J. Abernathy pointed the finger at management training, noting that the emphasis on management as a science had created a "false and shallow concept of the professional manager, a 'pseudo-professional' who erroneously believed he or she could step into an unfamiliar company and run it successfully through strict application of financial controls, portfolio concepts, and a market-driven strategy" (Hayes and Abernathy, 1980, p. 74).

Increasingly, corporate executives were portrayed as loose cannons incapable of effectively managing organizations. The Chicago School's market-driven philosophy permeated the discussion of American capitalism, as shareholder value and short-term financial results became the only valid measure of corporate performance. As economists exerted more influence in business schools, beginning in the late 1970s and early 1980s, agency theory dominated the curriculum of MBA programs. Under agency theory, managers are viewed as agents of shareholders, and they are seen as having their own conflicting values.

The secret to aligning the interests of shareholders and managers is to compensate managers by rewarding them for increases in share values. The use of stock options and incentives would ensure that managers would, in looking out for their own financial well-being, also be serving the interests of the shareholder. As Khurana argues, agency theory created a new class of managers who "were no longer fiduciaries or custodians of the corporation and its values. Instead, they were hired hands, free agents who, undertaking no permanent commitment to any collective interests or norms, represented the antithesis of the professional" (Khurana, 2007, p. 325).

Managers no longer had any sense of loyalty to the organization; instead, they viewed their work as one more emotionless, market-driven exchange devoid of human relations. In Drucker's words, the corporate world had become a jungle, and "you bring your own machete" (Harris, 1993, pp. 114–122). Corporate downsizing, right-sizing, reengineering—whatever term one chooses to use, the mass restructuring of American business in the 1980s and 1990s merely reinforced agency theory's concept of the temporary nature of work and the absence of relationships and community in the workplace. Employees of all stripes competed in a vast market for labor—and "corporations once built to last like pyramids . . . [were] more like tents" (Drucker, 1998b, p. 177).

The same market-driven philosophy permeated the business schools themselves. Just as humanities departments had to redefine themselves to remain relevant, MBA programs began to compete with each other in a grand marketplace where prospective students were seen as potential customers. *BusinessWeek*'s 1988 inaugural ranking of MBA programs in the United States launched a new round of self-evaluation, as schools battled for the top spots on the list to attract the best students. Instead of emphasizing the institutions' academic quality, the *BusinessWeek* rankings weighted more "user friendly" criteria, such as starting salaries of graduates and volume of job offers received. In keeping with the "greed is good" mentality of the 1980s, MBA programs that could prove a return on investment for students and/or parents fared better in the rankings than prestigious schools with strong research programs (Khurana, 2007, p. 336). The same pressures brought to bear on liberal arts programs, demanding that they prove their utility in terms of training in marketable skills, influenced graduate programs in business.

As the glory days of Wall Street in the 1980s led to the 1990s dot-com explosion of wealth production, the market-driven philosophy of American capitalism seemed to have permanently altered the nature of management and management training. An MBA was no longer about acquiring skills or learning the nature of a profession; instead, it was about obtaining a network of lucrative alumni connections. But as the bubble burst on Wall Street in the late 1990s, and as evidence of insider trading and other financial wrongdoing at AT&T, Enron, Tyco, and many other firms leaked out, the flaws of agency theory became apparent: rewarding all players for share value would lead some to employ questionable or illegal methods of increasing share value. The unemotional, rational model of management could not curb the irrational human emotions of greed and lust for power. As Bethany McLean and Peter Elkind show in their book *The Smartest Guys in the Room: The Amazing Rise and Scandalous Fall of Enron*, the ancient Greek concept of hubris is alive and well in twenty-first century American business (McLean and Elkind, 2003).

Management as a profession, as a discipline, and as a practice was broken and battered before the mortgage meltdown and credit crisis shattered the global economy beginning in 2007. Wall Street's continued payouts of bonuses while accepting government bailout money, Bernie Madoff's Ponzi scheme, AIG's lavish resort weekend for employees just prior to its financial downfall—the public image of management as a profession and capitalism in general plummeted along with the Dow Jones Industrial Average. Business schools, practicing managers, and the media provided a multitude of explanations for the failures of American business. Warren Bennis, management professor at the University of Southern California, stated that MBA programs place "an overemphasis on the rigor and an underemphasis on relevance," while McGill University professor Henry Mintzberg noted that the reliance on case studies, or "packaged versions of business problems," prevents students from acquiring applicable skills (Holland, 2009, p. 2).

Business schools are busy revamping their curriculum; Yale School of Management has joined with the Aspen Institute to develop courses designed to teach students to incorporate values into their work life. Harvard is revising its case list to include recent examples of the financial crisis (Holland, 2009, p. 4). And Brown

University has announced an experimental joint MBA program with the Instituto Empresa Business School of Madrid, Spain. The executive program will have its roots in the liberal arts and utilize faculty from all disciplines in its design and delivery (Kagan, 2010).

In his book *The Management Myth*, philosopher turned management consultant Matthew Stewart lambasts the entire notion of management theory, arguing that most of what is taught—and practiced—is gibberish (Stewart, 2009). Others place the blame for the financial debacle on the insulation of corporate executives and their out-of-whack priorities; *New York Times* business columnist Ben Stein and billionaire Carl Icahn both agree that American executives have become accustomed—even addicted—to obscenely high salaries and company perks (Mankiewicz, 2009). Whether one chooses to blame the direction of MBA programs, the market-driven compensation packages of CEOs, or the steady erosion of government oversight of corporate activities, it is clear that there is much hand-wringing over the state of management as a profession.

PARALLEL HISTORIES: LINKING MANAGEMENT AND THE LIBERAL ARTS

The parallel histories of the liberal arts and management show how management as a liberal art might begin to link the two together again. The key lies in recognizing the need for social relevance of both traditions, and restoring their most crucial components.

As early as the debate over "philosophers" or "orators," those fashioning the liberal arts idea encountered questions of the end of a liberal arts education. For centuries, those attempting to fashion a liberal arts education have been raising questions of what its aims should be: should it be merely to pursue some definition of virtue, or should it also be to model it? Or: How to reconcile the past and its traditions with change?

As we have seen in this chapter, the liberal arts tradition has embraced a variety of ends and virtues, including the "liberal-free ideal," emphasizing humanism and democratic values, and the "well-rounded" human being in a modern technological society. Yet, in each and every case, the liberal arts has had some kind of social relevance, whether that relevance has reflected the need for clergy members in a dominantly religious society, for an educated class of political leaders in a growing democracy, or for a broadly educated citizenry expected to participate intelligently and morally in the day-to-day life of modern society. Today, in many respects, the liberal arts struggle to be socially relevant, particularly in an academic world where specialized, individual intellectual achievement is valued but applicability to the general public (or students not specializing in the humanities) is not.

The business school tradition illustrates a similar trend toward lack of social relevance and intense specialization. In the early years of management education, its very validity relied on its ties to the liberal arts, which were seen as the bastion of virtue and morality. However, increasing specialization in analytical and technical skills led to a disconnect with the liberal arts after World War II. As a result, management education has turned out trained functionaries with no sense of their broader responsibilities to greater society.

Just as the liberal arts have been redefined to fit the needs of society, business schools have redefined their curricula to meet the requirements of an increasingly financially driven model of American capitalism. The result is that today, as that model comes into serious question on a number of fronts, management as a profession has no social relevance; the discipline has lost its connection to the human values and dimensions that were so crucial to its early existence.

In order to bridge the divide between the two, management as a liberal art must work toward making both the liberal arts and management socially relevant. The histories of the liberal arts tradition and management education illustrate similarities involving debates about the purpose of education; the nature of the curriculum; and most importantly what is valued by universities and students. Management as liberal art can help us answer these question for many individuals, institutions, and society as a whole, and in doing so, give relevance to liberal arts and ground management in concerns for the human condition. We can reaffirm and update the initial connections involving social relevance, such as the idea of creating "orators" or citizens in the sense of the "liberal-free ideal," as well as grounding managers in an understanding of the human condition and the social role and nature of organizations.

Drucker's concept of a "tolerable" society provides us with a way to practice management as a liberal art, and thus to make both the practice of management and the liberal arts socially relevant once more. This is clear from the link between Drucker's major intellectual influences and the primary concerns of liberal arts and management education. As we now know, business education once gained its credibility through its connections to the liberal arts and the aims of such academic training. Although the composition and aim of a liberal arts education has shifted over time, there are elements that have remained since the concept of the *artes liberales* originated with antiquity. Regardless of the time period, the liberal arts idea has included the transmission and/or retention of some system of values and morals; a balancing of individual freedom and development with an obligation to society; and the negotiation of a middle road between retaining traditions of the past and accommodating change. Interestingly, these three traits are also important themes found in the intellectual influences on Peter Drucker's work.

As discussed in Chapter 1, Kierkegaard, the three German thinkers, and Burke, Schumpeter, and Sloan contributed to Drucker's vision of a functioning society of well-managed institutions. Religious and philosophical morals and ethics, the social needs of free individuals, and the challenges of discontinuity (in political and other forms) are all components of Drucker's "bearable" society.

In the next chapter, we will see how management as a liberal art employs these components and contributes to eliminating the gap between academics and practicing managers.

CHAPTER 3

CONTRIBUTIONS OF MANAGEMENT AS A LIBERAL ART

As discussed in the previous chapter, management as a liberal art has the potential to reconnect management education with its historic link to the liberal arts. It can also reinforce the connection between a liberal arts education and functioning as a member of society or one of its constituent organizations. Management as a liberal art shows promise for practicing managers and those engaged in the liberal arts fields as well. This chapter presents some of the contributions of management as a liberal art to both managers and academics, as well as a discussion of the broader issues the subject raises: the nature of values, ethics, and the role of character; the importance of context and perspective; and the function and nature of learning and knowledge. Finally, we briefly describe some of the very real limitations of management as a liberal art.

CONTRIBUTIONS OF MANAGEMENT AS A LIBERAL ART TO THE LIBERAL ARTS

Those within the academic community have of late bemoaned the state of liberal arts education. The shift in students away from the humanities and social sciences toward business is well documented. In the 1970–1971 academic year, 7.6 percent of undergraduates majored in English, 18.5 percent in history, and 13.7 in business. Those percentages shifted in the 2003–2004 academic year to 3.9, 10.7, and 21.9 respectively; business has become the most popular major in America's institutions of higher learning (Chace, 2009, p. 32). More and more of these students are enrolling in public universities instead of smaller, private colleges; in both types of institutions, however, humanities course offerings are increasingly diminished in favor of more pragmatic classes, as pressure from parents, students, and alumni donors forces even small liberal arts colleges to offer more courses that will prepare students for a job.

What are the driving forces behind the decline in the liberal arts? Some are obviously financial. As tuitions have increased faster than the rate of inflation, a college education has become outrageously expensive for average middle-class families. Students and their families take on additional debt loads to finance a college degree, and the pressure mounts for matriculating students to find a job as soon as possible after graduation in order to pay off the accumulated debt. The appeal of a business major over a liberal arts course of study is clear if the goal of education is to obtain the skills necessary for a job. Alexander W. Astin, Professor of Higher Education Emeritus at the University of California, Los Angeles, found that in the mid-1960s, 80 percent of entering freshmen claimed that "developing a meaningful philosophy of life" ranked most important in their college goals. By 2001, over 70 percent of students cited "being very well off financially" as most important (Chace, 2009, p. 36).

One cannot deny the role of money in the decline of the liberal arts in America. Yet it is too easy merely to point to financial concerns as the sole reason for this state of affairs. Many within the liberal arts community have commented on the lack of vision or mission in humanities programs or liberal arts colleges. Christina Elliott

Sorum, who served as classics department chair and dean of faculty at Union College, wrote that her institution's mission was "muddled, especially with regard to the questions of whether we should or can teach values and of why the liberal arts are relevant beyond the teaching of skills" (Sorum, 2005, p. 27). As Sorum noted, during Union's accreditation review process, the faculty confronted a number of questions faced by many other colleges and humanities departments:

> Is our role to teach critical thinking skills or to imbue students with the wisdom and traditions that have shaped their culture? Or is it to open student minds to an ever changing world and to train them to cope with constantly expanding fields of knowledge? Or is it to train individuals in English or political science or biology and get them into medical or law school? Does or should a liberal arts education have an overt civic purpose? Should or can we teach values in our diverse world? (Sorum, 2005, p. 27)

Sorum wrestled with the broader question of how to make the liberal arts relevant to today's society. Of course, as discussed in Chapter 2, the liberal arts and liberal arts education have always been modified and adjusted to fit the times, and thus it should come as no surprise that there is a need to revitalize the humanities once again. It is our hope, however, that management as a liberal art is viewed as one means for the liberal arts to reassert its importance in the community and society. By connecting the benefits of a liberal arts education and approach to the practice of management, management as a liberal art can reinvigorate the humanities without losing the spirit of liberal arts inquiry.

Management as a liberal art can also bring the force of the liberal arts perspective to the study of management in its larger historical context. Using the disciplines of the humanities and social sciences, scholars can shed new light on the role of management in the development and reflection of broader trends in culture and society. Historians, literary scholars, and those engaged in the study of the visual arts and music could benefit by treating management itself as a topic of liberal arts inquiry. Students of popular music, for example, might explore how artists also function as managers. The Grateful Dead (or The Dead) band encouraged fans to make recordings of the band's live performances and then distribute these recordings to friends and relatives free of charge over the Internet. The band knew that distribution channels for music were changing, and they decided to encourage free distribution of their music to a vast worldwide audience. The band thus expanded its "brand recognition" and simultaneously its market for live performances (Kot, 2009).

There has been some new scholarship in this direction, although much ground remains to be covered. Some authors have begun to delve into the intellectual and philosophical origins of management concepts (Peskin, 2003; Augspurger, 2004; Linkletter, 2004; Immerwahr, 2009), while others have emphasized the transformative role of the rise of managerial capitalism in American culture and society (Trachtenberg, 1982; Davis, 2000; Hooper and Hooper, 2007). Barbara Czarniawska's creative work involves the analysis of how popular culture has influenced management practice and theory (Czarniawska and Rhodes, 2006). Czarniawska argues that elements of myths and common plot formulations impact decision making and attitudes within organizations, including attitudes about what constitutes appropriate leadership and gendered behavior.

In spite of this and other related scholarship, there is much room for additional work in studying management from a variety of perspectives. How have management practices in various organizations reflected broader social and cultural influences? How has popular culture (for example, movies, television, radio, and music) mirrored attitudes about management, or challenged those attitudes? How has public sentiment regarding corporate governance changed over time, and what factors have driven these changes? Have managers changed their practices in response to cultural influences? There are many avenues for study that would benefit the body of liberal arts scholarship as well as the knowledge of practicing managers.

Management as a liberal art provides an opportunity for practitioners in the liberal arts to consider the practice of management as a subject worthy of consideration. The study of management from a liberal arts perspective can help bridge the gap between the humanities and business. Furthermore, the practice of management as a liberal art can breathe new life into the importance and relevance of a liberal arts training in today's society. As much as those in the liberal arts may bemoan the state of affairs, it is clear that the trend toward occupational fields dominating undergraduate education is not likely to change. According to one recent study, it appears that "any rebirth of the arts and sciences as the center of undergraduate education probably lies well in the future, at a time when the bachelor's degree has become a preparatory degree for a majority of students who are planning to pursue postgraduate training rather than the mass terminal degree it is today. And even in this distant future it is possible that the arts and sciences will become the preserve of a still smaller number of students and faculty than they are today, if they are further devalued by a society that has turned away from the types of intellectualism they reflect and sustain" (Brint et al., 2005, p. 174).

CONTRIBUTIONS OF MANAGEMENT AS A LIBERAL ART TO MANAGEMENT

If the state of liberal arts education is in disarray, the status of management as a profession might be likened to a patient on life support. From 2007's mortgage meltdown to the outcry over 2009's bonus awards to employees of financial institutions that received government bailout funds, the private sector's apparent inability to function ethically or effectively has resulted in much collective hand-wringing about the state of American business.

Not surprisingly, perhaps, some have voiced the benefits of infusing the liberal arts into not just the *education* of management but also the *practice* of management. One author has noted that the broad aims of an education in the humanities would provide useful training for working managers, including an understanding of "the ultimate values behind our decisions," critical thinking skills, and improved ability to developing convincing arguments (Arenas, 2006, p. 127). Some of the nation's top business schools have recognized the potential for liberal arts graduates to succeed as managers; in 1997, Dartmouth's Tuck School of Business developed a Business Bridge Program to train liberal arts majors in business concepts, thus enhancing their ability to work in management positions. Recruited by a variety of companies, graduates from these programs clearly possess a blend of traits coveted by employers (Rafter, 2004).

Most often it is the character-developing, or moral, component of liberal arts training that interests those who would seek to link the liberal arts and management. Behind this is an understanding that management is inherently an activity involving human beings, not just technology and data. There seems to be an increasing discomfort with the tendency to extend the neutrality of markets to managers; as Khurana (2007, p. 364) has argued, efforts to align the self-interest of managers with that of shareholders have not met with universally happy results.

University of Reading Professor of Management John Hendry has made an excellent case for the values of the humanities for practicing managers. He argues that management education has not kept pace with changes in twenty-first-century organizations (Hendry, 2006). The bureaucratic structures of yesterday's organizations limited individual judgment, personality, and moral discernment. Today's "post-bureaucratic" organizations, relying less on hierarchy and more on shared leadership and authority, require the very types of human qualities that management training in the past sought to quash.

In spite of their desire to cast themselves as morally neutral, managers are anything but that, according to Hendry: "Moral management, then, is no easier in post-bureaucracy than it was in bureaucracy, but in a central and critically important sense, morality is now what management is all about" (Hendry, 2006, p. 31). The mundane, everyday work of organizations is now done by technology (computers), leaving the more human activity to people. This means that management now more than ever involves entrepreneurial decisions, managing relationships, building trust, understanding diverse needs and how to accommodate them fairly, and a whole host of other complex, human-related activities. The modern manager is anything but neutral. Says Hendry: "The moral dimension has to be managed directly, by managers, through the medium of personal relationships" (Hendry, 2006, p. 31).

Managers thus need to know not just about the nuts and bolts of finance and cost accounting but also about human nature, judgment, the role and source of values and morals, and other intangible qualities. Hendry argues that the humanities can provide the foundation for today's manager; particularly history and literature can do so, but so can social anthropology and sociology (Hendry, 2006, p. 37). Through exposure to disciplines that train students in understanding the human condition, a liberal arts education can prepare managers to be more effective in today's less-hierarchical organizations.

MAJOR ISSUES RAISED BY MANAGEMENT AS A LIBERAL ART

The imperative of morality in leadership is prominent in Drucker's work. And training in morality has historically been one of the features of a liberal arts education. This training played a prominent role in Drucker's education in the liberal arts. These issues and the influences upon Drucker related to them are explored in this section.

Values, Ethics, and the Question of Character

As discussed in Chapter 2, an education in the liberal arts has always included some degree of moral development as one of its aims. Although the character traits valued by cultures have varied over time, the overarching goal of fostering "good character," or developing people of "virtue," has remained a component of liberal arts training. Management as a liberal art, therefore, must raise the subject of values, ethics, and the definition of "character."

Such issues bring up all kinds of questions: If the study and practice of management as a liberal art involves inculcating values, whose values receive priority? What constitutes "character" in today's world, and does it vary from culture to culture? Are there timeless and universal morals or values that all can agree are good, or is there no such thing as a universally accepted value? Should one judge character by one's intentions or one's actions? Or both? Such broad questions are the stuff of philosophical inquiry, but they are also at the heart of practicing management as a liberal art.

If management is truly a liberal art, it must allow the individual a path of free inquiry into such broader questions. One of the hallmarks of a liberal arts education, after all, is its emphasis on so-called critical thinking skills, which include the ability to synthesize concepts, use higher-level reasoning and analysis to evaluate problems, and develop well-crafted arguments based on sound evidence. Such higher-order thinking inevitably involves making complex ethical and moral decisions. For example, is it acceptable to sacrifice one life to save an entire community? Is torture ever justified as a means to extract information? Should one engage in local business practices even if they violate the ethical norms of one's own culture? Are economic sanctions an effective form of diplomacy, or are they too harmful to the civilian population of the targeted country? Like these, most difficult questions in the management realm involve some ethical component, and they cannot be governed by a simple list of dos and don'ts that apply universally in all cases.

In a sense, then, management as a liberal art is in part an exercise in moral philosophy, specifically virtue ethics. Rather than prescribing a fixed set of rules for behavior, management as a liberal art focuses on developing the person as a whole so that decisions are made not just because the moral code says so but also because the person has the desire and disposition to make the right decisions consistently.

Virtue ethics derive from Aristotelian thought, specifically the *Nicomachean Ethics*. Aristotle argued that moral character requires education; one must learn proper behavior by practicing it. Thus virtuous behavior is formed by habit. Importantly, though, one must choose to practice virtuous behavior. In Aristotle's model, people of character aren't just born that way; they develop over time, coming to the realization that virtuous behavior is the right way to act in a given situation. Virtue is chosen for its own sake, not because of some fixed set of rules. Nor is virtue practiced "accidentally"; by definition, virtuous behavior is chosen behavior.

Aristotle defined virtuous behavior as that which falls within the mean: it is not extreme in any way (by nature of either its deficiency or its excess). He identified 12 specific moral virtues that he believed comprise a fulfilling life (*eudaimonia*). Each of the 12 virtues also has a parallel set of two vices associated with failing to achieve the mean. For example, truthfulness as a virtue can become either the vice of understatement or boastfulness, depending on to what degree one either exceeds or falls short of the mean. With training and practice, the virtuous person develops the sense and disposition to choose the virtuous mean for all of the 12 virtues.

Modern virtue theory does not simply advocate a return to Aristotelian philosophy in its entirety. In many respects, Aristotle's ideas were a reflection of his own time, and there is good reason to question their applicability to the modern world. For example, are Aristotle's 12 virtues adequate, complete, and relevant for today's society? Should his list be augmented, or should some of his virtues be replaced with others that we value more highly today? Such questions are not new, as philosophers through time have altered Aristotelian thought to reflect their own values. Thomas Aquinas expanded Aristotle's list of virtues in his *Summa Theologica* to include the Christian ideals of faith, hope, and charity as "theological" virtues. In *An Enquiry Concerning the Principles of Morals*, David Hume defined virtues as qualities deemed useful or approved of by human observers (and thus based on emotion rather than reason). Immanuel Kant's moral philosophy argued the opposite position, that moral codes were based on reason. More recently, Scottish philosopher Alasdair MacIntyre posited that virtues have varied according to time and culture. In his groundbreaking work *After Virtue* (MacIntyre, 1981), he postulated that society needed to return to Aristotle's philosophy in order to rectify the damage done by the overemphasis on individualism since the Enlightenment. MacIntyre argued that humans are the by-product of a shared historical narrative, and that developing agreed-upon shared values as a community is integral to human existence. While these values will certainly change, depending on the community and its unique history, there is nonetheless a need for grounding in shared values, as contrasted with a society where each individual forms his or her own values independently.

Management as a liberal art therefore involves an understanding of the historical context of values for different cultures and periods as well as an appreciation of agreed-upon virtues for a given organization or society. The spirit of liberal arts inquiry, while traditionally focused on the cultural production of the West, involves this kind of open exploration of larger philosophical questions. Made up of human beings, organizations must also consider these same broader cultural and philosophical questions. For example, as Elmer Johnson, former executive vice president of General Motors, has remarked, the General Motors–Toyota joint venture forced his company to confront larger issues of human motivation, dignity, and meaning:

> It is ironic that we were forced by competitive considerations to learn from a non-Western culture some rather basic truths as they apply to the workplace. The ideas behind the Toyota system, translated into the language of the Western religious and ethical traditions, are simple and yet profound. First, each employee of the enterprise has complementary gifts and talents and resources. The wealth-creating power of the corporation depends on the recognition of that complementarity. Second, while there are necessarily different levels of authority and responsibility in the enterprise, we are all equal as human beings and our spiritual side far transcends the narrow commercial purposes of the corporation. Accordingly, respect for all persons is fundamental. Third, while there may often be tension between these human values and our legitimate business purposes, there is no basic conflict. More often than not, the two are mutually reinforcing. (Johnson, 2005, pp. 62–63)

By analyzing the values of another culture, General Motors (at least during the 1980s) radically changed its management philosophy, and it subsequently discovered that "the business corporation best serves its stockholders and customers by creating a moral community" (Johnson, 2005, p. 63).

With its emphasis on open and liberal inquiry, management as a liberal art cannot prescribe a laundry list of virtues to be embraced. Rather, it embraces the exploration of the question itself. Such a proposition may gall practicing managers unused to or uncomfortable with such language, but the concept of the organization as a moral entity is not new. Adam Smith is well known for his argument against mercantilism in *The Wealth of Nations* (1776/1994); while advocating free trade, Smith points to competition as the regulating force to control the negative impacts of self-interest. However, in his earlier work, *The Theory of Moral Sentiments* (1759), Smith calls on human sympathy to regulate the tension between self-interest and the greater good; it is our understanding that our actions impact others that curbs self-interest in Smith's moral system. This part of Smith's philosophy has been lost by most, glossed over by vague references to the "invisible hand" and laissez faire capitalism as a moral system in and of itself. Self-interest itself, as many from Adam Smith on have noted, cannot serve as a moral force.

But, then, what can? There have certainly been attempts to create global standards of ethics and morals based on common religious values, concepts of human rights, and other virtues shared by those engaged in the process.[1] For example, the Hague Convention of 1899 and the Geneva Convention of 1925 were early international efforts to establish codes of conduct for warfare based on shared understanding of human rights. The Atlantic Charter of 1941 more explicitly sought to elucidate a set of universal human freedoms and rights, albeit framed from a decidedly Western (even, arguably, a distinctly American) perspective. Shortly thereafter, in December 1948, the United Nations issued its Universal Declaration of Human Rights, which detailed in 30 articles those rights the General Committee deemed to be common to all human beings. Drafted during the Cold War, the Universal Declaration was controversial; in the 1955 Bandung Conference, developing nations exerted increasing influence, developing their own statement of principles to foster human development and maintain rights. The fact that such documents were forged out of disagreement and controversy indicates that identifying truly universal values remains elusive, certainly at the geopolitical level.

Others have sought a solution at the organizational level. As Lord Griffiths of Fforestfach has detailed, there is a history of efforts to define a "new global ethic as the foundation for a global society" (Lord Griffiths of Fforestfach, 2005, p. 129). In 1973, at the third meeting of the European Management Symposium in Davos, Switzerland, members drafted a Code of Ethics, later referred to as the Davos Manifesto. Based on the stakeholder concept, this code emphasized the interrelationships between organizations and their suppliers, customers, competitors, and society at large. While the code emphasized the need for return on investment and profitability, it also highlighted the fact that "management has to serve its employees because in a free society leadership must integrate the interests of those who are led. In particular, the management has to ensure the continuity of employees, the improvement of real income and the humanization of the work place" (World Economic Forum, 2009, p. 16). Others have sought global solutions to self-interest; in 1988, a group of Muslim, Christian, and Jewish representatives developed an Interfaith Declaration on a Code for Ethics for International Business in Amman, Jordan. In a global, multicultural environment, the question of the source of values becomes complex in the twenty-first century. Nevertheless, that does not mean we can neglect the question, or that we cannot find some kind of consensus as we consider an increasing range of perspectives. For example, business ethics expert Bettina Palazzo has analyzed the cultural assumptions (which, quoting Alexis de Tocqueville, she refers to as "habits of the heart") inherent in American and German companies; she not only exposes the very real differences between the two but offers pointed suggestions for common ground (Palazzo, 2002).

As discussed in Chapter 1, Drucker's guiding set of virtues was firmly grounded in the Judeo-Christian religious tradition. In addition to the central influence of Søren Kierkegaard, Drucker was also influenced by the western philosophical heritage stemming from Aristotle. We turn now to examine these additional philosophical and religious influences.

Saint Augustine (354–430)

Augustine of Hippo was born in North Africa to a Christian mother and pagan father. He studied at the University of Carthage. Augustine converted to Catholicism in 387 after he moved to Milan and was mentored by Bishop Ambrose. He was appointed Bishop of Hippo in 395, and he formed a monastic community there. He is well known for defining Christian orthodox belief, such as the belief in original sin. Heavily influenced by Plato, Augustine delved into such questions as the nature and origins of evil, the role of free will, and the relationship between faith and reason. Augustine's influence on Drucker's work is most apparent in Drucker's discussions of freedom and responsibility. For Drucker, freedom and responsibility are intertwined; his is a positive definition of freedom, involving not merely the absence of limits on individual action but also the ability to decide to act for a greater purpose than one's own personal gain. Drucker's definition of freedom derived from Christian roots, particularly from the writings of Augustine and St. Paul: "The roots of freedom are in the Sermon on the Mount and in the Epistles of St. Paul; the first flower of the tree of liberty was St. Augustine" (Drucker, 1942, p. 113).

Drucker grounded his view of freedom in the Augustinian concept of original sin: humankind has inherited the taint of sin from Adam, and thus is prone to weakness and requires God's grace to gain salvation. This notion of human nature is crucial to understanding Drucker's entire body of work, as it infuses virtually everything he wrote. For Drucker, the natural human condition is that of original sin, after the Fall of Man:

The only basis of freedom is the Christian concept of man's nature: imperfect, weak, a sinner, and dust destined unto dust; yet made in God's image and responsible for his actions. Only if man is conceived as basically and immutably imperfect and impermanent, is freedom philosophically both natural and necessary. And only if he is seen as basically and inescapably responsible for his acts and decisions, in spite of his imperfection and impermanence, is freedom politically possible as well as required. (Drucker, 1942, pp. 110–111)

Augustine's doctrine of original sin dictated that humanity could not perfect itself; salvation could not come from one's own actions because of humankind's very nature, nor could humans divine truth without God's assistance. Yet, Augustine believed that humans possessed free will; evil, in fact, derived from poor human decisions, not God.

Thus, even though God possessed foreknowledge (and thus would know which decision a person would make before he or she made it), Augustine stated that this did not negate the existence of free will; God's foreknowledge did not necessarily dictate human choice. In Drucker's words, a person is "responsible for his actions and decisions, in spite of his imperfection." God's omnipotence, the Fall, or original sin does not get humanity off the hook for poor decisions; our decisions are our own.[2]

In *City of God*, Augustine contrasts the City of God (often interpreted as the Catholic Church or Christian faith) with the earthly, pagan City of Man. Written after the Visigoths sacked Rome in 410, *City of God* attempted to explain why, in spite of earthly turmoil, the Christian kingdom would triumph. As Rome experienced several waves of barbarian invasions, pagans increasingly blamed the Christian empire; when citizens sacrificed to the pagan gods, they claimed, Rome was a peaceful city. Augustine's response was to revisit Roman history, showing that even in its pagan heyday, Rome suffered from violence. The City of Man, Augustine concluded, could never find harmony or peace; perfection was possible only in the City of God, not in the material realm.

Existing on the same plane as the City of Man, Drucker's functioning society, too, can never attain perfection; one can hope only for a "livable" or "bearable" society. Freedom in this functioning society does not involve license to follow one's desires as one pleases. Freedom instead involves the Augustinian notion of free will: tainted by original sin, human beings cannot choose to do the right thing by their nature. Rather, they need the grace and guidance of God in order to properly exercise their free will. Freedom for both Drucker and Augustine, then, involves human alignment with divine purpose and authority.

Saint Paul (c. 10–c. 65)

Saul of Tarsus was a Roman citizen and Jewish Pharisee renowned for persecuting Christians. According to the Book of Acts, on his way to Damascus to round up members of the Christian sect, he heard the voice of Jesus speak to him (Acts 9:3–5). He eventually became a devout follower of Christ and an ardent missionary, traveling throughout the Middle East and Asia Minor and into Macedonia and Greece to establish numerous churches. He was arrested in Jerusalem, brought before the Jewish council, and imprisoned in Caesarea for two years, under Roman guardianship. Paul was tried in Rome, and martyred under the rule of Emperor Nero.

Like Augustine, Paul contributed important concepts of freedom to Drucker's idea of a bearable society. In particular, Paul's notion of Christian liberty, which involved willing submission to Christ's authority in service to one another, can be seen in Drucker's expectations for individual responsibility.

Paul's letters to the various early churches reveal his own, unique interpretation of Christianity. One of the images found in several of the epistles is that of slavery and freedom. In his letter to the Galatians (Galatians 4, verses 21–31, especially verse 4:31), Paul uses this juxtaposition to illustrate his vision of Christian liberty. Like many of the early Christian communities, the Galatians consisted of Jewish Christians and Gentiles, or non-Jewish converts. As these communities grew, disputes arose as to how to assimilate non-Jews into

Jewish life. Should Gentiles be subject to Jewish law, such as dietary codes and circumcision requirements? In some communities, these debates gave rise to deep divisions, as people argued over how the law should be interpreted and who was, in effect, a "true believer."

As he did in most of his epistles, Paul contrasted the role of law and faith in governing the Galatian community. In essence, Paul argued that the importance of Christ was inclusivity; Gentiles and Jews alike were to be included in God's community: "For in Christ Jesus neither circumcision nor uncircumcision counts for anything; the only thing that counts is faith working through love" (Gal 5:6, NRSV).

Importantly for our purposes, Paul used the language of slavery and freedom to illustrate this concept of inclusivity; he stated that Jewish law was a necessary step in the course of human development, but "now that faith has come, we are no longer subject to a disciplinarian. . . . There is no longer Jew or Greek, there is no longer slave or free, there is no longer male and female; for all of you are one in Christ Jesus" (Gal 5:25–28).

In Paul's language, Christ brings freedom, but with that freedom comes responsibility. Indeed, Paul claimed that in their newfound freedom, the Galatians were to "become slaves to one another" (Gal 5:13). The message is one of service; while no longer slaves to the old laws, the new spirit of freedom requires that "all must carry their own loads" in order for the community to function (Gal 6:5). In reality, Paul made the case that Christian freedom would, in fact, result in the keeping of Jewish laws, although through different motivations. The Galatians should do the right thing out of a sense of communal obligation and love for one another rather than fear of retribution. Thus faith became the source; the law became the course.

As we have seen, Drucker's assumptions about human nature played a pivotal role in his assessments of U.S. society, as well as his synthesis of management theory. Although he was not necessarily a utopian, Drucker nevertheless placed his faith in the responsible individual as he defined it: guided by a sense of humility, obligation to higher authority and community, and well aware of his or her own imperfection.

Gottfried Wilhelm Leibniz (1646–1716)

Drucker wrote "there are only two philosophers I subscribe to— those prophets of diversity, Leibnitz and St. Bonaventura" in order to emphasize that the point of his work "has always been that the right thing is what fits a particular institution at a particular time for a specific purpose" (Drucker, 1985, p. 28).

Gottfried Wilhelm Leibniz[3] was born in Leipzig, Germany. His father, Friedrich, was a university professor; following Friedrich's death in 1652, young Gottfried's mother took responsibility for the boy's education, turning him loose in the family library, where Leibniz read widely in philosophy, history, and science. He later attended the universities of Leipzig and Altdorf, earning his doctorate of law in 1667. Instead of pursuing an academic career, Leibniz worked for several German noble families. He served as a diplomat in Paris from 1672 to 1676, then returned to Germany, living in Hamburg, where he served as an advisor to the House of Brunswick.

Leibniz was a polymath. He discovered calculus independently of Newton (although accusations of plagiarism dogged him during his life), attempted to develop a blueprint for unifying the Catholic and Protestant churches, and served as a mining engineering consultant. But it is Leibniz's contributions in philosophy and metaphysics that influenced Drucker's work. In the words of biographer Maria Rosa Antognazza, Leibniz's life centered on a "master project" that focused his multiple interests:

Throughout his life Leibniz nursed essentially the same dream: the dream of recalling the multiplicity of human knowledge to a logical, metaphysical, and pedagogical unity, centered on the theistic vision of the Christian tradition and aimed at the common good. (Antognazza, p. 6)

Leibniz sought to develop a series of texts that would, taken together, encompass all knowledge and order it along a single, theological basis. This encyclopedia would bring order to the diversity of all human knowledge, aligning it with the source of all good: God. In essence, Leibniz's work can be seen as an effort to bring unity to chaos, or to draw diversity into the service of the unifying force of goodness.

Yet Leibniz was no utopian. His idea of "the best of all possible worlds," as described in his work *Theodicy: Essays on the Goodness of God, the Freedom of Man, and the Origin of Evil* (1710), bears a strong resemblance to Drucker's concept of the "bearable society." Just as Drucker dealt with the question of evil (in the form of fascism) and the need for individual meaning in the world, Leibniz tackled the theological question that lingered in his era: if God is good and all-powerful, then why does He permit evil in the world?

One cannot deny that there is in the world physical evil (that is, suffering) and moral evil (that is, crime) and even that physical evil is not always distributed here on earth according to the proportion of moral evil, as it seems that justice demands. There remains, then, this question of natural theology, how a sole Principle, all-good, all-wise and all-powerful, has been able to admit evil, and especially to permit sin, and how it could resolve to make the wicked often happy and the good unhappy? (Leibniz, 1710/1985, p. 98)

The end of the belief in salvation by society surely marks an inward turning. It makes possible renewed emphasis on the individual, the person. It may even lead—at least we can so hope–to a return to individual responsibility. (Drucker, 1993, p. 13)

Leibniz shared the view of Saint Augustine, that evil is merely the absence or lack of goodness (see Augustine, 1467/1984, p. 445). Therefore, God does not create evil; evil only exists as a privation. Leibniz took this argument further, stating that there are three kinds of evil: metaphysical evil (imperfection); physical evil (suffering); and moral evil (sin). If evil exists as a lack of good, then metaphysical evil (imperfection) gives rise to the other two forms of evil. We suffer because we are physically imperfect. We sin because we lack moral understanding, and we make mistakes.

So why would God create a world that was less than perfect, and thus susceptible to evil? Leibniz's answer was that God chose from among several possible worlds, and selected the most perfect one possible. Leibniz defined perfection as that which maximizes variety and harmony. Because both variety and harmony are important, God necessarily had to make trade-off decisions involving each attribute of the world. Thus, in some cases, variety, or diversity, may have been sacrificed for order, or harmony. As God made these trade-off decisions, He ultimately arrived at the perfect balance, and the best of all possible worlds. However, humans tend to view the world only in terms of how it impacts them, not in terms of the larger picture. As a result, we may see imperfection, where in reality, God chose the most perfect world that was possible, given the choices He had:

No substance is absolutely contemptible or absolutely precious before God. . . . It is certain that God sets greater store by a man than a lion; nevertheless it can hardly be said with certainty that God prefers a single man in all respects to the whole of lion-kind. Even should that be so, it would by no means follow that the interest of a certain number of men would prevail over the consideration of a general disorder diffused through an infinite number of creatures. This opinion would be a remnant of the old and somewhat discredited maxim, that all is made solely for man. (Leibniz, 1710/1985, pp. 188–189)

Leibniz's "best of all possible worlds," then, is not a utopia for humanity, although it has been interpreted as such. Voltaire's *Candide* features a character named Dr. Pangloss, a devotee of Leibniz, who pronounces this the best possible world despite one disaster after another; Candide famously responds, "If this is the best of possible worlds, what must the others be like?" (Voltaire, p. 16).[4] Although Leibniz arguably held an optimistic view of human existence, his thesis acknowledges the existence of imperfection, or evil. Drucker, too, recognized that imperfection is part of the trade-off for increased diversity. For Drucker, diversity was most visible in humanity, as evidenced by the variety of abilities and interests that distinguish us from one another. Rather than attempting to "fix" perceived imperfections, Drucker called on people to see the elegance in the balance:

Maybe the problem is that you, my friends, start out with the idea that there is or should be *one right way*. The whole point of the teaching of this old anti-Thomist, anti-Cartesian, anti-Kantian has always been that the right thing is what fits a particular institution at a particular time for a specific purpose. . . I profoundly believe that our job here on earth is not to try to improve the Lord's handiwork—however much we may carp about it—but to use it both to glorify the Lord and to do our work. (Drucker, 1985, p. 28)

Leibniz served as a "prophet of diversity" for Drucker through his construction of the "best of all possible worlds." Rather than attempting to find the "*one* infallible technique" that doesn't exist, or trying to "reform the boss (or even the subordinate)," Drucker advises executives to "*Stop bellyaching about what you cannot do. What can you do?*" (Drucker, 1985, pp. 28–29). Like Leibniz, Drucker, while optimistic about human potential, nevertheless recognized that human individuality necessarily involves fallibility. If evil is defined as human imperfection or weakness, then it is part of a diverse world: "human beings perversely insist on behaving like human beings, and that . . . means pettiness and greed, vanity and the lust for power and, yes, *evil*" (Drucker, 1985, p. 31). The best of all possible worlds can only be a bearable society.

Saint Bonaventure (1217–1274)

Drucker named Bonaventure as another "prophet of diversity." Born Giovanni di Fidanza in central Italy, Bonaventure studied at the University of Paris at a pivotal time in medieval history. During the twelfth and thirteenth centuries, Aristotle's writings became available in Western Europe, setting off a wave of interest in Greek classical literature in the increasingly important universities, including the University of Paris. Simultaneously, a wave of monastic reform movements swept the Catholic Church, led by the Franciscans, who embraced poverty as a way of life. The monastic movement led to the Lateran IV council, which established a program of church reforms, including the provision that every Catholic receive communion and attend confession at least once annually. As a result, the monasteries, including the Franciscan order, became centers of education, training friars in pastoral service to the laity.[5]

Bonaventure took his new name when he entered the Franciscan order in 1234. He studied theology at the university, receiving his *licentia docendi* (what we would refer to as a doctoral degree) in 1254. Bonaventure taught at the university and Franciscan convent, and in 1273 he was appointed Cardinal Bishop of Albano. At the time of his death in Lyons, he was one of the most prominent figures in the Catholic Church.

Bonaventure's theology addressed the enormous upheaval that resulted from the rediscovery of Aristotle's works in the West. Because there were discrepancies between scriptural and classical texts, conflict arose as to the use of the new documents; some attempted to prevent them from being taught, while others, such as Thomas Aquinas, were highly receptive. The study of Aristotelian and other Greek texts gave rise to Scholasticism, a method of teaching that sought to produce knowledge consistent with both reason and faith. Scholastics used Aristotelian logic to argue for the existence of God and other theological points. Scholasticism led to a burst of new questions about knowledge, the nature of God and man, and the role and place of theology and philosophy. How would one study God—through theology or through philosophy? Aristotle's work *Metaphysics* sparked this controversy: did reason or faith play the more important role in understanding God and the nature of existence? (Gracia and Noone, 2003).

Ultimately, Bonaventure viewed philosophy as a means, not an end. Truth, immutable truth as understood through God's wisdom, was the end of all inquiry. Without this truth, nothing could be understood or known. His primary contribution to Drucker's thought was this emphasis on truth, understood in the absolute sense. For Drucker, Bonaventure was a "prophet of diversity" because of his belief that in divine truth, all things are united and understood. Rational inquiry or human pursuit of knowledge is valid only if guided by the quest for this truth. Quoting Bonaventure (who paraphrased the Epistle of St. James), Drucker noted:

> "All knowledge leads back to the Source of All Light and to the Knowledge of Ultimate Truth." I must admit that I am not quite sure how cost accounting, or the study of tax

loopholes, or brand marketing, will lead back to the Source of All Light, let alone to the knowledge of Ultimate Truth. But I am quite sure that the spirit of St. Bonaventure's short sentence must animate all we do if management is to have results. (Drucker, 1988, p. 5)

For Bonaventure, all knowledge led directly to God through Christ; the goal of learning in any discipline was not learning for learning's sake, but to study God and the soul. One of Bonaventure's contributions was that one could find God, or truth, through not just scripture but also the arts and sciences. This "spirit" of learning and knowledge—focused on larger issues of truth and values—informs Drucker's concept of management as a liberal art. It looms over all that Drucker wrote and reminds his readers of the limitations of human rationality.

In *The New Society*, written in the throes of the Cold War, Drucker states that political action, while necessary, would not "overcome the profound spiritual crisis of Western man," nor was it a "substitute for the great Prophet who shall call this generation to repentance, [or] for the great Saint who shall turn our vision back to the source of all light" (Drucker, 1950, p. 352). Bonaventure served as Drucker's reminder that the crises of his time were not merely political, but spiritual, requiring a focus on the "source of all light" that unifies all. The union of wisdom with practical actions is, after all, at the very heart of Drucker's concept of management as a liberal art.

Reinhold Niebuhr (1892–1971)

Reinhold Niebuhr was a Protestant theologian who sought to apply Christian teachings to twentieth-century industrial society. He graduated from Yale Divinity School in 1914, and took a position in a Detroit parish, where he witnessed the realities of working-class life through his parishioners, many of whom worked for Ford Motor Company. From 1928 to 1960, he was on the faculty of Union Theological Seminary in New York. A member of the American Socialist party and a pacifist, Niebuhr was active in the burgeoning ecumenical movement of the 1930s. Increasingly, however, he distanced himself from the idealism of the Social Gospel Protestants, who sought to bring a Kingdom of God to fruition on earth. Like Augustine, Niebuhr delved extensively into the role of sin and the corruption of humanity, and its ramifications for modern society (Fox, 1985).

Niebuhr's theology clearly continued in the vein of many of Drucker's other influencers, such as Saints Augustine and Paul. Niebuhr, however, explicitly tied his Augustinian interpretation of human nature to capitalist society, and he overtly refuted the idealism of Marxism and many mainline Protestants.

Late in his life, Drucker acknowledged Niebuhr's influence on his work, referring to Niebuhr as "my great teacher" (Buford, 1991, p. 5). Both Drucker and Niebuhr embraced a similar view of the tension between individual existence and existence within society. Like Drucker, Niebuhr attempted to come to terms with humanity's capacity for violence and malice toward one another, in spite of various attempts to better society through education, technology, and political reform. Niebuhr's conclusions regarding human beings and society are instructive, as they clearly parallel Drucker's own views.

Although Niebuhr's political stance changed during his life (like many intellectuals, he repudiated his support of socialism following the Hitler-Stalin pact in 1939), he retained a consistent position regarding the relationship between individuals and society. In his 1932 book, *Moral Man and Immoral Society*, Niebuhr argues that, while individuals can be guided by genuinely charitable and selfless motives, society as a whole can never truly reflect these individual characteristics. He believed it was naïve to assume that larger forces, including religion, could curb self-centered impulses in every human being to the point of creating a perfectly benevolent society. In Niebuhr's view, sociologists, Social Gospel Protestants, and others who envisioned perfect social harmony neglected to recognize that there are "elements in man's collective behavior which belong to the order of nature and can never be brought completely under the dominion of reason or conscience" (Niebuhr, 1932/2001, p. xxvi).

Technological and educational advancements had not reduced conflict; in fact, argued Niebuhr, they had in many ways increased it. Furthermore, religion's ability to smooth over inherent power struggles was limited; he noted that religion tends to one of two extreme positions, neither of which is conducive to societal harmony. One tendency is toward defeatism, which Niebuhr illustrates using Augustinian thought: "the tendency of religion to obscure the shades and shadows of moral life, by painting only the contrast between the white radiance of divine holiness and the darkness of the world, remains a permanent characteristic of the religious life" (Niebuhr, 1932, p. 69). If all that is earthly is pure evil, hopelessly separated from the City of God, then all efforts to improve conditions on earth are a waste of time. The other extreme position Niebuhr refers to as sentimentality, which he ascribes to liberal Protestants who embrace "evolutionary optimism and the romantic overestimates of human virtue" (Niebuhr, 1932, p. 78). Religion, then, is highly personal for Niebuhr, and reminiscent of Drucker's Kierkegaardian individual before God.

Like Drucker, Niebuhr had no easy solutions to the problem of immoral society. Eventually, he placed his faith in the institution of democracy; in *The Children of Light and the Children of Darkness* (1944), Niebuhr set up another seemingly simple moral opposition that he proceeded to complicate. Just as *Moral Man and Immoral Society* did not merely show that individuals were moral and society evil, Niebuhr's 1944 book, while portraying Western democracy favorably against German, Soviet, and Italian totalitarianism, does not let the Children of Light (individuals who believe in a moral law beyond their own will) off the hook. Although Niebuhr believed that democratic institutions provided the best solution to the societal problems he had identified, he by no means posited that democratic peoples were inherently more moral than those in nondemocratic nations. The Children of Light were just as susceptible to evil doings as the Children of Dark. In fact, Niebuhr stated, the Children of Light had "underestimated the power of self-interest, both individual and collective," echoing his earlier argument in *Moral Man and Immoral Society* (Niebuhr, 1944, p. 10). Human beings, inherently flawed, would make mistakes; democracy, however, was a system that contained the capacity to curb those mistakes. In Niebuhr's often-quoted words, "Man's capacity for justice makes democracy possible; but man's inclination to injustice makes democracy necessary" (Niebuhr, 1944, p. xi).

Drucker, like Niebuhr, sought a functioning society while recognizing there would be no kingdom on earth. Both men witnessed and feared totalitarianism, and both also worried about the impacts of modern industrialization on human freedom and dignity. Both men also looked to democracy as a bulwark against the evils of modern society, but they came to different conclusions regarding what that society would look like. Whereas Niebuhr's experience in Detroit soured him on industrial capitalism, Drucker believed that the industrial sector could be managed effectively to provide humans with a place of citizenship and meaning. Thus, Drucker's idea of a functioning society of organizations built on Niebuhr's conclusion that democracy would harness humankind's best and worst tendencies.

Judgment and Values in Management as a Liberal Art

While not every organization or society has or will embrace the exact same virtues or values, Drucker's insistence and management as a liberal art's reliance on addressing questions of an ethical nature requires that individuals consider the history and source of what they value and consider to be virtues. Management as a liberal art will not provide the absolute answer as to the ultimate source of a society's, organization's, or individual's values, but it requires that the question be raised and considered thoughtfully.

It is this emphasis on the development of an understanding of what constitutes virtue that differentiates management as a liberal art from yet another exercise in business or managerial ethics. Most efforts aimed at increasing ethical behavior in the private sector appear to emphasize *consequences or rules rather than values or virtues*. *Business Ethics* is a publication dedicated to corporate responsibility; its mission is "to promote ethical business practices, to serve that growing community of professionals and individuals striving to work and invest in responsible ways" ("About Business Ethics," n.d.).

In the wake of the Sarbanes-Oxley Act of 2002, which imposed extensive requirements for financial disclosure and more stringent governance requirements on public companies, many companies have implemented ethics training programs aimed at preventing them from being the next headline maker related to corporate scandal. Yet Web-based education about money laundering, accounting fraud, or other illegal behavior does not always seem to work. Edward Petry, executive director of the Ethics Officer Association, reported that most large companies failed to adequately monitor their internal ethics programs (Schmitt, 2002). While most ethics programs emphasize the positive or negative consequences of a given action, or the function of rules governing decision making, management as a liberal art emphasizes the role of judgment and values. The emphasis is not on "ethical business practices" or training in a set of rules but rather the larger development of the human as a whole.

Just as the development of a virtuous individual was an ideal in Aristotle's time, it is for management as a liberal art nowadays. Grounded in the philosophy of Kierkegaard, St. Augustine, and others, management as a liberal art cannot espouse the possibility of a perfectible human being. Thus, while the practice of management as a liberal art involves dealing with the larger questions of character development, virtue, and values, it also involves understanding that achieving Aristotle's mean of virtuous behavior is an unobtainable goal. Nevertheless, that does not mean that we cannot improve.

THE IMPORTANCE OF CONTEXT IN MANAGING CONTINUITY AND CHANGE

Just as management as a liberal art forces us to address the question of the source and nature of values, it also requires us to consider whether or not there are truly universal aspects of human nature or whether context plays an important role. As we have seen, one of the important themes in Drucker's work is the need to find a balance between continuity and discontinuity or change. This question of balance is important in terms of assessing the relevance of the liberal arts tradition and its union with management. How much of the liberal arts ideal represents continuity, concepts, and ideas that exist regardless of time or space, and how much of that ideal needs to be modified to reflect modern realities? How many of modern management's questions involve situations that reflect changeless aspects of human nature and behavior, and how many are the result of discontinuities in specific organizations, cultures, or societies?

One of the major, and valid, criticisms of liberal arts study has been its traditionally Eurocentric viewpoint. The belief that Western societies were the sole standard bearers of beauty and culture has been considered narrow and elitist for some time. The reconsideration of the Western "canon" of literature, as well as the expansion of the study of history beyond Western civilizations, reflects the modernization of the liberal arts to include non-European perspectives. This richer curriculum can at times call into question the universality of values and human nature. How much are a given society's values a reflection of its specific culture?

Today's broader perspective on the liberal arts allows for a more nuanced reading of even the classic canon. For example, the comedies of Aristophanes reflect very specific attitudes, events, and values of Greece in the fifth century BCE; can one really say that the political values of citizenship of that society universally apply to today's American democratic system? Or India's?

If management is a liberal art, then, it involves considering the question of context. How much of a given situation is the result of organizational history, tradition, or culture? How much is driven by the individual personalities involved? How much is governed by cultural differences between the various players, or differences in gender perspective or class background and upbringing? How much are the parties being driven by what could be considered universal human motivations? Just as the humanities today require a consideration of the role of race, ethnicity, class, and gender, management as a liberal art also mandates that such issues of context be considered as well.

Philosophers of Discontinuity and Change

Drucker was certainly well read in philosophy, ranging from the ancient Greeks to Jean-Jacques Rousseau and Friedrich Nietzsche. Those philosophers with a theological bent are covered in the first part of this chapter. Here we have focused on those philosophers who most obviously influenced Drucker's concept of discontinuity. These philosophers all espouse a belief that change is a part of reality and must be accepted as such.

Henri Bergson (1859–1941), Alfred Whitehead (1861–1947), and Process Philosophy

Henri Bergson and Alfred Whitehead are two important representatives of what is known as process philosophy. The Frenchman Bergson began to develop his philosophy during the late nineteenth century, when there were essentially two diametrically opposed positions in the philosophical community. On one side stood the advocates of Herbert Spencer and John Stuart Mill, who emphasized material existence and an empirical, deterministic approach that discounted the role of human emotions. On the other side stood the German idealists, such as Georg Wilhelm Friedrich Hegel, who believed that the human mind, will, and imagination were crucial in understanding what was real; experience and human interpretation could not be divorced from knowledge and understanding.

Bergson resolved to develop a philosophy that would bridge the gap between these two schools of thought (Chevalier, 1928, pp. 1–36). Whitehead was an English mathematician, educated at Trinity College; he later taught mathematics there and at the University of London. Whitehead's interest in philosophy was sparked by the impact of Einstein's theory of relativity and the subsequent replacement of the Newtonian system of physics. Whitehead extended the concept of relativity from physical science into the realm of human existence, redefining the human experience as a series of constantly changing events rather than permanent and knowable. In 1924, he was invited to teach philosophy at Harvard in spite of the fact that he never studied the subject. Whitehead published his ideas in his 1929 work *Process and Reality*, the document that began the process school of philosophy (Lowe, 1962, pp. 3–31).

In essence, process philosophy emphasizes change and the passage of time as key to understanding reality. True to its name, the theory underscores the importance of processes; processes are, in fact, more important than things themselves. Human beings are thus viewed as the product of their experiences, or as processes themselves. Process philosophy has been applied to theology, in which God is seen not as a single entity but as a process as well. With its emphasis on change and time, contingency is a critical element of the philosophy; one cannot understand reality without taking into account human agency and creativity (Rescher, 2000).

Management professor Tony H. Bonaparte argued that Bergson's process philosophy appears in Drucker's work, particularly in Drucker's "organic approach" (Bonaparte, 1970, in Bonaparte and Flaherty, p. 28). Drucker noted the role of Bergson and Whitehead in his 1959 book *Landmarks of Tomorrow*, highlighting the importance of change in society (Drucker, 1959). Elsewhere as well, the themes of discontinuity, impermanence, and human agency and creativity reflect, at least in part, the permanence of change that is pivotal to process philosophy.

Drucker mentioned Bergson and Whitehead in the first chapter of *Landmarks of Tomorrow*, entitled "The New World-View." In this chapter, he set the agenda for the entire book, which is that the Western world must adopt a completely different and new point of view. The old point of view based on the philosophy of René Descartes, in which the emphasis was on analyzing the structure and mechanics of things, had been replaced by a new philosophy that emphasized qualitative factors and relationships between things. In short, according to Drucker, the new philosophy emphasized process, in which, he states, "may well lie the greatest departure from the worldview of the modern West that has been ruling us for the last three hundred years. For the Cartesian world was not only a mechanical one, in which all events are finitely determined; it was a static one" (Drucker, 1959, p. 9). Drucker ends the chapter stating that, while the new philosophy does not yet exist, "we may well have the new synthesis more nearly within our grasp than we think" (Drucker, 1959, p. 15). The remainder of the book contains Drucker's outline for this new synthesis, closing with the admonition that "if there is one thing we can predict, it is change. The coming years will be years of rapid change in our vision, the direction of our efforts, the tasks we tackle and their priorities, and the yardsticks by which we measure success or failure" (Drucker, 1959, p. 269).

In this important work, Drucker began to identify the knowledge worker and the knowledge society as the direction of this change. In

The Age of Discontinuity (1969), he more fully elucidated this shift, establishing the "knowledge society" as one of his primary areas of interest, and a place where process theory shows up repeatedly. Drucker argued that the first half of the twentieth century was a period of economic continuity based on knowledges developed during the last half of the nineteenth century. As he looked ahead to the end of the second half of the twentieth century, he saw a period of great discontinuity in the advancement of knowledge, which itself would create the reality of a knowledge society in developed countries:

> The growth industries of the last half-century derived from the scientific discoveries of the middle and late nineteenth century. The growth industries of the last decades of the twentieth century are likely to emerge from the knowledge discoveries of the first fifty and sixty years of this century. . . . The coming decades in technology are more likely to resemble the closing decades of the last century, in which a major industry based upon new technology surfaced every few years, than they will resemble the technological and industrial continuity of the past fifty years. (Drucker, 1969, pp. ix–x)

In an essay titled "From Information to Communication," Drucker discussed the human process of understanding language, invoking Whitehead's *Principia Mathematica* in the opening paragraph (Drucker, 2003, p. 179). The entire concept of "discontinuity" requires a sense of time to have meaning. Unfolding processes, changing situations, and human interactions and agency are pivotal elements of Drucker's writings on both management and society.

Jan Smuts (1870–1950) and Holism

Although Drucker credited Bergson and Whitehead for his "new world-view," he stated in *Landmarks of Tomorrow* that "the first to comprehend it, however, was probably that astounding South African, Jan Christiaan Smuts—the closest to the 'whole man' this century has produced" (Drucker, 1959, p. 11). Smuts was a Dutch South African military and political figure. He served two terms as prime minister of the South African Union. Smuts fought in the Anglo-Boer War of 1899–1902 and World War I, and he was a field marshal in World War II. He was instrumental in developing the structure of the League of Nations. For most of his life, Smuts advocated a segregated South Africa ruled by a united Afrikaner elite, although he did not support institutional apartheid. His political and military career reflected a belief that South Africa should be a nation of British and Dutch people who would uphold western European civilization (Ingham, 1986).

Drucker's interest in Smuts stemmed from the philosophical beliefs of the Dutch South African rather than his political and military career. Raised in a devout Christian house, Smuts was expected to become a minister. When he went to Cambridge, however, he decided to study law, not divinity; nevertheless he felt torn: how could one pursue a practical career and still find intellectual fulfillment, a sense of meaning in life? In an article titled "Law: A Liberal Study," Smuts (1893) argued that the legal profession was uniquely poised to address individual freedoms as well as the needs of the larger community. As he continued to work through his dilemma, he developed his philosophy of holism, which involved the view that objects are more than simply the sum of their components. Smuts saw deep connections between individuals and the world, connections that transcended what he saw as the constraints of Christian doctrine; in one biographer's words, "he came to identify his own conscience as the conscience of mankind" (Ingham, 1986, p. 7).

In their article entitled "Drucker, Holism, and Smuts," (Bonaparte and Flaherty, 1970), Edward J. Cook and Allen F. Chapman argue that Drucker's work reflects Smuts' concept of holism, particularly in its synthesis of existing ideas into something new. Cook and Chapman compare various quotations from Smuts and Drucker, pointing to similarities in the respective texts. For example, Smuts posited that "creative evolution synthesizes from the parts a new entity not only different from them but quite transcending them," while Drucker noted that "a great deal of new technology is not new knowledge; it is new perception. It is putting together things that no one had thought of putting together before, things that by themselves had been around a long time." Cook and Chapman also point out that Drucker's idea of discontinuity may have originated with holism; Smuts argued that "Creative Evolution seems to move forward by small steps or installments or increments of creativeness. Why there should be this *discontinuity* rather than a smooth continuous advance we cannot say" (Cook and Chapman, 1970, in Bonaparte and Flaherty, pp. 58–62).

The synthetic nature of holism certainly seems to have informed Drucker's work. For example, it finds its way into his warnings of the potential dangers of using techniques of management science that seek technical efficiency without recognizing the possibility of "suboptimization of the whole" that may result because the whole is very different than the sum of its parts.

There is one fundamental insight underlying all management science. It is that the business enterprise is a *system* of the highest order: a system the parts of which are human beings contributing voluntarily of their knowledge, skill, and dedication to a joint venture. And one thing characterizes all genuine systems, whether they be mechanical, like the control of a missile, biological like a tree, or social like the business enterprise: it is interdependence. The whole of a system is not necessarily improved if one particular function or part is improved or made more efficient. In fact, the system may well be damaged thereby, or even destroyed. In some cases the best way to strengthen the system may be to weaken a part—to make it less precise or less efficient. For what matters in any system is the performance of the whole; this is the result of growth and of dynamic balance, adjustment, and integration rather than of mere technical efficiency. Primary emphasis on the efficiency of parts in management science is therefore bound to do damage. It is bound to optimize precision of the tool at the expense of the health and performance of the whole. (Drucker, 1973, p. 508)

THE FUNCTION OF LEARNING

Liberal arts inquiry involves a process of challenging assumptions, developing judgment and values over time, and bringing this knowledge to bear upon problems confronted in the world of work.

Drucker could relate to the leader in Hermann Hesse's 1943 novel *Das Glasperlenspiel*. In Drucker's words, the novel depicts "a brotherhood of intellectuals, artists, and humanists who live a life of splendid isolation, dedicated to the Great Tradition, its wisdom and beauty." In the end, the leader defects to rejoin the real world—"the polluted, vulgar, turbulent, strife-torn, money-grubbing reality"— finding that the Great Tradition is but "fools gold" unless there is relevance on the ground (Drucker, 2008, pp. 515–516). No doubt Drucker thought bringing the knowledge and wisdom of the ages to bear upon problems confronted in the world of work was a wise thing to do.

Another crucial theme to Drucker's work is the importance of balancing social meaning and individual freedom in life. For Drucker's idea of management as a liberal art, knowledge must have some sort of social relevance as well as individual satisfaction. As we saw in Chapter 2, however, this does not mean that the "real world" necessarily must be devoid of the wisdom and beauty of the liberal arts; in fact, we argue that the liberal arts tradition can bring social relevance to the practice of management once again.

The educated person in the knowledge society does not look upon the liberal arts as mere ornaments with little practical relevance. The practice of management as a liberal art requires a person to synthesize from all knowledges those required to carry out a function at hand. With the rapid advance and splintering of knowledge, the ability to do so requires a commitment to continuous lifetime learning. Continuous learning becomes ever more important as one assumes greater levels of responsibility. And the earlier one acquires a mindset and practice of continuous learning, the better.

In many respects, the very nature of this process flies in the face of what has traditionally been included within the scope of the practice of management and a liberal arts education. If the manager has traditionally been viewed as a neutral and unbiased functionary, management as a liberal art involves exercising judgment and applying wisdom in a very nonneutral fashion. The process of learning management as a liberal art is therefore very different from traditional means of learning the skills and functions of management. Instead of focusing on quantitative skills, management as a liberal art emphasizes character formation and the qualitative abilities discussed earlier along with critical thinking skills discussed in subsequent chapters. Developing these abilities involves exposure, skill, and experience, and it often involves challenging long-held assumptions and preconceptions about leadership and management.

As a result, management as a liberal art involves a systematic, lifelong process of learning. It is not a set of tools to be employed in given situations, a laundry list of what to do and what not to do, but rather the cultivation of a mindset and systematic process for acquiring and applying knowledge from the humanities and social sciences to concrete problems of management.

WHAT MANAGEMENT AS A LIBERAL ART IS NOT

For all of its contributions, management as a liberal art is no panacea for organizations or the liberal arts. There is a tendency to romanticize the past when the present seems dysfunctional; many have waxed on about the golden age of the liberal arts, or a lost era when executives had character and "real" values. Management as a liberal art is *not* an attempt to recapture some lost, better time in the past. As should be clear by now, there is no utopian vision for management as a liberal art as derived from Drucker's ideas and influences.

Nor is management as a liberal art an effort to dictate some set of values or character attributes that constitute good or bad managers. But it does require its adherents to think through moral dilemmas and to grow both in intellect and in character.

Management as a liberal art does not seek to eliminate interpersonal conflict; instead, it recognizes that conflict is an inherent part of the human condition. We are not trying to change human nature by practicing management as a liberal art. Rather, we are trying to raise the level of vision and intellectual attainment, as well as the moral capacity of all members of an organization, especially those who occupy or aspire to positions of responsibility.

While not a magic pill to cure what ails either liberal arts education or the practice of management, management as a liberal art has the potential to refocus people in positions of authority on values, ethics, and the question of character. By restoring the historical connection between management and the liberal arts disciplines, management as a liberal art can perhaps inject new life into both the academic and practical worlds.

CHAPTER 4

FEDERALISM AND THE DISTRIBUTION OF POWER AND AUTHORITY

W e have argued elsewhere that there is a consistent set of philosophical assumptions underlying Drucker's work that have to do with human nature (Linkletter and Maciariello, 2009). While Drucker believed in humanity's capacity to organize and manage complex organizations for the betterment of both the individual and society, he never lost sight of the reality of humankind's foibles and weaknesses. Organizations, in Drucker's view, needed to be structured to counteract, minimize, or redirect the darker forces of human nature, including greed and the lust for power. Yet many of Drucker's readers missed this more pessimistic side of his writing, criticizing him for what they saw as a naïve, rather utopian view of human nature as it operated within large organizations, particularly the corporation.

In this chapter, we discuss the importance of federalism in Drucker's work. Federalism, the political philosophy behind the argument for the American Constitution, was first formally elucidated in the *Federalist Papers* of John Jay, Alexander Hamilton, and James Madison. Although federalism developed into a complex and not altogether cohesive view of the role of centralized power and the nature of individual rights, Drucker applied many of its principles to the complicated problem of managing the pluralistic institutions of a democratic society, which involves the organization and distribution of power. He did so because of his high regard for the relevance of the *Federalist Papers* to the complex problems faced by executives of society's institutions as they attempt to control greed and the lust for power through the distribution of authority and use of checks and balances (Drucker, 1954, p. 280; Drucker, 1985a, pp. 31–32).

Federalism, including constitutionalism, can contribute to creating a system of functioning organizations by acknowledging the darker side of human nature and identifying ways to curb abuses of power. Analyzing Drucker's work in terms of his use of federalist concepts refutes the critique of Drucker as a naïve utopian. He, as did Enlightenment thinkers and the founding fathers, wrestled with the role and nature of virtue in society, the potential for abuse of power, and the trade-offs between maximization of human liberty and protection of the greater interests of society.

We open with a look at an exchange between Drucker and Harvard Business School professor Rosabeth Moss Kanter that reveals the important role of federalism in Drucker's work. Following a discussion of the eighteenth-century debates on the American Constitution and the Federalists' arguments in support of the new government, we evaluate how Drucker applied federalist principles to his management theories. We then examine corporate federalism, the application of federalist and other related principles to corporations. We use General Motors, the subject of Drucker's own analysis of corporate federalism, and Drucker's concept of Management by Objectives as illustrations. Finally, we offer suggestions for applying federalist ideas to today's organizations, including restructuring the CEO and board of director positions.

Why was Drucker so drawn to the application of federalist principles? He advocated the practice of management as a liberal art, that is, as an endeavor that involves taking into account the fundamental aspects of human existence, and the ability to incorporate a wide array of viewpoints and disciplines in the process. Proper management of today's organizations requires not merely technical training in such areas as accounting, finance, and marketing but also an understanding of the history of people's successes and failures in organizing socially, politically, and economically, as well as other knowledge that leads to a greater wisdom of the human condition. Our synthesis of political federalism with Drucker's ideas and principles of corporate federalism illustrates the benefit of the larger framework of management as a liberal art. The result, we believe, is a reasonable solution for dealing with the challenges of managing today's institutions.

KANTER'S CRITIQUE OF DRUCKER

One of Drucker's most probing critics was Rosabeth Moss Kanter, a distinguished professor of sociology and management at the Harvard Business School. Her criticisms of Drucker's work appear in her article "Drucker: The Unsolved Puzzle" in the journal *New Management* (Kanter, 1985, pp. 11–12). Kanter begins her article by praising Drucker's vast contributions to the practice of management and expressing her admiration for his work. Then she lists the important dimensions of management that Drucker appears to have ignored, asking, "How could he possibly have ignored such vital issues?"

Kanter's primary criticism of Drucker is that his work assumed a too-rosy view of the modern business organization, depicting "a world of management as it ought to be, rather than it is." Kanter claims that Drucker blamed organizational problems on ignorance and relied solely on education to solve the dysfunctions of corporate governance. Such a view, she states, lacks an understanding of the reality of "human or organizational frailty." Humans cannot be made perfect through education, and many people are not "merely ignorant or misguided but are, instead, greedy or power hungry." According to Kanter, Drucker's management ideas and organizational concepts do not take this fact into account: "There is no evil in the world Drucker shows us."

Drucker's Rejoinder to Kanter

Drucker answers Kanter's criticism in the same *New Management* issue:

> As Rosabeth Kanter cannot probably know, I started out teaching religion. I am thus only too aware of the fact that human beings perversely insist on behaving like human beings, and that this means pettiness and greed, vanity and the lust for power and, yes, *evil*. My first book was on the rise of Nazism, after all. And I have been an active consultant for 40-odd years—too long, I am afraid, to remain as naive of evil as Rosabeth obviously thinks I am. . . . I long ago learned that the distinguished intellectual tradition of which Rosabeth Kanter is the heir—the tradition that goes back to Plato's Seventh Letter and was known for hundreds of years as "The Education of the Christian Prince"—is not an effective protection against evil. The only thing that works— admittedly only with indifferent success—is the other great tradition of Western political thought, the one that also goes back to Plato (or at least to Aristotle) and is known as "Constitutionalism"—limiting power by power, making sure that the units of power are kept small (for example, through decentralization), containing the danger of megalomania and of the lust for power through countervailing forces (for example, through a strong board of directors or through a

three-person top management team), and, above all, through making objectives and performance the touchstones rather than personality and "charisma." (Drucker, 1985, pp. 31–32)[1]

Finally, Drucker reconciles Kanter's criticisms by stating the underlying purpose of his work:

> What I have been trying to do is first to develop the *norm* (that is what ought to be) and then the constitutional principles that enable the well-meaning and virtuous to achieve it, and that will at least slow down and impede the corrupt and vicious. (Drucker, 1985a, p. 32)

This interchange between Kanter and Drucker provides valuable insights not available elsewhere in such concise form. Both are making accurate statements, but Drucker's rejoinder can only be understood in light of his entire body of work. Kanter leveled her criticisms of Drucker based, apparently, upon a close reading of Drucker's most important books on management, leadership, and innovation, such as *The Practice of Management* (Drucker, 1954), *The Effective Executive* (Drucker, 1966), *Management: Tasks, Responsibilities, Practices* (Drucker, 1973), and *Innovation and Entrepreneurship* (Drucker, 1985b).

Readers unaware of Drucker's early work, such as *The End of Economic Man* (1939), Drucker's analysis of the rise of totalitarianism to which he refers, or his works of social analysis, such as *The New Society* (1950), could easily come away with the impression that Drucker's management work fails to address the "human frailty that interferes with the implementation of ideal practice" (Kanter, *New Management*, 1985, p. 12). Because Drucker did not explicitly discuss his philosophical and intellectual framework in every one of his books, Kanter and others, such as Abraham Maslow (Maslow, 1998,

p. 44), charged Drucker with being overly optimistic in his assumptions about human nature.

In the exchange between Kanter and Drucker in the *New Management* journal, Kanter raised a number of very important issues that Drucker did choose to exclude from his most widely read books and articles on management; that exclusion did give many of his readers an incomplete account of the full scope of his work. Drucker's response provides his explanation for how his work did, in fact, take into account the role of frailty and evil. The explanation reveals that Drucker believed that limits on power through the structure of governance would allow virtuous people to accomplish their goals, and would "at least slow down and impede the corrupt and vicious" (Drucker, 1985, p. 32).

Kanter's arguments and Drucker's rejoinder lead us directly into the theme of this chapter: the role of federalism in promoting effective governance. Derived from American federalism, the political ideology in support of the U.S. Constitution, we use the term "corporate federalism" to apply to *the dynamics of shared power and authority among central organizations and their various operating units.*[2]

Because it derives from the eighteenth-century debates over the nature and structure of the American government, corporate federalism reflects several key elements of those historical debates from the 1700s, including the principles of constitutionalism, the rules of conduct for the center and its parts, and the *reservation of powers* specifically called out in an organization's constitution. *Reservation of powers* sets aside certain key decisions and designates them for executives of the central organization. Policies stipulated in an organization's constitution and in the charters of subunits spell out the domains of operation for each subunit and the checks and balances on both the central organization and the decentralized units.

Drucker's response to Kanter makes clear that he viewed federalism as crucial to curbing abuse of power and minimizing the potential for corruption within organizations. It is also clear, however, that Drucker did not see federalism as a guarantee against abuse and corruption.

DRUCKER'S OBJECTIVES

The purpose of Drucker's body of work was to develop the requirements for a society of functioning organizations. Bear in mind that he was never trying to construct a *utopian* society of institutions, but only a *tolerable* one.

This was not a new theme for Drucker in 1985; in his earlier writings, he continually referred to the need to organize around not an ideal, but a functional, tolerable society. In his 1942 book *The Future of Industrial Man*, Drucker defines a "functional society" made up of industrial institutions, but he makes no claim that any nation can achieve such a goal: "Man in his social and political existence must have a functioning society just as he must have air to breathe in his biological existence. However, the fact that man has to have a society does not necessarily mean that he has it" (Drucker, 1942, p. 26). A few years later, he likewise noted that "we are not however looking for perfection or for the ideal, but for the possible. . . . No society can ever realize its promises in full and for every one of its citizens; perfection does not pertain to the kingdom of man" (Drucker, 1946, p. 134). And in his 1949 essay "The Unfashionable Kierkegaard," Drucker states that, ultimately, life can only become "bearable by making it meaningful" through faith (Drucker, 1949, p. 602).

Consultant and writer Peter Paschek, a long-time friend, colleague, and student of Peter Drucker, prepared an essay for participants of the First Global Drucker Symposium in Claremont in June 2007. In this essay, Paschek incorporates quotes from a number of direct interviews and exchanges with Peter Drucker. Many of these quotes illustrate Drucker's pessimistic view of what is likely to be attainable in society. Drucker also expresses distrust in the use of power by leaders of society's institutions:

I have become increasingly skeptical of all promises to save the world through society. I think one of the main events of the last fifty years is that we increasingly became disenchanted with "Volksbegluckung" [trans.: system rendering the people happy] and increasingly have become convinced that there is no perfect society and that there is only a tolerable society and that there can be improvement but there can be no perfection. And this is a conservative view, but also because it puts the emphasis on the individual and the individual's own belief, which is essentially a religious view that sees the end not in this world but beyond this world. Therefore I call myself a conservative Christian and an Anarchist in the sense that I'm increasingly suspicious of . . . power. As a philosopher—which I do not pretend to be—I have always seen power as the central problem and the lust for power as the basic human original sin. (Drucker and Paschek, 2004, pp. 225–226; translated and cited in Paschek, 2007)

Drucker spent much of his life searching for ways to reconcile the tension between human existence as an individual and existence within society. How can a free society protect individual liberty while still watching out for the interests of the common good? In particular, how can a modern industrial society composed of large organizations provide both the freedom for individual growth and development and a meaningful existence as a member of a community? Drucker's answer lay in a society of well-managed organizations; federalism was one intellectual and operational pathway to effective management.

THE HISTORY OF FEDERALISM

Although the framers of the U.S. Constitution formalized its concepts into a new and innovative political philosophy, federalism originated long before the founding fathers drafted the new nation's core document. During the sixteenth and early seventeenth centuries, European intellectuals developed both competing and complementary political theories of the state. Jean Rodin's idea of the monarchical state (*Les Six Livres de la Republique*, 1576) and Johannes Althusius's contrasting model of sovereignty within the will of the people, not a divine monarch (*Politica Methodice Digesta*, 1614), inform eighteenth-century American federalism as much as Rousseau's concept of the social contract (1763) and Montesquieu's theory of separation of powers (1748).

Federalism developed into a complex political philosophy during the early years of the U.S. republic. In 1777, the former British colonies organized themselves under the Articles of Confederation. The Confederation was not a unified republic but rather a "firm league of friendship" among 13 sovereign states (Articles of Confederation, Article III); as historian Gordon Wood notes, the dominant political ideology was informed by that of French philosopher Montesquieu, who espoused the idea that only a small society without factions or diversity of interests could survive as a republic (Wood, 1969, pp. 356–357). Each state had its own respective government, its own unique interests, and was beholden to no higher authority than itself under the concept of sovereignty. The new republic was understandably distrustful of having anything remotely resembling a large, authoritative central government, given its recent experience with British rule.

By the 1780s, it was increasingly clear to many that the loose confederation was an ineffective means of governing the new republic. Economic conditions were highly unstable, and the lack of central government power prevented any coordinated effort to alleviate the situation. Shays' Rebellion, an armed uprising of farmers and other poor citizens in 1787 in western Massachusetts, highlighted the instability of the new republic and the impotence of the confederation to quell dissent. Many began to feel that perhaps the object of fear need not be an encroaching central authority but rather the lack of any central authority at all.

That summer, state delegates met in Philadelphia to develop a Constitution. Not surprisingly, the delegates had widely varying ideas as to what the document should contain. There was considerable disagreement regarding how much power should be vested in the states versus the central government, whether or not the country should continue to defend itself using state militias or have a standing army, and how each state's financial matters should be handled (for example, assumption of debt). Behind the arguments over the details loomed very real philosophical differences regarding human nature and the role of authority and power. These differences burst forth in the debates between those who favored a strong central government ruled by a qualified elite (the Federalists) and those who feared the erosion of state sovereignty and the concentration of power in the hands of a select few (the Anti-Federalists).

In order to address the concerns of the Anti-Federalists, John Jay, Alexander Hamilton, and James Madison wrote and circulated several essays now known as *The Federalist Papers*. These essays demonstrate the salient points in the Federalist–Anti-Federalist debate. There are five topics addressed in *The Federalist Papers* that directly inform Drucker's management ideas for constructing a tolerable society. These topics are the danger of unchecked majority power, the need for virtue in leadership, the legitimacy of power, the nature of sovereignty, and the separation of powers. Following a discussion of the eighteenth-century American debates regarding these topics, we turn to an analysis of how Drucker applied these federalist concepts to the management of organizations.

Factions and the "Tyranny of the Majority"

Eighteenth-century American intellectuals abhorred the very concept of political opposition. Factions, or parties, were unheard of, and they were thought to irrevocably split the country apart. As historian Richard Hofstadter has argued, this attitude began to change with the rise of Federalism and Anti-Federalism, but during the debates about the Constitution, both sides could agree that factions represented a danger to society (Hofstadter, 1970, p. 12). In Federalist Number 10, Madison argued that "among the numerous advantages promised by a well-constructed Union, none deserves to be more accurately developed than its tendency to break and control the violence of faction" (Hamilton, Madison, and Jay, 1788/1961, p. 77). Madison famously posited that factions were part and parcel of society, that "the latent causes of faction are thus sown in the nature of man" (Hamilton, Madison, and Jay, 1788/1961, p. 79). Only a large, diverse society could prevent any one faction, or special interest, from dominating society. A larger republic consisting of a multiplicity of interests rather than a smaller, homogeneous confederation not only would prevent violent minority factions from monopolizing the political arena, it would also prevent what Madison termed the "tyranny of the majority," or the dominance of a majority interest at the expense of dissenting minority opinions. This, Madison noted, was a benefit of having a larger representative government: "The influence of factious leaders may kindle a flame within their particular States but will be unable to spread a general conflagration through the other States" (Hamilton, Madison, and Jay, 1788/1961, p. 84).

In Federalist Number 10, Madison addressed one of the primary fears of the Anti-Federalists, which was that a minority interest in charge of the federal government would quash the interests of the majority of American citizens. Although numerous scholarly works on the demographics, attitudes, and attributes of the Anti-Federalists illustrate that they were not a homogeneous group, they clearly harbored suspicions of any new kind of power and influence that threatened the established system of hereditary privilege that existed in pre-Revolutionary America. Several historians, such as Stanley Elkins and Eric McKitrick (1993) and Gordon Wood (1969/1993), have pointed out that Anti-Federalists were particularly concerned with the social mobility and associated disruptions brought on by the aftermath of the Revolutionary War. The Anti-Federalist "Country" opposition (Elkins and McKitrick's term) feared the influence of the up-and-coming merchant and middle-class professionals who threatened their agrarian ideals of class structure and order. By showing that the new Constitution would protect minority interests from the will of the majority, as well as protecting the nation from the whims of an impassioned minority, Madison confronted this very real concern.

A Virtuous Society

There is no doubt that both Federalists and Anti-Federalists believed that the nation must be run by virtuous men: by definition, an elite, small group of people. The importance of a moral, upright populace was a prominent theme in the years surrounding the American Revolution, as intellectuals viewed the Revolution in moral as well as political terms. The new republic had to learn lessons from the past and not fall into the trap of decadence that led to the downfall of Rome. Self-abnegation became symbolic of virtue in the new republic; as Gordon Wood has stated, "the sacrifice of individual interests to the greater good of the whole formed the essence of republicanism and comprehended for Americans the idealistic goal of their Revolution" (Wood, 1969, p. 53).

Following Shays' Rebellion and other events pointing to a loss of self-control among the population, many political leaders began to question the morality of the American people. Just six months before the Massachusetts rebellion, George Washington wrote to John Jay from Mount Vernon, lamenting that "we have probably had too good an opinion of human nature in forming our confederation. Experience has taught us, that men will not adopt & carry into execution, measures the best calculated for their own good without the intervention of a coercive power" (Washington, 1786, p. 605). Not surprisingly, then, the theme of "virtuous leaders" appears over and over in *The Federalist Papers*. For example, in Federalist Number 57, Madison addresses the Anti-Federalist claim that the House of Representatives, comprising an elite group of men, will not understand the needs and concerns of the average citizens. Madison charges that this "strikes at the very root of republican government," which is to "obtain for rulers men who possess the most wisdom to discern, and most virtue to pursue, the common good of the society; and . . . to take the most effectual precautions for keeping them virtuous whilst they continue to hold their public trust" (Hamilton, Madison, and Jay, 1788/1961, p. 350).

Arguments regarding the nature of virtue in political leadership went only so far in the constitutional debates. The Federalists' eventual surrender to include a Bill of Rights in the U.S. Constitution illustrates that Madison and others recognized the need to include some protection of individual rights from potential abuse of power. The Federalists, too, were suspicious of human nature. While the Anti-Federalists worried about the concentration of enormous power in the hands of a new moneyed elite, the Federalists, such as Madison, understood the danger of unchecked power wielded by either minority factions or the majority of the population. The U.S. Constitution as finally produced reflected the prevailing belief in the need for virtuous leadership (defined as the ability to choose wisely by placing one's own interests behind those of society), but the recognition that human nature involved the pursuit of individual interests at the expense of the greater good.

Legitimacy of Power

The Americans participating in the constitutional debates did so in the context of their recent experience with Great Britain and the Revolutionary War. The entire question of legitimacy of authority was at stake during that conflict, and thus it informed questions regarding how authority could be appropriately wielded in the new government. This question was closely linked to the issue of sovereignty (see "Sovereignty," below), but also related to the American belief in an elite, virtuous cadre of leaders. As they debated the structure of the new government elucidated in the Constitution, the Federalists were extremely concerned with how to construct a government that embodied the will of the people yet maintained the virtuous qualities of leadership they so valued. Then, too, they needed to persuade the Anti-Federalists that the Constitution was valid. In other words, "this new government must have competence, authority, and respect, and all this must be *believed*" (Elkins and McKitrick, 1993, p. 32).

One of the most important elements contributing to the new government's legitimacy was its emphasis on merit rather than on rank and privilege. Government service was considered a responsibility, not an entitlement. Many historians have remarked on the unique role of George Washington as the first president. His even, sober temperament and long track record of military service, as well as his public service in the Virginia House of Burgesses and his position as a well-known member of the landholding community, established him as a man of "character" in that era. Washington alone brought legitimacy to the new government in that he was a "natural" for its first president. Imposing enough in stature and reputation to fill the position, yet lacking the flamboyance and charismatic personality that would have made some suspicious of his motives, Washington embodied the virtues of public service and self-control valued by Federalists and Anti-Federalists alike.

As Gordon Wood has succinctly put it, "Washington epitomized everything the revolutionary generation prized in its leaders. He had character and was truly a man of virtue. This virtue was not given to him by nature. . . . Washington was a self-made hero, and this impressed an eighteenth-century enlightened world that put great stock in men's controlling both their passions and their destinies. Washington seemed to possess a self-cultivated nobility" (Wood, 2006, pp. 34–35). There was little fear that George Washington would become like old King George from whom they had only recently been liberated.

The constitutional framers were careful to define the president's Cabinet members as assistants rather than as ministerial rivals. Washington and others worried about the way in which these assistants would be appointed; they were well aware of the problem of patronage, or rewarding friends and family members with plum political positions. Washington was careful to choose Cabinet members based on their record of public service and reputation. Indeed, as Elkins and McKitrick note, Washington had no choice; the people in power whose acceptance and help he needed were not "first families" but leading citizens who were well known in their respective communities. Washington refused to appoint his nephew to any position within his administration for this very reason: "his favors were to be bestowed on the basis not of *noblesse oblige* but of civic virtue" (Elkins and McKitrick, 1993, p. 55).

Sovereignty

The nature of sovereignty had been one of the primary disputes behind the American Revolution. The idea of sovereignty became established in British political thought after the Revolution of 1688. It was the belief that there was a single, indivisible source of power higher than any other; all entities are thus subject to this ultimate authority. While the location of this sovereignty had traditionally been the monarch, following the Glorious Revolution of 1688, Britain viewed Parliament as the ultimate sovereign power. However, as the colonists bristled under Parliament's increasing laws, many of which seemed arbitrary and unfair, they began to challenge the British notion of indivisible sovereignty. Parliament, some colonists argued, had the authority of external oversight but not of internal taxation. Ultimately, the American revolutionaries began to argue that true sovereignty lay within the people, and that governmental authority was necessarily restricted to certain areas.[3]

When the Federalists proposed that one government preside over the 13 states, the Anti-Federalists revisited the very same arguments that had taken place prior to the Revolutionary War. The British, the Anti-Federalists warned, had said the same thing about parliamentary sovereignty. The American Revolution, after all, had refuted that very principle: that one entity could possibly represent such diverse interests with respect to matters such as taxation. How possibly, the Anti-Federalists asked, could two sovereign governments—state and federal—preside equally if sovereignty was, in fact, indivisible? The question of sovereignty also drove the Anti-Federalist quest for a Bill of Rights; if limitations on the federal government's power were not spelled out, who was to say that the new sovereign power would not abuse its authority just as England had done?

Increasingly, the Federalists altered their argument to incorporate the revolutionary notion of popular sovereignty: that the true authority lay in the people as a whole. As a result, any power not expressly laid out in the Constitution remained in the hands of the people themselves. Madison makes this interpretation clear in Federalist Number 46, as he chastises the Anti-Federalists for their inability to see that "the ultimate authority, wherever the derivative may be found, resides in the people alone, and that it will not depend merely on the comparative ambition or address of the different governments whether either, or which of them, will be able to enlarge its sphere of jurisdiction at the expense of the other" (Hamilton, Madison, and Jay, 1788/1961, p. 294).

Alexander Hamilton spelled out his interpretation of popular sovereignty in Federalist Number 84:

It is evident, therefore, that, according to their primitive signification, they have no application to constitutions, professedly founded upon the power of the people and executed by their immediate representatives and servants. Here, in strictness, the people surrender nothing; and as they retain everything they have no need of particular reservations, "We, the people of the United States, to secure the blessings of liberty to ourselves and our posterity, do *ordain* and *establish* this Constitution for the United States of America." Here is a better recognition of popular rights than volumes of those aphorisms which make the principal figure in several of our State bills of rights and which would sound much better in a treatise of ethics than in a constitution of government. (Hamilton, Madison, and Jay, 1788/1961, p. 513)

Although a Bill of Rights was ultimately included, the debate revealed the remarkable change in attitude regarding sovereignty on the part of the Federalists. Popular sovereignty was a means to overcome the dilemma of indivisible sovereignty in the face of an emerging federal government. As Wood notes, "only by making the people themselves, and not their representatives in any legislature, the final, illimitable, and incessant wielders of all power, could the Federalists explain their emerging doctrine of federalism, where, contrary to the prevailing thought of the eighteenth century, both the state and federal legislatures were equally representative of the people at the same time" (Wood, 1969, p. 545).

Separation of Powers

Even though the concept of popular sovereignty existed in the early years of the American Revolution, most Americans were aware of the all-too human tendency to seek out more and more power. The separation of powers into different units as a form of preventing its concentration in the hands of one man or a few men was part and parcel of early American government. The constitutions of Virginia, Maryland, North Carolina, and Georgia included provisions for dividing power into legislative, executive, and judicial branches that were separate from one another (Wood, 1969, pp. 150–151).

The debates about the Constitution included a rather spirited discussion as to the nature of the separation of powers in the new federal government. Given the relatively long-standing history that Americans had with the concept, it is understandable that the Anti-Federalists would have paid attention to this aspect of the Constitution. Anti-Federalists pointed to connections between the three branches; for example, the executive and legislative branches both had the power to make treaties, and critics worried that this and other examples of power mixing would undermine the early American ideal of separation of powers.

Madison launched a direct response to these critics in Federalist Number 47. He noted that even though all of the state constitutions contained language guaranteeing separation of powers, "there is not a single instance in which the several departments of power have been kept absolutely separate and distinct" (Hamilton, Madison, and Jay, 1788/1961, p. 304). In short, just because the words are there doesn't mean the government will behave in such a way.

In Federalist Number 51, Madison suggested some specific ways in which separation of powers could actually be enforced. Madison recommended a clear chain of command, in which each department had "a will of its own" and also had "as little agency as possible in the appointment of the members of the others." But the best safeguard against abuse of power was in linking individual ambition to the goal of the organization, and in recognizing human nature itself:

> But the great security against a gradual concentration of the several powers in the same department, consists in giving to those who administer each department the necessary consti-

tutional means and personal motives to resist encroachments of the others. The provision for defense must in this, as in all other cases, be made commensurate to the danger of attack. Ambition must be made to counteract ambition. The interest of the man must be connected with the constitutional rights of the place. It may be a reflection on human nature, that such devices should be necessary to control the abuses of government. But what is government itself, but the greatest of all reflections on human nature? If men were angels, no government would be necessary. If angels were to govern men, neither external nor internal controls on government would be necessary. In framing a government which is to be administered by men over men, the great difficulty lies in this: you must first enable the government to control the governed; and in the next place oblige it to control itself. (Hamilton, Madison, and Jay, 1788/1961, pp. 321–322)

Because of the nation's early experience with the doctrine of separation of powers, the Federalists included this language in the Constitution. However, their vision of the concept shifted away from a static notion of linear checks and balances to a more realistic idea that acknowledged human nature, not just organizational structure.

FEDERALISM AND DRUCKER'S OBJECTIVES

America's experience with the debates on the Constitution during the eighteenth century dealt with questions that continue to trouble modern organizations. Just as the framers worried about the "tyranny of the majority" over the minority interests of society, or the possibility that an overly zealous minority could cause social disorder, today's organizations are concerned with encouraging alternative points of view without experiencing sabotage. Training in corporate ethics and development of leadership skills seems to attempt to instill similar values of stewardship and wisdom in today's executives, while understanding that the organization has a responsibility to at least keep an eye out for bad behavior. The periodic outcry over excessive executive compensation and unethical financial transactions brings to the fore the question of the legitimacy of managerial power; have executives earned their positions through merit and accomplishment, or are they simply there out of a sense of privilege? In today's flatter companies, authority and power are more diffused throughout organizations; as the founders struggled to define the nature of popular sovereignty with respect to central and state governments, organizations often deal with questions as to who makes the final decision on matters, or who will be held accountable for group projects. Finally, shared leadership in modern organizations makes separation of powers more fluid and less structured; as it was for Hamilton and others, it is more about managing human nature than about setting up the right structure of divisions or departments.

As he indicated in his rejoinder to Rosabeth Moss Kanter, correctly understood, Drucker's teachings are pragmatic and take into account both the *nature of man* and *organizational realities*. A point-by-point analysis of the role of federalism in Drucker's work on management and society demonstrates this. Like the Federalists, Drucker sought to design a blueprint for a society that would curb the worst tendencies in humankind while liberating people's potential for good. Whereas the framers wrestled with designing a framework for governance in a relatively homogeneous society, Drucker struggled to find a model of a tolerable society for a modern industrialized world.

Drucker on "Tyranny of the Majority"

In his early writings Drucker acknowledges the "great innovation" of Madison as "the thesis that *any one ethical principle of power will become an absolutist, i.e., a tyrannical principle unless checked, controlled, and limited by a competing principle*" (Drucker, 1942b, p. 485). Drucker took Madison's concept of unchecked power in the form of "tyranny of the majority" and adapted it to his work on the requirements for a functioning society of institutions. In Madison's America, pluralism was a thing to be feared; political pluralism was unheard of, and many, particularly those in the wealthy landowning class, lamented the growing class of nouveau riche in the new republic. In Drucker's twentieth-century America, however, pluralism was tolerated, if not accepted. Drucker's pluralist society was a society of diverse institutions competing for power. The tyranny of the majority and the factions of Madison to Drucker became the various sectors in which large organizations could operate: the private, government/public, and social/nonprofit sectors. Whereas Madison feared the unchecked power of any particular special interest, minority or majority, Drucker feared the unchecked power of any one sector (particularly government) exerting its authority without challenge. Drucker's concerns about the problem of unchecked power, both within organizations and within the larger society, led him to corporate federalism (or decentralization) to curb corporate power, and to pluralism to curb government power.

Drucker was particularly keen on the corporation's ability to curtail the spread of government power. Ever watchful of the threat of totalitarianism, particularly during the Cold War, Drucker saw the "emergence of the industrial enterprise" as the primary challenge to the "trend toward the State as the sole center, the sole focus and the sole power" in society (Drucker, 1950, p. 37). Later, Drucker went on to include other sectors as challengers to governmental authority; the new "pluralism of society is one of apolitical, performance-focused, single-task institutions," which include hospitals, churches, or other entities functioning in what Drucker termed the "social sector" (Drucker, 1989, p. 59). Just as Madison argued for the stabilizing benefits of diversity among states, Drucker believed that diversity of interest groups served society well, preventing "tyranny of the majority." In Drucker's case, however, he focused more on limiting institutional power whereas Madison focused on limiting the power of political factions that would emerge under a loose federation of states without a strong central government.

Drucker's institutional pluralism represents an interesting application of Madison's argument for a republican government. In Drucker's twentieth-century pluralism, each institution has its own mission, its own view of the world, its own agenda; while there may be some commonality, there are more areas in which the institutions do not see eye to eye. In Drucker's view, then, pluralism is not about political power but about function: "the new pluralist organization of society has no interest in government and governance. . . . It is an 'organ' of society. As such, its results are entirely on the outside. . . . The new institutions do not encroach on political power as did the old pluralist institutions" (Drucker, 1989, p. 84).

Such a perspective ignores the role of political lobbyists for public funding or legislation, but Drucker's point is well taken: modern institutions' focus tends to be on its own activities rather than on the greater public good. Nevertheless, just as Madison feared the unchecked power of self-interest in eighteenth-century American society, Drucker feared the unchecked power of self-interested institutions in twentieth-century American society. Pluralism, in the form of multiple functioning institutions in multiple sectors, was Drucker's antidote to "tyranny of the majority."

Drucker on Virtue

Drucker addressed his work on management to people of virtue. He thus limited his intended audience to leaders who abide by his fundamental principle of ethical responsibility—"not knowingly to do harm" (Drucker, 2008, p. 222). Stated positively, Drucker assumed the very essence of management to be integrity in leadership (Drucker, 2008, pp. 287–288). Yet his verbiage reveals that even the best leaders may unknowingly do harm. The most virtuous, well-intentioned managers may very well inflict significant damage because of their own best intentions.

Intention defined virtue for both the American Federalists and Drucker. Like the founders, Drucker defined virtue as the capacity for putting the needs of the greater good before one's own self-interest. In the case of managers, this involves putting individual egos aside and focusing on the needs of the organization and its constituents. Managers not only must be cognizant of their own behavior but also must always be aware of the organization's values:

> Direct results always come first. In the care and feeding of an organization, they play the role calories play in the nutrition of the human body. But any organization also needs a commitment to values and their constant reaffirmation, as a human body needs vitamins and minerals. There has to be something "this organization stands for," or else it degenerates into disorganization, confusion, and paralysis. . . . Value commitments, like results, are not unambiguous. (Drucker, 1966, p. 56)

Drucker placed great value in results, the end of one's aims. But managers' intentions are just as important; an executive may achieve stellar results on the job, but if the results are driven by the wrong motivations (for example, self-promotion and aggrandizement rather than advancing the needs of the organization and its employees), the manager does not exemplify virtue.

In spite of this emphasis on virtue, Drucker's assumptions about human nature did not lead him simply to entrust society's institutions to leaders of integrity and leave it at that. Because management necessarily involves people, Drucker was adamant that it must concern itself with matters of human nature, including the capacity for good and evil: "Precisely because the object of management is a human community held together by the work bond for a common purpose, management always deals with the Nature of Man, and (as all of us with any practical experience learned) with Good and Evil as well" (Drucker, 1988, p. 5).

As managers must acknowledge the existence of evil as well as good in human affairs, they must always be cognizant of the potential for even the virtuous to misstep. Federalism's safeguards against abuse of power also offered Drucker a way to curb the darker tendencies of the not-so-virtuous managers who inevitably populate modern organizations.

The turmoil during the Confederation period in eighteenth-century America illustrated that even a republic based on virtue needed a larger, guiding institutional framework to at least minimize the potential for disorder and corruption. Drucker, too, realized that even the most virtuous leaders required a structure that would enable them to remain virtuous. He believed that the only effective way to address the question of ethics in business was to emphasize the interdependence of relationships within and outside of organizations; by stressing this "ethics of interdependence," leaders understand the impact of their actions on others (Drucker, 1981). Only through an understanding of the larger, governing structure and order can organizations begin to combat the negative aspects of human nature. As Madison noted, only angels could govern without the need for external or internal guidance.

Drucker on Legitimacy of Authority

In a sense, both Drucker and the Federalists sought to legitimize a new source of power. The Federalists had to convince the states to ratify the Constitution, and in doing so, to accept a new federal government that would have some, albeit limited, authority over their own governments. Drucker recognized that the large industrial organization was the new constitutive entity of modern society, but he feared that its power would not be deemed legitimate. Thus, key to Drucker's approach to the design of a functioning society of organizations is that power exercised by leaders of institutions must be legitimate.

What is legitimate power? And how is legitimate power fashioned? According to Drucker:

> Legitimate power stems from the same basic belief of society regarding man's nature and fulfillment on which the individual social status and function rests. Indeed, legitimate power can be defined as rulership which finds its justification in the basic ethos of society. . . . .Unless the power in the corporation can be organized on an accepted principle of legitimacy, it will disappear. It will be taken over by the central government—not because the government wants the power but because it will be forced by the consumer to assume it. (Drucker, 1942, pp. 32, 96)

In America, Drucker argued, institutional power could only be legitimate if it reflected the accepted values of democratic society, including equality of opportunity and individual liberty. If managers wielded their power in a way that was contradictory to the broader tenets of American democracy, then that society would no longer acknowledge those managers—or their institutions—as legitimate organs of power.

Corporate scandals involving the abuse of power are one example of illegitimate authority. The desire to exercise power is a trait found in many leaders and aspiring leaders. Drucker worried about unbridled, unaccountable power: "no human being, no matter however good, wise or judicious, can wield uncontrolled, irresponsible, unlimited or rationally not determinable power without becoming very soon arbitrary, cruel, inhuman and capricious—in other words, a tyrant" (Drucker, 1942, pp. 35–36).

It follows that legitimate leadership involves *responsibility*— responsibility for the mission of an organization and for the people under one's domain. Drucker's conception of leadership is very similar to that of the Constitutional framers; leadership is responsibility, not rank or privilege.

One of the ways in which Drucker sought to "make the ruling, decisive power of our industrial system a legitimate power" (Drucker, 1942, p. 77) was to define the functions of executive leadership. Drucker stated that leadership is *hard work* and *a means* to a desirable end. Leaders are responsible for recruiting, organizing, and training common men and women to do uncommon things. In Drucker's view, effective leaders are not afraid of strengths in subordinates but rather seek and encourage the development of those strengths. The Federalists, particularly Washington, recognized the importance of appointing Cabinet members on the basis of merit and accomplishment rather than family connections. In a similar vein, Drucker emphasized the importance of managers and executives earning their positions rather than acquiring them through political means.

Drucker defines leadership in terms of its tasks. Leadership begins with formulation of purpose and objectives. Effective leaders nurture life-giving values, including those that contribute to the esprit de corps of the organization. Leaders set high standards of performance and conduct for themselves and others. They establish priorities for their organization. They exercise constant surveillance of progress through personal observation and the use of timely performance measurements and controls. Leaders also make sure that the current mission of the organization is still valid in the face of changes in the environment and in the competencies of their organization.

An effective leader earns the trust of followers. Trust is an essential ingredient of integrity. Leaders demonstrate integrity by making effective people decisions—hiring, placement, promotion, and severance decisions. Trust is earned by relentless pursuit of an organization's mission and by setting examples of conduct and performance for others to follow. Effective leaders are *exemplars*.

Notable by its absence in Drucker's definition of leadership and in its various tasks is the particular personality type required by leaders. Drucker despised the notion that authority figures had to have "charisma" or some personality characteristic: "Leadership is not magnetic personality—that can just as well be a glib tongue. It is not 'making friends and influencing people'—that is flattery" (Drucker, 2008, p. 288). The case of George Washington is instructive in our comparison with the Federalist model of legitimate authority. Washington was hardly a dashing figure; in fact, it was his rather dull personality that contributed to his reputation for reliability and *gravitas*. Washington's legitimacy as a chief executive lay in his accomplishments, not some collection of leadership traits.

Drucker on Sovereignty

The founders continued the process begun during the American Revolution of transferring the locus of authority from the state to the people themselves. In essence, Drucker's insistence on the importance of human dignity and fulfillment in the workplace places a remarkable amount of power in the hands of the individual. More pointedly, Drucker's identification of the knowledge worker as the driving force of the world's economy represents a transfer of authority from executives in the boardroom to the workers themselves—a form of popular sovereignty.

In much of his work, Drucker emphasized the different nature of knowledge workers, and the inherent challenges posed by their independence and autonomy. These workers possess specialized skills and knowledge that is uniquely theirs, and is transferable from organization to organization; thus knowledge workers are highly mobile and can be much less loyal. As Drucker noted, "knowledge workers can work only because there is an organization for them to work in. In that respect, they are dependent. But at the same time, they own the 'means of production,' that is, their knowledge" (Drucker, 1993, p. 64). Knowledge workers own their own assets, acquired through education and experience. They are much more mobile than manual workers because they own their capital—knowledge capital.

Shared leadership and self-leadership are emerging models of leadership for this fastest-growing segment of employees in developed economies and societies. The evidence of improved performance in knowledge work using self and shared leadership is mounting (Pearce and Simms, 2002; Manz and Simms, 1993). Vertical leadership simply will not work in successfully motivating this segment of employees. Knowledge workers are much more interested in *meaning* and *purpose* in their work than are their manual-worker counterparts. Performance and motivation of these knowledge workers thus requires *shared vision* and *values* and *group rewards*.

Organizations of knowledge workers tend to be flatter and more information based. The orchestra is one of the best examples of a knowledge-based organization. And the orchestra is organized in a radically decentralized way down to the level of teams and individuals. It is held together by a *conductor* and a *score* or mission. It is the purpose of the conductor to make sure that the mission is shared and internalized by orchestra members. The internalized score becomes the basis for self-leadership.

While the Federalists proposed the concept of popular sovereignty to temper concerns regarding the divided nature of authority between the federal and state governments, the idea of shared leadership also allows for authority to be internalized. In flatter organizations employing knowledge workers, in the words of Hamilton, "the people surrender nothing."

Drucker on Separation of Powers

Drucker extended the idea of federalism to curtail power within industrial organizations; he believed that separation of powers and focus on results of decentralized units within the corporation would serve to prevent the abuse of power and authority. Just as the founders understood, Drucker acknowledged the role of human nature in seeking out more and more power. By shifting power to separate divisions, organizations could empower divisional leaders to "resist the encroachments of the others," as Madison warned. Drucker argued that divisions (or "federal units," in his terms) should exist independently, and "where they touch it should be in competition with each other." When they are not in competition with each other but are rather dependent upon each other, Drucker believed that they should have a "right of nullification." For example, automobile divisions should have the right to purchase supplies from outside manufacturers rather than from an in-house division if the outside provider could compete on cost or quality (Drucker, 1954, p. 216). This "right of nullification," borrowing language from American political history, prevents one division from lording its power over another.

Although the framers included language regarding the separation of powers in the Constitution, they recognized (as did the Anti-Federalists) that there would at times be some overlap between the responsibilities of the three branches of government. Madison, however, argued that all three branches had to be unified in their objective of serving the interests of the people of the United States. Similarly, Drucker noted that "decentralization . . . requires a common citizenship throughout the enterprise. It is unity through diversity" (Drucker, 1954, pp. 221–222). Human nature may be for people to seek out individual power and increase their authority. The goal of separation of powers, whether in government or in the private sector, is to limit this potential by countering ambition with ambition, all aimed at the same ultimate higher objective.

PRINCIPLES OF CORPORATE FEDERALISM

Several authors (Handy, 1993; O'Toole and Bennis, 1992) have noted the increasing use of federalist principles in corporations. The principles of corporate federalism not only have their roots in the U.S. Constitution, *The Federalist Papers*, and the Renaissance theories of state and Enlightenment ideas previously discussed, but also the Enlightenment philosophy of David Hume and Edmund Burke,[4] as well as some more contemporary sources worthy of note.[5]

Principle of Subsidiarity[6]

The concept of subsidiarity has a very long history in the Catholic Church dating back to the 1891 Papal encyclical of Pope Leo XIII, *Rerum novarum*, as further developed in *Centesimus annus*, the 1991 papal encyclical of Pope John Paul II. The principle holds that any function that can be performed by a lower entity should be performed by that entity. It is the reverse of assumptions underlying empowerment. Under the principle of subsidiarity, power and authority are *assumed to belong at the lowest possible level* of the organization at which they can be carried out. Excluded are decisions that are so important to the survival of the organization that they must be reserved for a higher level authority.

Drucker cites the management practices followed for two centuries by the British in governing the Indian subcontinent as the best example of a flat, information-based organization (Drucker, 2008, pp. 272–273). The example also illustrates the principle of subsidiarity.

The British Civil Service was able to manage the affairs of the subcontinent using just three layers of management: 9 provincial secretaries, 100 district officers, and approximately 100 civil servants who reported to each district officer. The British did this by establishing a system of information flow in which each district officer did the following:

- Spelled out expectations for the past month in his district
- Described the actual events that transpired during the past month together with discrepancies between expectations and actual events
- Developed expectations of events for the next month
- Delivered the report to the appropriate provincial secretary, who in turn provided detail feedback to the district officer

Modern information technology and management methods allow for the principle of subsidiarity to work much more efficiently and effectively than in the India example, but the example provides conclusive proof of the feasibility of the principle in action.

Principle of Interdependence

Interdependence involves the question of divided sovereignty discussed earlier: "a federation is different from a confederation, where the individual states yield no sovereignty to the center and try to need nothing from their neighbors." Interdependence provides the justification for the various units in an entity to stick together; they "need one another as much as they need the center" (Handy, 1993, p. 168). Furthermore, there is no reason for decentralized units to be a part of the whole federation unless the federation contributes to the decentralized units and provides services to those units that only can be supplied effectively and efficiently by the center of the organization.

Coordinated Controls and Corporate Governance

The final principle of corporate federalism that Handy addresses is the need to establish *coordinated controls and corporate governance.* Controls create accountability for performance of executives in charge of autonomous units, as well as those for executives in charge of the corporation as a whole. As Handy affirms, the "monitoring and governance" of a business seeks to serve as the equivalent of the *separation of powers* in democratic governments:

> Management is the executive function, responsible for delivering the goods. Monitoring is the judicial function, seeing that the goods are delivered according to the laws of the land, that standards are met, and that ethical principles are observed. Governance is the legislative function, responsible for overseeing management and monitoring and, most important for the corporation's future, for strategy, policy and direction. (Handy, 1993, p. 170)

GENERAL MOTORS: AN ESSAY IN CORPORATE FEDERALISM

In Drucker's *Concept of the Corporation,* he portrayed the organization and operation of General Motors as an "essay in federalism—on the whole, an exceedingly successful one." What made it a successful essay in federalism? Says Drucker: "It attempts to combine the greatest corporate unity with the greatest divisional autonomy and responsibility; and like every true federation, it aims at realizing unity through local self-government and vice versa [responsibility]" (Drucker, 1946, p. 46). Drucker saw corporate decentralization as more than just another method of industrial organization. Because of its ancestry in political federalism and its application both to divisions inside the company and to dealers and other external partner organizations outside the company, it was considered by Drucker to be the pattern for a new social order.

General Motors Corp. was founded by William C. Durant as a holding company consisting of a number of "scattered facilities for making and selling automobiles, parts, and accessories" (Chandler, 1962, p. 115). Durant was a salesman who saw an opportunity to capitalize upon the growing market for affordable automobiles, but he had no organizing structure or process for doing so. Without a unified structure and process to rationalize the management of the various decentralized "factions" of General Motors, Durant's company fell victim to the post–World War I depression. The company was on the verge of bankruptcy when, with the assistance of J. P. Morgan, a deal was struck between Durant and Pierre S. du Pont of the DuPont Company to infuse capital into General Motors and avoid bankruptcy. Pierre du Pont took over as CEO of General Motors; eventually he adopted a reorganization plan prepared by Alfred Sloan, then a vice president of United Motors, an accessory division of General Motors, and a member of the board of General Motors and of its executive committee (Sloan, 1963/1990, pp. 24–25). Sloan became president of General Motors in 1923 and chairman in 1937.

Sloan designed a federal organization structure for the company, with decentralized operations and central control. In his report to Durant, Sloan described the ambiguity caused by the conflicting principles of independence of the divisions and interdependence of the federation:

1. The responsibility attached to the chief executive of each organization shall in no way be limited. Each such organization
headed by its chief executive shall be complete in every necessary function and enabled to exercise its full initiative and logical
development.
2. Certain central organization functions are absolutely essential to
the logical development and proper control of the Corporation's
activities. (Sloan, 1963/1990, p. 53)

Economies of scale in certain functions, the need for specialized
expertise, and assessment of legal risks are reasons for centralizing
certain services, such as treasury and legal. Furthermore, authority
for the formulation and implementation of expansion and abandonment strategies, for executive succession policies, and for obtaining
and allocating key financial and human resources must be reserved
for top management. Certain activities required to uphold the values
and standards of the entire organization, including applying rem-
edies for wrongful termination decisions, also must be reserved for
top management.

Sloan went on further to elaborate the principles and policies of
interdependence:

1. To definitely determine the functioning of the various divisions
constituting the Corporation's activities, not only in relation to
one another, but in relation to the central organization.
2. To determine the status of the central organization and to coor-
dinate the operation of that central organization with the corporation as a whole to the end that it will perform its necessary
and logical place [functions]. (Sloan, 1963/1990, pp. 53–54)

Sloan's model of corporate federalism has had an enormous
influence throughout the business world. This resulted from
Drucker's extensive description of federal decentralization, first in

his study of Sloan's General Motors published as *Concept of the Corporation* (Drucker, 1946, Chapters 3–5) and then as developed by Ralph Cordiner and Peter Drucker at General Electric Co. and described in Drucker's *The Practice of Management* (Drucker, 1954, Chapter 17).

In *Concept of the Corporation*, Drucker (1946, pp. 63–64) asked the question about the federal organization at General Motors that has threatened every form of federal government in history—the question that was at the core of the arguments for strong, central, national powers made by Federalist James Madison: how is the "deadlock between co-ordinated organs, the dangers of a break-up of the organization in factionalism, intrigues and fights for power to be overcome"? Drucker was following the warning of James Madison: "The inference to which we are brought is, that the *causes* of faction cannot be removed, and that relief is only to be sought in the means of controlling its *effects*" [that is, by creating a strong central government] (Hamilton, Madison, and Jay, 1788/1961, p. 80).

At General Motors, reductions in the potential debilitating effects of factions that often occur in a federally decentralized organization were made possible by including central monitoring. Also enabling reductions was insistence on the use of a factual basis for calculating performance—cost accounting methods for measuring *efficiency,* and marketing methods for calculating market share and for determining *effectiveness.* The very concept of good management to Sloan "rests on a reconciliation of centralization and decentralization, or 'decentralization with co-ordinated control'" (Sloan, 1963/1990, p. 429). And much of the coordination among divisions at General Motors took place by central management using standing committees for policy formulation and administration, and by the development and use of formal control systems. Thus, Sloan's structure for General Motors reflected Handy's three principles of corporate federalism: subsidiarity, interdependence, and coordinated controls and corporate governance.

As Drucker noted in his own analysis of General Motors, the company's structure also reflected many aspects of eighteenth-century American political Federalist thought. Sloan's decentralized structure helped General Motors avoid the pitfalls of "tyranny of the majority," or the proliferation of a specific personality type and/or style in the managerial ranks that can plague larger corporations. Drucker commented that there was "no 'General Motors atmosphere' and very definitely no 'General Motors type'" (Drucker, 1946, p. 56). He remarked on the tremendous variety of backgrounds of divisional managers, noting that "this variety is not only permitted, it is definitely encouraged by central management; for it is held that every man will do his best job when he does it his own way, and that each division will do its best job when it feels a pride in its tradition, manners and social climate" (Drucker, 1946, p. 57).

Although elsewhere Drucker wrote about the need for virtue in management, in *Concept of the Corporation* he deemphasizes the role of human morality, recognizing the limitations of human nature. In fact, Drucker criticized General Motors for placing too much emphasis on "the personality of the ruler or . . . the good will of the citizens. . . . If it were true that the General Motors' system rested on individual good will, it could hardly survive the life span of one man" (Drucker, 1946, pp. 64–65).

Drucker, like Madison, knew that men are no angels. General Motors' decentralized structure allowed for sovereignty within divisions ["no attempt is made to prevent Oldsmobile, for instance, from trying to displace the low-priced Buick car" (Drucker, 1946, p. 50)], but also within the people themselves in the form of a plant community, in which each worker has some semblance of authority and control over his or her own work (Drucker, 1946, pp. 182–191). Drucker remarked on the many ways in which Sloan's structure contributed to the legitimization of authority, notably the elimination of "'edict management' in which nobody quite knows why he does what he is ordered to do. Its place is taken by discussion and by policies which are public and which are arrived at as a result of the experiences of all the people concerned" (Drucker, 1946, p. 48).

As Drucker notes, General Motors displayed clear separation of powers, with distinct lines drawn between the roles of central management and the heads of each division. Although there is not much evidence that "theories of governmental organization or historical examples had any considerable influence on the development of General Motors' managerial organization" (Drucker, 1946, fn: p. 44), the decentralized nature of the firm's structure had a remarkable resemblance to the principles embodied in American Federalism.

Making Objectives and Performance the Touchstones

Inherent in the idea of federalism is the tension between the autonomy of individual states or divisions and the authority of the central government or management. For Drucker, this tension embodied the reality of life in a "tolerable" society, where one must negotiate between being a free, autonomous human being yet also a member of larger institutions/communities. Beginning with the publication of *The Future of Industrial Man* (1942), Drucker began to address the question, *How can individual freedom be preserved in an industrial society in light of the dominance of managerial power and the corporation?* Drucker commented on this freedom enjoyed by executives in his study of General Motors' policy of federal decentralization: "The impression that emerges from an analysis of the aims of General Motors' policy of organization is one of great individual liberty in which every man—at least among the three to five hundred first-and second-line executives—is to be allowed as much responsibility as he is willing to assume" (Drucker, 1946, p. 63).

The freedom provided executives by the use of federal decentralization at General Motors was accompanied by accountability for results. Sloan elaborated upon this in great detail but summarized its key aspects:

> It was on the financial side that the last necessary key to decentralization with co-ordinated control was found. That key in principle was the concept that, if we had the means to review and judge the effectiveness of operations, we could safely leave the prosecution of those operations to the men in charge of them. The means as it turned out was a method of financial control which converted the broad principle of return on investment into one of the important instruments for measuring the operations of the divisions. The basic elements of financial control in General Motors are cost, price, volume, and rate of return on investment. (Sloan, 1963/1990, p. 140)

While Drucker never specifically evaluated General Motors' principles of financial control, preferring his more comprehensive system of Management by Objectives and Self-Control, he did believe that in order to grant autonomy in federal organizations one must have accountability for results. *"To give autonomy, one must have confidence.* And this requires controls that make opinions unnecessary. To manage by objectives, one must know whether goals are being reached or not, and this requires clear and reliable measurements" (Drucker, 2008, pp. 445–446).

The development of Management by Objectives (MBO) and Self-Control followed shortly after Drucker's work with General Motors and the publication of *Concept of the Corporation*. With the assistance of Harold Smiddy and many others at General Electric, Drucker developed MBO as a philosophy of management to be implemented as an integral part of General Electric's reorganization from departments to federally decentralized units. Two fascinating passages from the third volume of the series *Professional Management in General Electric*: *The Work of a Professional Manager*, describe the early origins of MBO and self-control and its relationship to Corporate Federalism:

> One does not need to be "controlled" or "commanded" if he knows what is to be done and why; if he knows, from continual measurements of results, whether the work is getting done as planned, and on schedule, or if not, why not. (General Electric Co., 1954, quoted in Greenwood, 1981, p. 229)

> Decentralization of managerial decision making requires that objective goals and objective measurements of progress towards these goals be substituted for subjective appraisals and personal supervision. Through a program of objective measurements, managers will be equipped to focus attention on the relevant, the trends, and on the future. To the extent, therefore, that we are able to develop sound, objective measurements of business performance, our philosophy of decentralizing authority and responsibility will be rendered more effective. (General Electric Co., 1954, quoted in Greenwood, 1981 p. 229)

MBO coupled with self-control is the managerial philosophy Drucker proposed in *The Practice of Management* (1954, Chapters 7 and 11) for resolving the tension between individual freedom and the authority the individual must yield to the corporation upon employment. Even in the present knowledge society, MBO with self-control is the best solution we have to a central concern of Drucker: how to protect individual freedom in organizations by requiring individuals to assume personal responsibility for the results of their work.

Achieving freedom in the corporation and in other institutions of society requires responsibility at every level. MBO with self-control is a philosophy of management that incorporates methods of setting objectives and of monitoring performance by each organizational unit and by each individual. The MBO process, if properly designed, develops both responsibility and freedom for individuals in organizations.

The nature of individual responsibility required by MBO was precisely defined by Drucker in an interview with Jack Beatty:

> Responsibility is both external and internal. Externally it implies accountability to some person or body and accountability for specific performance. Internally it implies commitment. The Responsible Worker is not only a worker who is accountable for specific results but also who has the authority to do whatever is necessary to produce these results, and who, finally, is committed to these results as a personal achievement. (Beatty, 1998, p. 79)

A related feature of MBO is upward communications in which each manager clarifies the objectives of his or her superior and then sets objectives that are both achievable by the manager and congruent with the superior's objectives. Drucker proposed a semiannual "management letter" (Drucker, 1954, p. 129) that could be written by each manager to her superior to communicate how the manager's objectives fit into the overall objectives of her superior. The letter would contain proposed performance standards applied to the manager along with work the manager must do to attain these objectives. The manager would then identify the assistance she needed from her superior to attain her objectives. If the superior accepted the recommendations in the letter, these recommendations would become the agreed-upon set of objectives and actions for the manager during the period.

Next, the superior reviews all objectives and negotiates agreement with each manager while seeking to integrate the objectives of subordinates on whose performance the superior depends. In the process, the superior seeks to gain enthusiastic acceptance and commitment from each manager for agreed-upon objectives. If the superior is successful, this process of communication and participation will encourage subordinates to internalize these objectives. Ideally, achieving organizational objectives becomes identical to achieving one's own objectives.

Superiors then coach subordinates toward the achievement of objectives and seek to eliminate any known barriers to performance and achievement. Finally, the superior ensures that subordinates have timely and accurate information to assess progress toward objectives and to take corrective action without any interference from above. This last step attempts to fulfill the "self-control" dimension of MBO.

But MBO with self-control is extremely demanding to accomplish. It requires skillful executives at each level of the organization, people throughout the organization committed to their objectives, and the proper design and use of managerial information and controls. For Drucker, these were ideals (Drucker, 2008; compare pp. 70–71 and pp. 266–277). These and many additional difficulties in achieving both freedom and individual responsibility in organizations should eradicate any belief that Drucker proposed a "utopian" approach to the practice of management.

Nonetheless, clear objectives with appropriate performance measures allow top management to independently evaluate performance of *persuasive personalities* and *charismatic leaders*. Performance measurement itself, however, is in the best case imprecise, requiring both formal controls and a healthy dose of human judgment in order to achieve "imprecise" evaluations.

LESSONS FOR THE FUTURE FROM FEDERALISM: AN EFFECTIVE TOP-MANAGEMENT TEAM

The study "CEO Succession 2005: The Crest of the Wave" by the global consulting firm Booz Allen Hamilton (Summer 2006, Issue 43), presents evidence that turnover of CEOs of the 2,500 largest global public companies set a record in 2005. One out of every seven CEOs left his or her position, four times the rate of departure 10 years earlier. Furthermore, the rate of CEO dismissals in 2005 reached its highest point. This rate of failure and the trend over time indicates that perhaps the CEO position has become a job that has become unworkable and is in need of restructuring.

There are some hints as to the direction that restructuring of the CEO position should take. For example, Jack Welch of General Electric created a three-person top management team, each with specific responsibilities (Drucker, 2008, p. 467). Welch's two colleagues, before assuming their positions on the top-management team, agreed not to seek the position of CEO once vacated by Welch. That placed each member of the top-management team in a position to provide candid advice, and checks and balances on the actions of Welch as well as on the actions of one another. The visibility of the CEO team to General Electric's board of directors provided a safeguard that allowed each of the three members to be candid about one another's performance and about the performance of executives in the decentralized operating divisions. This arrangement provided a process for offsetting power with power, creating checks and balances on human conduct that are essential to the principles of federalism.

An Effective Board of Directors

Peter Drucker was adamant about the need for boards of directors to assume fiduciary responsibility, organize their work, and perform their duties effectively. But like the position of the American CEO, the position of a board member of a public company in the United States is also unworkable and in need of restructuring. Drucker saw this problem over 30 years ago, when he wrote this in an essay originally published in *The Wharton Magazine* in 1976:

> Whenever an institution malfunctions as consistently as boards of directors have in nearly every major fiasco of the last forty or fifty years it is futile to blame men. It is the institution that malfunctions. The large complex organization—whether business enterprise, university, or hospital—has changed so much that the traditional board, which law and custom envisage, no longer works and no longer can work. (Drucker, 1981b, p. 110)

In order for boards to function effectively, they must understand and organize their tasks. Ira M. Millstein, Holly J. Gregory, and Rebecca C. Grapsas (Millstein, Gregory, and Grapsas, 2006) have described the work and tasks of the board and in doing so they have placed a strong emphasis on the role of the board in ensuring integrity of the organization's management and its board members. The attempt to ensure the integrity of the organization in its activities, and in the organization's management, in itself would contribute to Drucker's mission to "enable the well-meaning and virtuous to achieve it [the norm]" (Drucker, 1985, p. 32).

The recommendations of Millstein, Gregory, and Grapsas for the work of the board are comprehensive and compressed. For simplicity, we have divided their recommendations into 10 items:

1. Set the agenda for the board so as to focus on the *areas critical to the success of the corporation.*
2. Arrange to have *appropriate information flows* to permit the board to set its agenda and to organize its own work.

3. Assess *the performance of top management* and of *individual board members.*
4. *Set compensation levels* that reflect performance against preset responsibilities of top management.
5. Designate a subcommittee of the board to focus upon issues related to *managerial succession* for key positions.
6. Go beyond matters related to *compliance in reporting* and insist on *ethical performance throughout the corporation.* This is principally a matter of *culture and integrity* that is established from the top, for, as the proverb has it, "fish rot from the head down." In other words, management, and top management in particular, sets the tone for the organization. Moreover, private behavior is indicative of moral beliefs and cannot be discounted in assessments of the integrity of corporation leaders.
7. Actively participate in reviewing the major strategies formulated by top management and then monitor the effectiveness of management's implementation of approved strategies. Board members also should critically evaluate these strategies and question management by providing expertise external to the organization.
8. Once strategies are approved, the board should identify critical success drivers that determine effective implementation and performance of these strategies. The board should ensure it has adequate information between board meetings to review the status of these drivers and to identify present or potential risk factors facing the corporation.
9. Directors should make certain that financial statements accurately reflect the true economics of the corporation and its parts. In other words, financial statements need to accurately represent the "true" financial status of the organization to investors, regulators, and the public at large.
10. Once compensation levels are determined, the compensation committee of the board and the board itself should help share-

holders, rating agencies, and regulators understand the logic and equity of executive compensation and provide reasonable justification for executive incentives and compensation.

Federalism in Networks and Alliances

As with so many of the issues raised in this chapter, the challenges of managing networks and alliances loom larger now than when Drucker first recognized them. It is the very nature of knowledge to constantly splinter into new specialties. That makes it very difficult for a knowledge-based organization to maintain all the specialties it requires at a scale that is economical. As a result, organizations partner with other organizations and create multiorganizational teams that are themselves embedded within multiple organizations and require a system of shared-leadership practices.

These alliances and networks are an extreme form of decentralized federalism. Central authority is very weak, and the burden of managing these organizations is placed upon *a system of leaders*, drawn from the various units of organization represented on an interorganizational team. Drucker has referred to these kinds of organizations as "system organizations," and he has enumerated the requirements and potential difficulties of managing these networks and alliances for success:

> Systems organization is an extension of the team design principle. . . . The systems organization builds the team out of a wide variety of different organizations. They may be government agencies, private businesses, universities and individual researchers, and organizations inside and outside the parent organization. . . . What organizations that use the systems structure have in common is a need to integrate diversity of culture, values, and skills into unity of action. Each component of the system has to work in its own way be [sic]

effective according to its own logic and according to its own standards. Or else it will not be effective at all. Yet all components have to work toward a common goal. Each has to accept, understand, and carry out its own role. This can be achieved only by direct, flexible, and tailor-made relationships among people, or groups of people, in which personal bond and mutual trust bridge wide differences in point of view and in what is considered "proper" and "appropriate." In no other organizational structure is the *ratio between output and effort needed for internal cohesion* as poor as in the systems structure. (Drucker, 2008, pp. 452–453)

Requirements for Managing the Systems Organization Structure

The requirements for successfully operating an organization based upon the systems structure are stringent. First, there must be a vision for the project, a vision that is shared by all members from the multiple organizational units and organizations involved on interorganizational teams. This vision must be converted into absolutely clear objectives for each person in the systems organization. Constructive interpersonal relationships among participants must be strong because they must substitute for the absence of formal authority—personnel in different organizations report to superiors in partner organizations. Interpersonal relationships must substitute for the lack of formal authority over people from different organizations.

Because of the loose, and often unclear, nature of responsibility and authority in a systems structure, *each member must assume responsibility for the success of the project* and be ready to fill gaps that develop during the project. Without shared vision, values, objectives, responsibilities, and personal loyalties, project success will be an unlikely occurrence, making these systems structures extremely vulnerable to failure.

Nevertheless, the systems structure has enjoyed significant success, such as on NASA's Apollo Project. *"It needs, however, clear goals, high self-discipline throughout the structure, and a top management that takes personal responsibility for relationships and communications"* (Drucker, 2008, p. 454).

CONCLUSION

Drucker's use of federalist principles embodied his own concept of management as a liberal art and its role in the creation of a tolerable society. By analyzing the ways in which people in the past struggled with the same issues we deal with today—questions of human nature with respect to leadership, the problem with reconciling the rights of the individual with the needs of the many, the problems associated with the abuse of power and authority—Drucker derived tangible solutions for the management of corporations and other organizations. He ultimately promoted the concept of a functioning society made up of decentralized, pluralist institutions. The difficulties leaders in government and business have had over time in achieving a society of functioning organizations led Drucker to be pessimistic and disposed to seek the conditions for a tolerable society, not a utopian one.

The central problem to be solved in creating a tolerable society of pluralistic institutions is the effective organization and distribution of power. Federalism offers one model for organizing and distributing power. In many corporations and governments alike, however, federalism is not without its defects. As we have seen, the framers of the Constitution placed sovereignty in the hands of the people. In doing so, they sidestepped the issue of inevitable conflicts between state and federal governments. Alexander Hamilton acknowledged that such conflicts would exist, but remarked that to engage in speculation was futile; better to "confine our attention wholly to the nature and extent of the powers as they are delineated in the Constitution. Everything beyond this must be left to the prudence and firmness of the people; who, as they will hold the scales in their own hands, it is to be hoped will always take care to preserve the constitutional equilibrium between the general and the State governments" (Hamilton, Madison, and Jay, 1788/1961, p. 197). The legacy of this ambiguity in the Constitution is patently obvious in the history of Supreme Court decisions involving judgments with respect to federal vs. state authority in a vast array of public and private matters.

Global applications of federalism offer even more profound lessons for dealing with the larger questions of power distribution and individual liberty. As Daniel Elazar has noted, the European Union has adapted federalist concepts to emphasize economic commonalities while retaining nation-state sovereignty (Elazar, 2001, pp. 35–42). Multinational federations such as India face the challenges and opportunities of multiculturalism as they work to balance conflicting views of federal government priorities (Burgess, 2006, pp. 123–125). Private sector organizations have struggled, and continue to wrestle with, ambiguities regarding authority. Who, in today's world of networks and alliances, has what degree of authority over what decisions? If nothing else, the lessons of federalism tell us that ambiguity is often inherent in organizations built to maximize individual liberty and central cohesion.

The practice of management as a liberal art as derived from the totality of Drucker's work offers a pragmatic and attainable model for managing society's institutions. Management as a liberal art takes into account the reality of human nature, the fact that humans are imperfect beings who at their very best require regulation, guidance, and some larger moral foundation to steer the course of their actions to desired ends. Practicing management as a liberal art will not prevent future scandals or poor decisions. However, it does offer a realistic approach for governing the behavior of individuals, organizations, and society. It can, perhaps, lead us in the direction of a tolerable society.

CHAPTER 5

THE HUMAN DIMENSION AND MANAGEMENT AS A LIBERAL ART

At its heart, management as a liberal art deals with questions of the human condition. The liberal arts ideal involves the study of disciplines that deal with human behavior, creativity, emotions, decision making, and moral values. Management necessarily involves organizing people for productive purposes, and thus it requires an understanding of what it means to be human. In this chapter, we discuss the role of the human dimension in management as a liberal art, specifically the concept of human dignity.

Drucker based his model of a functioning society on the Judeo-Christian concept of humans as created in the image of God and thus deserving of dignity and rightful treatment. Drucker's idea of human dignity follows in the trajectory of discussions of human rights, particularly in the United States. As we shall see, Drucker's Judeo-Christian view of rights presents its challenges for implementing management as a liberal art in today's diverse society. While not everyone will have the same vision of the human dimension as did Drucker, the issues he has raised regarding the source and nature of human rights and human dignity are valid ones that have been part of historical debates about liberty in America. If management as a liberal art is to work, it needs to squarely address the topic of the rights and dignity of human beings.

As we have seen in Chapter 4, Rosabeth Moss Kanter argued that Drucker, in his management writings, presented "an optimistic utopian view of human perfectibility" (Kanter, 1985, p. 12). Was his vision for bridging the gap between individual and collective existence in a society of organizations a dream doomed to failure? Or were his attempts to establish normative practices for leading and managing organizations of society realizable?

The bulk of this chapter is spent examining two companies that demonstrate the feasibility of Drucker's leadership and management practices. Both of these organizations adopted Drucker's Judeo-Christian view of the rights and dignity of human beings, and they translated that view into specific management practices. These examples illustrate the challenges associated with putting Drucker's worldview into practice, but they also indicate that his vision of a "bearable" society of functioning organizations was not just a utopian dream.

DRUCKER'S WORLDVIEW: JUDEO-CHRISTIAN FOUNDATIONS

Questions of worldview are particularly relevant to the work we all do and to the management of organizations in which we work. These questions were very relevant to Peter Drucker; they formed his understanding of human nature, the purposes of life, and the purposes of organizations.

Answers to the question of one's worldview are critical to attaining an understanding of oneself and reaching an understanding of how to manage people. As psychiatrist and Harvard University professor Armand Nicholi remarked:

Our worldview informs our personal, social, and political lives. It influences how we perceive ourselves, how we relate to others, how we adjust to adversity, and what we understand to be our purpose. Our worldview helps determine our values, our ethics, and our capacity for happiness. It helps us to understand where we come from, our heritage; who we are, our identity; why we exist on this planet, our purpose; what drives us, our motivation; and where we are going, our destiny. . . . Our worldview tells more about us perhaps than any other aspect of our personal history. (Nicholi, 2002, p. 7)

Drucker's vision for the individual was shaped by his worldview, which, as we have seen in Chapters 1 and 3, incorporated principles from the Judeo-Christian tradition, especially principles pertaining to the sanctity of human creation:

Social ecology is not value free. If it is a science at all, it is a "moral science"—to use an old term that has been out of fashion for two hundred years. The physical ecologist believes, must believe, in the sanctity of natural creation. The social ecologist believes, must believe, in the sanctity of spiritual creation. (Drucker, 1992/1993, p. 64)

Two implications for individuals follow Drucker's worldview:

(a) the promise of justice or, as we usually phrase it, of equal opportunities . . .
(b) . . . [and] the promise of individual fulfillment, of the "good life," or, in a perhaps more precise formulation, the promise of status and function as an individual. (Drucker, 1946, p. 136)

Status and *function* are related to each other, but they are not achieved in exactly the same way. In the Judeo-Christian tradition, status is inherent to the individual—the human being is made in God's image, frayed by his or her fallen nature but possessing inherent dignity and in search of significance. Function, on the other hand, is achievable only in society. But both status and function may be either significantly enhanced or substantially degraded by actions of management.

DRUCKER'S WORLDVIEW: THE CONCEPT OF HUMAN DIGNITY AND HUMAN RIGHTS

Drucker's Judeo-Christian foundation informed his view of human beings as possessing inherent qualities of value. The notion that all humans are created in God's image translates into the belief that all people have inherent worth, regardless of their behavior. This belief also served as the basis for discussions regarding the nature of liberty and rights, notably during the formation of the United States of America. Given Drucker's understanding of federalism (see Chapter 4), it is not surprising to find that his view of human dignity echoes that of the founding fathers. Drucker's concept of human dignity, and its function and role in the workplace, reflects early American debates about the source and composition of human rights. Understanding these historical connections makes the Drucker vision of the human dimension clearer for a contemporary audience.

Drucker's view of human dignity is clearly a derivative of natural-rights theory. The idea of natural rights, that all humans are born with some God-given rights inherent to their being products of divine creation, existed before the Enlightenment, but John Locke's 1690 *Second Treatise on Civil Government* was the first formal discussion of the concept. The founding fathers were well versed in natural-rights theory; they and other colonists not only read Locke, but also considered English common law, based on Locke's idea of natural law, as part of their colonial identity. Thus they embraced the idea of inherent rights as part and parcel of human existence.

But, as Bernard Bailyn argues, the colonists began to debate this idea as they progressed toward independence from England (Bailyn, 1967, pp. 184–197). If rights were natural, imbued in every human being by the Creator, then there would be no reason to write those rights down or to codify them. Yet without any documentation or codification, how could the colonists ensure the protection of those rights? And just what were those rights? Early understandings of natural rights were quite vague and generalized. John Locke's wording of natural rights as the right to "life, liberty and property," and Jefferson's "life, liberty, and the pursuit of happiness," are equally nebulous.

The discussion regarding the nature of human rights became more focused during the debates about ratification of the Constitution. In addition to the questions regarding the nature and extent of central control (see Chapter 4), the debates on the Constitution involved an extensive conversation about the nature of rights, and whether or not the Constitution should include a Bill of Rights. Those who favored a Bill of Rights were primarily Anti-Federalists, fearful of abuses of power by a strong central government. This group sought to protect individual liberties by specifically listing those rights that were considered to belong to all (although the founding fathers only included propertied white males in their definition of "all"). The Federalists, who opposed attaching a Bill of Rights to the Constitution, argued against such a document using natural-rights theory much like Drucker's view of human dignity. They noted that if God was the originator of these rights, if humans were already in possession of their natural rights, then there would be no need to produce a formal document stating what already was true. In one speech against the Bill of Rights, Benjamin Rush stated the following:

As we enjoy all our natural rights from a pre occupancy, antecedent to the social state, in entering into that state, whence shall they be said to be derived? Should it not be absurd to frame a formal declaration that our natural rights are acquired from ourselves? And would it not be a more ridiculous sole-cism to say, that they are the gift of those rulers whom we have created, and who are invested by us with every power they possess? (Rush, 1787/1993, p. 817)

The Anti-Federalists countered with the opinion that, if the Constitution were not specific regarding which rights were protected, at some point the government itself would define those rights, and to its advantage. As Bailyn states:

The antifederalists continued to believe that government *would*, inevitably, infringe on personal rights, that if rights were not specified but simply assumed to exist, in the end it would be up to someone in government to say, in any given situation, what precisely the rights were that should be protected; and that would mean that those who controlled the government could constitutionally silence anyone who disagreed simply by refusing to recognize the rights they claimed. (Bailyn, 1967, p. 350)

We have the Anti-Federalists to thank for our Bill of Rights. The colonists derived the idea of such a document, as well as some of the specific rights contained in it, from the 1689 English Bill of Rights. England, too, had wrestled with the concept of natural rights and the need to define more clearly exactly what those rights were and to whom they applied. Edmund Burke, the political theorist discussed in Chapters 1 and 4, argued against the idea of ill-defined, God-given natural rights, claiming instead that the English (and by exten-sion, the American colonists who carried with them the protections of English law) had inherited their rights from their forefathers who framed the English constitution and Bill of Rights, and thus were bequeathed a national, specific legacy.

As evidenced by the experience of the American colonists, as well as that of the English following the Glorious Revolution, a notion of divinely imbued human rights has certain inherent difficulties when implemented in specific moments in time. That is why natural-rights theory typically has defined God-given rights in very general terms, such as the right to "life, liberty, and the pursuit of happiness."

Defining *liberty* or *happiness* for a given culture at any given time will not necessarily result in the same answer. We saw this was the case for the liberal arts ideal, where definitions of an educated, moral human being changed depending on the values of the culture and the human beings who participated in the entire exercise. It has certainly been the case for the U.S. Constitution, which has been amended to, among other things, extend those protected rights to nonwhite males and women.

Due to the fact that the rights attributed to a divine hand are, in fact, explicated by human forces, they have changed as societies have changed. This is no more clearly evidenced than by the case of Abraham Lincoln, who guided his vision of the Union by the ideals contained in the Declaration of Independence, and who faced his own internal moral battle over human rights as his society underwent dramatic changes (see Chapter 6).

Therefore, if one begins, as did Drucker, with the belief that human beings have God-given qualities that must be respected and honored, at some point one must define what those particular qualities are, understanding that such a definition is informed by circumstances of time and culture. In other words, just as the founding fathers had to elucidate a set of rights in order to ratify the Constitution, a Drucker-centered model of management as a liberal art requires a clear definition of those qualities that are inherent to all human beings regardless of performance. Such a model does not require one to be Jewish or Christian, or to have any faith at all. But it does involve addressing questions that have loomed over discussions of human rights for centuries: from what source do our rights as human beings derive? What rights do we believe should be afforded to all people, regardless of what they do? How will we ensure the protection of these rights, or in Drucker's words, preserve human dignity?

In the following section of this chapter, we provide Drucker's definition of human dignity, the qualities he perceived to be uniquely human given his particular worldview. We show how Drucker specifically linked those qualities to organizations, the places where he believed human beings would find status and function in a modern industrial society. In Drucker's model, the "bearable" society would consist of well-managed organizations that fulfilled the human need for status and function: in short, that respected human dignity.

DRUCKER'S WORLDVIEW: HUMAN NATURE AND WORK

The human being has multiple characteristics and dimensions. People are not only biological and physiological beings but also social, spiritual, and moral beings. Individuals hold worldviews, beliefs about the purpose of existence, who they must ultimately answer to, and what they are responsible for. A person at work is still a biological person and a spiritual person, and these dimensions combine to guide her or his actions throughout the day. Management involves an acknowledgment of the multiple dimensions of human beings.

Crucial, therefore, to understanding Drucker's methodology as a social ecologist is grasping his assumptions about the fundamental nature of the human being. As discussed in Chapter 1, Drucker was so profoundly influenced by Kierkegaard that he came to the same realization about human existence as the Danish philosopher: it is an existence in tension. It consists of existence in time—that is in society—and in eternity where society is no longer relevant. God is outside of time and is eternal, as is the soul of the individual. Therefore, a true ecology of human-made existence must take into account the question of the existence of God in order for man to "fly right-side up." Individuals require personal answers to these existential questions of life both to achieve personhood in society and to resolve the questions caused by facing the reality of death.

While expressions of individual spirituality differ, recognition of people's spiritual nature is a necessary feature of Drucker's management philosophy. He believed that this recognition would help human beings gain a deeper understanding of what motivates and fulfills people in their work:

> In hiring a worker one always hires the whole man. . . . One cannot "hire a hand": its owner always comes with it. Indeed, there are few relations which so completely embrace a man's entire person as his relation to his work. . . . Only the relationship to his Creator and that to his family antedate man's relationship to his work; only they are more fundamental. (Drucker, 1954, p. 262)

In his article "The Unfashionable Kierkegaard," Drucker argued that people have a *responsibility* to make their own decisions about the existential dimensions of existence (Drucker, 1949). He believed that personhood, one's relationship to other human beings, requires recognition of the transcendental or existential dimensions of human existence. Although he regularly argued that a person's spiritual side was extremely private, Drucker noted that this private sphere had an impact on the public arena of the workplace. One's beliefs about ultimate existence, or existential tension, may be reflected in the workplace because of the way it embraces a person's entire being. One's spiritual viewpoint could also result in gaining a deeper understanding of oneself and of one's coworkers. In Drucker's words:

> If you accept the fact that you are one of God's creatures, no better, no worse than any other creature, it's not humility, that's the wrong word, but you accept the fact that you are

God's creature, and therefore the fact that the fellow who
works next to you doesn't have an MBA is irrelevant . . . this
is the brotherhood. (Buford, 1993, p. 7)

Drucker was concerned not only with people's spiritual side but
also with the physiological, material, and psychological aspects of
human existence. Each of these spheres is joined in an interlocking
web in the workplace such that action in one sphere may have reper-
cussions in other spheres. For example, a worker in the middle of a
divorce will likely experience difficulties in performing up to par on
the job. A manager dealing with the death of a family member cannot help but feel the impact of that emotional trauma in the workplace. It follows, therefore, that there are major differences between
managing the objective aspects of work, governed by establishing
standards for making work productive, and managing the subjective aspects of work, which require managers to establish conditions
so workers can experience a sense of achievement, fulfillment, and
growth.

Status and Function at Work

Individuals are not naturally designed to work in organizations.
Organizations are human-made structures for achieving desired
outcomes. The purpose of an organization is to make the strengths
of its members productive and to promote the growth and development of individuals while they are at work. To both make members
productive in their work and develop them requires a careful process
of selecting people to match their strengths to their assignments. The
positions so filled by these people should then be designed to permit
individuals to exercise the full scope of their strengths as they carry
out their responsibilities.

A major difference between the human being and other productive resources is that the human being actively participates in the

process of work. The human being has considerable discretion over how much to work and how hard to work—the degree of concentration and effort expended and the imagination applied. An employee may choose to simply get the job done, to get the job done well, or to improve upon the way in which the job is done. Outputs of human work may become more or less than the sum of human efforts. Says Drucker: "To get out more than is being put in is possible only in the moral sphere" (Drucker, 1954, p. 146).

Obstacles to Realizing Status and Function

Unemployment (or underemployment) is the most obvious example of the loss of function and status. According to Drucker, unemployment is "economic catastrophe . . . [along with] social disfranchisement." The unemployed worker is "an outcast—for a man who has no function and no status, for whom society has no use and nothing to do, has been cast out." (Drucker, 1942, p. 82). Unemployment is an affront to the dignity of the person, and if prolonged, can lead to the loss of self-respect for no reason having to do with the actions of the person.

Less obvious, however, is the employed worker who also may encounter loss of status and function. The employed worker often lacks status and function if he or she is treated as a "human machine" and perceived as the *object* of work. Using assembly-line production workers as an example, Drucker graphically illustrates the lack of status and function experienced by some workers whose jobs are so designed that they are treated as objects of work:

The productive labor is that of the man on the assembly line who, standing rigidly all day, holds in his outstretched hand a paint brush which automatically draws a red line on the flanks of slowly passing automobile bodies. He neither understands how an automobile works nor does he possess any skill which could not be acquired by everyone within a few days. He is not a human being in society, but a freely replaceable cog in an inhumanly efficient machine. (Drucker, 1942, p. 85)

This reality, most often observed in the design of production and service work, and to a lesser extent in knowledge work, is an offense to the inherent dignity of the human being who deserves respect merely for who he or she is. And it's a wasted opportunity; it fails to capitalize on the uniqueness of each individual as a potential source of great strength in the organization.

Responsibilities of Management

In Drucker's worldview, management is about being the employer, organizer, and developer of the whole person within human and social organizations. The organization is the central organ of a functioning society, and it serves as a structural link between the individual and society. An organization makes it possible for the combined efforts of human beings to be directed toward a desirable end. The problems and opportunities posed by organizations, therefore, are not merely technical problems but rather problems of organizing human relationships. Posits Drucker: "To borrow a metaphor from modern psychology, an institution is like a tune; it is not constituted by individual sounds but by the relations between them" (Drucker, 1946, p. 26).

People are the building blocks of organizations. Performance in organizations therefore depends upon the performance of people. A business may produce a highly technical product, but it is people who design, organize, and evaluate the work. The task of management, then, is to make people productive while developing their skills, character, and intellectual capacity. Taken together, the productivity and development of people should in turn contribute to the long-term success of the organization.

Management Practices and the Human Being at Work

There are five interrelated categories of practices in managing and developing the human being at work. The Drucker vision is to use these practices to maximize human potential for the common good. The first four practices are considered in this chapter and are ordered to coincide with ServiceMaster Company's four objectives, which are described later in the chapter.

These are the first four practices:

1. Integrity and values
2. People and their development
3. Strengths and opportunities
4. Performance and results

The fifth practice, self-management, is considered in detail in Chapter 7 and is there integrated with the four practices described in this chapter.

Integrity and Values

Drucker saw personal integrity and organizational values as crucial to the management of people. Maintaining personal integrity, or remaining true to one's own values, is a key component of living an ethical and meaningful life for many people. Translating that devotion to an organization is a more challenging proposition. How can managers ensure that their own values are aligned with those of their organizations? How can they attract and retain others who share the same values, and who are likewise committed to integrity?

Integrity. Drucker calls integrity the touchstone of management—its very essence (Drucker, 2008, p. 287). Imbedded within integrity is a moral code of behavior. The power of integrity in a leader is the example it provides for the rest of the organization, for as the old proverb goes, "An ounce of example is worth a ton of precept."[1] Alfred Sloan modeled executive integrity for Drucker, so many of the traits described here reflect Sloan's influence on Drucker (see Chapter 1).

Responsibility is a trait possessed by persons of integrity. And responsibility itself is not possible without a moral reference point to establish its meaning and scope. We are not suggesting, however, that a moral reference point should be established based only on legal and ethical codes. If that were the case, then Drucker would have embraced decentralization alone as a means for curbing the lust for power. As was discussed in Chapter 1, Drucker (and Sloan) did not believe that structures or codes alone would result in good management decisions. Instead, both men felt that it was important to have people with a strong moral compass in managerial positions.

Alexander Solzhenitsyn made a compelling case against reliance on legal codes as the only criterion for moral behavior:

> I have spent my entire life under a communist regime and I will tell you that a society without any objective legal scale is a terrible one indeed. But a society with no other scale but the legal one is not quite worthy of man either. A society which is based on the letter of the law and never reaches any higher is taking very scarce advantage of the high level of human possibilities. The letter of the law is too cold and formal to have a beneficial influence on society. Whenever the tissue of life is woven of legalistic relations, there is an atmosphere of moral mediocrity, paralyzing man's noblest impulses. (Solzhenitsyn, 1978, p. 4)

Drucker long ago made a complementary argument for the need of moral absolutes to guide responsible behavior in a free and functioning society: "The essence of freedom . . . is responsible choice.

And, . . . in order to have freedom, it must be assumed that there is absolute truth and absolute reason" (Drucker, 1942b, pp. 482–483).

One of the challenges of Drucker's view, however, is that moral values have changed in societies over time. Slavery was an accepted part of many "free" societies, as was the subjugation of women. The "absolute truths" of the biological inferiority of women and people of color have long been disproven, and the divergence of religious opinions on such issues as gay marriage indicates the range of moral stances within the community that sees itself as the guardian of values. Attempts to create declarations of human rights that cover all people in all cultures across the globe have, as we have seen, involved considerable discord (see Chapter 3). In American industrial organizations, child labor was considered acceptable until the early twentieth century, and incidents such as the Triangle Shirtwaist Fire of 1911 illustrate that early factory owners cared little for the health and welfare of their immigrant laborers. Nevertheless, Drucker's point is apt: in order to practice integrity, organizations must decide upon a set of moral values that are upheld and agreed upon. For Drucker, those values were very clear, and they reflect his belief in the concept of human dignity. Integrity, then, involves the recognition of each person as having innate value, and requires behavior to back up that recognition. Drucker valued Sloan, for example, because of qualities such as his fair treatment of employees, willingness to listen to others' opinions, and emphasis on people's strengths. In short, Sloan modeled integrity because of the way he treated others as well as the way he upheld his own responsibilities.

Integrity Is Demonstrated in People Decisions. Integrity is difficult to define, but its absence or presence is made plain in people decisions. People decisions, and not formal value statements, are the real indicators of what an organization and its executives value. There are five major ways in which the presence or absence of integrity is reflected in people decisions (Drucker, 2008, pp. 287–288):

1. A focus on weaknesses instead of strengths constitutes a lack of integrity. Integrity involves looking for what is good in a person and focusing on what a person can do well.
2. Placing personality above all else is corruption. It encourages politicking and cautiousness that result in mediocrity. A person who is more interested in "Who is right?" instead of "What is right?" lacks integrity.
3. Placing performance or intelligence above all else in people decisions demonstrates a lack of integrity. "This is immaturity—and usually incurable" [p. 287].
4. Promoting weak people because of the perceived threat caused by strong people constitutes a lack of integrity. Competent and performing subordinates can only serve to raise the performance of the whole organization and make the superior's performance shine brighter. It is the sign of a strong manager that he or she has strong people in the organization.
5. A manager's lack of respect for the individual constitutes a lack of integrity. A manager must show respect for the uniqueness of every human being in the organization.

In summary, there is no substitute for integrity in the effective leadership of an organization. Codes of ethical behavior are no substitute for personal integrity, for integrity requires honesty and morality in decision making. For "there is no interpretation of a rule or standard that can ever substitute for the integrity of the person who has to apply it" (Pollard, 2006, p. 148).

Values. Management deals with the human community; managing people requires values, commitment, and conviction. Values are what enable the organization to continue into the future, weathering the curveballs of discontinuities and radical change. Values that are merely opportunistic, greedy, and selfish, those that exist *to take and never to give*, will result in an organization that will not perform at an optimal level. In troubled times, people must call upon their reserves and put forth extraordinary effort, and people will not do this unless they believe in what they are doing—in other words, accept the values of the organization.

Drucker insisted that leaders of an organization should commit to those values that reflect deep compassion for people. The most significant and fundamental of those values is respect for the dignity and innate worth of the individual. This value is a basic human right. How to translate this natural right to dignity and respect in an organization is a larger, more complicated issue. Just as the founding fathers sought to define Americans' natural rights (for example, life, liberty, and the pursuit of happiness), Drucker sought to help managers understand the need to define organizational values clearly and then to establish structures and practices that uphold those values.

Instilling values in an organization involves creating a culture within that institution. The integration of people into a common effort leads to the formation of an organization's culture—the ways in which people in an organization solve the recurring problem of the organization. History, government, customs, and political systems of a specific region and country play a strong role in shaping the way management carries out its functions. Management may also shape the culture of its organization. The ability to shape culture offers management significant opportunities along with challenges, as Drucker observes:

Management is—and should be—culture-conditioned; in turn, management and managers shape culture and society. Thus, although management is an organized body of knowledge and, as such, applicable everywhere, it is also *culture*. It is not "value-free" science. (Drucker, 2008, p. 12)

Yet we have several examples of those who view management and business as a value-free enterprise. The fact that the market system is amoral is sometimes used as an excuse. For example, George Soros, commenting on his role in creating the crises in Asian financial markets in the late 1990s, said:

> I am basically there to—to make money. I cannot and do not look at the social consequences of—of what I do. And I don't feel guilty. Because I'm engaged in an amoral activity which is not meant to have anything to do with guilt? . . . There was no sense that I shouldn't be there, because that was—well, actually, in a funny way, it's just like in markets—that if I weren't there—of course, I wasn't doing it, but somebody else would be taking it away anyhow. . . . Whether I was there or not, I was only a spectator, the property was being taken away. . . . I had no role in taking away that property. So I had no sense of guilt. (Dinerstein, 2006)

In still another example of amoral market behavior, the CEO of Boeing, Harry Stonecipher, resigned on March 7, 2005, because of an improper sexual relationship with a woman at the Boeing Company. In clarifying the reasons for the resignation, Chairman Lew Platt noted, "The Board concluded that the facts reflected poorly on Harry's judgment and would impair his ability to lead the company." But Platt continued, "the affair *did not violate* [italics added] the company's code of conduct in and of itself, but that the board believed the relationship violated the code about hurting the company's reputation" (Isidore, 2005). It was the company's image with prospective customers that was the offense, not the negative moral consequences of the conduct of the CEO on other employees. In other words, the conduct was okay but the damage to the reputation of Boeing was not okay. Thus we see a clear separation between personal moral behavior and corporate moral behavior—Stonecipher's behavior was okay, merely a lapse in judgment, but it did harm the reputation of Boeing in the company's markets.

What did Boeing's code of conduct mean if that behavior did not violate Boeing's code? The chairman's response sounds like legal language, not ethical or moral language. The specific behavior in question is not illegal under the Sarbanes-Oxley Act (SOX), so it is not illegal executive behavior. But, a rule-based system for ethical behavior, such as SOX, will never substitute adequately for the high standards of integrity required by top executives.

The Boeing example illustrates why Drucker faulted the trend toward "business ethics" and away from an emphasis on integrity and moral behavior in business. Drucker believed that a business cannot have ethics, only its people can, and what is ethical personal behavior is often very easy to determine:

> There is only one code of ethics, that of individual behavior, for prince and pauper, for rich and poor, for the mighty and the meek alike. Ethics, in the Judeo-Christian tradition, is affirmation that all men are alike creatures—whether the Creator be called God, Nature, or Society. (Drucker, 1981, p. 19)

To understand Drucker's concept of values requires an understanding of his grounding in this Judeo-Christian tradition. For Drucker, what is immoral for the person should be immoral for the company—there can be no business ethics separate from moral personal behavior.

People and Their Development

A worldview that accepts the inherent dignity and worth of the human being will lead executives to treat individuals as assets and develop whatever strengths they possess. Observed Drucker: "It is typical of the most successful and the most durable institutions that they induce in their members an intellectual and moral growth beyond a man's [or woman's] original capacities" (Drucker, 1946, p. 28). When opportunities for growth and development are provided, and the mission of the organization linked to the growth and development of the individual, a job becomes an integral and meaningful part of life itself. Intellectual and moral growth so induced manifests itself in a person's life, both inside and outside of the organization.

Focusing the efforts of a person on realistic but challenging objectives is an essential element in the development of the person. The key question, "What can I contribute?" forms a pathway to self-development, as Drucker relates:

> Individual self-development in large measure depends on the focus on contributions. The man [or woman] who asks of himself [or herself], "What is the most important contribution I can make to the performance of this organization?" asks in effect, "What self-development do I need? What knowledge and skill do I have to acquire to make the contribution I should be making? What strengths do I have to put to work? What standards do I have to set myself?" (Drucker, 1966, p. 68)

Development of the human being is a two-way process, involving the cooperation and motivation of the individual and employer. The role of management is to provide opportunities for growth and development both by insisting that individuals focus on the unique contributions they can make and by investing in their further development.

Strengths and Opportunities

The executive sets standards for excellence—in ambition, aspiration, and impact. When an executive raises the demands on himself or herself, those around that individual do the same. Development of others and development of oneself can be tightly linked in a self-perpetuating cycle.

Focus on Strengths. Drucker thought that "to make strengths productive is the unique purpose of the organization" (Drucker 1966, p. 71). A focus on strengths is based on the belief that each individual is endowed with unique and specific abilities. A conscious choice to focus on what a person *can* do instead of what he or she *cannot* do is in full accordance with the social ecology of the person—the material, biological, and spiritual nature of human beings. A focus on strengths involves both an attitude and practices. It consists of making the worker productive and of helping the worker to achieve. A focus on the strengths of people gives executives an opportunity to participate in the transformation of individuals at work—in what people are *becoming* as a result of their work. Managers are able to witness people raising their sights and achievements beyond what they previously thought possible.

To enable this transformation to occur, an executive should exploit the strengths of people by providing them with training and opportunities that permit them to achieve higher levels of performance. A focus on strengths permits setting high standards whose attainment brings a sense of achievement and a "yes, I can" feeling. That sensation encourages a person to perform at even higher levels. In contrast, a focus on weaknesses leads to frustration and shame. It leads to lack of performance by shining the spotlight on what is wrong, not on what is right. It can create fatigue, cynicism, demotivation, and, eventually, disengagement.

The key is to hire a person who is an exceptional performer in an area that counts for the organization. Once hired, the executive should expect performance from the person based on known capacities. Executives can protect their organization from weaknesses of individuals by overlapping the strengths of others so that individual weaknesses are rendered irrelevant.

Rules for Staffing from Strength. What are the rules to follow in order to staff from strength? As Drucker notes in *The Effective Executive*

(1966, pp. 78–91), first, be on guard against the impossible job. Start with the acknowledgment that jobs are made by humans and are never designed perfectly. A job that thwarts two or three good people is an impossible one and should be restructured or abolished. Such a job may appear on paper to be reasonable, but often it requires a mixture of temperaments and talents that are rarely found in one person. That job might have been structured in the past to fit an unusually gifted person.

Second, it is important to make each job demanding and large. A job with adequate scope brings out the strengths of a person. If a job is large and demanding, it provides opportunities for an individual to stretch and to meet new demands and challenges. And that is how growth takes place. A demanding job is especially important at the beginning of one's career, as it allows the person to determine what she is good at, how she performs, and where she belongs. A small job does not provide that kind of experience and may leave the person frustrated, cynical, and unproductive. Worst of all, it may prevent a person from becoming all she can become.

Third, begin appraisals with strengths, with what a person can do well and has done well. A shortcoming of some performance appraisal systems is that they focus on what a person cannot do instead of what a person can do. Or, the appraisal system may place more importance on potential rather than on performance. Drucker advised that performance appraisals ought to emphasize the positive:

> Good appraisals should ask, "What has she done well and will therefore likely be able to do well?" "What does she have to learn or to acquire to be able to get the full benefit from her strength?" and lastly, "If I had a son or daughter, would I be willing to have him or her working under this person? Why, or why not?" (Drucker, 1966, p. 86)

A focus on strengths is particularly important when leadership positions are being filled. Leaders are highly visible in an organization. They set the standard; they are the exemplars. It is relatively easy to raise the performance of an entire organization by raising the performance of its leaders because, as standard setters, leaders establish performance targets for the entire organization. Leaders, therefore, should be appointed to positions that capitalize upon their strengths.

Focus on Opportunities and the Future. An organization that is focused on opportunities is one that is primarily on the offensive. It is marked by the excitement of what is possible, a sense of achievement, and satisfaction that comes from directing energies toward the future. A focus on opportunity creates an organization where people are willing to work hard. It creates an organization where people are enthusiastic and highly stimulated toward what is possible. It pulls together energies required to overcome obstacles and problems in the way.

An organization that is focused on opportunities stands in marked contrast to one that is purely problem focused and characterized by worry and defensiveness. Problems can never be ignored, but an excessive focus on problems can conceal opportunities. A problem-focused organization "is an organization that feels that it has performed well if things do not get worse" (Drucker, 2008, p. 284).

People in an opportunity-focused organization look for opportunities that involve measured risk but that are likely to produce results that really matter and are meaningful to both the individual and the organization. And they ask, "What are the opportunities that, if realized, will have the greatest impact on performance and results of the company and of my unit?" (Drucker, 2008, p. 284–285). They reject mediocrity and complacency.

An organization that focuses on opportunities does not consider the past to be the golden years and does not expend effort on preserving the memory of bygone times. It is not satisfied by maintaining yesterday's level of performance. It does not celebrate holding steady, or not doing worse than yesterday, nor does it see avoiding problems as the ultimate goal. Instead, it focuses on opportunities for moving ahead, up, forward, and toward the future; it demands that these opportunities be converted into results. It commits resources—time and, most importantly, people—to opportunities. It starves problem areas and feeds its opportunities with resources (Drucker, 2008, p. 285).

A focus on the future therefore begins by abandoning the past. For it is wasteful to expend resources on products and services that were productive in the past but cease to produce today and are unlikely to produce in the future. The key question then is, "Is this still worth doing?" Ask, "If I were not doing this right now, would I decide to do it today?" (Drucker, 1966, p. 104). If the answer is no, abandon the activity in question or reduce its scope significantly.

Establishing priorities is an essential part of focusing on the future. There are always more opportunities than there are resources to pursue them. The key is to decide which tasks are most important and which are least important; then concentrate efforts and resources on the best opportunities. Either the pressures or the executive will make the decision as to where to focus, and if the pressures win out, the organization loses.

A focus on the future demands that an organization focus on the one most important task that, if done with excellence, would make a huge difference in the performance of the organization. The organization then concentrates on this task until it is done and doesn't commit past this one task. Then it reassesses and chooses the next most important task, a first-things-first approach.

An organization with a clear focus on the future has clear priorities, has communicated these throughout the organization, and follows through with the application of appropriate resources. People then pursue with confidence what they know to be most important to the organization, thus facilitating the opportunity for real contribution, achievement, and motivation.

Performance and Results

There are three result areas: *direct results, development of values*, and *developing people*. For a bank, direct results are sales and profit. For a hospital, they are patients healed or cared for. For a school, they are students educated. Direct results should be made clearly visible and unambiguous. *Values* are commitments to certain beliefs and help to keep everyone pulling together in the same direction. *Development of people* is the way an organization renews its human capital and overcomes the limits on contribution that are imposed upon it by the mortality of its members. It requires continuously upgrading human resources to establish new levels of performance. It is one of the fundamental imperatives of an organization.

Performance and results are produced when people focus on contribution. People who focus on contribution make the connections between their personal skills, relationships, specialties, and function and the work of the entire organization and its purpose. They ask, "What can I contribute that will significantly affect the *performance and the results* of the institution I serve?" (Drucker, 1966, p. 52). A focus on contribution leads to an examination of the unused potential in a job relative to what constitutes true performance and results.

Cultivating a focus on performance and results is a critical component for creating and sustaining a highly spirited organization. But a correct definition of performance leaves room for failure and recognizes failure as a component of performance itself. The definition of performance is "the consistent ability to produce results over prolonged periods of time and in a variety of assignments" (Drucker, 2008, p. 281). Performance is therefore more like a slugging average, calculated as the magnitude of successes versus total attempts, including those attempts that were mistakes and failures. The more effective a person is, the more mistakes that person will make but the greater will be her or his overall contribution. At issue in performance appraisal is the magnitude of contributions over total efforts, not merely the number of successes over total attempts.

In summary, there are five categories of practices involved in the Drucker vision for managing and developing the human being at work. Four of them have been described in this chapter. We turn now to two examples that illustrate the four practices.

EXAMPLES OF THE DRUCKER VISION: SERVICEMASTER AND DACOR

C. William Pollard served as CEO and chairman of ServiceMaster from 1983 to 2002. During that time, ServiceMaster expanded its service offerings from residential and commercial cleaning, facility maintenance, and management for health-care, education, and industrial customers to a network of company-owned, franchised service centers and business units operating under such brands as TruGreen-ChemLawn, TruGreen-LandCare, Terminix, Service-Master Clean, Merry Maids, AmeriSpec, Furniture Medic, and ServiceMaster Management Services. Most of its operations were in the United States, but it also had operations in 45 foreign countries and ended 2001 with revenues that exceeded $6 billion.[2]

Pollard upheld and further developed the ServiceMaster values by following in the steps of his three predecessors: Marion Wade, Ken Hansen, and Ken Wessner. Their approach to leadership and management was based upon four objectives:

1. To Honor God in All We Do
2. To Help People Develop
3. To Pursue Excellence
4. To Grow Profitably

But it was not these four objectives that distinguished ServiceMaster from 1947 to 2002; rather, it was the depth in which these objectives, and the thinking behind them, were espoused and applied to the management of human beings at work. That made this American public corporation, and this example, a unique story in American business history and worthy of systematic study.

Most of the company's workers were unskilled laborers engaged in service tasks, such as cleaning hospital rooms and airport waiting areas.[3] This type of work is very different from that performed by knowledge workers (as discussed in detail in Chapter 7). One of the challenges Drucker identified was how to provide status and function to workers engaged in such tasks. How can such an organization prevent the all-too-common problem of viewing service workers as the "object of work"? How can service workers have demanding and large jobs that allow them to develop their strengths? How can organizations provide opportunities for growth and development for people who, initially, may lack educational backgrounds for advancement? How can organizations work to make these employees active agents in improving their work environment?

The ServiceMaster example is instructive in that it illustrates how Drucker's model of human development can be applied to workers who typically have little control over their day-to-day activities on the job, are paid low wages, and may be resistant to and/or suspicious of managerial efforts to change their behavior.

ServiceMaster's four objectives coincide with the four categories of Drucker practices described above:

1. Integrity and values
2. People and their development
3. Strengths and opportunities
4. Performance and results

Objective 1: To Honor God in All We Do

The first ServiceMaster objective, "To Honor God in All We Do," mirrors Drucker's first category of integrity and values. This objective provided ServiceMaster with a set of agreed-upon values that emphasized behavior at all levels of the organization. It also focused the company on the Judeo-Christian model of human dignity, which, as discussed earlier, assumes that every human being has certain innate rights that are endowed by the Creator. The first ServiceMaster objective is the most unusual and controversial; as Pollard noted, "it is the 'God language' that raises eyebrows" (Pollard, 1996b, p. 19). Pollard was very explicit that this value, for him, reflected his own Christian belief. Yet, in modeling Drucker's worldview, and Judeo-Christian assumptions about work and human nature, he stated that "my faith is personal to me and not a corporate belief, nor can it be mandated as such. However, our assumptions about human nature are fundamental to our assumptions about how work should be managed" (Pollard, 1996b, p. 21).

One of the challenges facing Pollard at ServiceMaster was to define those assumptions about human nature and work without mandating a belief system. As discussed in Chapter 1, Drucker believed that religious faith was utterly personal but that people needed to believe in something in order to have a functioning society. For Drucker, hope existed in the form of faith in well-managed institutions that provided meaning and status. ServiceMaster replicated Drucker's ideal, while more explicitly incorporating his Judeo-Christian influences. The point of the first objective is to unite the individuals in the firm through faith. Ultimately, at ServiceMaster, this faith was made operational by respecting "the dignity and worth of every person—every worker" (Pollard, 1996b, p. 21).

In essence, Pollard, and his three predecessors, found a way to apply their own personal faith within a secular economic organization, linking their faith in a personal God to the larger mission of the company. Assumptions about the existence and nature of God thus became fundamental to their assumptions about human nature and how work should be managed. Whether or not others in the organization shared Pollard's personal beliefs was not important so long as they understood that there was a difference between right and wrong, and had a desire to engage in right behaviors and to serve others. Pollard followed the Drucker blueprint for a system of values in organizations, but he more overtly tied it to Drucker's (and Pollard's) own Judeo-Christian tradition.

Drucker's model of integrity requires managers to focus on *what*, not *who*, is right. Although definitions of "right" have changed in cultures and societies over time, Drucker's emphasis on integrity and values dictates that people thoughtfully consider their own values and the source of those values.

For Pollard and ServiceMaster, the source was clear. "To Honor God in All We Do" was intended to remind the people of the company that they were under an authority higher than themselves. People were reminded that they are ultimately responsible to God for how they work and how they live. The first objective also established a reference point for the evaluation of behavior; that is, actions can be evaluated in terms of what is right and what is wrong. In the case of ServiceMaster, the organization's right and wrong behavior was defined by interpretations of Judeo-Christian traditions.

Putting that objective into practice can be a tricky business. First of all, in today's diverse American society, there is no guarantee that every employee of an organization embraces the same religious tradition (or any tradition at all, for that matter). Even if employees do share a religious affiliation, different interpretations of scripture or traditions can result in conflicting ideas regarding what is right or wrong in specific situations. For example, some would argue that Judeo-Christian values mandate a living, not a minimum, wage;

others would claim that the same values do no such thing. Also, some Christians interpret their scriptures to emphasize traditional gender roles, including the belief that women with young children should not work outside of the home. If an organization embraces such a value, that has significant implications for working women who seek to advance their careers within such a firm.

How are the values agreed upon in an organization? Are they mandated from above, or developed through consensus? Service-Master is an example of an organization that successfully incorporated religious traditions into its mission. Objective 1 provided a moral standard for establishing responsibility, a standard recommended by both Drucker and Solzhenitsyn. Yet, one of the challenges of Drucker's model remains its implementation: how does an organization establish a set of agreed-upon values that are not totally vague yet still can function as standards? Just as the English and Americans debated the definitions of natural rights in the seventeenth and eighteenth centuries, modern organizations will need to hash through this issue.

Drucker also stressed that integrity and values were reflected in people decisions. Objective 1 specifies how people should be treated and how they should treat one another. The faith of top management working through processes that enhanced human dignity and worth united the ServiceMaster organization and provided Drucker-like responsible freedom. As Pollard says: "When the purpose of the firm is linked to the growth and development of a person in God's image, it unleashes powerful forces in the mind and spirit of the worker" (Pollard, 1996). Thus, the ServiceMaster example provides a historical example of a management system that deeply integrated faith, the personal with the eternal, into the workplace and helped workers, so inclined, to acknowledge and resolve the existential tension of life. Objective 1 allowed ServiceMaster to incorporate its values into people decisions.

ServiceMaster's first objective challenged people to commit themselves to truth and honesty in all they do. This led ServiceMaster to declare that "Quality Is Truth" (ServiceMaster Co., 1994). Truth is debased if a person and organization knowingly delivers its services at levels of quality below what it is capable of and below what is known to be right.[4]

ServiceMaster's interpretation of its first objective also required that its leaders take responsibility and serve others. The philosophy of management at ServiceMaster in the very words of its name emphasizes both service and servant leadership—*masters of service* and *service to the master*. This is a clear example of the Christian interpretation of servant leadership (see Chapter 6).

Pollard embraced Drucker's model of the leader as a responsible servant of the mission of the organization. Pollard's vision of the effective executive, however, more explicitly folded in spiritual components. Invoking Aristotle, he upheld self-control as a necessary quality of leadership. However, it was Jesus' message of "Give thyself" that was more important for Pollard: "He taught His disciples that no leader is greater than the people he leads, and that even the humblest of tasks is worthy for a leader to do" (Pollard, 1996b, p. 130). Although both Pollard and Drucker believed in the management philosophy of servant leadership, it had a distinctly religious quality for Pollard. For Pollard and others such as Robert Greenleaf (1977, pp. 1–48), a servant leader does the following:

- Seeks to serve the best interests of all constituents and exhibits compassion for those served. The manager needs to be tough minded and results oriented but compassionate.
- Emphasizes leadership by example and encourages a servant's heart toward those served. One way for a manager to put this into practice is to display a willingness to perform the most menial tasks. Doing so not only gives the manager an under-

standing of the company's work but also enables him or her to empathize with the front-line service providers; it adds dignity to all the work of the company. The leader becomes the exemplar.

- Accepts, empathizes with, listens to, and learns from all constituents. Drucker says that "listening is not a skill; it is a discipline. Anybody can do it. All you have to do is to keep your mouth shut" (Drucker, 1990, p. 20).
- Focuses, not on the leader, but on the people who follow and the direction they are going in their work and lives.

Perhaps not surprisingly, part of the power of servant leaders comes from the very dignity they provide others because of the responsibility they assume for the development and enrichment of followers. Followers so served are more willing to yield authority to such a leader.[5] Servant leadership allows organizations to implement one of Drucker's key components of virtuous people decisions: avoiding the overvaluation of performance or intelligence. As leaders are willing to perform menial tasks, they show that such work is not "beneath" them.

Servant leadership also allowed Pollard and ServiceMaster to address the issues Drucker raised related to the legitimacy of leadership; servant leadership helps to justify the power of management. Power and authority are necessary for accomplishing the objectives of an organization. But the first objective also provides the moral compass for exercising power and authority. As Pollard relates: "Unless leaders earn the right to have the power and it is accepted as legitimate, they will fall into the trap of seeking to implement power through authority and might" (Pollard, 1996b, p. 101).

Objective 1 neatly unifies Drucker's method of legitimizing authority with the importance he placed on faith. The firm's mission, grounded in individual human development as a by-product of a creator God, aligns manager and employee through a larger purpose: "People want to work for a cause, not just for a living," says Pollard. "When there is alignment between the cause of the firm and the cause of its people, move over—because there *will* be extraordinary performance" (Pollard, 1996b, p. 45).

While it is difficult to arrive at direct measures of the effectiveness of servant leadership in any organization, it is clear from examples provided by Pollard in his two books, *The Soul of the Firm* (1996b) and *Serving Two Masters?* (2006), that ServiceMaster contributed to the transformation of employees into people who in their careers, inside and outside of ServiceMaster, have assumed high levels of responsibility and have realized high levels of self-esteem and personal fulfillment. These include individuals who began in low-wage positions in the firm and, through their own motivation and efforts, as well as with managerial support and development, worked their way into the management ranks of ServiceMaster.

In addition to personal development outcomes, the company increased cash distributions to shareholders for 30 consecutive years from 1970 to 2000 (ServiceMaster Co., 2001). For the 25-year period from 1963 to 1988, the company earned an 18 percent annual compounded growth rate in earnings per share. It achieved an average return on equity of 50 percent during the 20-year period from 1976 to 1996, a period of time in which ServiceMaster's share price increased from $1 per share to $28 per share (Maciariello, 2002, pp. 14–15).

For ServiceMaster, honoring God and respecting individuals encompassed a concern for the employees' families as well as its workers. This is especially important in the United States now given the fact that so many families do not resemble the traditional nuclear family. As more and more American households require two working adults to make ends meet, or consist of single parents raising children, changes in the workplace can have significant impacts on not just the employee, but also on his or her dependents. A company that seeks to enhance the dignity of the individual cannot be unmindful of the effects of work life on family life. But, many companies disregard these effects. And families in the United States need a great deal of help:

- More than 50 percent of mothers with infants less than one year old now work outside the home.[6]
- One in three children is born to a single parent.
- More than half of Americans today have been, are, or will be in stepfamilies.

Decisions made by firms, such as relocation and changes in job activities, affect not only the employee but also the employee's family. For example, unanticipated shift changes can significantly impact single parents' child care expenses as well as time with children when they are home. A job transfer may mean more income for an employee but also make child custody negotiations more difficult. By proactively seeking alignment between the values of the company and the values of the individual, a firm should seek to support rather than work against the well-being of the family unit. For example, ServiceMaster considered the family unit in employee relocation decisions. In so doing, the firm not only supported the family unit but in the process also increased worker productivity through this work-family alignment.

To summarize, the response to the question, What is the most significant positive contribution ServiceMaster's Objective 1 made to its practice of management as a liberal art? is to instill the importance of *leader as servant*. Its basis in the Drucker vision is found in Drucker's principles related to *responsibility*, *integrity*, and *values*.

Objective 2: To Help People Develop

The second ServiceMaster objective, "To Help People Develop," clearly reflects Drucker's second category of management practices involving the human dimension (People and their Development). Continuing in Pollard's Judeo-Christian tradition, Objective 2 follows naturally from the first objective; in this view, God is honored when his image in people is developed. In ServiceMaster, this was defined by respecting, developing, and serving people and by embracing diversity in the firm. In the ServiceMaster model, working was viewed as a process whereby the person gets the right things done and in the process becomes all she or he can be.

Many companies espouse values for developing their people, and they use slogans such as "people are our greatest asset." *But where do the passion and the power come from to develop people* and treat them as assets? Author Joseph Maciariello asked Frances Hesselbein, longtime head of the Girl Scouts of America and a student of the works of Peter Drucker, "Where did the power come from to do what you did for the development of young girls?" to which she answered, "From the spirit within."

This is where one's worldview is very important. If we employ Pollard's worldview, and to a large extent Drucker's, that worldview would include a belief in God, and this belief would require ultimate accountability to God. It then would be imperative for an executive to do the following:

1. Provide dignity to those led, as they too are created in God's image and are entitled to have that status recognized and enhanced.
2. Use the resources of the firm as an instrument for human development so far as the profits generated by that firm allow.
3. Recognize the need individuals have for community, to function as full members of an organization, a human society.
4. Adhere to a benchmark for determining *right and wrong* for the purposes of establishing responsible behavior.
5. Submit power and authority in the organization to a moral standard of responsibility.

If one's worldview does not include a belief in God or some divine power, then what motivates one to develop people? As we have seen, there are certainly other bases on which people may decide to develop people. The entire field of philosophy, notably moral philosophy, has provided numerous explanations for human compassion that do not require a Judeo-Christian belief system. We dealt with a few of these in Chapter 3, including the philosophy of Aristotle. In any event, executives need to understand what drives their desire to develop people; they also need to develop objectives that reflect their own beliefs and values.

ServiceMaster was so deeply committed to the development of people and to the application of *people development systems* that Peter Drucker saw the development of people as the essence of ServiceMaster's business. Indeed it was the answer to Drucker's prominent question, "What is your business?" (Drucker, 1994). It is not a simple process to determine why a business exists and what business one is in. Yet, it is very important to do so.

Accordingly, Drucker, during a meeting with the board of directors of ServiceMaster, asked the group to answer the question: "What is your business?"

After listening to this group provide various answers to this question, Drucker responded with this statement:

> Your business is simply the training and development of people. You package it all different ways to meet the needs and demands of the customer, but your basic business is people training and motivation. You are delivering services. You can't deliver services without people. You can't deliver quality service to the customer without motivated and trained people. (Pollard, 1996b, p. 113)

The board agreed, and the first sentence of Drucker's statement was boldly embedded on the wall of the main training facility at company headquarters.[7]

As an outsourcing firm, ServiceMaster is in the unique position of being able to undo the negative impact on people and their development as activities of firms are outsourced. Whenever a firm outsources a major function, the firm loses its ability to develop those people whose activities have been outsourced. If these organizations "lose their capacity to develop people, they will have made a devil's bargain indeed" unless the outsourcing firm concentrates on developing people (Drucker, 2002, p. 71). In a people-development approach, the person is viewed not merely as a factor of production to be "used up" in accomplishing a task but rather an asset to be "enhanced," to be developed in the process of serving the customer; the person will become the *subject* of work and not its *object*.

The recognition that people possess inherent dignity (and "status," in Drucker's language) is at the heart of the purpose of Objective 2—and is an element that is often missing in the practice of management. If one were to ask, therefore, "What is the harm of not bringing Objective 2 to bear on the practice of management as a liberal art?" the answer to this question would be *a loss of dignity accorded to people at work*.

In his discussions of the practice of developing people, Drucker highlighted the need to design large, demanding jobs that would stretch people and provide them with opportunities to grow. This requirement presents a challenge for firms such as ServiceMaster, where most of the jobs done by its employees involve physical, unskilled labor: how does one make the job of a housecleaner large and demanding? Pollard employed the idea of decentralization, tying it to Schumpeter's notion of creative destruction (Chapter 1) and to Drucker's admonition to practice abandonment, continuous improvement, and innovation (Drucker, 1999). As discussed in Chapter 1, Schumpeter's concept of creative destruction involved periods of economic disruption that not only destroyed formerly stable enterprises, but also made room for new business opportunities. As a follower of Schumpeter, Drucker believed that organizations must plan for the inevitable disruptions associated with creative destruction. Not surprisingly, Drucker charged that developing people requires a focus on the future, on opportunities and strengths rather than weaknesses.

Pollard argued that bureaucracy stifles entrepreneurial spirit and innovation. A flatter structure that supports the larger vision *of promoting human growth and development* will enhance innovation and continuous improvement. Importantly, innovation should be led by those closest to the customer: those on the front lines of the organization. By helping to facilitate change, frontline service workers help to ensure the survival and growth of the company, which in turn provides them opportunities for further individual growth and development. More importantly perhaps, empowering service workers like those at ServiceMaster with autonomy to exert control over significant aspects of their own jobs provides them with responsibility and authority leading to enhanced self-esteem. The workers themselves are often in the best position to design and improve the way they perform their jobs because they possess specific job-related knowledge and skill, and to this extent are able to manage themselves in a manner similar to knowledge workers.

In the ServiceMaster model the first two objectives are considered to be "end" objectives whereas Objectives 3 and 4 are "means" objectives. In other words, Pollard sought to give priority to applying God's standards to all activities and to developing the people of the company. This should be not glossed over lightly—the purpose of the firm is seen in terms of Objectives 1 and 2. Objectives 3 and 4 are means to achieving those purposes (honoring God and developing people), not ends in themselves. And, as discussed, Objective 1 is put into action by Objective 2; at ServiceMaster, employees developed the people in the firm as a way of honoring God.

Objective 3: To Pursue Excellence, and Objective 4: To Grow Profitably

Objective 3 mirrors Drucker's third practice of management related to the human dimension (strengths and opportunities), while Objective 4 reflects the fourth practice (performance and results). The pursuit of excellence involves a focus on strengths rather than weaknesses, and it provides employees with opportunities to grow as workers and as people. Growing profitably is one measure of performance and results, although Drucker also emphasized the development of values and people as two equally important measures of results.

As stated earlier, Objectives 3 and 4 were subsidiary objectives to 1 and 2. At ServiceMaster, Objective 1 ("To Honor God in All We Do") provided the spirit and energy for carrying out Objective 2 ("To Help People Develop") with real dedication. Objectives 3 ("To Pursue Excellence") and 4 ("To Grow Profitably") were means for accomplishing Objectives 1 and 2. Collectively, the *ends* and *means* objectives form a "system of objectives." And the objectives can function together as a dynamic system.

Here is how the system of objectives is supposed to function: Practicing Objective 3 faithfully results in service to customers, by providing tools and training required by employees to give excellent service. By providing value to customers, and with good management, the company is able to produce a profit (Objective 4). Profit then provides the resources required to develop people (Objective 2), by providing jobs and superior tools, and by creating opportunities for expanded responsibility for people. That in turn meets Objective 1: it honors God.

Pollard provides a persuasive example of the interaction between Objectives 2 and 3 through people, tools, and work and the dignity of the service worker:

During a trip to Leningrad in 1989, I met a custodian named Olga. She had the job of mopping a lobby floor in a large hotel. I took an interest in her task and engaged her in conversation. Olga had been given a T frame for a mop, a dirty rag, and a dirty bucket of water to do her job. She wasn't really cleaning the floor; she was just moving dirt from one section to another. . . . Olga was not proud of what she was doing. She had no dignity in her work. She was a long way from owning the result. But Olga had great untapped potential. . . . No one had taken the time to teach or equip Olga or to care about her as a person.

By contrast, I had the experience just a few days later while visiting a hospital that ServiceMaster serves in London, England. As I was introduced to one of the housekeepers as the Chairman of ServiceMaster, she put her arms around me and gave me a big hug. She thanked me for the training and tools she had received to do her job. She then showed me all that she had accomplished in cleaning patient rooms, providing a detailed "before and after" ServiceMaster description. She was proud of her work. She had bought into the result because someone had cared enough to show her the way and recognize her efforts when the task was done. She was looking forward to the next accomplishment. *She was thankful.* (Pollard, 1996b, pp. 246–247)

It appears that neither of these workers had the agency or inclination to independently seek out more dignified treatment on the job. In both cases, the workers required managerial assistance to show the way.

Human development at work may involve providing the worker with tools to do the job effectively. In the case of service workers, this may or may not involve the input of the workers themselves. Managers have to recognize the need and step in.

These examples of the integration of *people, tools* and *work* at ServiceMaster are examples of the dual processes of making work productive and the worker achieving. And they are examples of the steps necessary to fulfill Objective 3. Drucker describes this dual process as follows:

> The first step toward making the worker achieving is to make the work productive. The more we understand what the work itself demands, the more can we integrate the work into the human activity we call working. The more we understand work itself, the more freedom we can give the worker. There is no contradiction between scientific management, that is, the rational and impersonal approach to work, and the achieving worker. The two complement each other, though they are quite different. (Drucker, 1974, p. 199)

By making work productive and the worker achieving, we observe just how the ServiceMaster System of Management leads both to enhancing productivity (Objective 3) and advancing the dignity of the service worker (Objective 2). These are two of the most significant issues faced by executives in a developed economy, as Drucker notes:

> If there is a more important problem for the developed countries than the productivity of the service work, it is the dignity of the service worker. And the two are closely interwoven. Indeed, they can only be solved together. . . . ServiceMaster provides a purpose and ultimate objective for the worker and his or her work, and thus contributes to the essential ingredient of dignity that has been lacking in the past. (Drucker, 1989, p. 26)

Pursuit of the "means" objectives leads to the fulfillment of the "end" objectives. Practicing excellence in all activities leads to growth in profit. Profit provides the resources and opportunities for develop-ing people and honoring God. Viewed as a means, profit becomes an excellent measure of performance, *a moral measure*, and of contribu-tion toward *meeting the wants of society*. Just as Drucker interpreted profit as a moral force, as derived from the work of Schumpeter (see Chapter 1), Pollard linked profit to God:

> Profit is a means in God's world to be used and invested, not an end to be worshiped. Profit is a legitimate measurement of the value of our effort. . . . It is a requirement for survival of the individual, the family unit, and any organization of society, whether it be a for-profit company or a not-for-profit organization. . . . God and business do mix, and profit is a standard for determining the effectiveness of our combined efforts. (Pollard, 1996b, p. 20)

Linking profit to both individual and societal values, Pollard explicitly described free-market capitalism as a potential instrument of God, a force for good. Cast in this light, profit not only ensures the continuation of the organization but also provides the means for developing human potential. ServiceMaster's profitability was thus effectively linked to its first three objectives; profitability honors God because it provides the resources required for developing people, as well as the resources required for the pursuit of excellence. And as we have seen, ServiceMaster was very profitable during almost all of Pollard's tenure at the company.

But, while profit is a good measure of how well a company is converting resources into the wants of customers, the four objectives of the ServiceMaster Management System will not automatically lead to high levels of profit. In fact, the reverse may often be true. Warren Buffett, the distinguished investor, makes this latter point in a compelling way: "I have seen a lot of not-very-good human beings succeed in business" (Gunther, 2001, p. 64).

A recent example that Mr. Buffett could cite as evidence that profitability does *not* always honor God, human dignity, or moral values is the shoddy recent behavior of Goldman Sachs Group described in the introduction to this book. One of Goldman's employees, with the help of a hedge fund, developed a derivative, mortgage-investment product that Goldman sold to a client while Goldman itself engaged in a short-sale transaction of the very same product—in other words, Goldman made a very profitable bet against its client-customer.[8]

ServiceMaster was a highly unusual organization that took Drucker's Judeo-Christian view of human dignity to heart in its corporate objectives. Clearly, the ServiceMaster model will not work in every organization, nor can it be exactly duplicated, given the fact that all organizations have their own cultures and histories. However, some institutions may be able to link Drucker's four practices related to the human dimension with some variant of ServiceMaster's objectives through the use of the "service profit chain" concept.

IMPLEMENTING THE FOUR DRUCKER PRACTICES THROUGH THE FOUR SERVICEMASTER OBJECTIVES

Three researchers from the Harvard Business School set out to answer the question, *Why are a select few service organizations better year in and year out at what they do than their competitors?* They answered the question by interviewing a number of service managers at high-performing service organizations, including managers at ServiceMaster. The answers they found are contained in a set of relationships they call "the service profit chain":

> Simply stated, service profit chain thinking maintains that there are direct and strong relationships between profit; growth; customer loyalty; customer satisfaction; the value of goods and services delivered to customers; and employee capability, satisfaction, loyalty and productivity. . . . The

strongest relationships suggested by the data collected in early tests of the service profit chain were those between: (1) profit and customer loyalty, (2) employee loyalty and customer loyalty, and (3) employee satisfaction and customer satisfaction. They suggested that in service settings, the relationships were self-enforcing. That is, satisfied customers contributed to employee satisfaction, and vice versa. (Heskett, Sasser, and Schlesinger, 1997, pp. 11–12)

Imbedded within the service profit chain in high-performing service organizations is a reinforcing "Cycle of [employee] Capability" (Heskett, Sasser, and Schlesinger, 1997, Figure 7-3, p. 128). The reinforcing cycle of capability links "careful employee selection"; the supply of high-quality training, tools, and infrastructure for employees; and appropriate rewards for good performance to both employee satisfaction and customer satisfaction.

The service profit chain thus links the selection and development of people (Drucker Practice 2 and ServiceMaster Objective 2), to developing the capability of people to serve customers (Drucker Practice 3 and ServiceMaster Objective 3), to profit (Drucker Practice 4 and ServiceMaster Objective 4). The power to develop people comes from the values and integrity of leaders (Drucker Practice 1 and ServiceMaster Objective 1).

James L. Heskett, W. Earl Sasser, and Leonard A. Schlesinger use ServiceMaster as one of their examples of a functioning service profit chain. They note the role of servant leadership in ServiceMaster, as well as other organizations, in imparting the kinds of values and leadership practices derived from ServiceMaster's Objective 1:

Sam Walton proclaimed to anyone who would listen at Wal-Mart the importance of the manager as "servant leader." Not only did managers listen, but they led Wal-Mart's ascension to the top of the retailing world. The concept fits well with the thinking of ServiceMaster's management, where the most important characteristic that former-CEO Bill Pollard sought in his successor was a "servant's heart." At Southwest Airlines, management seeks to achieve what Herb Keller calls a "patina of spirituality" not only in selecting new employees into its "family," but in reaching equally fundamental decisions about which cities to serve. (Heskett, Sasser, and Schlesinger, 1997, p. 248)

To summarize, the four Drucker practices and the four Service-Master objectives create overlapping and dynamic practices and objectives that have the potential for developing human capacity and character for the common good. They will work differently from organization to organization. Pollard clearly derived his objectives from Drucker's management practices. The work of Heskett, Sasser, and Schlesinger further illustrates the ways in which Drucker's practices, and ServiceMaster's objectives, can work together to create a highly effective organization.

The four objectives may be applied to any organization. But the most frequently asked question posed by those who are interested in understanding the ServiceMaster Management System is, "Why can't the same leadership principles and the same results be achieved without objective number 1?" *The answer is that they can under certain special circumstances.* Without a culture that explicitly supports Objective 1, executives must supply integrity and moral values to do so, and these values must penetrate the organization. With that in mind, here are 10 principles of leadership that supported the implementation of the four ServiceMaster objectives.[9] The implementation of these leadership principles in any organization should lead to a management system similar to the one that existed at ServiceMaster.

Principle Number 1. We respect the dignity and worth of the whole person. The results of our leadership will be measured beyond the workplace in the changed lives of people.

Implementation of this principle goes to the heart of the ServiceMaster Management System; it recognizes the dignity and worth of every human being. Its implementation by any organization will go a long way toward fulfilling the spirit of Objectives 1 and 2.

Principle Number 2. We are values driven. We value truth, integrity, loyalty and doing the right thing. We believe our company is and should be a moral community for developing human character. As we lead, we are responsible stewards of the environment. We also value lifelong learning and our role as teachers.

This principle assumes that there is a right way and wrong way to carry out activities of an organization. It assumes that leaders of an organization should assume responsibility for developing the capacity and character of their people. Finally, it assumes that leaders have a responsibility to act as stewards of the environment and, accordingly, to remedy any damage done to the environment by activities of the enterprise.

Principle Number 3. "If you don't live it, you don't believe it" (Wade, 1966, p. 7). (In this Principle Wade is referring to the values of the organization.)

Many organizations have exemplary codes of ethical conduct.[10] These codes include integrity in dealing with various stakeholders, an open environment, an emphasis on quality and service, and treating employees as resources to be developed. The nagging question, however, is, *are these exemplary values really carried out in practice or are they merely window-dressing?* Marion Wade, the founder of ServiceMaster, put the matter very bluntly in this principle by asking: Do executives of the firm actively seek to convert espoused values of the firm into action? If they do not, then they do not really believe the values they espouse.

Principle Number 4. We are owners, and we lead accordingly. We believe in innovation, risk taking, and balancing short-term and long-term decision making. We strive for an effective and efficient organization. We invest in our company and encourage others to do the same.

The leaders of a public firm should take significant ownership in that firm. A remarkable aspect of executive leadership at ServiceMaster during Pollard's tenure is not only did executives invest significant amounts of money in the shares of ServiceMaster, but they tended not to diversify their investments (Pollard, 1996b, p. 145). This put most of their own wealth at risk and demonstrated major commitment to the company and its performance. In doing so, executives acted very much like owners, providing confidence to other investors; executives of the firm were acting to promote the interests of shareholders (Objective 4).

Principle Number 5. We believe in what we sell and strive to deliver extraordinary service. We are proud of the services and/or products we sell and deliver to our customers. We believe in using our own products and services and recommending them to others. We go beyond the ordinary service expectation and provide what is known as "extra" ordinary service. We want to provide service beyond customers' expectations and strive for continuous improvement.

A clear linkage has been established by Heskett, Sasser, and Schlesinger (1997) between providing excellent customer service (Objective 3) and profitability (Objective 4).[11] The very name of ServiceMaster emphasizes "masters of service," and therefore Objective 3. This principle is good advice for every organization.

Principle Number 6. Our future and our profits depend upon creating and keeping customers. Growth is a mandate, not an option.

There is a linkage between the need for growth in profitability (Objective 4) and the ability to develop people (Objective 2). People need expanded opportunities if they are to grow in their capacities and character. And the possibility of expanding roles comes from growing an enterprise and acquiring compatible ones. Growth is not an option for achieving Objective 2. To grow, an organization must keep existing customers and attract new ones. As a part of its growth strategy, an organization should know the incremental cost of retaining a customer versus the cost of acquiring a new one, which is part of the effort involved in pursuing Objective 3. We see the connection of three objectives in this single principle.

Principle Number 7. We reward and promote based on performance and potential. Compensation and promotion are based upon performance and one's ability to grow, develop, and do new things in the future. Personal beliefs, length of service, gender, or race should have nothing to do with compensation and promotion.

Drucker was adamant that rewards and promotions be tied to performance, not to personal politics or preferences. Adding language regarding the ability to grow and develop incorporates ServiceMaster's devotion to human dignity and development. Yet, this principle explicitly notes that one's gender, religion, or ethnicity will not impact the potential for rewards.

Principle Number 8. We plan for succession and develop our future leaders.

Developing future leaders is at the heart of Objectives 1 and 2. It is vital for retaining the values and vitality of an organization, and for achieving success. Both formal and informal systems for management development and succession planning are required. Also required is that people be offered opportunities to test themselves to see if they are ready for increased levels of responsibility.

Principle Number 9. We have a spirit of independence, and we realize we need each other.

As an organization grows, it is increasingly difficult to retain its values; discord and divisiveness tend to develop among various groups. That is especially true if an organization's growth is by acquisitions. Unity can be achieved through diversity if executives pay particular attention to the need to retain continuity of values while changing. Doing so takes constant communications, not only within an organization but with customers and suppliers. The ability to retain individuality and a sense of purpose while growing is essential to the achievement of Objectives 2 and 3.

Principle Number 10. Truth cannot be compromised.

Drucker, early in his career, argued for the need to establish standards of truth and conduct so that responsibility can be achieved. ("Honoring truth" has been used as a substitute for Objective 1; see Maciariello, 2002, p. 58.) It is our belief that Drucker never changed his mind on the need to constantly seek and apply truth. As he himself stated:

> The only basis of freedom is the Christian concept of man's nature: imperfect, weak, a sinner, and dust destined to dust; yet made in God's image and responsible for his action. . . . Also, in order to have freedom, it must be assumed that there is absolute truth and absolute reason—though forever beyond man's grasp. Otherwise there could be no responsibility. (Drucker, 1942b, p. 483)

Drucker clearly states that "absolute truth and absolute reason" are "forever beyond man's grasp." As fallen, weak creatures, we are, in his worldview, incapable of discerning the truth, or what is right and wrong in absolute terms. Instead, Drucker would have us wrestle with Principle 10 and come to our own conclusions that may differ from Objective 1, but would provide a moral standard of conduct in our organizations. In Drucker's "bearable" society, humans can never achieve perfect understanding of truth, or clear knowledge of ultimate "right" and "wrong." Recognizing their Kierkegaardian separation from God, they must muddle through in their attempts to personally discern, on an existential level, what is real, what is true.

Under its current leadership, ServiceMaster no longer reflects Pollard's vision. Indeed, a value system that raises the question of God in its objectives cannot easily be implemented within the United States in *public companies*. Yet, there are examples of public organizations in the United States in which value systems that are somewhat compatible with those found in the ServiceMaster Management System have operated successfully and profitably. Lincoln Electric managed to do so for a century (Maciariello, 2000). Nevertheless, the current paucity of public organizations that have managed to combine meaningful individual and social existence through some sort of faith, legitimate authority, ethical and well-structured management, and adaptability indicates that perhaps Drucker's vision is more difficult to implement than he imagined, at least in public organizations.

The Drucker vision is much more likely to be found in private companies, which are often extensions of the beliefs of their founders. Therefore, it is useful to look at an example of how one private company seeks to implement objectives similar to ServiceMaster's. This company, Dacor, illustrates a company whose management systems are moving in the same direction, although the company is much smaller than ServiceMaster and as a result their management systems are simpler.

DACOR

A number of executives have been inspired to emulate the Service-Master example, especially its Objective 1.[12] We cite just one, Dacor, a high-end kitchen appliance manufacturer in Diamond Bar, California, which in 2004 had sales approaching $200 million. Dacor developed its *Statement of Corporate Values* in 1999. The statement, as it appears below, is engraved in a highly visible position on a marble wall at company headquarters in Diamond Bar (Dacor, n.d.).

TO HONOR GOD IN ALL WE DO:
By respecting others
By doing good work
By helping others
By forgiving others
By giving thanks
By celebrating our lives

It is one thing to come up with the words in a value statement and quite another to put them into action. Here is a very brief sketch of how the value system was put into action by Dacor.[13] First, the company identified the values. The values were defined and elaborated by Michael Joseph, CEO of Dacor.

The principal value—"To Honor God in All We Do"—was borrowed directly from ServiceMaster. The subordinate values came from phrases that Joseph was drawn to from time to time and from various sources, including homilies of his parish priest.

After defining and elaborating these values, Joseph sought to obtain comments and buy-in from owners and members of the executive team and from middle managers, associates, dealers, customers, and other key stakeholders. (Dacor had 1,200 dealers at the time.) Then, Dacor articulated the values widely by including them in virtually every communication vehicle of the company. Also, an eight-hour training session was conducted with members of the executive team in March 2002. This session explained the values and implementation steps to make the values work. Dacor aligned the values at three different levels of practice: individuals, teams, and organization. Finally, the company adopted a process of continuously improving upon its adherence to the values.

The company is building an "egalitarian organization"—their words—in which dignity and respect for all is being sought both within the organization and with external stakeholders, such as customers, dealers, and members of the community. Profits are a very important by-product of Dacor's business, but they are not the essence of the business. The essence of the business is to improve the quality of life of Dacor's "CEOs"—an acronym for *c*ustomers, *e*mployees, and *o*wners and other stakeholders.

Behavior must reflect values, if the values are to be effective. In a company managed by values, Dacor believes, there is only one boss: the company values. The company attempts to make its people feel good about themselves and their abilities. Self-esteem is the issue. The company believes that if its people are to do their best they must feel good about themselves and their potential to contribute to the organization.

In an effort to test the effectiveness of implementation of the values within the company, Dacor participated in a study conducted by a team of researchers from the Max De Pree Center for Leadership in Pasadena, California. The research team conducted extensive formal and informal interviews as well as focus group studies to determine how closely Dacor was approaching successful implementation of its values with all stakeholders. As a part of this assessment, a training program was conducted throughout the organization to clarify the value system. The results of the study were published in 2004 by the Max De Pree Center for Leadership in the monograph *To Honor God* (Max De Pree Center for Leadership, 2005). While the empirical study is complex and hard to summarize concisely, the researchers concluded that the stakeholders of the company were getting closer to living their ideals. And the company is trying hard to improve how they live their values. One way to test the effectiveness of the values is to go out and ask stakeholders, as did the research team at Dacor.

Joseph's values, like Pollard's, represent his faith and "they're not out to convert anyone" (Max De Pree Center for Leadership, 2004, p. 69). Yet, it is informative to note that Joseph reported that "the company has nearly doubled in size since the inception of the Dacor Value Statement five years ago [in 1999]." Therefore, while these values represent Joseph's faith, they have been compatible with successful growth to the benefit of the company's "CEOs."

To summarize, the example of Dacor demonstrates that the objectives and philosophy of management developed at ServiceMaster can be transferred with benefit to another company. That is part of the legacy of ServiceMaster and its founder and leaders.

CONCLUSION

Drucker insisted that we consider the human dimension in management as a liberal art. This is the point where management and the liberal arts most clearly intersect. The liberal arts, historically, have involved matters of the human condition (hence the term "the humanities" in describing many of the academic disciplines covered under the liberal arts). Management, too, involves dealing with the messy business of human emotions, ethics, morality, and other subjective matters. Drucker approached this reality by focusing on the subject of human dignity. In doing so, he invoked earlier debates about the nature of human rights, and he injected his own Judeo-Christian perspective.

In order to understand Drucker's concept of management as a liberal art, we need to comprehend what qualities he ascribed to human beings as natural rights, or inherent to all people. His view of human dignity is most apparent in his discussions of those engaged in manual labor (service work or assembly-line manufacturing jobs). These workers, who may not have control over their day-to-day activities, or who may or may not care to be actively involved in their work communities, deserve the same level of respect as those who manage them, in the Drucker system. According to Drucker's definition of human dignity, which is driven by Judeo-Christian beliefs, all workers are valued regardless of status, education level, or intelligence.

Drucker defined dignity in terms of treatment by management, and accordingly dictated four management practices that would allow all workers to be treated properly. These practices required managers to define and embrace integrity and values, develop people, focus on strengths and opportunities, and emphasize performance and results. When implemented effectively (as in the case of ServiceMaster), these four practices allow all workers, including service workers, to be the subject, not the object, of work.

Implementing Drucker's vision of human dignity, of treating every human being as a product of divine creation, does presents its challenges. For example, how does a given organization define its values? In the cases of ServiceMaster and Dacor, the founders chose to advance their own personal religious views. Not every organization can, or would choose, to define its values this way. Those involved in government organizations are subject to separation of church and state. Other entities composed of many different cultures and religious traditions must be sensitive to the conflicting values that those cultures and traditions bring to the table. Imposing one value system will not work unless management works to seek consensus among employees and other constituencies. The 10 principles described in detail in Maciariello (2002) serve as a bridge between the Judeo-Christian focus of the ServiceMaster model and those organizations for which such a model will not work.

Implementation of the human dimension of management as a liberal art will differ from organization to organization. Nevertheless, institutions must recognize that management as a liberal art focuses on the human being, and as such, involves various aspects of humanity. Just as early British and Americans worked through their own definitions of natural rights, organizations practicing management as a liberal art will need to come to an understanding of what constitutes human dignity. They will then need to develop their own models for addressing the human dimension.

CHAPTER 6

❖

EFFECTIVE LEADERSHIP
AS A LIBERAL ART

It is typical of the most successful and the most durable institutions
that they induce in their members an intellectual and moral growth
beyond a . . . [person's] original capacities.

—*Peter F. Drucker,* Concept of the Corporation *(1946/1983, p. 28)*

Leadership is a concept that originated with the earliest civilizations. Its study, however, is linked to the rise of organizations during industrialization. The literature on the subject is vast; in recent years, there has been a virtual explosion of books and articles on leadership, as well as entire journals dedicated to the exploration of leadership qualities, styles, and models. There is practically an industry devoted to the publication of work on leadership.

In this chapter, we will briefly trace the history of leadership theory's development, followed by a discussion of Drucker's model of leadership. Once we have described the primary elements of effective leadership according to Drucker, we use Abraham Lincoln as a case study of leadership. By using historical analysis, we link management and the liberal arts, illustrating how leadership decisions made by figures in the past might allow one to assess how to implement Drucker's model of effective leadership. As will become evident, it is not always easy to be an effective leader. Historical examples can illuminate the difficulties leaders face in complex, real-world situations, even if they involve decisions that are very different from those leaders might face today.

LEADERSHIP: VARIOUS INTERPRETATIONS

Leadership has been the subject of study for centuries. Aristotle and Plato wrote on effective governance, Niccolò Machiavelli analyzed the nature of authority and power in his 1513 work *The Prince*, and Enlightenment authors such as Thomas Hobbes and John Locke explored the relationship between leaders and those who follow them. The rise of the large industrial organization, however, led to a more systematic study of leadership as part of management. As management theorists turned their attention to analyzing those at the top of new organizations, they developed a wide range of leadership models that often conflicted with one another. Initially, management theorists concerned themselves with administrative questions: how could organizations produce enough in an efficient cost-effective way? Increasingly, however, practitioners and theorists began to shift their interest from the productivity of nonhuman capital to the productivity of human capital. As a consequence, the study of management naturally turned to the study of leaders and leadership, as people strived to identify ways in which to best use the human resources available to them.

As discussed in Chapter 2, management as a profession emerged in the late nineteenth century with the creation of the first business schools. The curricula of these early programs emphasized the work of Frederick Taylor and scientific management, reflecting the new American world of mass production that materialized at the turn of the century. During the 1920s, however, Harvard Business School began to focus more on the role of human relations in organizations than on the traditional curriculum of training in finance, accounting, and other such skills. After developing a practice in clinical psychology, Elton Mayo was hired by the graduate school to lead this area of research. Mayo is most well known for his work on the Hawthorne experiments. The Hawthorne plant was Western Electric Company's largest manufacturing facility. Located in Chicago, the site made telephones and telephone equipment. From 1924 to 1927, the company conducted a series of studies to examine the relationship between factory lighting and worker productivity. Inspired by Taylor's scientific management, Western Electric management wanted to see if modifications in lighting within the workplace would increase output. One group of workers received changes in lighting, while a control group experienced the same lighting. The results of the studies were inconclusive; both groups of workers increased their productivity. Western Electric hired an outside consultant and set up its own test, taking into account all factors they believed relevant to worker productivity, including psychological and social elements. Western Electric later invited Mayo to observe the experiments. In 1928, Mayo, along with coworker Fritz Roethlisberger (Mayo, 1946/2003; Roethlisberger and Dickson, 1939), began to interpret the results of the latest round of Hawthorne studies.

Mayo and Roethlisberger's now-famous interpretation of the Hawthorne experiments revealed that simple attention to working conditions could have an impact on productivity. In a sense, this was Taylor's larger concept finally recognized: a partnership between labor and management, with the understanding that both sides benefited. Mayo and Roethlisberger, however, emphasized that monetary compensation had nothing to do with the increased productivity at Hawthorne. It was managers' interest and concern with the workers as human beings that created the increases in production. As a result of these interpretations, the human relations school, as it came to be known, advocated management's use of psychological techniques to influence the attitudes, and thus the behavior, of workers.

Drucker recognized the importance of Mayo's conclusions to his own vision of the industrial community. In *The New Society*, Drucker stated that Mayo and Roethlisberger "showed that in every industrial enterprise there is an 'informal' social organization of the workers as well as of supervisory and managerial personnel. They found that it is this informal organization rather than management which actually determines rates of output, standards, job classification and job content. Without employing formal sanctions other than the disapproval of the group, this organization effectively directs the members' behavior" (Drucker, 1950/1993, p. 174). The human relations work of Mayo forced managers to see employees as human beings, to acknowledge the reality of human resources.

One of the first people to systematically document the function of leadership was Chester Barnard. Although Barnard did not recognize the full extent of the human dimension of management, he foreshadowed Drucker's concern with providing dignity and meaning in the workplace. Barnard's 1938 *The Functions of the Executive* was a synthesis of his own experience as a manager with earlier writings on management. The book was his attempt to formulate a theory of cooperative behavior and explain why people work in organizations and how they can do so more effectively. Of paramount importance to Barnard's analysis is loyalty to the organization; organizations rely on cooperation to function. Barnard postulated that people have varying degrees of willingness to cooperate and that management must be able to maintain an individual's willingness to cooperate. Instead of arguing for a top-down dictatorial or charismatic model of leadership, he proposed a bottom-up model that required those working in lower levels of an organization to willingly submit to authority or to recognize the legitimacy of managerial authority.

Barnard described what he termed a person's "zone of indifference," a comfort zone in which an individual would unquestioningly respond to managerial demands:

> How is it possible to secure such important and enduring cooperation as we observe if in principle and in fact the determination of authority lies with the subordinate individual? It is possible because . . . there exists a "zone of indifference" in each individual within which orders are acceptable without conscious questioning of their authority . . . [and] the interests of the persons who contribute to an organization as a group result in the exercise of an influence on the subject, or on the attitude of the individual, that maintains a certain stability of this zone of indifference. (Barnard, 1938/1968, p. 167)

This rather clinical description of individual loyalty illustrates Barnard's understanding of the realities of human interactions within the workplace: dictatorial mandates from above will not foster employee loyalty; instead, managers need to understand each individual's zone of indifference and recognize that some decisions will require justification and explanation in order to be legitimized. Barnard explains that one of the worst mistakes leaders can make is poor communication; authority must be earned through trust and clarity of direction. He warns that "the determination of authority remains with the individual. Let these 'positions' of authority in fact show ineptness, ignorance of conditions, failure to communicate what ought to be said, or let leadership fail (chiefly by its concrete action) to recognize implicitly its dependence upon the essential character of the relationship of the individual to the organization, and the authority if tested disappears" (Barnard, 1938/1968, p. 174). Barnard clearly understood the importance of management showing its legitimacy through words and deeds; titles alone would not suffice to guarantee cooperation and loyalty.

The horrors of World War II and the rise of totalitarian govern-ments added a new dimension to leadership theory in the 1950s and 1960s. Abraham Maslow, the son of Jewish immigrants, sought to understand why people rallied around leaders such as Hitler and Stalin; his later work focused on human behavior within industrial organizations. Drucker referred to Maslow as "the father of human-ist psychology" (Drucker, 1974, p. 195).

Maslow is best known for his hierarchy of needs, which is based on a pyramid of human aspirations. At the top of the pyramid is human self-actualization, which Maslow defined as "the full use and exploitation of talents, capacities, [and] potentials" (Maslow, 1954, p. 150). He posited that people cannot achieve self-actualization until other needs below this level have been met, including physi-ological, safety, and social needs. Because these lower-level needs have been met, self-actualized people are well-adjusted, according to Maslow. They have a calling or vocation to which they are dedicated, are emotionally stable, accept themselves and others, and exhibit a high degree of creativity and independence.

Maslow later applied self-actualization to his analysis of indus-trial organizations through his observations of Non-Linear Systems and his readings of Drucker's *The Practice of Management* [quoted by Maslow as *"Principles of Management,"* Maslow, 1998, p. xxi], McGregor's *The Human Side of Enterprise* (1960), and texts in the field of social psychology. He wrote his observations in journal form, developing the concept of "Eupsychia," which he defined as "the culture that would be generated by 1,000 self-actualizing people on some sheltered island where they would not be interfered with" (Maslow, 1998, p. xxii). In essence, Maslow sought to identify the attributes of an ideal society to point the way for improvement and change in the modern industrial world. If a society of organizations were populated solely by self-actualizers, what would that society look like? This ideal would then serve as a blueprint for the actual management of society's organizations. In Maslow's words, "How good a society does human nature permit? How good a human nature does society permit? How good a society does the nature of society permit?" (Maslow, 1998, p. xxii).

Maslow described the qualities of "enlightened management" and the assumptions that underlay these qualities. As he did so, he took Drucker and others to task on many points. In particular, Maslow criticized the assumption that people in an organization would not be driven (or paralyzed) by fear: "On the whole, where fear reigns, enlightened management is not possible. In this and in may [sic] other places, Drucker reveals his lack of awareness or knowledge of psychopathology, of evil, weakness, bad impulses, etc. There are many people in the world, especially outside of the United States, for whom Drucker's management principles will simply not work at all" (Maslow, 1998, p. 26).

Drucker, Maslow argued, was not only too general in his assumption (that all people will be motivated by the same things) but also too naïve in his view that people will not exhibit bad behavior in organizations. Maslow showed that not all leaders would be "enlightened," and that not all followers would be driven by the same motivations.

Another important contribution to leadership theory came from Douglas McGregor's 1960 work *The Human Side of Enterprise.* McGregor claimed that there were two primary styles of management, "Theory X" and "Theory Y," and argued that Theory Y was the preferred style. Theory X managers assumed that people dislike work and would avoid it as much as possible; this management style embraces command and control from above. The problem with Theory X leadership is that it does not motivate people whose lower-level hierarchical needs have been met. Direction and control from above will be entirely ineffective if social interactions and the need for self-esteem motivate employees. As a result, employees will begin to dislike their work, learn to expect constant direction and supervision, and avoid taking any risks that might anger those at the top. In short, Theory X leadership is a self-fulfilling prophecy.

In contrast, Theory Y managers assume that work is natural and that people want to be productive; this style emphasizes fostering independence and creative abilities. Looking for self-esteem and social fulfillment, employees will actually seek out responsibility, and they genuinely will be interested in exercising their mental abilities. Expectations breed actions (as happens in Theory X situations), and employees respond favorably—as Theory Y leaders would expect.

McGregor's work received wide acclaim and was adapted to many organizations. The Scanlon Plan, for example, was an effort to apply Theory Y management to an entire organization. Companies adopting this plan implemented cost-reduction sharing plans and established formal means for employees to contribute ideas. William Ouchi's "Theory Z" (1982) was intended to be a combination of Theory Y and Theory X management styles. Kurt Lewin (1947, pp. 5–41), who worked with McGregor at MIT, popularized the theories of group dynamics embodied in "T-Groups," or training groups, which emphasize the diffusion of decision making throughout an organization.

In 1978, John MacGregor Burns published his groundbreaking work *Leadership*. In his book, Burns contrasted two styles of leadership: transactional and transformational. Transactional leadership emphasizes a relationship involving a mutually beneficial exchange between two people. Using this model, leaders and followers engage in discrete transactions that emphasize self-interest. Transformational leadership, on the other hand, appeals to people's higher ideals and values, which serve as motivators rather than self-interest. In Burns's words, "leaders engage with followers on the basis of shared motives and values and goals" (Burns, 1978, p. 36). In two connected passages in his book, Burns captures the essence of what leadership *is not* and what leadership *is*:

Many acts heralded or bemoaned as instances of leadership—acts of oratory, manipulation, sheer self advancement, brute coercion—are not such. Much of what commonly passes as leadership—conspicuous position-taking without followers or follow through, posturing on various public stages, manipulation without general purpose, authoritarianism—is no more leadership than the behavior of small boys marching in front of a parade, who continue to strut along Main Street after the procession has turned down a side street toward the fairgrounds. . . . The test of their leadership function is their contribution to change, measured by purpose drawn from collective motives and values. (Burns, 1978, p. 427)

Bernard Bass further developed Burns's concept of transformational leadership, describing the ways in which transformational leaders function. One of the important contributions of Bass was the role of charisma in transformational leaders; to Bass, charisma was an important component of transformational leadership, and not always a positive one. Bass argued that transformational leaders were not always aligned with a higher moral force (Bass and Riggio, 2006, pp. 1–18).

One of the issues that has loomed over the study of leadership has been whether leaders are characterized by some specific set of traits or whether leadership is a more complex process. Burns's and Bass's work on transformational leadership moved the discussion toward an analysis of process rather than simply a list of character traits, but certain personality attributes, such as charisma, remained pivotal. Warren Bennis and Burt Nanus studied 90 leaders they identified as transformational, and they developed a list of traits they had in common (Bennis and Nanus, 1985). Although the expanded list of leadership attributes contributed to the work on the subject, the primary innovation of Bennis and Nanus's work was the idea that leadership could be learned; the traits they identified were not innate qualities but rather obtainable through practice (much like Aristotle's concept of acquiring an ethical view of life).

More recently, the concept of servant leadership has gained ground. Although developed in the literature extensively in recent years, the idea came from the work of Robert Greenleaf, who published *The Servant as Leader* in 1970. Greenleaf's thesis is that effective leaders serve others, particularly those who follow them. Servant leadership is other focused, and it usually involves providing subordinates with a considerable degree of freedom based on trust and respect.

Jim Collins's 2001 book *Good to Great* advanced the idea of "Level 5 leadership." Collins evaluated the managements of 11 companies whose public stock had underperformed or tracked the market and then had consistently and significantly outperformed stock indexes for 15 consecutive years. In doing so, he postulated that leaders of these companies tended to focus first on selecting the best team of people; then decisions are made about the mission or direction of the firm. In Collins's lingo, Level 5 leaders focus on "who, then what" as opposed to Level 4 leaders, who focus on "what, then who." Level 5 leaders are less concerned with their own personal qualities than with surrounding themselves with the most capable people they can; thus, according to Collins, these leaders possess the quality of humility as well as attention to organizational mission.

PETER DRUCKER'S MODEL OF EFFECTIVE LEADERSHIP

Drucker's idea of leadership synthesizes many of these interpretations. For Drucker, the test of effective leadership is not getting one's way; it is not the frequency of media appearances, nor is it the amassing of wealth. Effective leadership does not involve coercing people, silencing individuals with fear, or utilizing humiliating tactics to carry out orders. Rather, effective leadership is assuming *responsibility* for *getting the right things done* ("Leadership Means to Get the

Right Things Done," 2002, p. ii).[1] It is about communicating with people, uniting them behind a shared mission and values, and mobilizing energies toward accomplishing the mission or purpose of an organization. It is not about "me" or "I" but rather "us" and "we." An effective leader leads followers with dignity, and inspires them toward achievement. Drucker says that "leadership is not magnetic personality—that can just as well be a glib tongue. It is not 'making friends and influencing people'—that is flattery.... Leadership is lifting a person's vision to higher sights, the raising of a person's performance to a higher standard, the building of a personality beyond its normal limitations" (Drucker, 2008, p. 288).

As iterated in the discussion of transformational leadership, Drucker's interpretation is that leadership responsibilities require that a leader seek congruency between his or her values and goals and the values and goals of followers—everyone must be "on the same page," or nearly so. Achieving congruency is the essence of leadership and followership. President Dwight D. Eisenhower emphasized this very point in his remark that "leadership is the art of getting someone else to do something you want done because he wants to do it" ("Great Leadership Quotes," n.d.).

Unlike Bennis and Nanus, Drucker believed that effective leadership is not about specific leadership qualities, despite this teaching found in numerous books, articles, and journals. He noted that some of the most effective leaders have little commonality of highly acclaimed leadership qualities or of a particular "leadership personality." Abraham Lincoln, Winston Churchill, Dwight D. Eisenhower, Franklin Roosevelt, George Marshall, Alfred Sloan, and the Reverend Theodore Hesburgh were all very effective leaders of public, private, and social sector organizations. They shared few distinctive personality characteristics.

As Bass notes, charisma remains a valued quality in leaders, in spite of the fact that not all charismatic leaders have been effective. Drucker, too, commented on the popularity of charismatic leaders: "Every CEO, it seems, has to be made to look like a dashing Confederate cavalry general or a boardroom Elvis Presley" (Drucker, 2008, p. 288).

Charismatic leaders easily attract followers because of their charm and presence. But charm, a magnetic and flattering personality, a glib tongue, and popularity among influential friends in high places are personality characteristics of many charismatic leaders. As Bass and Drucker have both argued, these personality characteristics have nothing to do with effectiveness.

A vice president of human relations once asked Drucker "to run a seminar for us on how one acquires charisma" (Drucker, 2008, p. 288). The question posed by the vice president implied that leadership requires the pursuit and successful acquisition of popularity among followers. It is a major error to substitute charisma for effectiveness.

Charisma may be "the undoing of leaders" (Drucker, 2008, p. 289), as it was in the case of Civil War general George B. McClellan. Charismatic leaders often become set in their ways and demand that things be done "their way." They become convinced of their superiority and of the infallibility of their ways, and as a result they are unwilling to consider conflicting opinions of others and to properly evaluate risks and feedback from their actions.[2] Unable to amend their ways and to change, these leaders become abnormally vulnerable to failure and to the creation of harm. Three of the most charismatic leaders of the twentieth century—Stalin, Hitler, and Mao—were "misleaders who inflicted as much evil and suffering on humanity as have ever been recorded" (Drucker, 2008, p. 289).

The importance of shared values in Burns's model of transformational leadership is reflected in Drucker's belief in the crucial role of the mission statement for an organization. In his model, the foundation of effective leadership is built upon a concise statement of the *purpose or mission* of an organization. "The leader's *first task*," says Drucker, "is to be the trumpet that sounds a clear sound" (Drucker, 2008, p. 289).[3] If the mission is wrong, the organization will be misdirected. So, leadership begins by defining the mission and purpose of the organization, then by thinking through the implications of the purpose for others. Once the leader clarifies the mission, then the leader's task is to implement it by following the repetitive leadership tasks of setting goals and priorities; organizing resources; communicating and motivating others to perform; establishing standards and measurements; and further developing the performance capacity in people, including himself or herself. That means that leadership is a means to an end—the mission it serves is the end. That view is championed again and again by some of the most effective leaders, and is prominent in the Level 5 leaders in Jim Collins's book *Good to Great* (Collins, 2001).

Drucker's favorite mission statement was written in 1917 and belonged to Sears Roebuck. This mission statement stated: "It is our function to be the informed and responsible buyer for the American farmer, and later on for the American middle class" (Buford, 1998, p. 4). Merchants adopted the perspective of the customer and in the process defined their role in the company as buyers for customers rather than as sellers to customers. If merchants bought the wrong merchandise—things the customer didn't want or need—nothing could be done to move it off the shelves and it would have to be sold at clearance. After establishing this mission statement, President Julius Rosenwald asked each of his store managers, "What does this mean for you and your people?" By doing so, he radiated the impact of the mission statement throughout the organization. This mission statement effectively captured what the organization was about, and it brought it to life in the day-to-day work of each person within the company.

A mission statement should lead to agreement among team members, guide formulation of strategy, direct the mobilization of all resources, and utilize the energies of people to accomplish the mission. The well-known credo of Johnson and Johnson (J&J), for example, illustrates the phenomenal power of a good mission statement (Johnson and Johnson, n.d.). It helps the people of J&J to make a difference, to make the world a more caring and self-respecting place.

Mission statements do not last forever; they must be revisited and amended. Most have a short life because change is a universal aspect of organizational life. For example, in 1908 AT&T began with the mission to bring a telephone to every household and to make telephone service affordable. It achieved this goal in 1960, but it failed to revisit its mission. AT&T floundered until in 1982, when it was the target of a lawsuit brought by the Antitrust Division of the U.S. Department of Justice. When the lawsuit was settled AT&T agreed to break itself up into several firms. Seven other regional (or "Baby Bell") companies were created, and AT&T became the long-distance provider.

The second requirement for Drucker's model of effective leadership is acceptance of the fact that true leadership is *responsibility* for the mission and *support* of those led. It is not primarily *status* and *power*. Effective leaders do not fear strength in subordinates or associates; rather, they seek it. They know that strong subordinates create strong outcomes. Effective leaders support, push, encourage, and glorify in strong subordinates and are generous with recognition when a job is well done. But they accept responsibility for the outcomes under their command. A widely quoted phrase succinctly summarizing the ultimate responsibility of the leader, even for failures of subordinates, is Harry Truman's "The buck stops here." According to Drucker, "Effective leaders are rarely permissive. But when things go wrong—and they always do—they do not blame others"[4] (Drucker, 2008, p. 290). By emphasizing responsibility, not rank, "the effective leader sees leadership as *responsibility*" (Drucker, 2008, p. 290). This comes very close to Greenleaf's idea of servant leadership, defining the leader as *servant*, first to the mission and then to subordinates whose effort he or she must encourage and support to accomplish the mission.

The third requirement of Drucker's effective leaders is that they earn *trust*. Trust is earned when leaders effectively pursue the mission of their organization and are true to their word. Trust is derived from belief in the *integrity* of the leader. It is based primarily on being consistent to the mission and to followers. A leader is always on display before followers. Therefore, there must be consistency between a leader's action and what he or she says—in other words, between the leader's professed beliefs and actions. The need for the leader to earn the trust of followers is nothing new—it reflects the wisdom of the ages, but it is a critical ingredient for achieving effectiveness.

Integrity is so critical to leadership that Drucker considered its absence a major disqualifier for positions of responsibility, for, "by themselves, character and integrity do not accomplish anything. But, their absence faults everything else" (Drucker, 1967, p. 87). This consideration does not minimize the need for other talents in effective leaders, but it does emphasize that other talents of leaders can be rendered ineffectual by lapses in integrity. The qualities of character and integrity in leadership are featured prominently in this chapter, given their importance to success.

Misleaders—or "toxic leaders" (Lipman-Blumen, 2006, p. ix)—exist at every level of the organization and they are contaminating influences. How can you tell if you are following an effective leader or a misleader? Misleaders do not believe in their mission; instead, they seek personal power. Often the most important thing to a misleader is self-aggrandizement. Frequently, misleaders display "histrionics," an attempt to maintain a stage presence; therefore, it is not uncommon for misleaders to possess charismatic personalities. Many effective leaders also possess charismatic personalities, but they use their charisma in pursuit of the mission.

Effective leadership is critical in times of crisis. As Indian cricket commentator Navjot Singh Sidhu notes, "Anybody can pilot a ship when the sea is calm" (Sidhu, n.d.). The inevitable event in an organization is the crisis. The most important thing for the leader to do is to try to anticipate the crisis and to make her or his organization capable of averting it through anticipatory actions. The essential preemptive action for overcoming the inevitable crises is to create an organization that is opportunity focused and on the offensive at all times, rather than an organization that is constantly on the defensive. Becoming battle alert requires that an organization shed its unproductive products, processes, services, and people. It then demands that an organization institutionalize processes of change—entrepreneurship and innovation at every level.

If it is not possible to avert a crisis, the leader must have belief in the worthiness of the ultimate purpose of the organization and confidence and optimism in his or her ability to lead the organization through the crisis. How does one gain such confidence? First, there is no substitute for having gone through one or more crises in one's life and having learned successful adaptive behaviors. That requires the presence of technical as well as interpersonal competencies. Second, being thrust into a culture in which a person is essentially a foreigner requires a person to learn adaptive behaviors in order to succeed in the new culture.[5] Finally, a third approach for gaining confidence and direction is to anchor the organization in a solid credo that provides life-giving *values* and *direction* to help the organization in both good times and bad. From these kinds of experiences and values, the leader should know how to behave in a crisis, possess self-confidence for decisive action in the midst of a crisis, and have gained the trust of others so that both leader and followers can successfully navigate a crisis.

Leadership succession is the toughest problem facing any organization. According to Drucker, the focus of leadership succession should be on choosing a leader who will maintain or build a high spirit of achievement. Maintaining the spirit of an organization depends on maintaining *continuity* in leadership with leaders who share similar values and who are willing to embrace necessary change. Succession is especially difficult when new leadership is following that of a founding entrepreneur. Organizations should be aware of the danger of trying to duplicate exactly the style and behavior of someone, such as the founder, who has made a lasting impact on the organization. Conditions facing an organization in the future may call for a person to have entirely different strengths.

How should an organization go about selecting a new leader? One must think through the strengths required by the assignment that the new person will assume. It is best to have open and honest conversations with some people who previously have worked with each candidate to determine that person's strengths and weaknesses. A good appraisal of a candidate's record of past performance will include an assessment of both successes and failures.

The highly spirited organization, one with a high esprit de corps, creates the right practices and the right "soil" for the development of new leaders. Strong leaders develop the full capacities of the people who follow them, and they lead their people to accomplishments that exceed even the highest expectations of those led. Observed Drucker:

> It is typical of the most successful and the most durable institutions that they induce in their members an intellectual and moral growth beyond a . . . [person's] original capacities. (Drucker, 1946, p. 28)

Such an achievement is possible by using *right leadership practices*, not through personality traits, charisma, or luck. Right practices include providing challenging assignments, having high expectations for those led, and granting the autonomy required for people to develop their strengths. Max De Pree summarizes role of leaders in simultaneously granting individual autonomy and achieving organizational goals:

Delegate with a certain abandon so that people have space in which to realize potential, in which to be accountable, in which to achieve. I don't believe we can achieve organizational goals without that congruency. I believe it is more the responsibility of the leader to forge that integration [of individual development and organizational goals] than it is the individual. (Drucker, 1990, pp. 39–40)

The teachings on effective leadership just described are closely aligned with servant leadership as described in Chapter 5. Yet, servant leaders, while exhibiting empathy and compassion toward those served, also retain a pragmatic orientation toward results. It is toughness and compassion at the same time, so-called *tough love*. Servant leadership places great emphasis on listening, empathizing, and really "leaning in" toward the experience of those being led while pursuing results. Through servant leadership, leaders raise the dignity and self-respect of those being led. They do so by assuming responsibility for the development and enrichment of the people served. Servant leaders encourage those being led to assume high levels of responsibility and to realize self-esteem and fulfillment as they perform.

Robert Greenleaf describes the origins of servant leadership from Hermann Hesse's novel *Journey to the East*. In the book, Hesse tells the story of Leo, a servant who tends to a group of travelers on a journey. During the course of the story, Leo is lost, and the travelers find that they are unable to function without him. As Greenleaf remarks, the message he gained is that the servant was, in fact, the leader of the group, even though he performed the more mundane and routine tasks on the journey (Greenleaf, 1977, pp. 21–22). Although it is clear that Greenleaf's concept of servant leadership is grounded much more in existential and process philosophy than religion, many have chosen to interpret servant leadership in the context of the Judeo-Christian tradition.

Other examples of servant leadership in organizations abound. Wal-Mart positioned itself as a "national Christian icon" through its systematic implementation of a Judeo-Christian model of servant leadership (Moreton, 2009, p. 122). In mostly Muslim Malaysia, Francis Yeoh uses his Christian values to guide YTL Corp., insisting on ethical behavior throughout the organization (Karlgaard, 2004, p. 2). Servant leaders who model themselves in the Judeo-Christian tradition typically do so as a reflection of their own personal beliefs, striving to fulfill the moral obligations of their faith in every aspect of their lives.

In servant leadership, providing dignity through leadership is very instrumental to the development of the person, and to the achievement of the mission of an organization. When asked about his reputation for developing people, Max De Pree, then chairman of Herman Miller, Inc., said:

> I would have to begin with a very personal observation, which is I believe, first of all, that each of us is made in the image of God. That we come to life with a tremendous diversity of gifts. I think from there, a leader needs to see himself in a position of indebtedness. Leaders are given the gift of leadership by those who choose or agree to follow. We're basically a volunteer nation. I think this means that people choose a leader to a great extent on the basis of what they believe that leader can contribute to the person's ability to achieve his or her goals in life. This puts the leader in the position of being indebted—in the sense of what he or she owes to the organization. (Drucker, 1990, p. 37)

Theologian R. C. Sproul makes the link between the treatment of a person and the performance of that person. Sproul demonstrates that when a person's dignity and self-worth are respected, increased production and higher quality are its by-products.

When treated without respect, a person is downtrodden and uncommitted, and little production and bad qualities are the by-products (Sproul, 1991, p. 17). C. William Pollard, while in the process of writing his book *The Soul of the Firm* (1996), offered the view that "when the purpose of the firm is linked to the growth and development of a person in God's image, it unleashes powerful forces in the mind and spirit of the worker" (Maciari-ello, 1996). He provides numerous examples that affirm this view from his work at ServiceMaster.

While there are many reasons why leaders like De Pree and Pol-lard believe it is so important to be able to raise the issue of God in the workplace, the development of the human being at the work-place is the central issue. In the Judeo-Christian tradition, being created in the image of God recognizes that the human being has inherent dignity and status. As with other religious traditions, it provides guidelines for establishing right and wrong actions—and thus standards for what are considered responsible behaviors.

Judeo-Christian interpretations of servant leadership typically emphasize the role of a higher spiritual authority in guiding an organization's mission. They also provide the moral basis for rec-ognizing the potential for human development; by seeing all as created in God's image, these leaders have a religious imperative for upholding standards of equality and fairness in the workplace. Finally, the Judeo-Christian tradition creates the imperative for developing a healthy sense of community in the workplace within which the individual can find status and personal fulfillment through meaningful associations as part of a highly motivating organization. We have addressed this topic at length in Chapter 5, but here we see how some leaders have connected their reli-gious beliefs to their leadership philosophy.

We turn now to discuss a specific example of an outstanding leader, a historical figure who has been the subject of much scholarly inquiry and public interest—Abraham Lincoln.

ABRAHAM LINCOLN: A CASE STUDY IN LEADERSHIP

Abraham Lincoln is perhaps the most prominent figure in collective American memory. In spite of those who have said that nothing new can be said about the man, the Lincoln publications continue. In his April 1876 dedication of a statue of Lincoln, Frederick Douglass stated that "no man can say anything that is new of Abraham Lincoln" (Douglass, 1876). Sixty years later, historian James G. Randall published an essay titled "Has the Lincoln Theme Been Exhausted?" Nevertheless, historians celebrated the bicentennial of Lincoln's birth in 2009 with considerable hoopla, including a special issue of the *Journal of American History* ("Abraham Lincoln at 200," 2009). There has also been no shortage of Lincoln publications since Randall posited that the subject was "exhausted" in 1936. As historian Eric Foner wryly notes, "More words have been written about Lincoln than any historical personage except Jesus Christ" (Foner, 2008, p. 11).

One of the benefits of this continued exploration of the life and times of Abraham Lincoln is that we are gaining a much more nuanced portrait of the man and the people around him. Some historians, such as Brian R. Dirck (Dirck, 2009) and Mark E. Steiner (Steiner, 2006), have focused on the nineteenth-century context of Lincoln's early career, emphasizing the important role of his contemporaries and their attitudes in shaping his own beliefs. Others, such as Stephen Berry (Berry, 2007) and C. A. Tripp (Tripp, 2005), have chosen to write about Lincoln's personal life, delving into the private world of his psychology, marriage, or early romantic relationships. In recent years, several authors, such as Lerone Bennett (Bennett, 2000) and William Marvel (Marvel, 2008), have directly challenged the traditional depiction of Lincoln as a saintly figure in American history. Instead, they argue, he held racist views, was a political opportunist, and violated constitutional principles of freedom. It often surprises nonhistorians that so many scholars can read the same primary source documents and end up with such divergent conclusions with respect to historical events and personalities. Such is the nature of liberal arts inquiry.

One of the topics about which historians disagree is the nature of Lincoln's leadership leading up to and during the Civil War. By analyzing various decisions made by Lincoln, and the differing interpretations of those decisions, we can begin to evaluate how Lincoln functioned in terms of Drucker's leadership model.

Congruence between Values and Goals

The first element of Drucker's model of leadership was the congruence between the leader's and followers' values and goals. In evaluating Lincoln's performance with respect to this aspect of leadership, it is important to clarify which "followers" are being discussed. Obviously, the seceding Southern states did not share Lincoln's goal of preserving the Union. Political opponents in the Democratic Party, too, condemned him regularly. Border states did not wholeheartedly share Lincoln's goals either; the governors of Kentucky and Missouri both refused to send troops in response to Lincoln's 1861 request for support. But even some among his supporters in the North questioned his goals. An April 25, 1861, *New York Times* editorial lamented that "in every great crisis, the human heart demands a leader that incarnates its ideas, its emotions and its aims. . . . No such hero at present directs affairs" (White, 2009, pp. 415–416). As the Union experienced a wave of losses, from Lee's stellar win at Second Bull Run to the Confederate invasion of Maryland, Lincoln came under fire for his military decisions, ability to lead, and moral fiber (Donald, 1995, p. 373). Clearly, not all of Lincoln's "followers" shared his goals and values throughout the Civil War.

In such a fractious environment as the United States was during the Civil War, one would be hard pressed to come up with a group of followers who consistently shared Lincoln's values and goals. A more apt evaluation of Lincoln's ability to mesh his goals and values with those of his constituents would involve an assessment of his ability to find commonality in an atmosphere of divisiveness. One example of this is Lincoln's timing of the Emancipation Proclamation (January 1, 1863) and the nature of the debate on slavery.[6]

Lincoln's own position on slavery changed over the course of his career. As he came to the conclusion that slavery was morally wrong, he believed that he needed to act on those convictions. However, Lincoln was fully aware of the political climate of his time, and he knew that the vast majority of Northerners would not support a sudden transformation of the war into a "crusade for abolition" (Donald, 1995, p. 368). Lincoln's preparation for and timing of the Emancipation Proclamation illustrates his understanding of the importance of shared goals and values between leaders and their followers. Without such a shared understanding of the nature of the war, most Northerners would have withdrawn their support.

The issue of slavery was ever present in Lincoln's senatorial and presidential campaigns. The new Republican Party, created by former Whigs and some Democrats who believed that Southern plantation owners held a monopoly on Washington politics, began to catalyze around a moderate antislavery position in early 1854. All but the most radical believed in containing, not eliminating, slavery; if slavery could be prevented from expanding, they believed, it would eventually disappear. This policy of containment faced a direct challenge from the Kansas-Nebraska Act. Sponsored by Illinois Senator Stephen A. Douglas, the Kansas-Nebraska Act would allow the people of each of the two new territories to decide whether Kansas and Nebraska would be slave or free. The bill met with considerable opposition, but it passed both the House and Senate and was signed into law on May 22, 1854. As a result, the fragile compromises that had crafted a balance between slave and free states fell apart, and slavery entered the fore of national debates.

When Lincoln ran against Douglas for U.S. Senate in 1858, slavery was the major topic during the famous Lincoln-Douglas debates.

During the seven debates, Lincoln and Douglas staked out their positions. Lincoln expressed his belief in the Declaration of Independence as a standard for which the nation should strive: "All men are created equal. . . . I say . . . let it be as nearly reached as we can" (Lincoln, 1858, in Basler, p. 501). Douglas, on the other hand, maintained the states' right to decide whether or not they believed slavery was right or wrong.

Lincoln by no means advocated the outright abolition of slavery (which was favored by radical Republicans); he believed that those states that already had the institution were protected under the Constitution. Lincoln's primary concern was to control the spread of slavery into new territories, a position favored by moderate Republicans and many northern Democrats. However, because Lincoln grounded his argument against Douglas in the language of the Declaration of Independence—"all men are created equal"—he established a clear moral difference in their views. While few voices in Lincoln's time would have argued for racial equality, Lincoln pointed out that Douglas had "no very vivid impression that the negro is a human; and consequently has no idea that there can be any moral question in legislating about him" (Donald, 1995, p. 176). What established Lincoln's position as different from that of other moderate Republicans of his day was his "tone of moral outrage," his conviction of the "monstrous evil" of slavery (Donald, 1995, p. 176).

In spite of his personal convictions, Lincoln continued to answer to the political climate of the day. In response to prodding by Douglas, he confirmed that he was not "in favor of bringing about in any way the social and political equality of the white and black races," nor was he "in favor of producing a perfect equality, social, and political, between negroes and white men" (White, 2009, p. 276). Only the most radical voices would have proposed any sort of equality for the races in the 1850s. But by the time the Civil War was underway, some Republicans criticized President Lincoln for not waging a war on the institution that was considered to be the cause of the war.

Pennsylvania Republican Thaddeus Stevens and many others took Lincoln to task for not attacking slavery; Francis W. Bird lamented that "the key of the slave's chain is now kept in the White House" (Donald, 1995, p. 342).

Although his personal convictions were very much in line with his critics, as president and commander in chief Lincoln had to walk a tightrope to maintain his political constituencies for prosecuting the war. The problem was severe in the border states of Kentucky, Maryland, and Missouri because, although these states remained in the Union, they favored the status quo on slavery. Any move by Lincoln to abolish slavery would have forced the secession of these three states into the Confederacy. And Lincoln lamented, "these all against us, and the job on our hands is too large for us" (Lincoln, 1861, in Basler, p. 532).

Radical Republicans continued to argue that the issue of slavery was very important to the outcome of the war because slaves provided direct support for the South in fighting the war. Slaves provided support for the Southern economy, and they provided logistical support for Confederate armies. Radicals therefore argued that a strike against slavery would further the national policy of preserving the union.

The matter came to a head when Illinois Democrat Lyman Trumbull proposed a bill that would emancipate all slaves. There was a great uproar as to what to do with fugitive slaves, who ran away from their owners to join up with Union forces. The Fugitive Slave Act, passed in 1850, was still in effect, requiring that escaped slaves be returned to their rightful owners. As Northerners began to argue that these escaped slaves could, in fact, be used against the Union cause as "contraband," Lincoln and others had to consider what to do with the runaways. Returning them to their slaveholders seemed out of the question, but Trumbull's proposal for complete emancipation worried those in the North whose racial attitudes reflected those of the time: that blacks and whites were not and could never be social equals.

One solution Lincoln proposed was colonization, to ship runaway slaves off to another location away from the United States. Eventually, Lincoln's resettlement program evolved into an idea to abolish slavery in the border states. These arguments gradually gained acceptance in the North and with Lincoln. Fugitive slaves from Confederate States were not returned, and they became an important part of the Union Army.

Lincoln slowly began to change national strategy from preventing the expansion of slavery to abolishing slavery in states that were in rebellion against the Union. Describing his plan for emancipation as voluntary for the border states, and backed by the endorsement of Postmaster General Montomery Blair, Republican Senator Charles Sumner, and Secretary of the Treasury Salmon P. Chase, Lincoln effectively overcame objections from his opponents. Initially, he succeeded only in passing a bill for compensated emancipation in Washington, D.C. As biographer David Herbert Donald states, Lincoln was increasingly pressured to resolve the problem of fugitive slaves, and deal with the moral wrong of slavery through emancipation, but he was careful: "Always reluctant to be out in front of public opinion, always hesitant to assume positions from which there could be no retreat, Lincoln deliberated long before making a hard choice" (Donald, 1995, p. 347).

Clearly unsure that he had anything remotely like a mandate of support, Lincoln invoked his war powers as commander in chief to seize the slave property of Confederate States, while still compensating slave owners for that seizure once they were restored as loyal to the Union. After consulting his cabinet members about wording of the documents, and after making several personal revisions that took into account only a few of his advisor's comments, Lincoln issued the Emancipation Proclamation on January 1, 1863.

Eventually, the Emancipation Proclamation became the crowning glory of Lincoln's presidency. However, in the first few days after he began floating the idea of the proclamation, "Lincoln's leadership was more seriously threatened than at any other time, and it was not clear that his administration could survive the repeated crises that it had faced" (Donald, 1995, p. 377). Lincoln thus waited for public opinion to come into support of a national strategy to ban slavery in rebellious states before making the actual decision to abolish slavery. The timing was right at the beginning of 1863; it would certainly have been wrong and would have undermined the Union's position in the war had Lincoln acted against slavery much earlier.

The decision to emancipate slaves is an example of a decision that had to meet *certain boundary conditions* in order to be effective—it had to be shown to diminish the capability of the Confederacy to wage war against the Union *and* it had to wait upon public support for the measure. For this reason, the final Emancipation Proclamation freed only a select few slaves: those who were out of reach of the Northern Army. Border states were exempted. In the words of historian Ronald C. White, "the proclamation was not so much a fact accomplished as a promise to be realized" (White, 2009, p. 540).

Initially, the public reaction to the Emancipation Proclamation was positive through much of the North. However, as individuals scrutinized the speech, they found items of concern. One of the strengths of the Emancipation Proclamation, and one of its selling points to the American public, was its provision to include black soldiers in the Union war effort. But this raised concerns: how could freed slaves fight alongside Union soldiers? A massive campaign of educating and training black soldiers helped to alleviate Union concerns; nevertheless, this provision remained a concern for both Republicans and Democrats. As Donald has noted, the public debate about the Emancipation Proclamation was muted after Lincoln issued the proclamation suspending the privilege of habeas corpus, authorizing the arrest of any person deemed "guilty of any disloyal practice, affording aid and comfort to Rebels against the authority of the United States" (Lincoln, 1862, in Basler, p. 437). However, in the short term, the Emancipation Proclamation and suspension of habeas corpus cost the Republicans votes in later elections.

Yet, Lincoln managed to reframe the Civil War around the question of slavery rather than simply the preservation of the Union, and he did so in a brilliant manner. By arguing that the war effort (to preserve the Union) required the participation of slaves who chose to leave the Confederate cause, Lincoln assuaged the concerns of many constituencies. He pleased the Abolitionists, who saw the eventual move toward the end of slavery stated in the Emancipation Proclamation. For those concerned with the issue of property loss and compensation, Lincoln included language to acknowledge the government's role in providing compensation to former slave owners for the loss of their property. Finally, Lincoln acknowledged those who worried about achieving military victory for the North, which seemed elusive. By bringing in trained and loyal African-American soldiers, the North could remove the threat of black soldiers fighting for the enemy, and it would gain a significant force of manpower. The linking of emancipation with war service for the Union, as well as compensation for loss of property to Confederates who rejoined the Union, established boundaries for achieving the moral objectives identified by Lincoln: preservation of the Union and the end of slavery.

Drucker recognized that the identification of certain boundary conditions is a critical element in making effective decisions (Drucker, 1967, p. 122). The recognition that slaves were used by the enemy against the Union and should be freed using the war powers of the presidency as justification, and the right timing for issuing the Emancipation Proclamation, were constraints on the decision to free the slaves as a means for achieving the mission of the Civil War.

The Irrelevance of Charisma

As Drucker emphasized, specific character traits, notably charisma, do not play a role in determining effective leadership. Although an effective orator, Lincoln can hardly be characterized as a charismatic leader. In fact, many historians have commented on his analytical nature, his need to see problems from all angles before making a decision. In his important biography, David Herbert Donald describes Lincoln as a highly reactive individual, one who was essentially a passive responder rather than a proactive problem solver; Lincoln was reluctant "to take the initiative and make bold plans; he preferred to respond to the actions of others" (Donald, 1995, p. 15). Ronald C. White prefers to present Lincoln as "not passive but prudent" (White, 2009, p. 409), but he also acknowledges that Lincoln was not a commanding, charismatic presence. Richard Carwardine refers to Lincoln's "reticence and secrecy," commenting that "discretion in politically sensitive matters, including racial issues, marked his handling of men and measures" (Carwardine, 2008, p. xiii). Indeed, the repackaging of Lincoln as "the Rail Splitter," the homespun frontiersman from pioneer stock, instead of "Honest Abe" or the successful attorney that he actually was, shows how his political image needed a boost from his handlers (Donald, 1995, pp. 244–245).

Lincoln's lack of personal charisma can be contrasted with the personality of one of his generals, George B. McClellan. By most accounts the tenure of charismatic Major General McClellan, general in chief of the Union Army during the Civil War, was characterized by indecisiveness and by the lack of courage to make decisions to take offensive action against the enemy. He constantly overestimated the strength of the enemy and the risks of engagement, which led to overall ineffectiveness in achieving the Union's mission of defeating the Confederate Army. As to his magnetic personality, however, Herman Hattaway, Archer Jones, and Jerry A. Vanderlinde note that "McClellan had an aura that drew men to him. Admirers said he was the only general who by merely riding up could induce enlisted men to leave their breakfasts and follow him. . . . The President confided in him and 'Georged' him [reinforced his self-image of invincibility], the press fawned upon him, and people trusted him"

(Hattaway, Jones, and Vanderlinde, 1991, p. 80). Abraham Lincoln's selection of McClellan as general in chief of the Union Army was a major mistake, and it prolonged the war at enormous humacost.

Responsibility and Accountability

In Drucker's model, leaders accept responsibility and accountability for their mission and surround themselves with strong subordinates whom they support. Although Lincoln underestimated the severity of the problem, it was clear that one of his primary missions would be to deal with the threat of secession of the South and perhaps war. As southern states, beginning with South Carolina on December 20, 1860, seceded from the Union, Lincoln was forced to assume executive responsibility months before his inauguration on March 4, 1861. Shortly after his election, he began to assemble his team of advisors, selecting those with whom he would work most closely.

Historians have delved into Lincoln's selection of cabinet members, and not all agree regarding his motivations or thought processes. Doris Kearns Goodwin emphasizes the fact that Lincoln sought help from his most able political rivals. As Goodwin argues, he surrounded himself with a "team of rivals," a cabinet made up of men whom he believed were best qualified to assist him in meeting these challenges. Lincoln was not deterred by the fact that they were his fiercest political rivals who believed they were more qualified to be president than he was. He felt they were the most qualified executives to help him lead the nation during the time of national peril. He put the purpose of unifying the nation above personal grievances with these people and above attempts to achieve harmonious relationships in his cabinet. In Goodwin's assessment, it was an effective working group for arriving at and implementing the best decisions and for pursuing Lincoln's mission to preserve the Union. However, it was not a cast of characters that brought peace and harmony to Lincoln's cabinet and life.

David Herbert Donald's interpretation is that Lincoln recognized his own limitations, and he knew he would need his former rivals in order to function effectively. The biographer notes that Lincoln told William Henry Seward's principal political advisor, Thurlow Weed, that Seward, Salmon P. Chase, and Edward Bates, men whom he proposed to occupy positions in his cabinet and administration (see below), possessed "long experience in public affairs," which gave them "higher claims than his own for the place he was to occupy" (Donald, 1995, p. 262). Donald also argues that Lincoln's selections reflected his awareness of the diverse nature of the Republican Party. The new political party was hardly unified, its members holding conflicting beliefs over what to do about slavery, tariffs, and a host of other questions.

Lincoln made his cabinet choices to balance these various interests and also to reflect a fair geographic distribution. His list included men from the Northeast, Northwest, and border slave states (Donald, 1995, p. 262). Yet Donald highlights the disorderly way in which Lincoln chose his cabinet; he reminds us that Lincoln's process was far from smooth. Because Lincoln took so much time to offer Seward the position of secretary of state, Seward's political opponents in his home state of New York began to circulate rumors that Lincoln would not offer Seward the job. By the time Lincoln spoke with Seward, his future secretary of state was leery of accepting the position right away. Political jockeying from allies in Illinois and Indiana who had helped get Lincoln elected, as well as factional backbiting in Pennsylvania, resulted in competition for key positions and a bit of horse trading on Lincoln's part. Senator Simon Cameron of Pennsylvania campaigned for a spot in Lincoln's cabinet. When allegations of bribery and other wrongdoing surfaced, Lincoln withdrew his offer; later, however, he decided it was more important to have someone from Pennsylvania in his administration, and he made Cameron his secretary of war (Donald, 1995, pp. 265–267). In hindsight, this was not one of Lincoln's better decisions.

Not every scholar agrees that Lincoln carefully and thoughtfully handpicked his cabinet members on the basis of their personal characteristics; political considerations certainly were involved as well. For example, Lincoln polled the Republican senators for their top choice for secretary of the treasury; 11 of the 19 who responded recommended Chase, sealing his appointment (Donald, 1995, p. 281). But most scholars accept that Lincoln was well aware of the strengths and weaknesses of his cabinet members, and he was prepared to manage the inevitable disagreements between them. In fact, as historians have pointed out, Lincoln cut his leadership teeth on his first cabinet, in a sense; his second administration contained no rivals or major party figures but rather men who were supremely loyal to Lincoln. In his first term, the inexperienced chief executive needed the most competent people he could find, even if that resulted in personal rivalries and infighting (White, 2009, p. 649; Donald, 1995, p. 551).

In selecting his cabinet members, Lincoln followed three of Drucker's categories for executive effectiveness: *focus on strengths, focus on contributions*, and *make decisions effectively*. Lincoln decided to select people who had the ability required to carry out an important part of the mission and strategy of his administration. Choices were made regardless of the shortcomings that came with these people. Lincoln then insisted that each person contribute in areas of his strengths. Weaknesses had to be overcome by others, but strengths had to exist in the person appointed to a cabinet position.

By focusing on strengths and by emphasizing contribution, Lincoln did delegate much of the business of his administration to his trusted cabinet members. They in turn were expected to make decisions to implement relevant aspects of the overall mission and strategy. When proven ineffectual in their positions, they were eventually removed from them by Lincoln.

Clearly, Lincoln made mistakes in appointing Simon Cameron as secretary of war and George McClellan as general in chief of the

Union Army (a critical noncabinet appointment). He reversed the first decision quickly but delayed too long in replacing McClellan.

Focus on Strengths and Contributions

The four key cabinet appointments considered in the following paragraphs illustrate just how successful Lincoln was in filling these cabinet positions based upon the strengths of the individuals chosen in spite of some notable weaknesses. The weaknesses of Salmon P. Chase as secretary of the treasury were especially pronounced, but Lincoln needed his strengths, and Chase delivered.

William Henry Seward

Lincoln's first and most important cabinet appointment was that of secretary of state. This position was offered to and eventually accepted by New York State's esteemed U.S. Senator, William Henry Seward. Seward was a Phi Beta Kappa graduate of Union College in Schenectady, New York, and a successful criminal lawyer, before beginning a lifelong career of public service. Seward served in the New York State Senate for four years, was elected twice governor of New York, and then served as U.S. Senator from 1850 to 1861. Because of his tenure in state government, his stature in national politics, and his experience in both legislative and executive branches of government, William Seward was probably the best qualified Republican candidate for president in 1860 (HarpWeek, n.d.).

Seward was the most prominent leader of the new Republican Party and the pick of political professionals to win the nomination. After the severe disappointment of losing the nomination to Lincoln, having been the preconvention favorite to win both the nomination and the presidency, Seward was coaxed back into public service by Lincoln. He campaigned strenuously and successfully for the election of Abraham Lincoln even though they did not know each other very well at the time. Seward was committed to the Republican platform and to restrictions on the spread of slavery contained in the platform.

Lincoln chose Seward as secretary of state "in view of his ability, integrity and commanding influence" (Goodwin, 2005, p. 283). Seward's ability, integrity, and influence were especially demonstrated during Lincoln's long transition period between election day (November 6, 1860) and inauguration day (March 4, 1861). It was during this long transition period when Seward almost single-handedly kept the secessionist forces from disrupting the federal government. He obtained valuable information from Edwin M. Stanton, attorney general in the Buchanan administration, about planned plots of secessionist forces to overtake the federal government during the period prior to Lincoln's inauguration. Seward took the steps needed to foil the plots of these secessionists.

In Lincoln's private letter in which he offered Seward the premier cabinet appointment, the president-elect spoke of Seward's "position in the public eye, your integrity, ability, learning, and great experience, all combined to render it an appointment fit to be made" (Lincoln, 1860, in Basler, p. 149). These strengths continued to be evident as Seward worked closely with Lincoln and eventually became the president's chief counselor and dear friend. He served as secretary of state throughout Lincoln's presidency, and upon Lincoln's assassination he served throughout the Johnson administration until March 1869.

Seward's relationship with President Lincoln did not start out harmoniously. Believing himself to be more competent and experienced than Lincoln, Seward sought considerable influence in a number of Lincoln's early decisions. After Lincoln asked Seward to read over his inaugural address, Seward responded with a seven-page letter with his recommended changes, including two alternate closing paragraphs (White, 2009, p. 383). Registering his displeasure with Lincoln's selection of his rival Salmon Chase as secretary of the treasury, Seward resigned the night before the inauguration. Lincoln convinced Seward to change his mind, demonstrating his ability to manage the many personalities in his administration—a skill he would need to employ again and again.

Seward was one of five members of the cabinet to dissent on Lincoln's first consequential decision: whether or not to resupply Fort Sumter, South Carolina. Seward argued that significant Union sympathy existed in South Carolina and called on Lincoln to appease the South by abandoning Fort Sumter. To test Seward's assumption, Lincoln sent a scout into South Carolina to assess Union sympathy. Finding little, Lincoln overruled Seward.

Eventually, Seward realized the effectiveness of Lincoln as chief executive. In a letter to his wife, Francis, in May 1861, Seward said of Lincoln that "his confidence and sympathy increase every day." He told her again in early June [1861] that "executive skill and vigor are rare qualities. The President is the best of us; but he needs constant assiduous cooperation" (Goodwin, 2005, p. 364).

Seward was the first of Lincoln's rivals to recognize Lincoln's developing energy and executive competence. The secretary of state continued "to debate numerous issues with Lincoln in the years ahead, exactly as Lincoln had hoped and needed him to do." Seward "would become Lincoln's most faithful ally in the cabinet" (Goodwin, 2005, p. 364).

Like Lincoln, Seward was a man with strong moral values, and these shared traits permitted Lincoln to trust Seward and to grant him significant autonomy as secretary of state. Perhaps the best illustration of Seward's integrity was during the 1862 cabinet crisis when Salmon Chase, jealous of Seward's high standing with Lincoln, tried to engineer Seward's ouster from the cabinet. Rather than trying to right the wrong done to him by Chase, Seward put the interests of the country ahead of his own and resigned. When Chase's shenanigans and maneuverings with the Republican caucus were cleverly uncovered by Lincoln, Seward resumed his position as secretary of state.

Salmon P. Chase

An 1826 graduate of Dartmouth College, Salmon P. Chase, like Seward, was educated in one of the finest colleges in the United States. He studied law in Washington, D.C., and practiced it in Ohio. He was a fierce, antislavery Democrat, defending slaves who escaped to Ohio (Ohio History Central, n.d.).

Chase was elected to the U.S. Senate in 1849, and he infuriated Democrats with his strong denunciation of the Kansas-Nebraska Act of 1854, believing it to be a campaign to spread slavery throughout the nation. When the Republican Party formed in 1854 around an antislavery platform, Chase, along with other like-minded Democrats, changed his political affiliation and joined the Republican Party. He was elected governor of Ohio as a Republican in 1855 and then was reelected in 1857. Like Seward, he had judicial, legislative, and executive experience.

Chase was a determined candidate for the Republican presidential nomination in 1860, and he continued to pursue his presidential aspirations after his bitter defeat by Lincoln and while serving as a member of Lincoln's cabinet. Lincoln thought Chase to be an able executive with significant stature among the public. As a result Lincoln appointed him secretary of the treasury. With the South seceding from the Union, the finances of the United States were strained just at the time that massive financing was required to support the Union's war effort. In 1863, Chase played a crucial role in establishing a national banking system and in inspiring confidence among investors in the Union's cause; his efforts eased the financial burden of the war. Chase remained as secretary of the treasury until the spring of 1864.

Chase threatened to resign his office four times during his tenure. His offers to resign were always schemes to have his way on specific issues. Lincoln rejected Chase's first three attempts to resign because he needed Chase's strengths as treasury secretary even though Chase attempted to undermine Lincoln's authority. Finally on June

29, 1864, Lincoln accepted Chase's fourth attempt to resign. That shocked Chase and sent him into a depression, as he believed his political career to be at an end. Latter in that same year Chase ran against Abraham Lincoln, again unsuccessfully, for the Republican presidential nomination.

Shortly after Chase resigned as secretary of the treasury and then was defeated for the Republican nomination for president, Lincoln nominated him to become the sixth chief justice of the United States, a position that he occupied from December 15, 1864, to his death on May 7, 1873. He administered the oath of office to President Lincoln at Lincoln's second inaugural on March 4, 1865.

When Lincoln was advised to bypass Chase as chief justice, Lincoln focused not on the man's contemptuous personal behavior toward the president but rather on the man's strengths and on what Chase could do well and contribute to the nation. According to one biographer, Lincoln stated that "'Mr. Chase is a very able man. He is a very ambitious man and I think on the subject of the presidency a little insane. He has not always behaved very well lately and people say to me, '*Now is the time to crush him out.*' Well, I am not in favor of crushing anybody out! If there is anything that a man can do and do it well, I say let him do it. Give him a chance. Of all of the great men I have known, Chase is equal to about one and a half of the best of them" (Thomas, 1952/2008, p. 492).

Edward Bates

Edward Bates, a Missouri elder statesman and lawyer, served in a number of state positions as well as in the U.S. Congress. He was selected by Lincoln to be attorney general of the United States. A very humble man he, unlike many others, understood the dangers posed by high political office, as he stated:

> My pecuniary circumstances (barely competent) and my settled domestic habits make it very undesirable for me to be in

high office with low pay—it subjects a man to great tempta-
tions to live above his income, and thus become dishonest;
and if he have the courage to live economically, subject his
family to ridicule. (Goodwin, 2005, p. 286)

A patriotic man, Bates was encouraged by fellow Missourians
and a number of other national leaders to seek the nomination for
the presidency from his important border state. Bates did not later
seek a cabinet position. Yet his patriotism and the domestic turmoil
at that time led him to reconsider his initial inclination to decline
Lincoln's offer. When his acceptance of the nomination was leaked
to the press, and received positively by the public, Lincoln realized
that Bates would be readily accepted by the American people as
attorney general.

Edwin M. Stanton

Edwin Stanton, a brilliant lawyer who practiced as a defense attorney
in Pennsylvania, Washington, D.C., and Ohio, had early on intimi-
dated Lincoln by his learning, legal stature, and courtroom presence.
Stanton served as attorney general in the Buchanan administration.
And, although serving in that position for only a short period of
time, he is credited with changing President Buchanan's mind from
tolerating secession to taking a strong legal stand against it.

Stanton politically opposed Abraham Lincoln during the election but agreed to serve as an advisor to Secretary of War Simon
Cameron. As a strong ally of fellow Ohioan and presidential rival
Salmon Chase, he once again came to the attention of Abraham
Lincoln. Lincoln replaced Cameron with Stanton as secretary of war
in January 1862. Stanton was not seeking the position in the cabinet,
which required him to leave a very lucrative law practice, but knew
he would be able to help the country at its time of greatest need as
secretary of war.

Once Virginia seceded from the Union, the president lost his best hope to secure the services of Robert E. Lee as general in chief. As a result, Lincoln and Stanton played a hands-on role in determining military strategy, operations, and detailed battle tactics until Ulysses S. Grant became general in chief of the Union Army in early 1864. Stanton dealt with traitors with a very heavy hand. Lincoln did not always agree with Stanton's decisions, but the president only occasionally challenged the secretary of war because of his confidence in Stanton's judgment.

It was Stanton who upon Lincoln's assassination uttered the memorable tribute "now he belongs to the ages." And it was Stanton who among all of Lincoln's cabinet officers suffered prolonged grief over Lincoln's death. The two men ultimately shared a deep mutual affection for each other.

Lincoln and His Generals

In selecting his general officers, Lincoln also focused on strengths and capabilities. As Donald points out, "in making military appointments he tried to select commanders on the basis of military expertise rather than on what he called 'political affinity'" (Donald, 1995, p. 313). Nevertheless, Lincoln made a huge number of mistakes appointing general officers. Many of his chosen officers turned out to be failures. These failures often led him to assume the role of general in chief as well as commander in chief.

One such failure was none other than the charismatic George B. McClellan. McClellan was only 34 when he came to Washington, and he soon established himself as a heroic figure. Lincoln appointed McClellan to build a new army out of volunteers following General Irvin McDowell's disastrous loss at Bull Run. McClellan was popular with the troops, and Lincoln believed that he would be able to build a competent army. McClellan certainly had the admiration of his soldiers, who called him "Little Mac"; according to Ronald C.

White, McClellan's troops "offered a cheer when he approached, to which he would respond by raising and twirling his cap" (White, 2009, p. 441). Although full of confidence, McClellan shared little of his war plans with anyone, and when he took ill with typhoid fever, the entire Union Army's strategy was a mystery to all. Under criticism from the Committee on the Conduct of the War, as well as his political opponents, Lincoln began to study military strategy with the desperate thought that he might personally have to lead the Union campaign. When McClellan still failed to craft any meaningful plan after he regained his health, Lincoln issued his General War Order No. 1, which called for the military to begin a general advance against Southern forces on February 22, 1862.

Lincoln's order forced McClellan's hand, and revealed a wide gap in the two men's strategies for prosecuting the war. McClellan was against a direct assault on the Confederate army at Manassas, believing that such a move would replicate the disaster at Bull Run. Lincoln, however, believed that the Union forces should attack the Confederate forces where they were, focusing on fighting the army rather than taking specific territory. This essential difference in strategy made for an impossible relationship between the two men, as McClellan refused to engage the enemy directly, and Lincoln privately seethed. Notes Donald:

> Over the next few months the general did everything in his power to promote acceptance of his strategy, while the President dragged his feet. Self-absorbed and insensitive, McClellan seemed totally unaware that in a democratic society military commanders are subordinate to civilian authorities, and he felt no need to keep the President informed, much less to seek his advice. For his part, Lincoln, reluctant directly to interfere with military matters when he had no expertise, failed to make McClellan understand that when he made a suggestion he expected the general to follow it. This mutual

distrust destroyed any chance for a successful campaign. (Donald, 1995, pp. 338–339)

Lincoln demoted McClellan as general in chief, but he later reinstated the general to that position. When Union forces suffered defeat after defeat, and General Lee's army closed in yet again on the nation's capital in Washington, D.C., Lincoln turned to McClellan. As Donald states:

> Lincoln harbored no illusions about the general; he thought McClellan was the "chief alarmist and grand marplot of the Army," ridiculed his "weak, whiney, vague, and incorrect despatches," and considered his failure to reinforce Pope [Union General assigned to assist McClellan at Manassas] unpardonable. Yet he knew that McClellan was a superb organizer and an efficient engineer. And—what was equally important—he recognized that nothing but the reinstatement of McClellan would restore the shattered moral of the Army of the Potomac. (Donald, 1995, p. 371)

Virtually every one of Lincoln's advisors opposed McClellan's reinstatement, believing the general to be incompetent. McClellan did achieve victory at Antietam, but then he failed to pursue Lee and his Confederate forces. Frustrated and suspicious that McClellan's allegiance lay not entirely with the Union cause, Lincoln replaced McClellan in November with Ambrose E. Burnside.

Why did McClellan fail so? James McPherson has speculated that McClellan and other generals who commanded the Army of the Potomac were overwhelmed by the media attention and government scrutiny in Washington, D.C., and were thus fearful of taking any kind of risk (McPherson, 2008b, p. 30). Others have pointed out that McClellan was completely averse to Lincoln politically and personally; he referred to the president as "an idiot," "a well meaning baboon," and "the *original gorilla*," and, as a Democrat, found much to criticize in the Lincoln administration, from the Emancipation Proclamation to the president's involvement in military details (Carwardine, 2003, pp. 187–188). In the case of McClellan, having a rival on the team did not serve Lincoln's cause at all but rather resulted in costly foot dragging and delays.

What did Lincoln see in McClellan? He may have believed that the young general was the future of the military. Notes White: "It was as if he saw potential greatness in this young man and hoped he could nurture his abilities" (White, 2009, p. 447). Most likely, Lincoln recognized the relationship McClellan had with his soldiers. The president selected McClellan because of his ability to form a loyal, functioning cadre of soldiers, and Lincoln's primary reason for reinstating the general was to boost troop morale.

McClellan was indeed a popular general. When Lincoln first removed McClellan from his position, there was great public outcry as well as dismay among his soldiers. When word spread of McClellan's dismissal, soldiers left their regiments in droves, milling about in the streets of the nation's capital (Marvel, 2008, pp. 274–275). When Lincoln reinstated the general in September, his soldiers cheered and spread the word that "Little Mac" was back (White, 2008, p. 508). Historian William Marvel notes that most Union soldiers sympathized with McClellan's conservative politics, as well as his more methodical approach to waging war (Marvel, 2008, p. xii).

When Lincoln finally sacked McClellan, the president suffered from criticism not just from McClellan's loyal soldiers but also from the public. By 1863, a demoralized public saw Lincoln's decision to remove McClellan as a cause of the Union's many military defeats (Marvel, 2008, p. 335).

McClellan's popularity helped Lincoln sway public opinion toward supporting the war, but the general's military ineptitude eventually forced Lincoln to make a decision that was unpopular. Lincoln's focus solely on one of McClellan's strengths—his relationship with his soldiers—led to the ineffective decision to retain him in the job too long and at too great a cost. In this case, a rival was a liability, not an asset.

Lincoln's 1864 appointment of General Grant as general in chief of the Union Army was a much more effective choice, despite the general's reputation as a drinker.[7] Grant lacked the pompousness of McClellan, and he didn't complain about conditions or question Lincoln's direction. The two men shared political views as well, notably on the subject of emancipation. Finally, Grant was also from Illinois (Donald, 1995, p. 497).

The change in Union strategy with Grant led to other achievements, including Sheridan's successful campaign in Virginia's Shenandoah Valley in September 1864, General Sherman's effective and demoralizing campaign from Atlanta to Savannah in December 1864, and General Thomas's stunning victories in Tennessee in December 1864. It is noteworthy that each of these officers had records of both defeats and victories. The distinguishing characteristic of these "winners" over the "losers" is that they regrouped after a loss and pursued the armies of the enemy even after losing initial battles. Lincoln sought just that kind of general over those who did not understand that offensive attacks against the armies of the Confederacy involved calculated risks, and that these calculated risks involved the real possibility of failure. But there was no other way to bring the war to a successful conclusion.

Grant's performance in various positions in the Union Army, including his tenure as general in chief, illustrates very important dimensions of effectiveness. Effectiveness is not a "batting average," the number of successes over the number of attempts. Rather, effectiveness is a "slugging average," actual contribution to the mission of the organization over potential contribution. As Drucker stated:

Performance is not hitting the bulls-eye with every shot—that is a circus act that can be maintained only over a few minutes. Performance is rather the consistent ability to produce results over prolonged periods of time and in a variety of assignments. A performance record must include mistakes. It must include failures. It must reveal a man's strengths. (Drucker, 1973/1974 p. 456)

Lincoln was well aware of Grant's failures, but the president saw in Grant the strengths to persevere and, eventually, to succeed. Viewed through an accurate lens of effectiveness, Grant and Lincoln were very much alike. Both succeeded in their missions while suffering numerous failures along the way. Both were very effective leaders.

Integrity

As stated at the beginning of this chapter, effective leaders begin by establishing purpose or mission—"the trumpet that sounds a clear sound." They then accept leadership as responsibility for the mission. Finally, they earn trust. Trust is earned when leaders are true to their word and take responsibility for their mission. Trust is a belief in the integrity of the leader.

Peter Drucker considered *integrity of character* to be the very essence of good leadership. Here is the way Drucker states the importance of integrity of character:

INTEGRITY, THE TOUCHSTONE
The final proof of the sincerity and seriousness of an organization's management is uncompromising emphasis on integrity of character. . . . For it is through character that leadership is exercised; it is character that sets the example and is imitated. Character is not something managers can acquire; if they do not bring it to the job, they will never have it. It is

not something one can fool people about. A person's coworkers, especially the subordinates, know in a few weeks whether he or she has integrity or not. They may forgive a great deal: incompetence, ignorance, insecurity, or bad manners. But they will not forgive a lack of integrity. Nor will they forgive higher management for choosing such a person. . . .

This is particularly true of the people at the head of an enterprise. For the spirit of an organization is created from the top. If an organization is great in spirit, it is because the spirit of its top people is great. If it decays, it does so because the top rots; as the proverb has it, "Fish rot from the head down." No one should ever be appointed to a senior position unless top management is willing to have his or her character serve as the model for subordinates. (Drucker, 2008, pp. 287–288)

Unlike other characteristics of effectiveness, such as focus on contribution and strengths, and effective decision making, *integrity* is an internal quality and not an external executive skill. One cannot be trained in integrity in the classroom; a person either has *integrity* or does not. Drucker held this belief, but in one of his very last interviews he considered the possibility that an executive may be *mentored* in *integrity*.

We have talked a lot about executive development. We have been mostly talking about developing people's strength and giving them experiences. Character is not developed that way. That is developed inside and not outside. I think churches and synagogues and the 12-step recovery programs are the main development agents of character today. (Karlgaard, 2004, p. 1)

Mentoring in integrity is a much longer and more uncertain process than developing executive skills. A 12-step program similar to that used by Alcoholics Anonymous requires acknowledgment of the need for help, assistance of a higher power, and accountability to a group or to an executive who possesses integrity of character and who is willing to shoulder the responsibility of the process (Alcoholics Anonymous, 1976).

Let's consider the constituent parts of integrity of character. Henry Cloud, a well-known clinical psychologist, has mentored people in integrity, and he has described the attributes that must be acquired. He links integrity to our ability to make our strengths productive and to become effective leaders:

> If we do not have integrity of character, wholeness of character functioning in ways that we will describe it, *then our ability to capitalize on our strengths will be severely affected.* (Cloud, 2006, p. 33)

Cloud delineates six character traits that integrate to create integrity. None of us has all these traits neatly woven into our personalities, but we do see many of them present in the life and work of Abraham Lincoln. These are the six traits:

1. The ability to connect authentically (which leads to trust)
2. The ability to be oriented toward the truth (which leads to finding and operating in reality)
3. The ability to work in a way that gets results and finishes well (which leads to reaching goals, profits, or the mission)
4. The ability to embrace, engage, and deal with the negative (which leads to ending problems, resolving them, or transforming them)
5. The ability to be oriented toward growth (which leads to increase)
6. The ability to be transcendent (which leads to enlargement of the bigger picture and oneself) (Cloud, 2006, p. 33)

Abraham Lincoln is an American icon of integrity and trust; he earned the moniker "Honest Abe" when he stood by his debts as a young store owner in Illinois. Later on, he stuck to his mission, which was to save the Union. He absolutely refused to compromise on the matter (unlike many members of his own party, who were willing to consider concessions to the southern states to dodge the threat of secession). He was willing to reevaluate his positions on slavery and emancipation, developing a more finely tuned sense of moral right and wrong on the subject as he matured. In the words of Eric Foner, "He changed as his society changed, but his own actions helped remake his world. He was a man of his time yet able to transcend it, probably as good a definition of greatness as any" (Foner, 2008, p. 14).

Lincoln's reputation for greatness of virtue (only enhanced by his assassination and subsequent martyrdom) began not long after his death. Ida M. Tarbell's glowing biography, *The Life of Abraham Lincoln*, was published in 1900, and by 1909, Lincoln had replaced Washington as the greatest American in public perception (Guelzo, 2009, p. 400). His mythological status was not confined to the United States. Latin American countries in the late nineteenth century saw Lincoln as the symbol of broader republican values, not just American ones (Miller et al., "Interchange: The Global Lincoln," 2009, p. 479). In a 1908 documented conversation in the North Caucasus, Leo Tolstoy, one of the most renowned writers of his time, shared stories of history's great leaders with an inquisitive tribal chief and his associates. After Tolstoy described several great leaders, he was surprised when the chief asked him to tell him about Abraham Lincoln. How did he know of Lincoln in this far-off land? As Tolstoy observed:

This little incident proves how largely the name of Lincoln is worshipped throughout the world and how legendary his personality has become. Now, why was Lincoln so great that he overshadows all other national heroes? He really was not a great general like Napoleon or Washington; he was not a skilful statesman like Gladstone or Frederick the Great; but his supremacy expresses itself altogether in his peculiar *moral power and in the greatness of his character* [emphasis ours]. (Tolstoy, 1909, p. 389)

Tolstoy attributed Lincoln's greatness and worldwide renown to his moral attributes and character.

Yet Lincoln is no simple model of integrity, as evidenced by the range of historical interpretations of his values, particularly with respect to human rights. Some scholars, such as William Lee Miller (Miller, 2002) and Richard Striner (Striner, 2006), argue that Lincoln consistently opposed slavery on moral grounds, and posit that his more racist remarks were the necessity of political expedience. Others, such as George M. Frederickson (Frederickson, 2008) and William E. Gienapp (Gienapp, 2002), counter that Lincoln never placed the same importance on emancipation as he did on his ultimate mission: the salvation of the Union. Dorothy Ross has made an interesting case for Lincoln's belief in the nation as a moral force, and emancipation as merely one tactic for accomplishing his ultimate goal of redeeming the Union: "Lincoln surely welcomed the opportunity to strike a blow at the institution of slavery when 'necessity' promised. But keeping the nation intact had always been his paramount moral concern, toward which freeing the slaves at any time might, or might not, contribute" (Ross, 2009, pp. 395–396). The Lincoln of today's scholarship is thus not simply the man who "saved the Union" or "freed the slaves," but a complex individual whose motivations remain elusive to the modern interpreter. In the words of David W. Blight:

Despite all the efforts to pin Lincoln down ideologically, psychologically, religiously, legally, linguistically, sexually, and morally, the Lincoln of change, growth, and contradiction (even a self-described malleability) makes possible his endurance as symbol and as scholarly subject. And despite the considerable labors of devotees of the political theorist Leo Strauss, who crave a principled and consistent Lincoln to advance conservative agendas, his power over us derives from his splendid inconsistency. Certainly this is what has made Lincoln so useful to opposite ends of the political spectrum. (Blight, 2008, p. 273)

In spite of this difficulty, we can use Cloud's six components of integrity as one way of assessing Lincoln's integrity as a leader.

Authentic Connections with Others

Lincoln connected authentically with his cabinet, military officers, soldiers, political rivals, and the people of the United States. There is consensus that he was a highly approachable, likable man who, while conscious of his appearance and demeanor, was genuine in his dealings with others. Lincoln took great pains to remain connected to the American public in spite of his lofty title. In fact, his willingness to engage with the everyday citizen at times frustrated his own advisors. William Seward complained that "there never was a man so accessible to all sorts of proper and improper persons" (Carwardine, 2008, p. 197). Lincoln refused to deny anyone access, calling his open public receptions "public-opinion baths." Because of his willingness and ability to engage with the average American, Lincoln was viewed "more as a neighbor to be dropped in upon than as a remote head of state" (Carwardine, 2008, p. 197).

As a lawyer, Lincoln was well known for his ability to remember names, his love of storytelling as a means of relating to people, and his empathy with the concerns of everyday citizens. Although he certainly capitalized on the "railsplitter" persona during his political campaigns, the image was based on a very real ability to connect with people. Lincoln's rather awkward, gangly physical appearance only served his cause; unlike the dashing McClellan, Lincoln looked out of place on horseback, and he often wore ill-fitting pants and jackets. His folksy image may have been politically expedient, but, as historian Richard Carwardine states, "this did not mean that there was anything contrived about his interest in the common folk" (Carwardine, 2008, p. 50). Lincoln's empathy was genuine. He met regularly with Union soldiers, visiting them in the hospital, in the field, and in private sessions in Washington. Importantly, these soldiers believed that their president had their interests at heart. Lincoln made a number of efforts to improve the conditions of Union troops; in 1864, he changed the sentence for desertion from execution to imprisonment for the duration of the war. Lincoln's authentic connection with his advisors, as well as with the soldiers fighting the war and the American public, allowed him to weather the changing political climate in a remarkably difficult chapter in American history.

Orientation toward Truth

Historians agree that Lincoln made decisions in a careful manner, analyzing and considering various opinions and evidence. As we have seen, certainly by the Kansas-Nebraska Act in 1854, he clearly wrestled with the moral questions involved with slavery, attempting to arrive at some resolution in his own mind. In two notes he wrote, Lincoln mulled over various arguments in support of slavery, testing their veracity. In one of these notes, he commented that "although volume upon volume is written to prove slavery a good thing, we never hear of the man who wishes to take the good of it by being a slave himself" (Lincoln, 1854, in Basler, p. 222).

As he gradually developed his position on emancipation, Lincoln sought to align himself with what he saw were true moral principles, particularly the principle of equality as ideally set forth in the Declaration of Independence. Lincoln's obsession with weighing alternatives, considering conflicting viewpoints and opinions, and wrestling with the larger moral questions behind the Civil War point to his desire to make the right decision, not just the most expedient one.

Achievement of Results

Ultimately, Lincoln achieved his primary mission of preserving the Union, and he also settled the question of slavery through the resolution of the war. As we have seen thus far in this section on Lincoln's leadership, he oriented his presidency toward accomplishing objectives as he defined and refined them. In selecting his cabinet members and in calculating the timing of the Emancipation Proclamation, Lincoln showed his astute political sensitivity, a gift that helped ensure that his goals were accomplished with relatively broad support. By learning from his mistakes in selecting generals, Lincoln finally found the right officers to conduct the war according to his objectives and strategies. His change in military leadership, as well as his growth in knowledge and expertise in military strategy, turned the direction of the war in favor of the Union forces. In large part because he kept his goals few and focused, Lincoln achieved remarkable success, even though that success involved flexibility and recognition of the limits of power. As James McPherson remarks, "He enunciated a clear national policy, and through trial and error evolved national and military strategies to achieve it. The nation did not perish from the earth but experienced a new birth of freedom" (McPherson, 2008, p. 36).

Ability to Deal with Negative Events

Some scholars have speculated that Lincoln's early life prepared him to deal with the trials of secession and war. Abraham Lincoln experienced grief at a very early age. He was nine years old when he experienced a string of deaths of his loved ones. His mother died. He had previously lost his baby brother who died in infancy. Then, when he was 19, his older sister died giving birth. To add to his sorrow his fiancée, Anne Rutledge, died in 1835 shortly before they were to marry.

This series of losses had a profound effect upon Lincoln. Doris Kearns Goodwin argues that "Lincoln's early intimacy with tragic loss reinforced a melancholy temperament. Yet his familiarity with pain and disappointment imbued him with strength and under-standing of human frailty. . . . Moreover, Lincoln possessed a life-affirming humor and a profound resilience that lightened his despair and fortified his will" (Goodwin, 2005, p. 49). Goodwin uses the writings of Leo Tolstoy to bolster this claim. In his book *Childhood, Boyhood and Youth*, Tolstoy discussed the relationship between the potential ability of a person to love and his or her ability to heal from the events brought on by devastating personal tragedies:

> Only those who can love strongly can experience an over-whelming grief. Yet their very need of loving sometimes serves to throw off their grief from them and to save them. The moral nature of man is more tenacious of life than the physi-cal, and grief never kills. (Tolstoy, 1852/1991, pp. 87–88)

Tolstoy provides a plausible explanation of Lincoln's ability to overcome numerous tragedies. Another likely source of Lincoln's capacity to deal with negative events was his fatalism, a trait that Lincoln ascribed to himself and that was confirmed by his contem-poraries. He believed that there was very little human agency in affairs, that events were controlled by "Divine Providence," or the will of God. This particular theology allowed him to view traumatic events as inevitable rather than the cause of human actions. Such a belief system was especially helpful in Lincoln's ability to cope with the growing casualties of the war, as the conflict stretched out longer than any had anticipated. In his second inaugural address, Lincoln places the cause of the conflict on human affairs (slavery), but the punishment (the casualties and duration of the war) are God's doing: "The Almighty has His own purposes." As Donald summarizes, "Again and again he reverted to the idea that behind all the struggles and losses of the war a Divine purpose was at work" (Donald, 1995, p. 514). Lincoln's theology thus allowed him to deflect the blame for the horrors of war, as well as other events, from human actions to the mysterious, unknowable actions of an intervening God.

Orientation toward Growth

Lincoln's orientation toward growth is evidenced by his early self-education, as well as his continuous personal and professional growth while serving as president. The image of a barefoot Lincoln reading while propped against a tree is a popular image in his iconography, and there is sufficient historical evidence to support this characterization. A member of the post-revolutionary generation who firmly believed in the concept of the "self-made man," Lincoln valued education as a path to achieving success in America; he pursued book learning well beyond that typical for his peers. As a law student, Lincoln continued this tendency, reading and paraphrasing standard law texts until he mastered them (Donald, 1995, pp. 54–55).

Lincoln's emphasis on personal growth continued during his presidency, as we have seen. He realized his own inexperience as a chief executive, and surrounded himself with the most experienced men in his cabinet, even though several of those advisors were his political rivals. As he gained more confidence, Lincoln relied less on his "team of rivals," selecting a second-term cabinet made up of those who were not only competent but also loyal to Lincoln personally. As commander in chief, Lincoln took on a remarkably active role, educating himself in military strategy and tactics through the same methods of book learning he employed as a youth and as a law student. While Lincoln's self-education and involvement in the conduct of the war irked many of his generals, he did, it seems, grow into the role remarkably well. On one occasion when McClellan had failed yet again to act, Lincoln developed his own plan to capture Norfolk, Virginia. The May 9, 1862, offensive, devised and directed by Lincoln himself, was successful. Salmon Chase informed his daughter, "So has ended a brilliant week's campaign of the President; for I think it quite certain that if he had not come down, Norfolk would still have been in possession of the enemy" (White, 2009, p. 485).

Lincoln grew ethically, too, as he wrestled with the question of slavery through his career. Initially, he sought merely to end its spread through the nation. However, by 1854, as we have noted, there was a marked tone of moral outrage over the matter in his speeches. Finally, as president, Lincoln began to see the complete eradication of slavery as the only hope for saving the Union. His own personal growth led directly to a shift in the definition of the war's purpose, from merely saving the Union to saving the Union through emancipation:

> The story of the evolving purposes of the Union's war is also the story of Lincoln's personal development. Those who withstood unmoved the buffeting of war were rare indeed. Inevitably, Lincoln's private understanding of his moral obligations, and of the meaning of the conflict itself, evolved under the grueling burden of leadership, the wider suffering of wartime, and personal grief. Unfathomable as the private Lincoln has to remain, there is every sign that his understanding of providential intervention both shaped the thinking by which he reached the most profound of his decisions, for emancipation, and—even more powerfully—steeled his nerve to stand by the implications of that decision once made. (Carwardine, 2006, p. 193)

Achievement of Transcendence

Cloud's concept of transcendence involves leaders who recognize that they are but a small part of a larger picture. Leaders who achieve transcendence comprehend that they are a piece of a larger puzzle, not the center of the universe or their organizations. Lincoln not only recognized his own limitations as a chief executive, he also clearly saw himself as beholden to higher principles not of his own making. His moral aversion to slavery was a direct consequence of his reverence for the principles embodied in the Declaration of Independence, a document he viewed "as a near-sacred statement of universal principles, one consistent with his belief in a God who had created all men equal and pursued his relations with humankind on the principles of justice" (Carwardine, 2006, p. 229). Founded by this near-sacred document, the Union itself transcended any single human being's importance, and thus had to be preserved at all costs, in Lincoln's eyes. Finally, Lincoln's belief in divine providence, his fatalistic outlook, informed his view of human events; guided by the mysterious hand of God, human affairs, including the Civil War, could ultimately never be decided by mere mortals. Lincoln's theology, as well as his reverence for the ideals behind the United States, reinforced his own humility, leading him to achieve Cloud's trait of transcendence in leadership.

Crisis Management

Drucker identified that strong leaders have the ability to either avert crises or weather them. He also stated that, in times of crisis, effective executives must know how to make effective decisions. Effective decisions are not made by acclamation—they are made by considering alternatives. Observed Drucker: "They are made well only if based on the clash of conflicting views, the dialogue between different points of view, the choice between different judgments. The first rule in decision making is that one does not make a decision unless there is disagreement" (Drucker, 1967, p. 148).

A Case Example of Lincoln's Effectiveness as Decision Maker: Fort Sumter

Lincoln was confronted with his first major decision as president and commander in chief the day after his inauguration. Major Robert Anderson notified the president that only a few weeks of supplies remained at the federal garrison at Fort Sumter. The Union soldiers guarding the fort would have to surrender to the Confederate forces unless they were provided with provisions quickly.

The new president, by all accounts, had a difficult time just dealing with the everyday requirements of the job, much less this onerous threat. Lincoln insisted on personally meeting with every individual desiring a position with his administration (and there were many), and he made multiple errors in procedure, which hindered the smooth conduct of daily business. Overwhelmed by the demands of the position early in his tenure, Lincoln relied heavily on his cabinet for advice regarding what to do about Fort Sumter.

Lincoln could have simply attempted to provide the supplies requested by Anderson and refortify the fort, or he could have sent additional military personnel to thwart a potential attack on the fort by Confederate forces. The second alternative would have provided the appearance that Lincoln was ready to engage in an act of war. Finally, Lincoln could have decided to simply evacuate and surrender the fort to the Confederate Army, which would have appeared to be a recognition of the legitimacy of the Confederacy.

Lincoln solicited opinions from his top military and civilian advisors on the proper course of action to take. General Winfield Scott, Union general in chief, saw no other feasible alternative than to evacuate the fort. Montgomery Blair, postmaster general, and his politically influential father, Francis Blair, believed that evacuating and surrendering Fort Sumter would be the equivalent of surrendering the Union. Secretary of State William Seward was opposed to the fortification of Fort Sumter for fear that this would lead additional states to secede from the Union and start a civil war. Treasury Secretary Salmon Chase equivocated by favoring refortification of Fort Sumter so long as it did not lead to civil war. All other cabinet members, except Blair, thought that saving Fort Sumter would be a useless effort and a waste of men and money.

Lincoln mulled over these various opinions, guided by the intentions expressed in his inaugural address. In that speech, he stated that he would not surrender garrisons under Union control. However, he also said that he would not instigate a war with the Confederate forces. Thus, the Sumter situation posed quite a dilemma for Lincoln. If he gave up on fortifying the fort, he essentially surrendered that garrison. However, if the Union launched an all-out effort to provision Fort Sumter, the Confederacy would no doubt view such an act as one of aggression, and act accordingly. Lincoln decided to notify Jefferson Davis that he was going to resupply the fort but without sending in military reinforcements. Lincoln thus made the very risky decision to attempt to resupply Fort Sumter but without the use of force. This course of action was consistent with the conviction Lincoln expressed in his inaugural address not to use force against the South, but also not to yield Union territory.

As Richard Carwardine states, "In debating Lincoln's intentions within this framework for action, historians have spilled gallons more ink than the blood shed at the time of Sumter's fall" (Carwardine, 2003, p. 158). Did Lincoln intentionally draw the South into a war, forcing them to fire the first shot? Did he believe he would avoid conflict entirely? Did he honestly believe the plan to resupply the fort would work, in spite of the fact that there were, in fact, two resupply missions launched at the same time (Fort Sumter and Fort Pickens), managed by two separate divisions, and involving an overextension of military capabilities? We can never be sure; nor can we second-guess his decision, for "whether he would have [attempted to resupply Sumter] had he known the scale of the human suffering that would follow is as much an imponderable for the historian as the moral rightness or wrongness of the decision that he took" (Carwardine, 2003, p. 159).

Lincoln's leadership in the Sumter crisis was highly criticized at the time and has been criticized subsequently by historians. Many argued that Lincoln took too long to act, that he vacillated, that he was indecisive. However, others take note of the fact that his ultimate decision adhered to the goals set forth in his inaugural address. In this sense, Lincoln exhibited one quality of effective decision making: he went back to first principles in that he attempted to maintain the Union and to do so without the use of force. He attempted to resupply the fort and to maintain the sovereignty of the United States over its territories. Lincoln thus shifted the decision for peace or war to the Confederacy. By taking Fort Sumter by force, the South fired the first shot and was identified as starting the Civil War. The Confederacy therefore was seen to be the aggressor, which built popular political support for the war in the previously divided North.

Lincoln displayed a deep understanding of the wider consequences and complexities of the national policy to preserve the Union; the strategy to build support for the war, if it became necessary; and the use of military strategy as a means of national policy and strategy. Lincoln and his cabinet wrestled with the decision for a number of weeks. In the final analysis, it was a decision that took full account of the complexities and constraints involved. As an inexperienced chief executive, Lincoln confronted a dilemma with few good solutions. While his decision, in fact, began what would become an all-too-long and bloody conflict, we can, through management as a liberal art, begin to understand his decision-making process to a certain degree.

Servant Leadership

The last component of effective leadership identified by Drucker is succession planning, which leads directly to the idea of servant leadership and the importance of developing people within an organization. There is a strong emphasis on treating people with dignity, whether that emphasis derives from Judeo-Christian beliefs or other moral and religious foundations. Servant leadership involves an understanding of the value of every contribution regardless of status, and the pivotal role of helping others within an organization.

Lincoln's role as a servant leader is particularly apparent in his behavior toward his generals and the Union soldiers. Although he was unusually involved in military tactics (often by force of necessity), Lincoln preferred to give his officers the benefit of the doubt. As we saw in the case of McClellan, Lincoln's desire to uphold troop morale by maintaining popular generals at times cost him substantially in terms of war objectives. However, Lincoln clearly kept the soldiers' human dignity in the fore of his mind as he made key decisions, including the ones to promote and later reinstate McClellan.

We also saw how Lincoln's concern with troop welfare led to a number of specific actions on his part, such as eliminating the death penalty for desertion. Lincoln found positions within the administration for disabled veterans, and had a reputation among the soldiers for being sympathetic to their complaints about conditions or pay (Carwardine, 2008, pp. 284–285). While Lincoln certainly knew the value of high troop morale in fighting the war and maintaining positive public opinion, he may also have been motivated out of a sense of moral obligation.

In his interactions with even his ineffective officers, Lincoln treated subordinates with dignity and respect. Joseph Hooker, appointed to replace Burnside as commander of the Army of the Potomac in January 1863, had a checkered reputation. Although highly respected for his bravery in battle and his concern for his soldiers' well-being, he was also renowned for drinking and womanizing (the slang term for a prostitute derives from the women who hung around Hooker's camp). Hooker was also known for voicing his opinions, and he had criticized Burnside behind his back when serving under his command. Lincoln was well aware of Hooker's good and bad qualities; he knew that the man's "chief assets were that he was an independent and outspoken soldier" and that his "chief liabilities were the same two qualities" (White, 2009, p. 538). When Lincoln appointed Hooker, he told him directly of his concerns regarding the general's liabilities but that he was willing to trust him.

Hooker seemed to embody servant leadership, securing better food and updated hospitals for the soldiers. As he said, "My men shall be fed before I am fed, and before any of my officers are fed" (White, 2009, p. 544). Hooker's strong points came through, but unfortunately, so did his weak points. Like McClellan, he was slow to pursue the Confederate enemy, preferring to see cities as targets rather than the Southern army itself. Overconfidence to the point of hubris resulted in Hooker's downfall. Armed with 70,000 soldiers and grand plans for a victory, Hooker suffered a crushing defeat at the Battle of Chancellorsville in May 1863. Instead of launching an offensive against Lee's force of 25,000, Hooker took up a defensive position, leaving his soldiers open to Confederate attack. Hooker was injured, and for a time, his troops were in disarray without leadership. The Union army was forced to retreat.

Rather than deal with the bad news from afar, Lincoln met Hooker at his headquarters. Although distraught by the loss, Lincoln expressed his concern for Hooker's injury, and he noted that this may have played a part in the defeat. Supportive in spite of the turn of events, Lincoln attempted to give Hooker the freedom to conduct military strategy, yet he let the general know that he would assist him, if needed. Yet Hooker could not muster a feasible plan, and Lee's army began to move into Maryland and Pennsylvania by June. Lincoln shortly thereafter removed Hooker from his position, replacing him with George Meade.

While Hooker was incapable of formulating a meaningful strategy to pursue the Confederate Army,[8] he did improve the morale and conditions of the Army of the Potomac, something Lincoln believed the general could do well. In this respect, Lincoln's servant leadership served him well; he and Hooker both saw the dignity and human needs of the troops. However, Lincoln's attitude of service toward his general in the field may have done him a disservice. As Donald notes, Lincoln expressed his "wishes as suggestions, rather than commands," and deferred to his military men, not wishing them to see him as interfering in their area of expertise (Donald, 1995, p. 439). By giving Hooker ample room to develop as a military commander, by giving him the benefit of the doubt after Chancellorsville, and by putting aside rumors of his unseemly behavior, Lincoln practiced servant leadership, treating Hooker as a unique human being with potential. Unfortunately, not every person will thrive under servant leadership, and part of that model of leadership may require the "tough love" of recognizing that the individual is ill-suited to a particular position or organization.

CONCLUSION

Management theorists have attempted to discern the elements of good leadership for decades. Peter Drucker's model of effective leadership involves not only a list of character traits or habits but also the cultivation of an attitude that leads to certain behaviors. Drucker's model requires that one view leadership from a holistic perspective, seeing the relationship between the leader and followers, the leader and the mission, the leader and the organization, and the leader and his or her own values. Viewed in such a way, leadership is part of management as a liberal art, emphasizing the development of human beings and their relationships with one another.

One way to begin to understand one's own leadership strengths and weaknesses is to study leaders in the past and present. History offers many such figures, including political leaders such as Abraham Lincoln. Students from all disciplines of management and the liberal arts can benefit by a close study of this man, his life, and his work. Lincoln's life and career are illustrative of Drucker's model of leadership; by surveying the extensive secondary literature on Lincoln, one can begin to see the challenges involved with truly implementing

Drucker's vision, as well as how leadership functions in real-world situations. By incorporating the work of historians into management theories of leadership, we begin to get a sense as to the complexities behind putting the ideals of effective leadership into practice.

Although lionized in popular imagination, Lincoln was not a perfect leader. Like all human beings, he developed as he aged, maturing into his various roles in life.

Most biographies of Lincoln end with some reference to Stanton's eloquent comment after Lincoln's death: "Now he belongs to the ages." Larger than life in the eyes of most Americans, Lincoln nevertheless remains a very human—and thus very useful—model of leadership.

CHAPTER 7

———— ❖ ————

SOCIAL ECOLOGY AND THE PRACTICE
OF MANAGEMENT AS A LIBERAL ART

When asked, "How would you classify yourself?" Peter Drucker replied, "I am a social ecologist" (Drucker, 1992b, p. 57). Human ecology is defined by Merriam-Webster.com as "a branch of sociology dealing especially with the spatial and temporal inter-relationships between humans and their economic, social, and political organization" (Merriam-Webster.com, n.d.). Human ecology, Drucker's primary concern, is in contrast to natural or scientific ecology, which is defined as "a branch of science concerned with the interrelationship of organisms and their environments." According to Drucker, "Social ecology is a discipline. It has not only its own subject matter but also its own work. But it is easier to say what the work is not than to specify what it actually consists of" (Drucker, 1992b, p. 61).

While this definition is vague, Drucker indicated that the discipline of social ecology should focus on its findings or results: "Social ecology as a discipline also deals with action" (Drucker, 1992b, p. 64). Although social ecology involves analyzing human relationships and institutions, Drucker's version of the discipline emphasizes the implications of those relationships. As a result, his methodology involves a highly pragmatic approach focused on actions rather than on theory. Drucker applied the practices of management and entrepreneurship to specifically address the challenges he saw as by-products of changing relationships between people and society.

Drucker's idea of social ecology was influenced by intellectual concepts. His methodology was informed by all the disciplines discussed thus far in the book. In addition, Drucker's practice was colored by specific methodological practices of other prominent social ecologists, as well as the works of prominent practitioners of management. He specifically identified eight "leading practioners" of social ecology; "The discipline itself boasts old and distinguished lineage. Its greatest document is Alexis de Tocqueville's *Democracy in America*. I count among its leading practioners another Frenchman, Bertrand de Jouvenel, two Germans, Ferdinand Toennies and Georg Simmel, and three Americans, Henry Adams, John R. Commons (whose "Institutional Economics" was not too different from what I call Social Ecology) and, above all, Thorstein Veblen. But none of these is as close to me in temperament, concepts and approach as a mid-Victorian Englishman: Walter Bagehot" (Drucker, 1992b, p. 57).

This chapter considers the influences on Drucker's methodology of these eight practioners of social ecology, as well as the impact of the work of his close friend Karl Polanyi. We also discuss seven key management practitioners whose ideas shaped Drucker's practice of social ecology. Following the evaluation of the historical and contemporary influences, we analyze Drucker's particular method of social ecology, and provide three examples of his methodology in action.

METHODOLOGICAL AND SOCIAL INFLUENCERS

The nine influencers mentioned previously modeled social ecology for Drucker. Their primary role was to serve as examples of people who observed their respective societies (or, in some cases, specific institutions that comprised their societies), and they noted developing trends, potential threats or challenges, and new approaches to emerging conditions. Working in such diverse fields as sociology, economics, and history, these nine individuals all showed Drucker the observational techniques involved in social ecology: the process of analyzing relationships between human beings and various institutions of society.

Alexis de Tocqueville (1805–1859)

Alexis de Tocqueville is probably the best-known foreign observer of American culture. Although he was born into the French aristocracy after the French Revolution, he was well aware of its impact; Tocqueville's father was sympathetic to the revolution's cause, but, as a government official, he was imprisoned briefly during the Reign of Terror. Alexis de Tocqueville's France also experienced political change; the revolution of 1830 overthrew King Charles X and installed Louis-Philippe, whose reign was characterized by a combination of liberal reforms, a powerful ruling middle class, and an increasingly unhappy lower class. As a member of the aristocracy, Tocqueville understood that his class's power was waning in French society, and he wanted to study the form of government that he felt would likely replace his country's monarchy: democracy. What better place to study democracy than America, which practiced its most pervasive form?

Tocqueville traveled to America in 1830, ostensibly to study its new penitentiary system to help France reform its own prisons. The by-product of his 10-month visit was a two-volume work, *Democracy in America* (Tocqueville, 1835/1840/2003), which contained Tocqueville's detailed observations of American politics, culture, and society. Drucker referred to Tocqueville's *Democracy in America* as social ecology's "greatest document" (Drucker, 1992b, p. 57). As a work of social ecology, *Democracy in America* may have served as a model for Drucker's own work. Tocqueville's analysis of how democracy impacted American culture, attitudes, and behavior certainly influenced Drucker's model of a functioning society. Specifically, Tocqueville's assessment of America's love of equality, and how that obsession potentially threatened the health of the country's democracy, seems to have informed Drucker's concept of a modern society of knowledge workers.

In *Democracy in America*, Tocqueville characterized the nature of American democracy in order to educate the French not just about America but also about the direction French society and government was likely to head. One of the most crucial observations Tocqueville made about Americans was that they valued equality more than liberty; he noted that they would tolerate slavery and other conditions that nineteenth-century Europeans would find unacceptable as long as there was what Tocqueville described as "equality of conditions," which we would define as equality of opportunity:

> I think that democratic communities have a natural taste for freedom; left to themselves, they will seek it, cherish it, and view any privation of it with regret. But for equality their passion is ardent, insatiable, incessant, invincible; they call for equality in freedom; and if they cannot obtain that, they still call for equality in slavery. They will endure poverty, servitude, barbarism, but they will not endure aristocracy. (Tocqueville, 1835/1840/1993, p. 97)

In Tocqueville's France, one's family background mattered; Tocqueville's own aristocratic heritage ensured his position in government service, for example. In contrast, American society placed no value on one's family lineage; instead, nineteenth-century Americans believed in the concept of the "self-made man" who adhered to middle-class values of hard work and restraint in order to succeed in the expanding nation.

While Tocqueville admired some aspects of America's idea of equality of conditions, he feared the end results he foresaw. Because human beings inherently desire to be seen as individuals, Tocqueville argued that Americans strove to single themselves out despite their love of equality. In American society, material success was the most obvious way of signaling individualism; thus, Tocqueville said, Americans were a highly materialistic bunch obsessed with individual success. The upshot of this for Tocqueville was that this glorification of money led to a gradual withdrawal from society, as people chose to spend time with others like them in mindset. Eventually, Tocqueville observed, Americans would become so consumed with pursuing material goods that they would stop participating in the democratic process; without lively debate in the community, democracy would cease to work as a system:

> The reproach I address to the principle of equality is not that it leads men away in the pursuit of forbidden enjoyments, but that it absorbs them wholly in quest of those which are allowed. By these means a kind of virtuous materialism may ultimately be established in the world, which would not corrupt, but enervate, the soul and noiselessly unbend its springs of action. (Tocqueville, 1835/1840/1993, p. 133)

Thus Tocqueville feared that equality of conditions contained the very seeds of democracy's destruction. The more people sought equality, the more they would seek ways of differentiating themselves, pulling people farther and farther apart. The more people pursued their individual materialistic desires, the less they would involve themselves in matters of governance. A healthy democracy, Tocqueville pleaded, required the active participation of all citizens.

If Americans withdrew from the democratic process, they subjected themselves to tyranny and despotism.

Drucker embraced Tocqueville's idea of "equality of conditions," noting that "the central difference between America and Europe may well be in the *meaning* rather than the *extent* of social mobility. When the boss's son is made a vice president in this country the publicity release is likely to stress that his first job was pushing a broom. But when a former broom pusher, born in the Glasgow slums, gets to be managing director in a British company the official announcement is likely to hint gently at descent from Robert Bruce" (Drucker, 1952, p. 76). Drucker's entire idea of a knowledge society rests on the reality of equality of conditions; a functioning society of knowledge workers must be "open-ended. . . . Indeed it is a society that demands equality of opportunity" (Drucker, 1959, p. 104).

As European observers of America, Tocqueville and Drucker applauded the unique aspects of American democratic society. Both social ecologists observed the impacts of egalitarian sentiments on American politics and culture in times of great change.

Walter Bagehot (1826–1877)

Drucker compared his practice of social ecology to that of several other men, but he claimed that "none of these men is as close to me in temperament, concepts, and approach as the mid-Victorian Englishman Walter Bagehot. Living, (as I have) in an age of great social change, Bagehot first saw the emergence of new institutions" (Drucker, 1992, p. 57). Bagehot was an aspiring British politician who became the editor and director of *The Economist*. He studied law and worked in journalism and banking, serving as a government advisor while in the financial services industry.

Just as Tocqueville before him, Bagehot believed that America's emphasis on equality was destroying the country's pluralism. Assessing the state of America during the Civil War, Bagehot warned that "the masses are everywhere omnipotent; and the masses in most part are only half educated, and in many parts are as ignorant as those of Europe and far more ruffianly." The emphasis on a sovereign American people, in Bagehot's eyes, had resulted in what Madison termed the tyranny of the majority. And, given this state of affairs, Bagehot bemoaned the future of an American political system governed by the people: "How can men who are where they are because they have truckled and temporized and cajoled and cringed and fawned upon the mob, now coerce that mob to do its duty, or overawe it into obedience and order?" (Brogan, 1977, p. 339).

Although Drucker's words are less strident, he, too, worried about the unchecked power of direct democracy. Drucker wondered, "Is such a theory of majority rule compatible with a free government and a free society? The answer is undoubtedly: No. The majority principle as it is commonly accepted today is a despotic and tyrannical, and unfree principle. . . . The mistaken identification of unlimited majority rule and free government is at the bottom of a great many of the troubles which beset our society today" (Drucker, 1942, p. 487). Bagehot's nineteenth-century world seems utterly far removed from Drucker's twentieth-century environment. Yet, as Drucker noted, the two men shared "temperament, concepts, and approach" driven by their respective times.

Thorstein Veblen (1858–1929)

Thorstein Veblen was born in Wisconsin to Norwegian immigrants He is best known for his 1899 work *The Theory of the Leisure Class*, in which he coined the term "conspicuous consumption" (Dorfman, 1934).

Drucker claimed that, "above all," Veblen was the leading practitioner of social ecology (Drucker, 1992, p. 57). One reason Veblen appealed to Drucker was likely Veblen's methodology, which involved incorporating multiple disciplines, as well as revising traditional methods of inquiry. Although Drucker disagreed with some of Veblen's conclusions (notably Veblen's analysis in *The Engineers and the Price System*), he praised him as the sole sociologist or anthropologist to view technology as important (Drucker, 1992, p. 57). Veblen thus modeled cross-disciplinary analysis as vital to social ecology.

Veblen's economic analysis incorporates a wide variety of other disciplines and fields, notably anthropology, history, and the practice of business. In the words of one scholar, "He thought economics could embrace all these territories in which he was himself keenly interested" (Riesman, 1953, p. 162). Veblen was writing when the canons of "natural law" and social Darwinism were routinely invoked to justify America's Gilded Age. Laissez-faire language of the laws of competition, supply and demand, and free markets ruled the day, and the success of corporate tycoons such as Andrew Carnegie and John D. Rockefeller pointed to the role of Darwin's evolutionary theory at work in society: the "fittest" members were clearly surviving.

In this environment, Veblen turned his social ecologist's eye toward America's burgeoning capitalists in two key works: *The Theory of Business Enterprise* (1904) and *The Theory of the Leisure Class* (1899). In *The Theory of Business Enterprise*, Veblen took aim at the disruptions caused by industrial capitalism, using economic, cultural, and historic tools of analysis. In the better-known *The Theory of the Leisure Class*, he employed anthropological arguments to show that the hallmarks of the "leisure class," including "conspicuous consumption," have origins in earlier societies. He also pointed out the role of culture in reinforcing materialistic practices: "There grows up a code of accredited canons of consumption, the effect of which is to hold the consumer up to a standard of expensiveness and wastefulness in his consumption of goods and in his employment of time and effort" (Veblen, 1899, pp. 89–90). Veblen used as evidence of such consumption such varied things as manicured lawns, pagan shrines, Angora cats, Hawaiian feather mantles, and foot binding. By tracing tendencies of American's Gilded Age culture back to "barbarian and savage state" societies, Veblen constructed an analysis of the human condition, not just of one particular society.

Drucker, too, used a wide range of disciplines and examples in his work. For example, drawing upon his understanding of history, government, and economics, Drucker knew that the twin policies of glasnost and perestroika—or freedom of speech and economic restructuring, respectively—would not rescue the economy of the Soviet Union and prevent it from collapse. In Chapter 4 of his book *The New Realties* (Drucker, 1989) Drucker predicted the demise of the Russian Empire ("When the Russian Empire Is Gone?"), which did indeed occur at the end of 1991. How did Drucker know that the Soviet Union was doomed? He knew from his knowledge of history that it was very difficult to hold together by economic cooperation alone a diverse group of ethic nationalities, such as those that made up the Soviet Union.

Bertrand de Jouvenel (1903–1987)

Drucker included Bertrand de Jouvenel in his list of social ecology practitioners (Drucker, 1992, p. 57). Jouvenel was born a few years before Drucker, and he grew up in a similar intellectual environment. Jouvenel studied law and mathematics at the Sorbonne in Paris. He published extensively on international relations, documenting the rise of totalitarian governments in Italy and Germany. After World War II, Jouvenel left his career in journalism to focus on political theory (Anderson, 2001).

In his political works, Jouvenal, like Drucker, drew on the future to argue his points. Jouvenel is a fascinating example of a social ecologist who used futurist material to evaluate the present, a technique also found in Drucker's writings.

In 1967, Jouvenel published *The Art of Conjecture*, a work in which he explored the then-budding field of future studies. Jouvenel famously stated that the future consisted of a fan of possibilities

(Jouvenel, 1967). While he vehemently argued against the possibility of predicting the future, he believed that human intuition and intellect could be used to anticipate larger trends, which can help guide political and social policy. Jouvenel stated that future studies would aid in preventing knee-jerk decisions in the public realm, when conditions have reached a point where society has no choice but to make a decision:

> It seems natural and even reasonable in such a case to take the questions in order of urgency—but the results show that this is a vicious practice. No problem is put on the agenda until it is a "burning" issue, when things are at such a pass that our hand is forced. . . . The means of avoiding this lies in acquainting oneself with emerging situations while they can still be molded, before they have become imperatively compelling. In other words, without forecasting, there is effectively no freedom of decision. (Jouvenel, 1967)

Jouvenel linked forecasting the future with individual liberty; the more choices of action remained, the more freedoms would be preserved. Drucker, too, was very much concerned with forecasting, not predicting. In most of his books and articles on society, he sketched long-term trends for the future, such as the rise of the knowledge society, the increase in distance learning, and the growing importance of the large, pastoral churches in American society. Like Jouvenel, Drucker used forecasting to help buffer the impacts of change, particularly those affecting the worker. For example, in "The Next Society," written in 2001, Drucker warns of "a shrinking life expectancy for businesses and organizations of all kinds" (Drucker, 2003, p. 205). Social ecologists Jouvenel and Drucker both acknowledged the importance of anticipating future trends to maximizing human liberty and potential.

Henry Adams (1838–1913)

Drucker included the historian Henry Adams in his list of social ecologists. A child of privilege, Henry Brooks Adams counted two former U.S. presidents in his lineage: John Adams, his great grandfather, and John Quincy Adams, his grandfather. He graduated from Harvard and studied law at the University of Berlin. He taught history at Harvard for seven years, and published both academic and political material, including his massive *History of the United States, 1801 to 1817* and *The Education of Henry Adams.*[1]

Adams was a product of his time—the late nineteenth century. Well traveled and well read, he was a true intellectual in a time of enormous intellectual upheaval. All intellectuals were adrift in this period, but, as Henry Commager noted, "No American of his generation embarked more earnestly on the search for truth or labored more disinterestedly to rationalize history into a science" (Commager, 1950, p. 133).

It was this very quality of Adams's, this desire to bridge the world of his lineage with the world of his present and future, that links him to Drucker. Adams's observations of his changing, industrializing, chaotic world no doubt impacted Drucker's own efforts to rationalize the twentieth century's irrationality.

Adams, the historian of the nineteenth century, had, like others in his time, believed in the "unity of natural force" (Adams, 1906/2008, p. 222). In the new world of Einstein's relativity and technological innovation, what formerly had been fixed and understood was now impermanent and "drifting." Adams, too, noted the impact of industrialization and modernization on the American economy:

Once admitted that the machine must be efficient, society might dispute in what social interest it should be run, but in any case it must work concentration. Such great revolutions commonly leave some bitterness behind, but nothing in politics surprised Henry Adams more than the ease with which he and his silver friends slipped across the chasm, and alighted on the single gold standard and the capitalistic system with its methods; the protective tariff; the corporations and Trusts; the trades-unions and socialistic paternalism which necessarily made their complement; the whole mechanical consolidation of force, which ruthlessly stamped out the life of the class into which Adams was born, but created monopolies capable of controlling the new energies that America adored. (Adams, 1906/2008, pp. 269–270)

Although Adams's tone is more nostalgic than Drucker's, the two social ecologists recognized the dramatic changes their respective Americas were experiencing. A pessimist, Adams ultimately feared the revolution of mass production and technology, but he recognized that there was no going back. Drucker understood Adams's reaction, in part because he, too, worried about the negative impacts of industrial society, but also because he recognized the revolutionary nature of the new business enterprise of the late nineteenth century. It was understandable to Drucker that Adams would portray "the new economic power as itself corrupt and, in turn, as corrupting the political process, government, and society" (Drucker, 1993b, p. 156). Both men dealt with power and irrational forces, albeit in different ways.

Georg Simmel (1858–1918)

As did the other social ecologists that Drucker cited, Georg Simmel used unconventional methods of observing his environment and the people within it. He studied at the University of Berlin when a remarkable number of renowned scholars taught there. As a result,

Simmel had a broad education in history, philosophy, anthropology, psychology, the social sciences, and art from some of the world's finest professors (Frisby, 1992, pp. 23–25).

Simmel was working to define the discipline of sociology during a time of academic debate in Europe. During the late nineteenth century, scholars challenged prior assumptions that history and the social sciences could be understood using the same methods as the physical sciences. Those in the social sciences began to redefine their disciplines to include the irrational side of human behavior.

It was during this time that sociology as a field came into existence. The early founders of the discipline wrestled with how to define and describe human society, particularly the new modern society that they faced. Simmel's contribution was to view society as a series of interactions between individuals. He posed the vexing question, "How Is Society Possible?" (Frisby, p. 14). He focused on the nature of modern life itself; he described it as fragmented, disjointed, and consisting of fleeting experiences. More importantly, Simmel emphasizes the "inner world" of human existence: how people react to the nature of modernity itself. The experience of modern life results in a particular internal reaction, which, in turn influences human relationships and interactions. Emphasizing the transactional nature of the modern industrial economy, Simmel states that "the slot machine is the ultimate example of the mechanical character of the modern economy" (Frisby, 1992, pp. 64–73).

Drucker, too, concerned himself with the human element, including the interior life of people. He worried about the impacts of modernity, using at times the same language as Simmel (for example, Chapter 20 of Drucker's *The New Society* is called "Slot-Machine Man and Depression Shock"). Just as Simmel sought to capture the emotional experience of modern life, Drucker uses this term to describe the management-worker relationship as transaction oriented:

When management looks at the worker, it does not really see the worker but sees the caricature of the "slot-machine man" instead: a greedy, lazy, shiftless automaton interested only in the pay check. And when the worker looks at management, he too sees what the "slot-machine man" concept has conditioned him to see: a fat parasite in cutaway and striped trousers, clipping coupons. (Drucker, 1950, pp. 198–199)

Neither stereotype is true, according to Drucker; the point is that modern industrial society has altered people's interior experience and thus their interpersonal relations. Simmel and Drucker, commenting on their respective modern societies, note the role of psychology, aesthetics, or other factors in economic transactions.

Ferdinand Toennies (1855–1936)

Ferdinand Toennies is referred to as the founding father of sociology. Toennies's best known work is his 1887 book *Gemeinschaft und Gesellschaft* (*Community and Society*), which was the second book (other than Burke's *Reflections on the French Revolution*) that Drucker stated "permanently changed my life" when he was 18:

It was obvious even to a totally ignorant eighteen year old that the "organic" community which Toennies hoped to save with his book—the rural community of pre-industrial days— was gone for good beyond any hope of renewal. As my own work on community and society evolved over the next few years, my concepts of both became very different from Toennies' pre-industrial and indeed, pre-capitalist views with their roots in eighteenth-century German romanticism. But what I learned from Toennies—and never forgot—is the need for both, a community in which the individual has status, and a society in which the individual has function. (Drucker, 2003, p. viii)

From Toennies, Drucker gleaned an important message of the individual's need for status and function.

Toennies's *Community and Society* elucidated a theory of human relationships that centered on two primary forms: *Gemeinschaft* (community) and *Gesellschaft* (society). Each of the two forms of relationships involved a particular type of human will: essential will (community), or arbitrary will (society). Familial relationships are the most obvious expression of community; essential will thus involves the natural tendency of people to form bonds based on kinship and local affiliations. Economic-based relations involving the conscious choice of individuals to engage with others (to barter, trade, or otherwise interact) characterize societal relations. Although he posited that human development involved a movement from one form (community) to the other (society), central to Toennies's theory is the premise that both types of relationships coexist.

Drucker saw that Toennies argued for the importance of retaining a sense of community within society. Human beings need to have an alternative to the ideal types that Toennies presented in his work. As Drucker noted, the idealized preindustrial community was a thing of the past, and Toennies's depiction of bourgeois society was equally stereotypical. Drucker's vision of a functioning society of institutions did not involve atomistic humans treating each other as objects of economic exchange. Toennies's archetypes of community and society showed him that a functioning industrial society would require capturing some sense of familial, communal bonds between individuals and the institutions in which they served. This overarching emphasis on bridging individual and collective meaning is one of the most important features of Drucker's work, and derives in part from Toennies's influence.

John Commons (1862–1945)

John Commons was an economist trained under Richard Ely at the University of Chicago. Ely and others at Chicago in the post–World War I era criticized the inequities of modern capitalism, particularly the unbridled individualism epitomized by the captains of industry who headed America's powerful trusts. Commons taught at Indiana University, Syracuse, and the University of Wisconsin; his ideas influenced the progressive and labor reform movements in Wisconsin during the early 1900s.

Although Drucker does not overtly mention Commons as a specific source of influence, he does acknowledge that his concept of social ecology is "not too different [from Commons's concept of Institutional Economics]" (Drucker, 1992b, p. 57). Commons's search for a functioning industrial community echoes Drucker's language of a functioning society of institutions.

Commons saw the industrial organization as a human enterprise, and he advocated many of the same attitudes that Drucker did in his writings. Commons seems to have foreseen the shift toward a knowledge society as early as 1919:

> The new America promises to be an educated America. "Americanization" means the spread of independence in the shop. The individuals cannot be swung in a mass by the boss, or the labor agent, or the padrone, but may be expected to assert themselves. Great and exceptional personalities there will be. But they will work through hundreds and thousands of lesser ones. (Commons, 1919, p. 163)

While Drucker wrote primarily about white-collar workers, Commons articulated the same trend toward worker education and inclusion on the shop floor. He, like Drucker, observed that worker loyalty cannot be assumed. "Thus, education, interesting work and loyalty go together. . . . Loyalty is not gratitude for past favors, nor a sense of obligation, but is expectation of reciprocity" (Commons, 1919, p. 150). Importantly, Commons pointed out that work is not simply about a paycheck, but is about dignity and meaning. Like Drucker, Commons rejected the oversimplified view of the industrial employee as an "economic man," driven only by remuneration and the hope of advancement.

Karl Polanyi (1886–1964)

Drucker devoted an entire chapter of his memoirs, *Adventures of a Bystander*, to the Polanyi family. Elsewhere, he noted that "perhaps I learned the most from Polanyi, although not formally because we were friends" (Drucker, 1995, p. 2). Among other things, Drucker described in Polanyi a talent for the practice of social ecology: "He analyzed, with an uncanny knack for seeing the importance of inconspicuous developments at an early stage" (Drucker, 1997, p. 133).

Economic historian Karl Polanyi lived a similar life to Drucker's, but he developed a different philosophy of capitalism and society. Born in Budapest, Polanyi moved to Vienna, where he met Drucker while he worked as senior editor of *The Austrian Economist*. Polanyi was a socialist, and thus he lost his job when Hitler came to power. He emigrated to the United States, where he joined Drucker on the faculty of Bennington College in the early 1940s. While at Bennington, Polanyi wrote his seminal book, *The Great Transformation* (1944), in which he challenged the tenets of free-market liberalism.[2]

Polanyi and Drucker both recognized the dangers of utopian solutions to social problems. Drucker's primary target was the irrational promise of totalitarian government, whereas Polanyi took on nineteenth-century free-market capitalism. In *The Great Transforma-*

tion, Polanyi's thesis is that the error of classic nineteenth-century economic theory is its belief in economic self-interest as the primary motivator: "Nineteenth-century civilization," says Polanyi, "chose to base itself on a motive only rarely acknowledged as valid in the history of human societies, and certainly never before raised to the level of a justification of action and behavior in everyday life, namely gain" (Polanyi, 1944, p. 256). Polanyi argued that humans are not merely economic beings, motivated purely by the pursuit of wealth; more importantly, wealth represents status and membership in a larger community:

> The outstanding discovery of recent historical and anthropological research is that man's economy, as a rule, is submerged in his social relationships. He does not act so as to safeguard his individual interest in the possession of material goods; he acts so as to safeguard his social standing, his social claims, his social assets. He values material goods only in so far as they serve this end. (Polanyi, 1944, p. 48)

Polanyi's assessment of the value of material goods echoes Drucker's emphasis on the need for industrial organizations to provide people with status and function; a job is not so much about a paycheck as it is about finding meaning in society: "Industrial society itself will not be able to function or even to survive unless . . . the members see the relationship between their own work and purpose and the purpose and pattern of their society" (Drucker, 1950, p. 26).

While both Drucker and Polanyi saw the impact of social forces on the economy, they came to very different conclusions regarding how society should respond. Polanyi believed in harnessing the power of government to shape the economy; for example, he proposed an alternative to free-market capitalism and Marxist socialism that involved significant elements of government planning, or "economic collaboration of governments" at the international level (Polanyi, 1944, p. 262). Drucker, in contrast, had little faith in humanity's ability to engineer a better society through regulation or other government interference. He saw Polanyi's conclusion as a belief in "salvation by society"; Polanyi, according to Drucker, viewed Drucker's belief in an "adequate, bearable, but free society" as "a tepid compromise" (Drucker, 1978, p. 140). Yet both men shared the same goal of finding an alternative to the false promises of totalitarianism, promises they believed had brought the regimes of Hitler and Stalin to power.

What Did These Nine People Teach Drucker about Social Ecology?

These nine social ecologists helped Drucker to develop his methodology as a social ecologist. Importantly, all of the influencers reflected the importance of human relationships within economic, social, and political organizations. The overarching goal of social ecology as a discipline and practice is the creation of a functioning society in which individuals are accorded dignity and status within a community and a meaningful place within a society. While not all of the social ecologists examined here mirrored Drucker's pragmatic approach to the discipline, they were certainly all concerned with better understanding their respective societies in terms of how those societies provided opportunities for human development and fulfillment.

These early social ecologists also lived in times of change, and they sought to understand the impacts and meaning of that change. Drucker fashioned a more pragmatic style of social ecology, one that involved applying his own ideas about the practice of management and entrepreneurship to address the implications of change. Seeing the future that has already happened is an important goal for the social ecologist as he or she seeks to assist executives and policymakers to proactively manage the demands on them and to advance the welfare of society. The objective is to prevent knee-jerk reactions to problems by providing analysis, warning, and policy prescriptions that allow for thoughtful action. Executives and public officials will then have time to formulate and implement courses of action to maintain continuity in the midst of inescapable change.

Even though change is certain, continuity was also a concern of the nine social ecologists evaluated here. Each one expressed an interest in retaining some of the earlier values, structures, beliefs, or qualities in the face of dramatic economic, political, or social upheaval. As Drucker learned from these influencers and others, there needs to be some degree of continuity in a functioning society of institutions. In many cases, that involves balancing personal, individual interests with the needs of the greater community. As the earlier social ecologists showed, it was important to understand which aspects of the past ought to be preserved in the face of change and which ought to fall by the wayside.

Balancing change and continuity in such a way as to foster human dignity and development is a tall order, but not a utopian vision. All of the nine early social ecologists identified by Drucker had a vision for reconciling the conflicts they saw in their own environments. Some of them were broad in their visions, while others had more specific advice about how to solve the problems of their time. For example, Tocqueville had very specific observations and concerns about the trajectory of American democracy, and Commons wrote extensively regarding his suggestions for improving industrial America. In contrast, Toennies's vision of human community and Simmel's concern with the inner world are much more general observations of the human condition in modern society. Drucker's vision represents a blend of the general and the specific, the theoretical and the pragmatic. His concept of social ecology involved not only the kind of liberal arts thinking represented by the nine men discussed here but also the influence of early practitioners of management. Drucker's goal was to seek a bearable society of functioning institutions in which individuals can achieve dignity and status, and make positive associations with the purposes of society at large. Because his focus was on a bearable society of functioning organizations, Drucker built upon the work of prominent, early practitioners of management, individuals who taught him the pragmatic, day-to-day challenges of running a business.

PRACTITIONERS

The following seven management practitioners also had a strong effect on Drucker and helped shape his management philosophy. The first four were pioneers in the development of scientific management.

Frederick Winslow Taylor (1856–1915), Henry Laurence Gantt (1861–1919), Frank Bunker Gilbreth (1868–1924), and Lillian Gilbreth (1878–1972)

Frederick Winslow Taylor was born to a wealthy Philadelphia family. Although he attended preparatory school, he chose not to attend college. Instead, he became an apprentice, first for Enterprise Hydraulic Works, a manufacturer of hydraulic pumps, and then in the steel industry. Taylor worked his way up to a supervisory position on the shop floor, where he began to analyze the way in which individual workers performed a given task. As he inspected, measured, and recorded each element involved in a job, such as shoveling coal, Taylor developed a description of how best to perform the task. Using a stopwatch to time workers' movements, Taylor identified what he believed to be the most efficient way to complete each job.

Taylor published his ideas in 1911 as *The Principles of Scientific Management*, and he became an overnight celebrity. As more and more companies rationalized their production processes, Taylor was hailed as a master innovator. But he came under increasing fire, particularly from workers who chafed at his methods and demeanor. His focus on technology meant that he failed to see the workers as human beings; laborers to Taylor were merely units of production to be made as efficient as possible. Andrea Gabor remarked, "In Taylor's mechanistically oriented imagination, the common laborer wasn't a potential source of ongoing ideas and process improvements but rather a particularly problem-prone piece of the machinery" (Gabor, 2000, p. 19).

Henry Gantt was a mechanical engineer who worked with Frederick Taylor at Bethlehem Steel. Gantt was responsible for designing the "task and bonus" plan, an incentive compensation system that rewarded workers for productivity. Following his term at Bethlehem, he became a management consultant, during which time he developed a system of charts (Gantt charts) to track production schedules (Rathe, 1961, pp. 238–281).

Frank and Lillian Gilbreth also applied scientific management principles in the early twentieth century. A bricklayer and engineer, Frank Gilbreth broke the process of bricklaying into several discrete movements and, through processes similar to Taylor's, devised the most efficient ways to perform each one. Lillian Gilbreth, Frank's wife, applied scientific management to domestic duties, analyzing household tasks using the same techniques. The Gilbreths pioneered the use of motion pictures to analyze workers' actions, analyzing films frame by frame to dissect the various actions involved in a given task. They coauthored the 1948 book *Cheaper by the Dozen* (later made into a film), in which they described how they applied scientific management in their home with their 12 children (Gilbreth Network, n.d.).

Drucker saw both positive and negative contributions of scientific management. His positive assessments emphasize Taylor's place in history, particularly the role of modernization in lifting up the industrial worker. In the longer term, however, Drucker viewed the legacy of scientific management as something that needed to be overcome; Taylor's view of the worker as a piece of machinery troubled Drucker, and gave him ammunition to demand that humans be treated with dignity.

In a chapter titled "From Capitalism to Knowledge Society" in *Post-Capitalist Society* (1993d, pp. 19–47), Drucker marks several points in the development of the modern economy. He describes three key revolutions: the Industrial Revolution, the Productivity Revolution, and finally the Management Revolution. Taylor was instrumental in bringing in the Productivity Revolution of the early twentieth century, as he "first applied knowledge to the study of *work,* the analysis of work, and the engineering of work" (Drucker, 1993d, p. 33). Drucker also noted that what motivated Taylor to study work was the antagonism between workers and owners that existed in the late nineteenth century. In Drucker's words, "Taylor's motivation was not efficiency. It was not the creation of profits for the owners. . . . His main motivation was the creation of a society in which owners and workers, capitalists and proletarians, could share a common interest in productivity and could build a harmonious relationship on the application of knowledge to work" (Drucker, 1993d, p. 34). Taylor's motivations were distorted over time by those who portrayed him as solely a prophet of efficiency. Taylor's words in *The Principles of Scientific Management* support Drucker's assessment:

The majority of these men [industrial workers and employers] believe that the fundamental interests of employees and employers are necessarily antagonistic. Scientific management, on the contrary, has for its very foundation the firm conviction that the true interests of the two are one and the same; that prosperity for the employer cannot exist through a long term of years unless it is accompanied by prosperity for the employee, and *vice versa*; and that it is possible to give the workman what he most wants—high wages—and the employer what he wants—a low labor cost—for his manufactures. (Taylor, 1911, p. 10)

Drucker credits Taylor with creating a blue-collar middle class: "It was Taylor who defeated Marx and Marxism. . . . Without Taylor, the number of industrial workers would still have grown fast, but they would have been Marx's exploited proletarians" (Drucker, 1989, p. 189). While social and labor historians might disagree with Drucker's rosy interpretation of the status of the American late nineteenth-century working class, the historic importance of scientific management to Drucker is clear. Taylor's vision of a more productive society that was mutually beneficial to worker and owner informed Drucker's own idea of a society composed of industrial organizations that offered individual status and meaning.

Yet Drucker did not believe that what he described as "Taylor's Productivity Revolution" was an entire success; Drucker noted that the increasing productivity of manual workers resulted in a subsequent loss of those very jobs: "The Productivity Revolution had become a victim of its own success" (Drucker, 1993d, p. 40). Taylor's emphasis on productivity, in fact, resulted in fewer and fewer productive workers who were gainfully employed. While Drucker acknowledged Taylor's contribution to the historical progression of labor development, he recognized the limitations of Taylor's approach. One of the most important limitations was Taylor's emphasis on reducing jobs to individual motions that could be tracked and measured. Such an emphasis created a "blind spot" to the need to understand the worker's job as a whole. The second, and more important, blind spot was the belief that human beings function as machines: "The human being does individual motions poorly; viewed as a machine tool, he is badly designed" (Drucker, 1954, p. 283). As long as the worker is expected to "do rather than to know," in other words, treated as a piece of machinery that merely produces outputs through a series of discrete actions, he or she will be resistant to change and will not be truly used as an effective human resource.

Lyndall Urwick (1891–1983)

Educated at Oxford, Englishman Lyndall Urwick worked in his family's glove-making business, and served in World War I. He left the family business in 1920, and began a career devoted to studying innovations in management theory and practice. He worked as a management consultant, including nearly 30 years with the British firm of Urwick, Orr and Partners Ltd. During World War II, Urwick advised the U.S. Treasury and the Petroleum Warfare Department. Following his military service, he focused his energies on management education, publishing and lecturing prolifically (Lyndall Fownes Urwick Archive, 2009).

Urwick argued that management should be a science, based on rational analysis rather than trial and error. He is careful to note that management is remarkably unscientific in its subject matter, "dealing with men and women, of inducing them to co-operate" (Urwick, 1943, p. 25). Yet, Urwick stated, management must be based on rational decision making: "management *can* use the scientific temper and the scientific method," which involves the "substitution, as far and to the full extreme which our knowledge allows, of an analysis and a basis of fact for opinion" (Urwick, 1943, pp. 20–21).

Drucker's description of the job of management clearly indicates the lessons he took from Urwick. Drucker agreed that "there are . . . distinct professional features and a scientific aspect to management," and that management was not "just a matter of hunch or native ability" (Drucker, 1954, p. 9). Yet he clearly refuted Urwick's statement that management was a science: "Management is a *practice* rather than a *science* or a *profession*, though containing elements of both" (Drucker, 2008, p. 11).

Mary Parker Follett (1868–1933)

Mary Parker Follett was a prominent management theorist in the 1920s. While at Radcliffe, she conducted a detailed study of American government, which she published as *The Speaker of the House of Representatives* (1896); that book caught the attention of many notable figures, including Theodore Roosevelt. As a social worker in Boston, she was active in a number of reform movements, chairing the Women's Municipal League. Well connected internationally, she devoted herself to a life of publishing and scholarly production while maintaining an active life in social work. Follett analyzed the democratic process and the role of informal groups and individuals. Her 1918 work *The New State: Group Organization the Solution of Popular Government,* established her as an important author on political matters, and led to a number of positions in public service. Follett turned her attention to business and became a respected consultant to the private sector, applying many of her previously worked-out principles of democracy to business (Graham, 1995; Tonn, 2003).

Drucker's acknowledgement of Follett's work is problematic (Drucker, 1954, p. vii). While he lauded her work and recognized the debt that many owe her pioneering work, Drucker claims that he and others "worked without any knowledge of Follett" (Drucker in Graham, 1995b, p. 8). However, the Mary Parker Follett Foundation indicates that Drucker "discovered Follett's work in the 1950s," and claims that he referred to her as his "guru" (Mary Parker Follett Foundation Web site, n.d.). The timing of Drucker's "discovery" is important, given that so much of Follett's material appears in Drucker's own work. Nevertheless, the fact remains that Follett's ideas are remarkably similar to many of Drucker's concepts.

Two important and related themes in Follett's work are the role of power in organizations and the inevitability of conflict. Follett devised the contrast between "power-with" and "power-over"; power-over described a coercive or authoritarian model of power, and power-with, "a jointly developed power, a co-active, not a coercive power" (Follett, 1925, in Graham, p. 103). She was adamant that power-with did not involve abdication of one's power; in fact, she argued, that was impossible: "If we have any power, any genuine power, let us hold on to it, let us not give it away. We could not anyway if we wanted to. We can confer authority; but power or capacity, no man can give or take" (Follett, 1925, in Graham, p. 115). Power is not to be diffused in the Follett organizational model, but rather pooled.

In many respects, Follett's ideas about power and conflict, particularly with regard to the tension between the individual in society, mirror Drucker's idea of the functioning society of organizations. Just as Drucker saw individual membership in an organization as the road to individual meaning and communal membership, Follett discussed her own solution for human meaning: "Our definition of individuality must now be 'finding my place in the whole': 'my place' gives you the individual, 'the whole' gives you society, but by connecting them, by saying 'my place in the whole,' we get a fruitful synthesis" (Follett, 1920, in Graham, p. 258). Drucker and Follett saw membership in the industrial organization, the business community, as key to human development.

Long before Drucker wrote on management integrity, Follett posited that "if business offers so large an opportunity for the creation of spiritual values, and I think it offers a larger opportunity than any single profession in the possibilities of those intimate human interweavings; . . . should we any longer allow the assumption . . . that the professions are for service and business for pecuniary gain?" (Follett, 1925b, in Graham, pp. 277–278). No wonder Drucker referred to Follett as "the prophet of management" in his introduction to the writings of Mary Parker Follett (Drucker, 1995b, in Graham, p. 9).

Robert Owen (1771–1858)

Robert Owen was a successful textile manufacturer in Britain during that country's industrial revolution. In 1800, he took control of the New Lanark Mills in Scotland, and he instituted several reforms, including higher wages, shorter hours, and child labor restrictions. New Lanark not only remained highly profitable but also became the subject of scrutiny, as investors and manufacturers wondered how such an enterprise could function. Although criticized for his paternalistic attitude toward his workers, Owen nevertheless became well known as a philanthropist and advocate for industrial reforms (Harrison, 1969; Morton, 1963).

Drucker referred to Owen as a "prophet" of the industrial community; Owen's influence is most clear in Drucker's own idea of the self-governing plant community (Drucker, 1995). Drucker and Owen shared the belief that people's economic status is not an indicator of their moral status. While this was a more novel concept in Owen's day, twentieth-century advocates of capitalism often retained basic moral judgments regarding the poor or working class. As Drucker remarked:

> In its refusal to concern itself with the unsuccessful majority, the market society was a true child of Calvinism with its refusal to concern itself with the great majority that is not elected to be saved. . . . But this does not alter the fact that the philosophy of the market society only makes sense if the unsuccessful are seen as "rejected by the Lord" with whom to have pity would be sinful as questioning the decision of the Lord. We can only deny social status and function to the economically unsuccessful if we are convinced that lack of economic success is (a) always a man's own fault, and (b) a reliable indication of his worthlessness as a human personality and as a citizen. (Drucker, 1946, p. 153)

Like Owen, Drucker challenged the strict Calvinist notion that one's financial status was always the reflection of one's morality. While Owen's socialist vision of planned community certainly did not mirror Drucker's vision of a functioning society of industrial organizations, the idea behind communities such as New Lanark did mesh with Drucker's concept of the plant community, where workers had a chance to have meaning and dignity.

What Did These Practitioners Teach Drucker about Social Ecology?

If the nine intellectual social ecologists taught Drucker the methodology of social ecology (observing one's society and surroundings in order to better understand human relationships and human institutions), the seven management practitioners taught Drucker that functioning organizations could potentially address the issues raised by the early social ecologists. All of the management practitioners were concerned primarily with human relationships in industrial organizations. All seven also noted the impact of change in their era, from Taylor's and Owen's newly modernized environments to Follett's and Urwick's more mature industrial societies. The practitioners, like the social ecologists, were aware of the discontinuity inherent in capitalism; all seven sought to minimize the impact of industrialization on the human condition.

SOCIAL ECOLOGY

What is social ecology? As defined at the beginning of this chapter, social ecology is the investigation of relationships between people and economic, social, and political institutions. Drucker's concept of social ecology was informed by nine earlier practitioners of the discipline, as well as seven management practitioners. This combination of influences resulted in Drucker's emphasis on the tangible results of social ecology as well as the observations inherent in the discipline. For Drucker, the end result of the practice of social ecology was more important than the methodology or process. The end objective of the work of social ecology is to improve the functioning of all the institutions of society. While influenced by great intellectual figures, Drucker was also a pragmatist, and he was not always content to wait for his recommendations to be put into action. Building on the work of early practioners, Drucker extended the work of social ecology to prescriptive advice. In the process, he created his own methodology, which consisted of identifying an important trend, calling attention to it, addressing the associated, specific management challenges posed, and developing broad, general management principles for the benefit of executives of institutions of society.

Drucker arrived at the practice of management in the course of his work as a social ecologist. He sought to provide leaders of society's institutions with the policies, practices, and executive competencies they needed to shape the future. Each of Drucker's management books, with the exception of his *Managing for Results* (Drucker, 1964), integrates his work in social ecology with detailed prescriptive advice for leaders of society's institutions. Drucker rarely separated identification of changes in the environment—demographic, economic, technological, political, and social—from specific advice for exploiting these changes through the practice of management.

The social ecologist, as defined by Drucker, helps find and promote continuity in the conserving institutions of society (such as the family, religious institutions, and the Supreme Court) while advocating innovation and change in the inherently destabilizing institutions of a free society, especially business but also social and public-sector institutions:

Society, community, family are all conserving institutions. They try to maintain stability and to prevent, or at least slow down, change. But the organization of the post-capitalist society of organizations is a destabilizer. Because its function is to put knowledge to work—on tools, processes, and products; on work; on knowledge itself—it must be organized for constant change. It must be organized for innovation. (Drucker, 1993d, p. 57)

Drucker sought to promote values that have stood the test of time while always prodding executives of institutions to innovate, become change leaders, capitalize on the new realities, and thereby advance the interests and effectiveness of society. The subtitle of his monograph on Julius Stahl, "A Conservative Theory of the State" (Drucker, 1933/2002), reflects Drucker's desire to promote continuity in society by emphasizing traditional values that have stood the test of time.

The end goal of the social ecologist is always action to improve the welfare of members of society—to create wealth, to heal a patient, to educate a student—and to seek to promote the functioning of the institutions of society, as Drucker explains:[3]

The social ecologist must aim at impact. His goal is not knowledge; it is right action. In this sense social ecology is a practice—like the practice of medicine, or law. . . . Its aim is to maintain the balance between continuity and conservation on the one hand, and change and innovation on the other. Its aim is to create a society in dynamic disequilibrium. Only such a society has stability and cohesion. (Drucker, 1992b, p. 63)

Wealth creation is not a zero-sum game. New wealth is created by improvements in productivity and innovation. Healing is advanced through new medications, improvements in productivity, and medical innovations. Learning is advanced by application of breakthroughs in understanding the brain, by advances in learning theory, and by the use of information technology as a tool to enhance learning.

Innovation and change are necessary to avert the persistent, entropic tendencies toward decline and to maintain continuity. Entropy is the natural tendency in physical, human, and organizational systems toward decline. Innovation and change are necessary to provide a counter-offensive to these entropic tendencies: to continue to make progress in spite of the downward drag of entropy.

One of the most important duties of a social ecologist is to identify major trends that have already emerged but have not yet made their impact felt on the institutions of society. Drucker identified these emerging trends ("the future that has already happened"[4]). He also projected them into the future well before others recognized them, and he alerted individuals to the opportunities and dangers these trends were about to create for institutions and individuals. Because he identified these trends as they were beginning to emerge, there was time to test his findings carefully and repeatedly against facts as they emerged. Working as a consultant, teacher, and writer, he was often able to provide advice to help executives and individuals take full advantage of emerging trends and changes in these trends, always differentiating important trends from fads.

DRUCKER'S METHODOLOGY OF SOCIAL ECOLOGY: "BORN TO SEE; MEANT TO LOOK"

Drucker's methodology can help us become keen observers of events occurring around us. Drucker was very skilled as a social ecologist in large part because of his broad knowledge of the humanities, social sciences, and technology. He had both the desire and the ability to see the implications of emerging trends and to think and work through the implications. Drucker's motto; "Born to See; Meant to Look" (from Goethe's *Faust*), is the motto of a social ecologist and of the discipline of social ecology. And the discipline is one of action and results (Drucker, 1992b, p. 64).

As we have argued throughout this book, Drucker's thinking on management was deeply influenced by ideas synthesized from many disciplines. However, Drucker typically emphasized the pragmatic over the academic in his teaching and writing. For example, he stressed the importance of having army generals present on the front line to illustrate that a good leader should provide an example to subordinates. He compared organizational values to vitamins—they help keep an organization alive and healthy. He claimed he learned more about religion, and about the forces of good and evil, by consulting with organizations and its executives than by teaching religion. Reality was a better teacher about these moral qualities than simply reading religious documents. Therefore, even though we have stressed the intellectual influences in Drucker, it is important to remember that his work was *not* intellectual in nature but rather firmly rooted in the pragmatic world of human organizations.

Similarly, Drucker did not have a traditional academic approach to learning and scholarship. (That trait earned him critical scorn at times; many reviewers have noted the absence of source citations in his written work.) He had wide-ranging interests, and he shifted to new subjects from time to time. Drucker described himself as a person always trying to pick up or keep up on "knowledges." In religion, he read books on Saint Francis of Assisi, Saint Bonaventure, Thomas Aquinas, and studied the Epistles of St. Paul. He studied mathematics for a few years, including complexity theory and chaos theory, just to understand these fields and their importance to the work of social ecology. Chaos theory examines numerous aspects of complex systems, one of which is the "butterfly effect." The butterfly effect "is the propensity of a system to be *sensitive to initial conditions*" and to *become unpredictable over time*." This idea gave rise to the notion of a butterfly flapping its wings in one area of the world, causing a tornado or some such weather event to occur in another remote area of the world" ("The Butterfly Effect," n.d.). Chaos theory confirmed to Drucker that it is futile to try to predict the future; we are better off embracing change and using it as an opportunity to create our own future (Drucker, 1964, p. 173).

Drucker studied art for most of his adult life. A catalog of Drucker's collection of Japanese paintings, *Song of the Brush: Japanese Paintings from the Sanso Collection*, includes an article by Peter Drucker, "A View of Japan through Japanese Art" (Drucker, 1979). He had a strong affection for Japan, and he had a lot of influence on the development of post–World War II Japan. He marveled at the way Confucian ethics operated in the workplace, creating a sense of community and individual responsibility. The Japanese loved his emphasis on human beings and on management's responsibilities to develop people. He thought China and India were countries that were going to have a major impact on global events in the twenty-first century.

Drucker synthesized and brought knowledge from various fields to bear upon problems of management and society. He was a master at seeing these connections and weaving ideas together. He worked on two or three book ideas at a time. He would create a draft, and then develop it through his teaching and consulting, bringing together ideas from his knowledge of history, economics, politics, technology, art, religion, business, psychology, international relations, mathematics, and other disciplines. He used the pedagogical practice of storytelling, weaving around subjects in a circular manner. Then, after surrounding a problem, defining it using the whole history of knowledge that influenced his thinking about the problem, he would reach full circle and communicate penetrating insights. This method could take considerable time in the classroom. In a three-hour seminar, Drucker would often take the entire period to complete his circular thought process, much to the bewilderment of many a student. Students who did not listen carefully often did not see the connections he was making.

Out of that teaching process and out of his consulting came his writings. Drucker's written works are, of course, more concise than his classroom presentations were, but they reflect the same convergence of multiple disciplines. In his review of Drucker's *The New Society* (Drucker, 1993c), George G. Higgins speaks to Drucker's synthesis of four specific social science disciplines:

> He is thoroughly at home in economics, political science, industrial psychology, and industrial sociology, and has succeeded admirably in harmonizing the findings of all four disciplines and applying them meaningfully to the practical problems of the enterprise. (Higgins, in Drucker 1993c) [5]

Drucker's close friend Theodore Levitt, editor of the *Harvard Business Review* and a pioneer in modern marketing, described the entire breadth of Drucker's work in a magnificent tribute:

> But what is even more impressive is the dignity, learning, grace, and cultivation he brings to each subject he approaches. Everything he writes has a glow of the Renaissance man for whom nothing is new. He sees the connection with other times, other disciplines, other cultures, and other values, but he marvels at and delights in the new twists that are perceptible in the old relationships; the new meanings and policies suggested by the unexpected conjecture of old opposites; the new expression taken by the assertion of venerable values and ancient morality; the new imperatives in politics, economics, morality, management, and world affairs imposed by science, technology, population change, weapons of mass destruction, and communication. (Levitt, 1970, in Bonaparte and Flaherty, p. 6)

Higgins's and Levitt's observations speak eloquently of Drucker's ability to employ various disciplines to analyze his environment, to function as a good social ecologist in the spirit of management as a liberal art.

APPLICATION OF DRUCKER'S METHODOLOGY

Drucker's methodology involves looking carefully at the world around us through the lens of the humanities, social sciences, and technology. Then it proceeds to ask five questions about discernable changes:

1. What changes have already happened that do not fit "what everybody knows"?
2. What are the paradigm changes?
3. Is there any evidence that this is a change and not a fad?
4. Are there results of this change? Does it make a difference, in other words?
5. If a change is relevant and meaningful, what opportunities does it offer? (Drucker, 1992b, p. 62, numbers added)

A contemporary example illustrating this methodology is contained in Drucker's article "The Next Society" (Drucker, 2001, pp. 3–20; Drucker, 2002b, pp. 235–299). This article demonstrates Drucker's methodology as a social ecologist. It also demonstrates what it means to use social ecology to bring action, not mere knowledge, to bear upon discernable trends in management and society.

The *Economist's* editors introduce the article with the words "tomorrow is closer than you think. Peter Drucker explains how it will differ from today, and what needs to be done to prepare for it" (Drucker, 2001, p. 1). One of the ways the next society will differ from the society of today is the emergence of knowledge as the key wealth-producing resource. Drucker describes the full emergence of the knowledge society and its implications for all three sectors—public, private, and social—of developed countries as well as for individuals. What is interesting to note, however, is that Drucker actually started to *track* the emergence of the knowledge worker, the knowledge economy, and the knowledge society almost a half century before the article appeared in the *Economist*.[6] Drucker's work on knowledge as the key resource of a developed society is one of the best examples of the application of the methodology of a social ecologist.

In his book *The Age of Discontinuity* (1969), Drucker focused his perceptive ability on the forces of change that were transforming the economic landscape and creating the next society. In each part of a four-part book, Drucker recognized a major area of discontinuity underlying social and cultural reality:

1. the explosion of new technologies resulting in major new industries;
2. the change from an international to a world economy;
3. a new sociopolitical reality of pluralistic institutions that posed important political, philosophical, and spiritual challenges; and
4. the new universe of knowledge work based on mass education along with its implications. (Drucker, 1969, Parts One to Four)

Drucker thought through the impact of each of these four *discontinuities* on institutions and people, including what should be done about these trends to produce *positive change* in society while retaining *continuity with the past*. *The Age of Discontinuity* thus provided a powerful blueprint for shaping the future that was discernable in 1969.

APPLICATION OF THE METHODOLOGY OF SOCIAL ECOLOGY: THE EMERGENCE OF KNOWLEDGE WORK

Peter Drucker began to track the emergence of knowledge work and the knowledge worker[7] in his *Landmarks of Tomorrow* (Drucker, 1959).[8] He continued to follow these changes right through to his last book *The Effective Executive in Action* (Drucker and Maciariello, 2006). He was convinced that the emergence of knowledge work, the knowledge worker, and the knowledge society meant that raising the productivity of the knowledge worker would become a major source of competitive advantage for people, organizations, and nations. It followed that raising the productivity of the schools and their teachers would also be critical to the effective functioning of a knowledge society.

In *The Age of Discontinuity*, Drucker lamented "the productivity of education is too low even for the richest country. It imposes intolerable burdens on the poor ones, and constitutes a major obstacle to their growth and development" (Drucker, 1969, p. 335).

Drucker continued the themes of improving the productivity of knowledge and schools in Chapter 11 ("The Accountable School") of his book *Post-Capitalist Society* (Drucker, 1993d, pp. 194–209). Indeed, the post-capitalist society is a knowledge society where human capital is beginning to replace tangible capital as the source of competitive advantage for individuals, organizations, and nations.

As a result of this shift to knowledge as the key resource, Drucker went to work showing how to improve the productivity of the knowledge worker. Much of this work appears in Chapter 5 of *Management Challenges in the 21st Century* (Drucker, 1999) and in "Knowledge Worker Productivity" (Drucker, 2002).[9]

We see the convergence of the two aspects of his methodology. Identifying knowledge as the emerging capital provides an example of Drucker's *perceptive ability to see* "the future that has already happened." Providing prescriptive advice for individuals and institutions allows society to adjust to the realities of the knowledge economy in the least disruptive way—in a way that promotes continuity with the past.

New Demands on the Individual in the Knowledge Society: Managing Oneself

As the nature of work began to shift toward knowledge, Drucker started encouraging knowledge workers to assume the task of managing themselves in a proactive way rather than leaving personal development to employer-designed-and-sponsored programs. Drucker's first systematic treatment of this new responsibility appeared very early, in his book *The Effective Executive* (Drucker, 1967). His final discussion of the topic appears in his last book, *The Effective Executive in Action* (Drucker and Maciariello, 2006) which was released one month before his death on November 11, 2005.

Self-management is the new demand placed on the individual in the knowledge society. It is the responsibility of the knowledge worker to manage herself for effectiveness. And doing so requires knowledge of herself. It requires understanding of her strengths, weaknesses, and values. It requires understanding of how she works to achieve objectives. This information then helps her know where to place herself for effectiveness, how to focus on contribution to achieve effectiveness, and how to take responsibility for relationships.

Know Oneself

The first demand to manage oneself is to know oneself; to know one's strengths; to know what one must do to maximize strengths; and to remedy bad habits that impede full development of strengths. Identifying strengths is very important because knowledge workers should focus their performance in areas where their strengths give them the best chance to optimize their contributions. Individuals, however, may have difficulty accurately identifying what they are good at without help from others.

Drucker recommended *feedback analysis* as a tool for identifying one's strengths. It is not a new tool. It was used over 450 years ago by Ignatius of Loyola, founder of the Jesuit Order. Each Jesuit imbedded the practice of feedback analysis and continuous learning into his work, which Drucker suggests is the explanation for the success of the Jesuits (Drucker, 1999, pp. 164–165). Clearly the Jesuits mastered self-management, feedback analysis and continuous learning a long time ago. As former Jesuit and managing director of J.P. Morgan & Company, Chris Lowney notes:

Every early Jesuit dedicated an intensely focused week each year to revitalizing his core commitment and assessing his performance during the previous year. Moreover, Jesuit self-awareness techniques [that is, spiritual exercises] accommodated change by instilling in recruits the habit of continuous learning, of daily reflection on activities. These techniques remain relevant today precisely because they were designed to allow busy people to "reflect on the run." (Lowney, 2003, p. 28)

Drucker believed that feedback analysis should be used by knowledge workers to improve decision making. Before making major decisions or taking critical action, a person should write down what he thinks will happen (that is, the prognosis). Then, after some time has passed, he should review his decisions and expected results and compare results to what actually happened, paying close attention to areas where he performed better than expected and to areas where he performed worse than expected.

Following the results of feedback analysis, one should concentrate on demonstrated strengths, shore up weaknesses that limit the full effectiveness of strengths, and place oneself where one's strengths will produce results, even exceptional results. One should then continue to improve strengths. This may mean acquiring new knowledge or skills, and taking action to remedy bad habits that limit full development of strengths.

Feedback information provides the knowledge worker with information as to what not to do. One should not take on assignments that rely on known weaknesses; rather, one should use energy to turn strengths into excellent results.

How Do I Perform?

Understanding the way one performs is key to achieving results. We all perform differently, so it is critical to understand one's own manner and method of performing. For example, a person should understand whether she is a reader or a listener or both. A reader prefers written memos and reports, while a listener is partial to oral briefings and brainstorming. Not understanding that a person performs better as a listener than as a reader, and vice versa, can be damaging to performance and result in frustration. It is important that knowledge workers understand this aspect of their performance and the performance of colleagues.

Another area to understand is how one learns. There are many different ways to learn; it is a highly individualized characteristic. One person may learn most by writing and rewriting an argument. Another may learn by talking out a decision, an idea, or his or her confusion with a group of people. Still another may learn best by giving an uninterrupted presentation, followed by a period of solitude to reflect on the experience. Almost all of us learn as we try to teach others.

What Are My Values?

Managing oneself also requires being aware of the answer to the question, "What are my values?" There should be compatibility between the values of the organization and the values of an individual. A mismatch can result in frustration and nonperformance.

Ethics are a dimension of values—but only one dimension. Ethics have their root in personal value systems, not in organizational codes. The value system of the individual should not vary among different situations or organizations. What is ethical in one situation or organization is ethical in another. The "mirror test" is the test of ethics. It requires asking, "What kind of person do I want to see when I look in the mirror in the morning?" (Drucker, 2008, p. 488). In the case of a conflict between placing oneself according to values and placing oneself according to strengths, placing oneself according to values should dominate. Our motivation is enhanced when our values are in sync with the values of the organization.

Where Do I Belong?

Understanding strengths, performance, and values is a prerequisite for answering the question, "Where do I belong?" By the time a person understands where he has strengths, how he performs, and what his values are, he should be able to say no to the job or assignment that goes against these. The person who works well in a small organization should say no to an assignment in a large multinational one. She should decline a role that emphasizes her weaknesses and limits the use of her strengths. In addition, understanding these aspects of managing oneself enables a person to describe to others how best to move forward with assignments to realize the highest levels of performance. The knowledge worker should be able to say, "This is how you should structure my job, communicate with me, and form relationships with me; finally, here are the results you can expect."

Take Responsibility for Relationships

Because most knowledge workers work with other people and are made effective through cooperation with other people, *taking responsibility for relationships is key to managing oneself effectively.* The first part of taking relationship responsibility is to understand the strengths, performance, and values of those one works with. Look closely at them and think through each of these elements. Understanding the strengths, performance, and values of colleagues is important to effectiveness.

The next task is to take responsibility for communications. After thinking through our own strengths, performance, values, and contribution, we must convey this information to those on whom we depend and to those who depend on us. Both the subordinate and the superior should take responsibility for relationships, and this responsibility should be evaluated in performance appraisals.

Many organizational conflicts arise because one person does not understand what another person does or should do, how the other does it, what his or her contribution is, and what results should be expected. Knowledge workers should approach others and say, "This is what I am good at. This is how I work. These are my values. This is the contribution I expect to concentrate on and the results I should be expected to deliver" (Drucker, 2008, p. 496). The trust that is necessary to build performance in today's organization is grounded in understanding one another's work. Doing so demands that everyone take responsibility for relationships.

In summary, Drucker recognized that demands on the worker in the knowledge society are fundamentally different from demands placed on the manual worker. Today, knowledge workers must manage themselves. They must determine what their strengths are through feedback analysis. They must understand the ways in which they work most effectively, and they need to be aware of their values. Then they must determine their potential contribution, or how to best place themselves as opportunities arise. Lastly, they must take relationship responsibility to fully realize their contribution.

Revitalization

Knowledge is very perishable—if a knowledge worker doesn't grow and learn, he simply can't keep up; he is no longer effective. The ways tasks are done are changing at breakneck speeds. In addition, it is often boring for people to work in the same field for a long period of time. Knowledge workers work with their minds and have longer working life spans than do most manual workers. It is unlikely that knowledge workers will remain in a narrow area for their entire career. So they need to change for two reasons: because they need stimulation and because knowledge is changing.

Revitalization is necessary for keeping oneself mentally challenged and engaged throughout a long working life. How can a person continue to grow and change over so many long years of life and work? What are the keys to keeping oneself effective? The answer is to take responsibility for one's own development and placement, and to revitalize oneself. The organization is no longer responsible for determining what challenges or experiences are best for each individual. Development is *self*-development, and placement is *self*-placement. It is the responsibility of the individual to ask, "What assignment would be useful at this time for my growth? What new challenges do I need? What new skills do I need to acquire?"

Drucker provides seven personal experiences for revitalizing oneself:

1. Strive for perfection, knowing that it will surely elude.
2. Have self-respect in the integrity of your work.
3. Pursue continuous, life-long learning.
4. Take time to review your performance—what you did well, what you could do better, and what you did not do but should have.
5. Think through what the new job requires.
6. Use feedback analysis to learn strengths. Then, focus on improving these and only these.
7. The one thing worth being remembered for is making a difference in people's lives. (Drucker, 2008, pp. 505–513)

Drucker believed that knowledge workers should "repot" themselves from time to time as a part of their own revitalization. His own major turning point illustrates this repotting process. In the late 1970s he began to shift slowly away from his heavy work in business and began devoting his attention to the leadership and management of social sector organizations. He consulted with organizations such as CARE, the American Red Cross, the Girl Scouts of America, Catholic Charities, and World Vision International. Initially, the consulting work was routine; later on, he either returned the consulting fee or performed the work pro bono. And during this period of repotting, Drucker also tried his hand at writing two novels.[10]

Managing oneself even requires thinking through what one should do in the "second half" of life. The second half occurs after a person has reached a sense of completion or after she or he has attained a certain amount of financial success from a primary profession. Many years of productive life may be left. But, what to do? By understanding our strengths, our values, and where we belong, we can all begin to move from success to significance with confidence.[11]

Figure 7.1 combines the practice of managing oneself as a knowledge worker, discussed here, with the four practices of management for developing the human being (see Chapter 5). Figure 7.1 contains the sum total of Drucker's five practices for maximizing human potential.

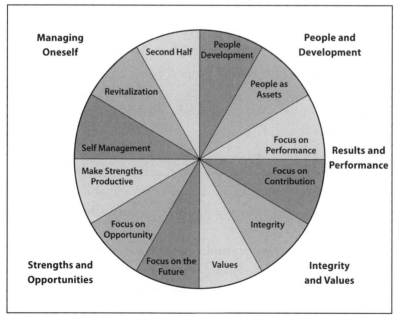

Figure 7.1   Maximizing Human Potential for the Common Good

APPLICATION OF THE METHODOLOGY OF SOCIAL ECOLOGY: THE MEGACHURCH

The last major institution that Drucker identified is the megachurch in the United States. His work on the megachurch also provides one of the clearest examples of the application of Drucker's methodology.

Drucker spent a good portion of the last two decades of his life identifying, understanding, and assisting the growth and development of the megachurch movement. He observed the growth in importance of the megachurches in the United States in his *Management Challenges for the 21st Century*:

> The pastoral mega-churches . . . have been growing very fast in the United States since 1980. . . . They are surely the most important phenomenon in American society in the last thirty years. . . . And while all traditional denominations have steadily declined, the mega-churches have exploded. They have done so because they have asked, "What is value?" to a *nonchurchgoer.* (Drucker, 1999, p. 29)

Research studies have continued to confirm Drucker's observations about the growth of the megachurch movement. A study by Hartford [Connecticut] Seminary, titled "Megachurches Today 2005," reported the existence of over 1,210 Protestant churches in the United States with weekly attendance exceeding 2,000—nearly twice the number in existence five years earlier (Thumma, Travis, and Bird, 2005, p. 1).

The same authors report that in 2006 there were in excess of 7,200 Protestant churches in the United States with weekly attendance over 1,000 (Thumma, Travis, and Byrd, 2007b, p. 35). And they state:

> On any given weekend during 2007, some 5 million U.S. churchgoers will worship in a megachurch—defined [tra-

ditionally as congregations that average] 2,000 or more in adults and children in weekly attendance. Thus almost one out of every 10 Protestant church attendees (8 percent) will be in a megachurch this weekend. (Thumma, Travis, and Bird, 2007b, p. 34)

A relatively small number of megachurches accounted for a very large percentage of church attendance in Protestant churches in 2007. As noted in the Hartford Seminary study:

In 2007, there were 1,250 megachurches out of a total of 335,000 U.S. congregations of all religious traditions. This relatively small number of very large Protestant Christian Churches has the same number of attendees at weekly services (roughly 4.5 million) as the smallest 35 percent of churches in the country. (Thumma, Travis, and Bird, 2007b, p. 1)

Drucker's observations about the megachurch illustrate how his methodology of social ecology works to improve the effectiveness of the institutions of society. In the mid-1980s Drucker observed Pastor Bill Hybels of Willow Creek Community Church in South Barrington, Illinois, and, a little later, Pastor Rick Warren of Saddleback Community Church in Lake Forest, California, organize the ministries of their churches around the spiritual needs of knowledge workers. Spiritual needs of knowledge workers and their families are somewhat different from those of the rest of the population. And Willow Creek and Saddleback excel at providing ministry support to this demographic.[12]

The knowledge society is creating a new and different constituency which the likes of Rick Warren, Senior Pastor of Saddleback Community Church, and Bill Hybels, Senior Pastor of Willow Creek Community Church, recognized and organized. All I [Drucker] had to do was to take a look. (Maciariello, 2006, p. 182)

Drucker saw the emergence of the megachurch well before it became a widely recognized phenomenon. When he understood the forces behind the development of these early megachurches he simply made the projection of their importance. Then he applied the principles of leadership and management he previously developed for other institutions to these new organizations. These principles have proven to be extremely useful to the megachurches as they seek to empower and release the excess energy of knowledge workers for service, and to deliver customized ministries to people in the areas they serve.

Drucker provided advice and counsel to pastors and other leaders of this movement over a 20-year time period. He did this by separating the issues faced by these churches into theological, cultural, and managerial topics. He concentrated his consulting activities on the managerial and cultural dimensions where he had competence. His objective was to help these churches operate in a more effective manner, contending, as Drucker did, that "the purpose of management for churches is not to make them more business-like but to make them more church-like" (Leadership Network, 2005). He offered no advice on the theological dimensions of these churches.

Thumma and Travis have persuasively demonstrated that the megachurch has created disruption for mainline Protestant and Catholic churches in the United States, while also creating opportunities for smaller, mainly Protestant churches. As they note, "The ministry activities and worship styles of the megachurches affect tens of thousands of smaller churches in the country and thanks to the Internet, literally millions of pastors around the world" (Thumma and Davis, 2007, p. 1).

In addition, the Purpose-Driven Paradigm developed by Rick Warren for the management of the megachurch provides an important blueprint for professional management of social sector organizations. Rick Warren's best-selling book *The Purpose-Driven Church* (Warren, 1995) is not only a handbook for managing churches according to their mission but also contains principles that are almost completely transferable to the management of other social sector institutions. Over 200,000 pastors and lay pastors worldwide have been trained by Warren and other Saddleback pastors in the use of the Purpose-Driven Paradigm (Saddleback Church, n.d.). It is not surprising, then, to learn that Drucker consulted with Rick Warren for over 20 years and was involved in discussions leading to the formulation of the Purpose-Driven Paradigm, originally called the Life Development Model (Buford, 1991).

This Purpose or Mission-Driven management approach represents a revolution in the way social sector institutions are managed and can be managed—that is, professionally, with a focus upon *mission, customer values, performance*, and *results*. These and other topics, such as leadership, strategies, and planning for orderly succession, are also addressed directly by Peter Drucker in his book, *Managing the Non-profit Organization* (Drucker, 1990) as well as in Drucker's numerous articles and talks on "Managing the Social Sector Institution."[13]

To sum up, the megachurch is another example illustrating Drucker's methodological sequence:

1. Identify the trend.
2. Call attention to it.
3. Deal with the management challenges it poses.
4. Extend its principles to other institutions of society that can beneficially use the knowledge and wisdom.

Pastors of megachurches must have, or must develop, a combination of talents and strengths to match the challenges they face as their churches grow and as demands upon them increase. Scott

Thumma and Dave Travis enumerate a number of talents required of senior pastors to deal with these challenges. Among these are the following:

1. Learn to test and adopt innovations from other churches and pastors to meet the changing needs of their churches,
2. Learn to manage themselves by focusing on their strengths and by delegating responsibilities to other staff members and volunteers, and
3. Develop leaders who are able to sustain the growth of the church and assume senior-level responsibilities, eventually succeeding members of the senior, pastoral staff. (Thumma and Travis, 2007, pp. 66–67)

SOCIAL ECOLOGY EXAMPLE: GENERAL MOTORS

Published early in 1946, *Concept of the Corporation* was the culmination of an 18-month study of the General Motors Corporation; it was Drucker's first major study of a corporation. He assumed the role of social ecologist and looked inside one of society's most powerful and important organizations, evaluating the policies and structures of General Motors. His primary purpose was to achieve a greater understanding of the role of the corporation within society. The General Motors example is still another example of Drucker's deep and enduring skill as a social ecologist, and of his powerful perceptual abilities.

He first recognized the vulnerabilities of General Motors in 1946, and he continued to offer his opinions for at least another 50 years. Drucker saw very early the likely future of this corporation, and he tried to change its trajectory. In the 1983 epilogue to *Concept of the Corporation*, Drucker listed three primary reasons for the rejection of the book, and its advice, by most top executives of

General Motors: "(1) the book's attitude toward GM's policies; (2) the recommendation on employee relations; and (3) the treatment of the large corporation as 'affected with the public interest'" (Drucker, 1993, p. 293).

Drucker criticized General Motors for not questioning its policies, especially those that had been in place for decades. Drucker knew that corporate policies are human-made, not eternal truths. They must adapt to changing circumstances. One such policy had to do with the attitude of the company toward its Chevrolet Division.

Drucker made a number of specific recommendations in a 1946 letter to executives of General Motors accompanying the published book. In one of these recommendations, Drucker suggested that the company spin off its Chevrolet Division (Drucker, 1993, pp. 294–295). Drucker believed the spin-off necessary in order to alleviate the stagnation that would almost certainly result from General Motors' success-induced restraints.

General Motors was then dominating the U.S. automobile industry, and its executives became concerned that the U.S. government would take antitrust action to break up the company. By spinning off Chevrolet, General Motors would have encouraged "freedom to attack, to innovate, and to compete" (Drucker, 1993, p. 295). The Chevrolet Division would in turn become one of the largest corporations in the United States.

General Motors rejected this idea as well as a number of other Drucker recommendations. Two of the most prominent of the remaining recommendations were that of the "responsible worker" operating in "the plant community." These ideas were intended to provide workers in General Motors with both status and function, two of the major themes found in Drucker's prior book *The Future of Industrial Man* (1942b), and developed at length in Parts Four and Eight of his subsequent book, *The New Society* (Drucker, 1950/1993c).

In *Concept of the Corporation* (Drucker 1993, pp. 182–191) and in *The New Society* (Drucker, 1950, pp. 151–201 and pp. 281–316), Drucker proposed the idea that the front-line worker could, if properly led and trained, develop a managerial attitude and managerial competence. With such an attitude, front-line workers could become part of a self-governing plant community. Attaining that goal required that workers be treated as assets, to be trained and developed. Executives at General Motors and the leaders of the United Auto Workers strongly opposed this recommendation, the merits of which have been amply proven by Japanese automobile manufacturers and by other American companies (Maciariello, 2000). Rejection of the responsible worker and of the plant community made General Motors very susceptible to continual demands from its unions *without* the offsetting achievement of gains in productivity that could have led to continuous reductions in wage costs per vehicle. Ironically, for General Motors and for the entire automobile industry, Drucker thought it relevant in the introduction to the 1993 edition of *The New Society* (Drucker, 1993c) to report the following:

> *The New Society* was the first of the author's books to have a major impact on Japan, in its discussion of . . . labor as a resource and of the need to create a plant-community. It is still considered in Japan to have been the guide to the restructuring of Japanese industry; to the development of modern Japanese management; and above all, to the radical reform in the "fifties" of Japan's employment and labor policies and practices. (p. xiii)

Finally, by taking a limited view of social responsibility, General Motors became a legitimate target for corporate critics such as Ralph Nader, who, in his 1965 book *Unsafe at Any Speed* criticized General Motors for the lack of safety of automobiles the company manufactured. General Motors also failed to respond early enough to the urgent need of society for more fuel-efficient vehicles to help the nation reduce its dependence on foreign oil.

Drucker asserts in his 1993 introduction to the Transactions Edition of *Concept of the Corporation* that "the 1983 Epilogue has been proven right in its prediction that, ten years later, General Motors would still be on the defensive" (pp. xi–xii). Moreover, in his conclusion to the 1993 introduction he describes the attempt by General Motors to sidestep its problems by "the old—and always unsuccessful—attempt to 'diversify.' Acting on the oldest delusion of management: 'If you can't run your own business buy one of which you know nothing.' General Motors has bought first Electronic Data Systems and then Hughes Aircraft" (Drucker, 1993, pp. xi–xii). The problems at General Motors could be solved only by the company becoming again "a truly effective automobile manufacturer. . . . And General Motors shows just how hard it is to overcome fifty years of success, how hard it is to break a monopoly mindset" (Drucker, 1993, p. xii).

Drucker concludes his introduction with a pessimistic warning about the future of the company: "I am increasingly coming to ask whether anything short of a General Motors breakup, either voluntary or through a hostile takeover, is likely to enable General Motors (or its successors) to make a successful turnaround" (Drucker, 1993, p. xii). We witnessed the demise of the great General Motors Corp. in 2009. After $19.4 billion dollars in initial aid from the U.S. government (Isidore, 2009), on June 1, 2009, General Motors filed for bankruptcy under Chapter 11 of U.S. bankruptcy law. As of April 2, 2010, the company received government assistance of over $50 billion, and it has reorganized itself into a much smaller company with four major product lines: Chevrolet, Buick, Cadillac, and GMC. Ironically, Chevrolet sales, according to estimates of the new General Motors Co. accounted for 44 percent of the company's sales in 2009, a 21 percent increase over the previous year.[14] Drucker's recommendation in 1946 to spin off Chevrolet seems all the more prescient in 2010. In an irony, the new General Motors Co. has shrunk to a size to accommodate the success of the Chevrolet Division, without antitrust pressure!

What Drucker saw at General Motors seems obvious in retrospect. Yet, it was never obvious to Alfred Sloan, otherwise one of the most effective executives in U.S. history and architect of General Motors' management system. Simply put, Drucker saw a company that was unable to *innovate sufficiently* and unable to overcome its significant operating cost disadvantages in comparison to Japanese auto manufacturers such as Toyota and Honda. And he saw a company whose employees were not allowed to develop according to their potential. Hobbled by work rules, high total wage costs, and adversarial relations with the United Auto Workers union, the company was at a severe operating disadvantage vis-à-vis its foreign competitors.

Drucker saw General Motors as an example of a company that was *unable to change* even in the face of very *real discontinuities* in its environment. It had been lulled into complacency by its own monumental, historic successes. This tendency is not uncommon—it afflicts individuals and organizations alike. All Drucker did was look and ask hard questions about empirical facts. But top management of General Motors simply did not listen.

Drucker extended the lessons learned from General Motors to other organizations through his writing and consulting work. The problems he observed at General Motors, including the lack of worker autonomy and dearth of innovation, were problems that would plague other institutions, including those engaged in not-for-profit activities. The solutions Drucker devised and published in the form of management practices thus applied not only to General Motors but also to a host of other organizations.

CONCLUSION

We have reviewed the influence of a number of social ecologists and management practioners on the methodology used by Peter Drucker. What is clear from this review is that Peter Drucker was not only a person with a Renaissance mind; he also was a pragmatist who desired to convert his work into action and results. He was both a theorist and a pragmatist.

He joined his grasp of the liberal arts with his desire to convert his ideas to results by practicing what he called social ecology. Social ecology included the twin objectives of identifying future trends that were likely to have major impacts on society, organizations, and individuals and then working out prescriptive advice for executives and policymakers. Drucker sought to provide advice in time to avoid the need to take hasty and ill-considered actions to cope with changes and disruptions to society. He practiced social ecology through his activities of teaching, consulting, and writing.

There are numerous examples of Drucker's brand of social ecology in action. A major example is his identification of changes in the nature of work itself, along with the steps necessary to prepare for life and work in the knowledge society. Drucker worked for almost a half century on the emergence, problems, and opportunities created by knowledge as a source of capital that rivaled tangible capital in importance. He was most concerned that individuals prepare for the demands of the knowledge society and that executives of organizations treat human beings as resources and assets to be developed.

Drucker's work with megachurches is another example of social ecology in action. He recognized the change in church attendance in America, but he also saw the opportunity to apply his own management theories to a new sector of society. Drucker also realized the diminishing role that corporate America could play in providing meaning to knowledge workers. He envisioned the burgeoning megachurch as a source of status and dignity for this growing cadre of Americans.

Finally, Drucker's early study of General Motors demonstrates his social ecology methodology, his blend of management practice with more intellectual theory. In *Concept of the Corporation*, Drucker clearly sought to identify solutions to the problems of discontinuity, continuity, and human status and dignity in modern industrial society. Drawing on the nine early social ecologists as well as the seven management practitioners, Drucker began to draft his idea of a functioning society of well-managed organizations as a means of combating the forces described by his intellectual forbearers.

CHAPTER 8

APPLIED SOCIAL ECOLOGY: INNOVATION AND CHANGE FOR A HOPEFUL AND BEARABLE SOCIETY

D rucker's master project was to fashion a blueprint for a moral society of well-managed institutions that would fulfill the human need for belonging and status (see Chapter 1). Drucker's writings on society and management were driven by his desire to provide concepts, principles, and methods that would allow executives to manage their organizations effectively, ensuring that those institutions would survive. One of the recurring themes in Drucker's work that derives from several of his intellectual influencers (for example, Stahl, Radowitz, Humboldt, Burke, and Schumpeter) is the balance between change and stability (discontinuity and continuity).

Like many of his influencers, Drucker recognized the permanence of change; he sought to find ways to manage discontinuities while simultaneously advancing the welfare of society. Drucker saw change and continuity as a continuum; he believed that society needed both in the appropriate balance. According to Drucker, to accomplish continuity and change, society must have both stabilizing and destabilizing institutions:

Society, community, and family are all conserving institutions. They try to maintain stability and to prevent, or at least slow down, change. But the modern organization is a destabilizer. It must be organized for innovation, and innovation, as the great Austrian-American economist Joseph Schumpeter said, is "creative destruction." (Drucker, 1992, p. 96)

Drucker thus saw a way of achieving balance between change and continuity by capitalizing on what he believed to be the nature of institutions. Conserving institutions should perform that role, while destabilizing institutions should be managed to function as forces of innovation and entrepreneurship. Drucker didn't relegate innovation solely to the private sector, however; taking his cue from Stahl, Burke, and others, he argued that government and other entities needed to practice innovation in order to avoid the more radical alternative of revolution. Drucker disagreed with Thomas Jefferson's statement that "every generation needs a new revolution" to rid itself of the consequences of tyrannical abuses of power. Drucker vastly preferred *systematic innovation* by every institution of society and peaceful *continuity* with the past as alternatives to revolution. Systematic innovation, he thought, was a prescription for renewing the institutions of society to make revolutions unnecessary:

> [Revolutions] cannot be predicted, directed or controlled. They bring to power the wrong people. . . . The main consequences of the Russian Revolution were new serfdom for the tillers of the land, an omnipotent secret police, and a rigid, corrupt, stifling bureaucracy—the very features of the czarist regime against which Russian liberals and revolutionaries had protested most loudly. . . . And the same must be said of Mao's macabre "Great Cultural Revolution." . . . We now

know that "revolution" is not achievement and the new dawn. It results from senile decay, from the bankruptcy of ideas and institutions, from failure of self renewal. . . . Innovation and entrepreneurship are thus needed in society as much as in the economy, in public service institutions as much as in businesses. . . . They achieve what Jefferson hoped to achieve through revolution in every generation, and they do so without bloodshed, civil war, or concentration camps, without economic catastrophe, but with purpose, with direction, and under control. (Drucker, 1985, pp. 253–254)

But Drucker's primary focus was on ensuring that private sector institutions, those engaged in for-profit activity (that is, wealth production), were well managed. Yet these were the very institutions subject to Schumpeter's process of creative destruction—a process that is necessary in a capitalist society if economic development is to occur. As mentioned in Chapter 1, Drucker turned creative destruction into an explanation for the moral value of profit. He also used Schumpeter's ideas to validate the destabilizing impact of American capitalism. In Drucker's model, innovation, or destabilization, actually becomes a force for stabilization, or continuity. In this view, the only way the modern organization can prevent chaos from ruling in its ranks is by continuously innovating, which requires that the organization establish "systematic, organized innovation into its very structure" (Drucker, 1992b, p. 59).

Consequently, it is not surprising that he pointed to his book *Innovation and Entrepreneurship* (Drucker, 1985) as a methodological guide that executives should follow for systematically introducing change. Drucker remarked that "my book *Innovation and Entrepreneurship* (1985) shows how to look systematically for changes in society, demographics, meaning, science and technology, as opportunities for the future" (Drucker, 1992b, p. 61).

While Chapter 7 of this book emphasized examples of Drucker's work as a social ecologist, this chapter describes Drucker's process of managing innovation within organizations. Drucker had a methodology for identifying and capitalizing upon inconspicuous and conspicuous developments in order to launch innovations that create new wealth, offset the processes of creative destruction, maintain continuity in institutions, and advance the welfare of society. In this chapter, we discuss the seven sources of innovation that Drucker identified; four of these sources derive from *within* organizations, and three from *outside* them, from external events. Through specific examples, we demonstrate how organizations have used these sources of innovation effectively to manage change and capitalize on opportunity. Finally, we discuss the role of technology in managing discontinuity.

PARALLELS BETWEEN METHODOLOGIES OF SOCIAL ECOLOGY AND INNOVATION AND ENTREPRENEURSHIP

Drucker notes that "the method used by the social ecologist has to be a rigorous method of looking, of identifying, of testing" (Drucker, 1992b, p. 62). Jim Collins underscores the rigor of the method followed by Peter Drucker: "Drucker immersed himself in empirical facts and then asked, 'What underlying principle explains these facts, and how can we harness that principle?'"(Drucker, 2008, p. xii).

Drucker developed this rigorous method of looking, identifying, and testing in his book *Innovation and Entrepreneurship* (Drucker, 1985). In doing so, he created a direct relationship between the work of the entrepreneur and the work of the social ecologist. That book not only serves as a valuable source of advice on entrepreneurship and innovation but also models his systematic and disciplined method for performing the work of social ecology.

SEVEN SOURCES OF OPPORTUNITY

For Drucker, "systematic innovation . . . consists in the purposeful and organized search for changes, and in the systematic analysis of the opportunities such changes might offer for economic and social innovation" (Drucker, 1985, p. 35). He specifies seven interrelated sources of opportunity for potential innovations: four within the confines of an organization and three in the environment. We provide examples of each source as a guide for applying Drucker's methodology.

Drucker identified four sources of opportunity and innovation that could be found within organizations:

1. The unexpected event
2. Incongruities
3. Process needs
4. Changes in industry structure

Each of these is discussed in the paragraphs that follow.

The Unexpected Event

First, and most important, is the *unexpected event*—an unexpected success, an unexpected failure, or an unexpected change in the environment. The unexpected success or failure offers the best opportunity for success when the event is followed up, understood fully, and effectively worked on by the innovator (Drucker, 1985, p. 37).

Reporting systems should be designed to highlight these unexpected events. Then innovators must look hard at these events to determine why they occurred and what steps are necessary to capitalize upon them. Good examples of the unexpected event—unexpected failure, unexpected success, and a change in the environment—can be found throughout organizational history. We will look at three.

The first is the car models introduced by Ford in the 1950s. Ford introduced its sports car, the two-seater Thunderbird, in 1955. It enjoyed limited success, merely break-even sales. Ford quickly learned that while consumers liked the sports car, they had need for more space than the two-seater provided. In 1958, Ford redesigned the Thunderbird as a four-seater luxury sports car. The Thunderbird became a big success.[1]

In parallel, with great fanfare, Ford introduced its pricy Edsel sedan in 1957 and abruptly discontinued it in 1960 because of poor sales; only 2,846 units were sold over the entire life of the car (Auto Editors of Consumer Guide, n.d.). The Edsel was priced between a high-end Ford and a low-end Mercury. Ford turned the lessons it learned from the unexpected failure of the Edsel, the limited success of the two-seat Thunderbird, and the significant success of the four-seat Thunderbird to its advantage. It learned of a shift in the socioeconomic environment: car buyers in the United States were no longer making purchasing decisions along socioeconomic lines but rather based upon lifestyle considerations. The four-seat Thunderbird was named "Motor Trend Car of the Year" in 1958 ("Motor Trend Car of the Year Complete Winners List," n.d.) because it was a sports car with a lot of passenger room.

A second example of capitalizing on an unexpected event is the Post-it note. The invention of Post-it notes by 3M Corp. was the result of an unexpected success that followed an unexpected failure. In 1970 Spencer Silver, a researcher at 3M Corporation, was trying to develop a strong adhesive product, but he found that the one he developed had weaker adhesive qualities than those on existing products—an unexpected failure for him and for 3M.

In 1974, Arthur Fry, another 3M researcher, was singing in his church choir and became frustrated because the place markers in his hymnal kept falling out. Fry was aware of the adhesive that Silver developed four years earlier, and he used some of Silver's adhesive to create place markers for his hymnal. For that purpose the adhesive was perfect—strong enough to hold a place in the hymnal but not so strong that it could not be moved from one place in the hymnal to another ("Post-it Notes," n.d.). Six years later, after successfully testing the market for the adhesive notes inside 3M and among CEOs of other large companies, 3M began to market Post-it notes. The product became one of the most successful personal and office products in history 10 years after the adhesive failed to meet Silver's specifications.

The 3M approach to the unexpected success is especially instructive. Neither Fry nor the management of 3M knew that it had a successful product. But, given 3M's systematic innovative processes, Fry obtained permission to carry out a low-cost probe of the market for the product within 3M itself. After the success of the probe within 3M, they broadened their market research to include CEOs of large companies. With success in the broader market they decided to launch the product commercially.

The last example is Reading Recovery. Reading Recovery is a reading program for first-grade students who are identified as "students at risk" for achieving reading literacy. The program was introduced in 1976 in Auckland, New Zealand, by Marie Clay, a doctoral student, and later head of the Department of Education at Auckland University. Clay focused her attention on individualized instruction based on an assessment of the reading status and the strengths of each learning impaired student. Her work with six-year-old students "revealed that children had diverse problems with print, and they also had diverse strengths and skills. By emphasizing the strengths of students, what students could do, teachers discovered they could design individual instruction to accelerate learning."[2] Marie Clay wrote of this time, "By the end of 1977 we had a well documented miracle full of surprises."

These surprising results led Clay and her colleagues to promote the expansion of Reading Recovery throughout New Zealand, Australia, North America, and Europe. The program's success in bringing reading-impaired students up to average grade-level reading performance, and then maintaining their performance at that level over time, has been replicated across many parts of the world. Reading Recovery is thus a remarkable example of an unexpected success, a program "full of surprises," that is being exploited to great social advantage and increasing literacy rates worldwide (Reading Council of North America, 2000, p. 8).[3] More recent evidence from the California Early Literacy Learning (CELL) program confirms again that Reading Recovery, when accompanied by necessary training and development of teachers, "has been a powerful demonstration of what might be accomplished with school restructuring and different teaching methods" (Swartz, n.d.).

Incongruities

The second opportunity for innovation is found in *incongruities*. Incongruities are products, processes, or services that are not what they ought to be. One of the best examples of this is the incongruity between what is and what ought to be in the economics of steel production.

Global demand for steel increases, approximately, at the rate of growth in global gross domestic product (Taccone, 2007). As sales increase, all things being equal, profits should increase as well. Once an integrated producer of steel is at full capacity, however, any significant increase in its demand requires the company to incur an enormous expenditure of capital for additional blast-furnace capacity. By the late 1970s, high capital costs together with relatively high labor costs per ton of steel put integrated producers in the United States at a disadvantage against foreign producers. As a result, the United States slowly lost its competitiveness in one of its strategic industries. Between 1978 and 1998, steel capacity in the United States declined from 160 million tons to approximately 95 million tons (Maciariello, 2000).

Electric-arc furnace technology developed by steel mini-mills has reduced the minimum size furnace necessary to achieve optimal scale for many kinds of steel products. The removal of the incongruity in the production of steel, along with the use of recycled scrap metal as raw material by these mini-mills, led to a revival of the steel industry in the United States. The cost advantages of the steel mini-mill over the integrated producer reached approximately 22 percent in the year 2000 (Crandall, 2002, p. 6). Nucor Corp., headquartered in Charlotte, North Carolina, has led the way since 1972 and is now the leading mini-mill, and one of the largest overall steel producers in the United States. The steel mini-mill has permitted the United States to regain competitiveness in the intensely competitive global steel industry.

Process Need

The third source of innovative opportunity, related to the second, is *process need*. A process need arises out of a "missing link" in an existing process. The innovation is supplying the missing link; need becomes the mother of invention.

The human heart has a natural pacemaker that regulates the heartbeat. Arrhythmia, or an irregular heartbeat, may result from a malfunction of the natural pacemaker. Working with cardiologist William Chardack, Wilson Greatbatch invented an implantable cardiac pacemaker in 1958 to deliver electrical impulses to the heart to correct irregular heartbeats. This pacemaker, patented as the Chardack-Greatbatch Implantable Pacemaker, was implanted in a human patient in 1960 at Millard Fillmore Hospital in Buffalo, New York (Drucker and Maciariello, 2009b, pp. 188–190). The implantable pacemaker is an example of a successful innovation based upon new knowledge (see below), *but it created a need for a process innovation.*

A battery powered by mercury and zinc, with an estimated life of five years, was the power source for the initial pacemakers. The actual life of the battery turned out to be only 18 to 24 months, less than half its estimated life. The need for a longer-lasting and more reliable battery thus emerged.

In 1970, Greatbatch made his second great contribution to implantable pacemakers by inventing the lithium-iodine battery, which has double the voltage capacity of the mercury-zinc battery along with an actual duration in excess of 10 years. By allowing patients with irregular heartbeats to maintain a normal heart rate, the implantable pacemakers with reliable batteries have saved millions of lives.

The cardiac pacemaker and its battery powered by lithium and iodine illustrate the integration of process-need-based innovation together with innovation based on new knowledge (see below). This provides an example of a complex phenomenon identified by Drucker: "The risks even of high-tech innovation [i.e., the Pacemaker] can be substantially reduced by integrating new knowledge as a source of innovation with one of the other sources defined earlier, the unexpected, incongruities, and especially process need" [i.e., the mercury-zinc powered battery] (Drucker, 1985, p. 129).

Changes in Industry Structure

The fourth source of opportunity for innovation is *changes in industry or market structure*. As an industry expands rapidly, it is difficult for the leader to serve all segments of the market, which creates opportunities for competitors. That is what happened with the growth in the volume of time-sensitive letters and packages. The U.S. Post Office was slow to respond to the unique requirements created by this new demand. That slow response time created opportunities that were exploited by FedEx, UPS, and DHL. These newcomers innovated and captured large segments of the market for time-sensitive letters and packages. Federal Express began offering delivery service for time-sensitive packages in 1971. The U.S. Post Office partially recovered when it responded with Express Mail delivery service in 1977. These four providers now account for 94 percent of the volume of time-sensitive letters and packages (Department of Homeland Security, n.d.). The market structure for time-sensitive packages remains highly concentrated, but it now has four strong suppliers rather than one.

In addition to the four sources of innovative opportunity internal to organizations there are three sources that are external and detectable in the environment, namely:

1. Demographics
2. Changes in perception, meaning, or mood
3. New knowledge

Each of these will be examined in the paragraphs that follow.

Demographics

The first and perhaps most important external source of innovation is a *change in demographic trends*. Demographic trends, as defined by Drucker, are "changes in population, its size, age structure, composition, employment, educational status, and income" (Drucker, 1985, p. 88). Demographic trends are the least able to be reversed. Therefore, determining the consequences of demographic trends are the first place to find, from seemingly inconspicuous events, those trends that are likely to produce very conspicuous developments.

In *The Pension Fund Revolution* (Drucker 1996, originally published as *The Unseen Revolution*, 1976), Drucker introduced two major trends in the United States that have had significant implications for the American economy and for society. The implications of these trends are still unfolding.

The first trend, which occurred during the 1970s and 1980s, was the emergence of pension fund capitalism, which gradually replaced entrepreneurial and managerial capitalism. Knowledge workers own their human capital, and, together with production and service workers, they have become owners of tangible capital. Workers became owners, initially, through their investment in the assets of their pension funds.

Ownership by workers through pension investments now occurs in two ways. Most public employees are still enrolled in defined-benefit pension funds that are administered by public pension fund administrators. The trend in private corporations, however, has been to eliminate defined-benefit pension plans in favor of defined-contribution plans. Investments in defined-contribution plans take the form of investments in stocks, bonds, and mutual funds directed by the individual through 401(k) plans or, in the case of smaller businesses or the self-employed, simplified employee pensions (SEPs).

Pension assets are thus managed by institutional investors: pension funds and other financial institutions such as investment companies, insurance companies, banks, and foundations. In 2006, institutional investors owned approximately 67 percent of U.S. equities, a 10-fold increase from 1980. Pension funds accounted for more than half of institutional ownership. And because of the shift away from defined-benefit plans by private corporations, state and local pension fund administrators are now the ones exerting the most pressure on corporate governance (The Conference Board, 2006).

To illustrate: The California Public Employees' Retirement System (CalPERS) is the largest public pension fund in the United States with more than $200 billion in assets under management in

2010. CalPERS assumes a very active posture in the management of its corporate investments, attempting to bring changes in corporate governance when it thinks it is desirable. The organization states:

> We believe good corporate governance leads to better performance. We seek corporate reform to protect our investments. The corporate governance team challenges companies and the status quo—we vote our proxies, we work closely with regulatory agencies to strengthen our financial markets, and we invest with partners that use corporate governance strategies to earn value for our fund by turning around ailing companies. [California Public Employees' Retirement System (CalPERS), n.d.]

Drucker saw the emergence of pension fund capitalism, as illustrated by the CalPERS example, and projected the implications of the pension fund revolution onto corporate governance—corporate goals should reflect the needs of future pension beneficiaries, and pension funds should be run for the long-term interests of their beneficiaries. The needs of pension beneficiaries, whether enrolled in defined-benefit plans or in defined-contribution plans, are long term, so the goals of the firm should reflect these long-term needs. That is simply good advice for corporate officers and for institutional investment managers.

The impact on management of the shift in ownership of corporations to institutional investors and their beneficiaries was first felt on the governance of the corporation about 10 years after the publication of Drucker's 1976 book *The Unseen Revolution*. Underperforming corporations, those failing to meet minimum standards of profitability, became candidates for hostile takeovers and leveraged buyouts. While pension funds do turn over their portfolios substantially from year to year, it is very difficult for them to sell major blocks of stock in highly capitalized companies simply because other institutional investors are likely to be owners of the same company. Today, large-cap mutual funds that typically are the most popular investments in defined-contributions plans— 401(k) plans and SEPs—face the same difficulties; portfolios in larger mutual funds lack flexibility because they cannot unload large blocks of shares in major corporations. Who will buy these shares, when most pension funds and institutional investors have large positions in the same companies? As a result, when a company is not earning sufficient profit to cover its opportunity cost of capital, executives of pension funds may agree with other large institutional investors to have the company acquired by new owners who promise better performance.

The almost immediate result of the pension fund revolution was decades of financial and economic turbulence: hostile takeovers, leveraged buyouts, purchases of public corporations by private equity firms, and restructuring of corporations to enhance returns to shareholders.

That has been a mostly healthy development for owners of pension assets, because executives of takeover-target corporations often were destroying the wealth of investors. However, as Drucker noted, a by-product of this focus on financial returns has led to a period of remarkable upheaval, one that has taken a substantial toll on the human beings within the impacted organizations. Drucker was distinctly critical of the trend toward leveraged buyouts and takeovers that occurred during the 1980s. Always concerned with the human dimension, Drucker saw that corporations were less concerned with the long-term welfare of their employees and communities and more concerned with the short-term financial success of their organizations. Corporate executives should indeed focus on adequate profitability, but they also should focus on value to their other stakeholders—employees, vendors, communities, and so on. By adopting an enlightened form of shareholder wealth maximization, the corporation could attempt to maximize its long-term wealth-producing capacity while also serving the interests of all its stakeholders. That is consistent with Drucker's overall advice: what is best for society should be made the objective of the corporation, because the corporation is a creature of society and is therefore an organ of society. And no organ can prosper in a dying body!

The second trend that Drucker discussed in *The Unseen Revolution* (1976) was the aging "baby boomer" generation. He then projected the implications of this demographic reality onto the Social Security and Medicare systems. When originally created in 1935, Social Security was intentionally designed to be funded through employee and employer contributions. President Franklin Roosevelt insisted that the program not result in any future unfunded liability; as a result, Social Security initially exempted many workers, including domestic and agricultural workers, in order to avoid the problem of underfunding. However, Social Security was expanded several times since then. Following the World War II, coverage was extended to most of the previously excluded workers, and disability and Medicare and Medicaid benefits were also added. By 1973, Social Security faced its first deficits, and there were widespread warnings of a shortfall in the trust fund's ability to meet future obligations.

Drucker showed that *demographic pressures* would put tremendous demands on both the Social Security and Medicare systems, and he drew the logical conclusion that the U.S. domestic political debate would focus increasingly on how to meet the needs of an aging population. The demographic "time bomb" in the United States is now ready to explode upon us. The time bomb resulted from the gradual but predictable decrease in the number of workers paying for the social security pensions of a relatively large number of retirees. This demographic is a result of the post–World War II baby boom generation—the number of payers per recipient has fallen and will continue to fall dramatically until these social systems become insolvent or are restored to fiscal health.[4]

Figure 8.1   Decline in Workers per Beneficiary under Social Security

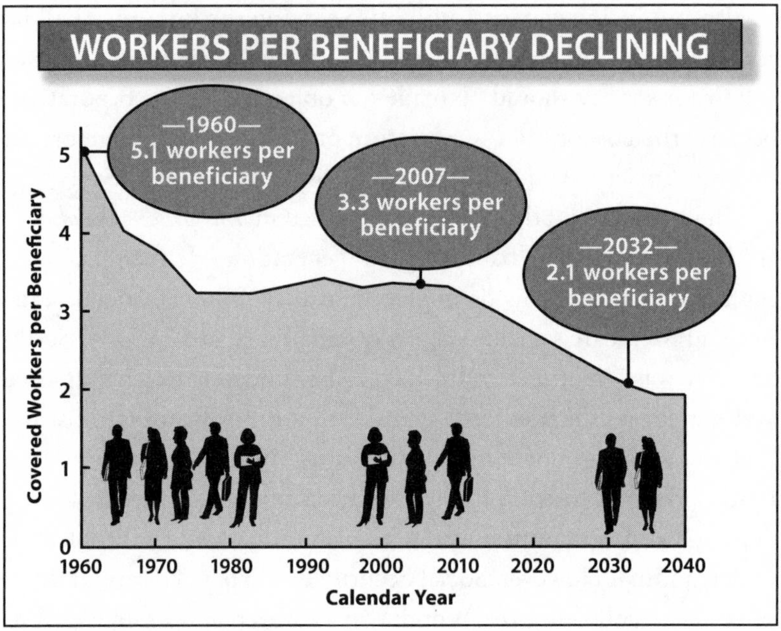

Source: Social Security Online, accessed July 15, 2008

Figure 8.1 illustrates the decline in workers per beneficiary under Social Security. In 1960 there were 5.1 workers per beneficiary, whereas in 2007 that number was reduced to 3.3 workers per beneficiary; under the current system the number is projected to decrease to 2.1 workers per beneficiary in 2032.

The Social Security system is a pay-as-you-go system, with current workers paying for current beneficiaries. It is still collecting more than it is paying out, but, based upon current projections, that situation is projected to change and the numbers turn negative in 2017. The surplus in the trust fund—money collected for Social Security but borrowed by the government to meet other budgetary obligations—is likely to be exhausted in 2041.[5]

The debate over how to handle Social Security entitlements has been ongoing for some time; in his 2005 State of the Union address,

President George W. Bush called for major reforms in the program, including the creation of 401(k)-like, individually directed accounts in which Americans could invest directly in the stock market. Bush's ideas were met with public outcry, as Social Security has—and continues to be—an untouchable third rail of politics in the United States for a variety of reasons. In spite of the fact that Drucker and others recognized the demographic-driven problem in the 1970s, American citizens have essentially tied the hands of their elected officials. The result is that a once potentially manageable problem is increasingly becoming more and more difficult to address; fixing the problem will likely now cause major discontinuities, as gradual solutions are no longer sufficient.

Although the results were not what Drucker wished, this illustrates again the work of the social ecologist: use demographic information as a source of opportunities to *create positive change* and avoid major *discontinuities*, which allows policymakers time to adapt to the inevitable changes in an orderly way so as to *maintain continuity*. Unfortunately, for the United States and for many other developed nations, Congress and the American people failed to act on Drucker's and others' warnings; as a result, extraordinary discontinuities now await policymakers, U.S. taxpayers, and future recipients of benefits. Payroll and self-employment taxes have been increasing over time, and the retirement age for full benefits has been slowly increasing, but these changes have been insufficient to address the shortfalls. More drastic changes will have to be made in the future to taxes, retirement ages, and benefits.

The United States is not the only nation that faces a crisis related to demographic shifts and entitlement spending. Many European nations are feeling the impact of such shifts, and they are facing staggering financial crises of their own. Because we all live in a global society, we must pay attention to *global demographic changes* and their effects on politics, economies, and societies of the developed countries of the world. In Drucker's important article "The Next

Society" (Drucker, 2001), he picks up the same argument he made for the United States in his 1976 book *The Unseen Revolution* and applies it to all developed countries:

> In the developed countries, the dominant factor in the next society will be something to which most people are only just beginning to pay attention: the rapid growth in the older population and the rapid shrinking of the younger generation. Politicians everywhere still promise to save the existing pensions system, but they—and their constituents—know perfectly well that in another 25 years people will have to keep working until their mid-70s, health permitting. (Drucker, 2001, p. 1)

As of this writing, the credit ratings of the sovereign debt of Greece, Spain, and Portugal have been cut as a result of the 2008–2010 (and beyond) global recession, in large part because of current and projected future spending on entitlements. In 2010, Greece's public debt was 124 percent of gross domestic product, and Standard and Poor's rating of that country's government bonds was downgraded to junk status (Tross, "The Euro Can Survive a Greek Default," *The Wall Street Journal*, pp. A1 and A12). As was the case with the United States, there is plenty of blame to go around for the meltdown of the Greek economy. Goldman Sachs and others aided and abetted the Greek government's overspending, loaning the country funds through deals that were hidden from European Union officials (Story, Thomas, and Schwartz, "Wall Street Helped to Mask Debt Fueling Europe's Crisis," p. A1). In response to the Greek government's efforts to raise taxes, cut entitlement spending, and reduce public employee's wages, Greek citizens took to the streets in protest by the thousands; three people were killed when protestors torched the Marfin Bank building in downtown Athens. Enabled by Wall Street and captive to entitlement obligations, by the spring of 2010, the Greek government was in the process of a meltdown that posed a threat to the stability of the entire European Union. An understanding of the global demographic changes driving entitlement spending might not have stopped Goldman Sachs' shady deals or citizen protests from taking place, but would at least have warned of the need to plan for (and possibly minimize) such discontinuities.

Demographic trends are also important as sources of innovative opportunity for many organizations. What opportunities do these trends, and changes in them, present for entrepreneurs? We will focus our example of opportunities on Hispanic households, since the growth in the number of Hispanics has been one of the most significant demographic shifts in the United States.

A 2009 study by Jeffrey Humphreys of the Selig Center of the University of Georgia allows us to gain an understanding of the opportunities created by the growth of the Hispanic population in the United States. For Humphreys, a "Hispanic" is "a person of Mexican, Puerto Rican, Cuban or other Spanish/Hispanic/Latino culture of origin, and is considered an ethnic category rather than a racial group" (Humphreys, 2009, p. 10). The Humphreys' study focuses on Hispanic buying power defined as "the total personal income of residents that is available, after taxes, for spending on virtually everything they buy, but it does not include dollars that are borrowed or that were saved in previous years" (p. 1).

In 2009, Hispanics comprised 15.7 percent of the population in the United States. Based upon projections of fertility and immigration rates, the percentage of Hispanics in the United States is forecasted to rise to 17.2 percent in 2014 (Humphreys, 2009, Table 4, p. 14). This is almost double the 1990 Hispanic population, which was 9 percent of the U.S. population.

In 2009, Hispanics had buying power of $978 billion, 26 percent of which was concentrated in California. The top five states (California, Texas, Florida, New York, and Illinois) had 60 percent of the total Hispanic buying power, whereas the top 10 states had 80 percent (Humphreys, 2009, p. 10). Furthermore, according to Humphreys, the direction of Hispanic buying power is different from the rest of the population:

> Despite markedly lower average income levels, Hispanic households spent more on telephone services, men's and boys' clothing, children's clothing, and footwear. Also, Hispanics spent a higher proportion of their money on food (groceries and restaurants), housing, utilities, and transportation. Hispanics spent about the same as non-Hispanics on housekeeping supplies, furniture, appliances, women's and girls' clothing, and personal care products and services. Compared to non-Hispanics, they spent substantially less on alcoholic beverages, health care, entertainment, reading materials, education, tobacco products, cash contributions, and personal insurance and pensions. (Humphreys, 2009, p. 11)

The likely direction of expenditures of the growing Hispanic population would seem to create marketing and innovation opportunities for cell-phone manufacturers; for designers of clothing and footwear; and for producers of automobiles. Yet such broad ethnic categories, and subsequent behavioral conclusions, must be evaluated carefully. The buying behaviors Humphreys details may change due to a number of factors. For immigrant families, the second generation often will assimilate more into the general American culture; these Hispanics may spend proportionately more on education and reading materials than their parents did. If Hispanic income levels rise, as more achieve middle-class status, we might expect to see an increase in health care and entertainment spending.

Self-identification is also important. The Pew Hispanic Center conducted a study in which they found substantial differences in self-identification among Hispanic ethnic groups. For example, 42 percent of U.S.-born Mexican Americans in California identified themselves as white. In contrast, 63 percent of U.S.-born Mexican Americans in Texas self-identified as white. Such self-categorization is important, because those Hispanics who viewed themselves as white typically had higher incomes and levels of education (Tafoya, 2004).

Regional and other differences complicate efforts to categorize Hispanics and other ethnic groups for marketing purposes. Nevertheless, demographic trends can help to identify both opportunities and warnings to executives trying to market and produce innovative products and services for the Hispanic market in various geographical regions of the United States.

Changes in Perception, Meaning, or Mood

The second external innovation opportunity comes from *changes in perception, meaning, or mood*. When there is a change in perception, "the facts do not change. Their meaning does" (Drucker, 1985, p. 104).

Politicians are notorious for creating or capitalizing on existing, changes in perception, meaning, and mood. One particularly acrimonious political topic was the American debate over health-care reform during 2009 and 2010. Much of this debate revolved around not facts, but people's perceptions of the meaning of those facts, as well as the mood of Americans during a difficult economic downturn. On both sides of the aisle, the "facts" were agreed upon, for the most part. What ruled the discourse was their meaning.

According to various estimates, there are as many as 47 million people in the United States without health insurance. These people do not have insurance for many reasons. One might be cost; they cannot afford to buy their own policy or pay the shared premiums mandated by their employer. Another is unemployment; perhaps their coverage under the Consolidated Omnibus Budget Reconciliation Act—COBRA—has expired and they can no longer afford to maintain it, or they are excluded for other reasons. Other reasons might be underemployment—they are ineligible because of part-time status. Or there might be another reasons, such as pre-existing conditions, or being employed by an organization that does not offer coverage.

Lack of health insurance is a major cause of personal financial distress in the United States; a Harvard study showed that half of personal bankruptcies filed in 2001 were medically related. Many of those fortunate to have had insurance lost their coverage, along with their income, when they became ill (Himmelstein, et al., 2010).

In 2010, Congress passed comprehensive health-care reform legislation that is projected to reduce the number of uninsured by approximately 32 million. This legislation was highly controversial, criticized from both the right and the left. The "facts" of America's problem (the high cost of health care, people losing coverage because of preexisting conditions and unemployment, inefficiencies in the system) were, for the most part, agreed upon. What fueled the controversy was exactly what Drucker identified as an issue of perception, meaning, and mood.

Some perceived the system of health care in the United States to be outstanding; these people we term the "half full" crowd. They felt that, because we live in an age of extreme health consciousness, others erroneously see that the glass still seems "half empty" and that we are experiencing a crisis in health care. The half-full group perceived that reality is quite different. For evidence, they point to the fact that life expectancies have increased dramatically in the United States because of better health and nutrition. The national Center for Health Statistics reports that, "from 1900 through 2004, life expectancy at birth increased from 46 to 75 years for men and from

48 to 80 years for women" (National Center for Health Statistics, 2007, p. 50). They also note the increased availability of information through the Internet. The massive flow of information on psychological and physiological wellness and the mind-body connection enables us to acquire knowledge regarding our health, well-being, and lifestyle habits that have an effect on our health. Major disciplines, such as medicine and psychology, are providing us new knowledge that we can use to help take control of our own well-being, to enhance our functioning, and to improve the quality of and prolong our lives.

The half-empty crowd perceived a different reality. To them, the American health-care system was dysfunctional, driven by profit rather than concern for well-being and value of human life. As evidence, they cite the growing obesity rate, particularly among children; First Lady Michelle Obama even got involved, launching a campaign against childhood obesity called "Let's Move." While the death rates for women giving birth are falling around the world, women in the United States are dying during childbirth at increasing rates, for a variety of reasons (Associated Press, 2007). They also note the fact that many working-class families have no Internet access, and thus are unable to tap into the flow of information on wellness and treatment available to those in the upper and middle classes. Race and ethnicity also play a role in health care. For many reasons, non-whites have less access to new technologies and information, and thus they are prevented from improving the quality or length of their lives. For the half-empty group, the American health-care system does not treat everybody equally, and thus it has inherent problems; those without the means to pay for treatment, or the knowledge of how to prevent illness, end up suffering.

Regardless of which group one may be in (the half-full one or the half-empty one), the health-care crisis presents opportunity because of the perceptions and opinions of the two camps. One thing everybody can agree upon: the debate over health care forced the American people to address the question of medical treatment and its costs. Is health care something valued as a human right? Or is it a marketable commodity that exists for the benefit of the companies that provide it? Or is it some combination of both? The health-care debate brought these perceptions and meanings to the forefront rather than any new set of facts. For corporations, the explosion of interest in "wellness" of the body and mind, together with an increase in useful *knowledge* (discussed next) has created all kinds of opportunities for innovation in everything from health-care magazines, to aerobic equipment, to vitamins of all kinds, and to books for and instructions on meditation exercises for managing the stresses of life. Regardless of perception, the health-care reform debate in America certainly increased awareness of the subject of wellness, providing opportunities for innovation.

New Knowledge

The last and most glamorous window of opportunity for innovation is *new knowledge*. The example here is the creation of management as a discipline by Drucker himself.

Drucker's used new knowledge to develop the discipline of management. A knowledge-based innovation is often based on a "convergence of several different kinds of knowledge" (Drucker, 1985, p. 111). Knowledge-based innovations will not come together until all the needed pieces of knowledge are in existence and are able to converge. Here is Drucker's illustration from his own innovation in the field of management:

My own success as an innovator in the management field was based on a similar analysis [to that of other innovators] in the early 1940s. Many of the required pieces of knowledge were already available: organization theory, for instance, but also quite a bit of knowledge about managing work and worker. My analysis also showed, however, that these pieces were scattered in half a dozen different disciplines. Then [I] found which key knowledges were missing: purpose of a business; any knowledge of the work and structure of top management; what we now term "business policy" and "strategy"; objectives; and so on. All of the missing knowledge, I decided could be produced. But without such analysis, I could never have known what they were or that they were missing. (Drucker, 1985, pp. 115–116)

As implied in Drucker's quotation, first came his understanding of what the discipline and practice of management is all about: what does it have to accomplish? Only then could he identify the parts that were required and separate them into those that were known and those that had to be discovered:

Every discipline has as its center today a concept of a whole that is not the result of its parts, not equal to the sum of its parts. . . . The central concepts in every one of our modern disciplines, sciences and arts are patterns and configurations. . . . These configurations can never be reached by starting with the parts. . . . Indeed, the parts in any pattern or configuration exist only, and can only be identified, in contemplation of the whole and from the understanding of the whole. . . . "Management," similarly, is a configuration term. (Drucker, 1959, pp. 4–5)

Drucker had a conception of the liberal arts and management that was holistic, one that involved viewing disciplines or practices from a larger perspective. In this view, management is an entire system that is greater than its individual components. Drucker referred to this as a "configuration," or a pattern. In developing his concept of the practice of management, he began with the "configuration term" of management, and in 1973 defined this term. In doing so, he made explicit what to him previously seemed implicit. Drucker defined the configuration of management as "a system the parts of which are human beings contributing voluntarily of their knowledge, skill, and dedication to a joint venture" (Drucker, 1973, p. 508). In other words, Drucker's work did not start with the parts; rather it started with "a concept of the whole," a "pattern." Then Drucker described the parts, or knowledges, required for the configuration to be carried out effectively.

Drucker first noted the knowledge that already existed in organization theory. As we have seen in Chapters 6 and 7, both Barnard and Follett established a substantial body of knowledge on the design of formal and informal organization. In addition to the works of Barnard and Follett, there was the important early work of Henri Fayol,[6] a Frenchman, who focused on organizational administration. Fayol, an engineer, published his book *Industrial and General Administration* in France in 1918. The book was translated into English in 1930. Fayol developed 14 principles of organization. He emphasized the division of labor and specialization and the creation of the functional organization structure for the accomplishment of work.

Fayol generalized the functional organization for all manufacturing organizations. Each manufacturing organization required certain distinct functions, each function with its own specialized work. These functions included engineering, manufacturing, sales, finance, and personnel. These functions operated independently and were integrated at the top by a general manager or chief executive officer.

Next, Drucker mentioned the research completed on the subjects of work and working, which was carried out by Frederick Taylor and

Elton Mayo, respectively. We discussed the influence of Taylor on Drucker in Chapter 7 and of Mayo in Chapter 6.

It is also interesting to note that the works of Taylor, Mayo, and Fayol all resulted in increasing the productivity of labor; the first by direct application of the *scientific method to work*; the second by increasing *worker motivation*; and the third by application of *systematic organization and administration* to work.

Synthesis of existing knowledges was necessary, since the knowledges required for the innovation were located in "a dozen different disciplines" (Drucker, 1985, p. 116). These include industrial engineering, manufacturing, psychology, industrial psychology, sociology, political science, history, government, and one discipline Drucker did not specifically mention: economics. Not only did Drucker draw upon the work of economist Joseph Schumpeter but he was very aware of the extraordinary early work in managerial economics by Joel Dean (1906–1979), who in 1951 published his groundbreaking book *Managerial Economics*.[7] Joel Dean was a professor of economics at Columbia University and management consultant in the fields of managerial economics and the economics of strategy. He is also known for his works in pricing, capital budgeting, and statistical cost estimation. He formed his management consulting firm, Joel Dean Associates, in 1940.

So, when Drucker wrote *Concept of the Corporation* and *The Practice of Management* (1954) he was building on the very formidable work of numerous predecessors, those described in Chapters 4, 6, and 7 as well as those described in this chapter. He then added the parts that were missing. He developed a good deal of his own work on decentralization, Management by Objectives, the structure of top management, and business strategy while working at General Motors on what became *Concept of the Corporation*, and when working with Harold Smiddy at the General Electric Co. on what became *The Practice of Management*. Drucker's work with Smiddy also resulted in the definition of the purpose of the business. In his autobiography Drucker states:

> At GE, there was something else I'd like to record here, which was not just a terminology but the fundamental question of what exactly the purpose of the business is. This is the question that no economist, including John Maynard Keynes, whose lectures I once listened to, could ever answer. While working with Smiddy, I redefined the purpose of the business in terms of market or customers rather than technology, and concluded that decentralization should also be based on that concept.
>
> One of my best known phrases is "the purpose of the business is to create customers." I thought that seeing profit as the purpose of businesses was missing the mark. Smiddy, who thought that this was a fresh idea, urged me to publish a book based on the series of volumes I wrote and edited for his department. In 1954, I published *The Practice of Management*, using my experiences working for GE and other major corporations. (Drucker, 2009)

Drucker's innovation in the discipline and practice of management is an example of the need for several kinds of knowledge to converge if there is to be a successful innovation based upon new knowledge. First, there is knowledge of purpose or configuration. Then there is the need to synthesize existing knowledges so that they converge. Third, there is the need to identify and to develop the missing pieces in order for new knowledge-based innovation to be successful. Drucker added "new knowledge" to existing knowledge and developed the practice of management.

Drucker's example of his own innovation illustrates that innovation based upon new knowledge is *only possible* when sufficient foundations have been established by others. The innovator works to synthesize knowledge and add the missing pieces. The maxim of Sir Isaac Newton was as true for Drucker as it was for all innovators who innovate using new knowledge: the innovator "stands on the shoulders of giants." This is a lesson for each of us.

TECHNOLOGY: THE GREAT DESTABILIZER OF SOCIETY

Drucker's interest in mastering destabilizing influences, or discontinuities, by holding on to continuities and by harnessing change so that it was positive for individuals, organizations, and society led him directly to the study of the influence of technology on society. Drucker's approach to technology was "to view technology as a human, nay a social, phenomenon rather than as a merely 'technical' one, and society as shaped by, and formed around, work and work bond" (Drucker, 1993, p. 276).

Technological change is inherently destabilizing. New technology itself brings forth the need for *additional social change and innovation*. New technology can transform the economic, social, and political landscape and shape the future of society. Any aspiring social ecologist must be attentive to technology and its profound potential for creating opportunities for personal, organizational, and social advancement but also for creating potentially disruptive discontinuities.

For Drucker, there could be no general understanding of technology unless it was understood *as tools applied to work*:

> It [technology] is about work: the specifically human activity by means of which man pushes back the limitations of the iron biological law which condemns all other animals to devote all their time and energy to keeping themselves alive for the next day, if not for the next hour. (Drucker, 1959–1960, p. 30)

The way we organize work is also an important tool of mankind, and Drucker recognized that Frederick W. Taylor's scientific management was a major technological breakthrough for the world:

> Scientific Management focuses on the work. Its core is the organized study of work, the analysis of work into its simplest elements and the systematic improvement of the worker's performance of each of these elements. Scientific Management has both basic concepts and easily applicable tools and techniques. . . . Indeed, Scientific Management is all but a systematic philosophy of worker and work. Altogether it may be the most powerful as well as the most lasting contribution America has made to Western thought since the Federalist Papers. (Drucker, 1954, p. 280)

Finally we arrive at the systems concept that appears so much in Drucker's methodology—in this case the mutual influence of *task*, *tools*, and *social organization*:

> But we have already learned that the task, the tools, and the social organization of work are not totally independent but mutually influence and affect one another. (Drucker, 1959–1960, p. 32)

THE LESSONS OF TECHNOLOGICAL CHANGE: A STREAM OF INNOVATION POTENTIAL BASED ON NEW KNOWLEDGE

Technological change is often a big disruptor to organizations, society, and people while bringing great benefits along with potential dangers. Technological change of significant scope requires changes in values, organization structures, and the behavior of people. Significant technological change therefore calls for numerous additional social and technical innovations in order to make the new technology beneficial for society, its organizations, and its people. This section explores the impact and opportunities created by technological change.

The Irrigation City[8]

Historians in the twentieth century explored the phenomenon of urban development, tracing its origins back to ancient civilizations. In 1961, Lewis Mumford published *The City in History: Its Origins, Its Transformations, and Its Prospects,* in which he discussed the role of irrigation in fostering social and economic change in early agricultural communities. Following in suit, in an article on the lessons of technological change, Drucker traced the influences of the first technological revolution—irrigation and the irrigated city, an invention of ancient culture: "First in Mesopotamia, and then in Egypt and in the Indus Valley, and finally in China," Drucker continues, "no other change in man's way of life and in his making of a living . . . so completely revolutionized human society and community" (Drucker, 1959–1960, p. 143). This was a great period of change in society, which revealed the tensions between the needs for *innovation and change,* and for *continuity.*

The irrigation city, because of its influence on the development of agriculture, resulted in agricultural communities and therefore the need for government and for property rights and for the rule of law. The irrigation city was susceptible to attack from enemies and therefore required military force to protect it. As a result social-economic classes of farmers, soldiers, and government officials developed. As a city developed, any surplus over consumption resulted in trade with other cities. This in turn created the need for a standard of exchange (that is, money) and provision for credit and banking. Trade also required writing and bookkeeping. Engineering was required to regulate and control the flow of water.

Each of these innovations required new knowledge. But, according to Drucker, most importantly the irrigated city created the person, the individual, and the citizen. It created the need for social justice and compassion. It also resulted in the development of the world religions.

Drucker concludes:

> Technological revolutions create an objective need for social and political innovations. They create a need also for identifying the areas in which *new institutions* [emphasis ours] are needed and old ones are becoming obsolete. . . .
>
> But the values these institutions attempt to realize, the human and social purposes to which they are applied, and perhaps most important the emphasis and stress laid on one purpose over another, are largely within human control. (Drucker, 1966, p. 50)

The irrigation city was created by innovation and required numerous additional innovations and the application of human values to the *management of society's institutions.* The study of technology and its influence on society and its institutions is therefore one of the most important tasks of the social ecologist.

Technological Change: The Internet

The Internet, an innovation in our time, has and will continue to have enormous impact on individuals, organizations, and society. By substantially reducing and almost eliminating the cost of communication, the Internet has practically eliminated distance as a factor in commerce for certain kinds of goods and services. While the invention of the steam engine and railroad *reduced* the impact of distance on commerce, the Internet has almost *eliminated* the impact of distance on the ability to conduct commerce globally. Practically all knowledge-related products and services—such as education, accounting, advertising, design, and research—may be conducted using e-commerce. In addition, e-commerce is making it feasible for individuals and organizations to distribute almost any product or service whether they produce it or not.

The Internet has

1. contributed to flattening organizations, removing layers that previously served as mere communication links;
2. made outsourcing of goods and services less expensive and therefore much more common;
3. changed strategies of corporations from ownership and control to alliances and partnerships;
4. increased the accessibility of knowledge to anyone able to access the Internet, thus intensifying global competition for goods and services;
5. altered social relationships by the widespread availability of social network sites; and
6. made individuals, organizations, and nations much more vulnerable to cyberwarfare.

While the effects of the Internet have already been felt in commerce, medicine, social relationships, terrorism, and politics and government, many of its implications remain to be played out, including understanding its full impact on globalization, as witnessed by the unexpected massive impact of the current financial crisis on developed and developing nations around the world.

Technology has played the role of great disruptor, creating opportunities and dangers for individuals, organizations, and society at large. The social ecologist should be on alert for changes such as these.

CONCLUSION

Drucker, the social ecologist, recognized that change, or discontinuity, was a given part of existence and that organizations must recognize this fact in order to survive. His methodology as a social ecologist involved viewing change as a source of opportunity for innovation; Drucker identified four sources of innovation that came from within organizations, and three that originated from the external environment. Harnessing the forces of technology also allows organizations to effectively negotiate the reality of discontinuity, while maintaining some level of continuity in order to minimize disruptions.

At times, the disruptions seem greater than others, particularly for the generation living through its time of discontinuity. This is indeed a period of great change, perhaps more significant than that brought on by the irrigation city. The social ecologist seeks to extrapolate these great changes into the future and alert executives and individuals to the *discontinuities* that are and will be created as well as to the need to *embrace change* in order to *retain continuity* and *viability* as a functioning entity. After 2008, we have witnessed the failure of organizations large and small to change fast enough. They have succumbed to the discontinuities brought about by the subprime global financial crisis. Global information and money flows have created positive global growth, but they have also created the dangers of chain reactions that intensify crises.

Against all this change comes the increased need to be vigilant: to abandon products, services, and processes no longer serving their intended function; to develop and perfect processes of systematic innovation and change while seeking to retain continuity with values that have helped to maintain cohesion and stability in times of rapid change.

The work of the social ecologist seems more important than ever because the opportunities and dangers of change are now greater. This chapter has provided the tools individuals, executives, and organizations need to change. Our hope is that they will contribute to a hopeful and bearable society.

CONCLUSION

What a piece of work is a man! How noble in reason! How infinite in
faculty! In form and moving how express and admirable! In action
how like an angel! In apprehension how like a god! The beauty of the
world! The paragon of animals! And yet, to me, what is this quintes-
sence of dust? Man delights not me.

—Hamlet

The theme of an imperfect world populated by "fallen" beings
permeates many of the liberal arts disciplines, including literature. Shakespeare's Hamlet laments the evil nature of humanity
in spite of what Drucker might have described as human dignity,
or creation in the image of God. In Mark Twain's *A Connecticut
Yankee in King Arthur's Court*, Yankee time-traveling Hank Morgan
believes that his era's technology and democratic ideals will solve
sixth-century England's social inequalities, only to find that human
nature prevails; Morgan falls prey to his own lust for power, and
the country devolves into a war of catastrophic proportions. Often
the most "holy" characters are the most "fallen"; Sinclair Lewis's

Elmer Gantry is a hopelessly corrupt Protestant preacher, and the man engaged in adultery with Hester Prynne in *The Scarlet Letter* is none other than Arthur Dimmesdale, the Puritan minister.

Peter Drucker found inspiration for his vision of a "bearable society" in a wide variety of liberal arts disciplines, including religious and political philosophy, sociology, history, psychology, and economics. Beginning with Kierkegaard's existentialist view of life in constant tension, Drucker found a host of other interpretations of human existence that attempted to reconcile—or at least come to terms with—this tension. Ultimately for Drucker, the most important tension was the one identified by Kierkegaard: the acknowledgement that earthly existence is separate from the spiritual realm, and that that translates into a life of disappointment. Only faith can overcome the despair that comes with understanding the irreconcilable tension of human existence. Using the ideas of Kierkegaard and other religious philosophers, as well as other disciplines, Drucker constructed a more accessible, secular vision for dealing with the change, dissonance, and disruption that is a given in modern society. His "bearable society" pivoted on well-managed institutions that would not just create wealth but also provide meaning—existential, philosophical, quasi-religious meaning—to people searching for a reason to be on this planet.

Given the intellectual process that informed his view of management, it is no wonder that Drucker envisioned management as a liberal art. It is also not surprising that understanding Drucker requires understanding his *moral* perspective; management for Drucker was a force for good, a way of staving off evil. To some, this seems utopian and unrealistic. Yet when we consider the role of the liberal arts in Drucker's thinking, his moral viewpoint becomes clearer. The liberal arts ideal from its inception to today has involved the inculcation of some set of agreed-upon values for a given society at a given point in time. If the historical purpose of the liberal arts has been to develop the human capacity to recognize the right and good, management's only hope to be a moral force for right and good is to ally itself with the liberal arts. The early business schools recognized that, and they required training in the liberal arts as a prerequisite to an advanced degree. Even before the burgeoning of business schools, there had been a long history of enlisting the liberal arts in the cause of producing more educated citizens, virtuous leaders, and people with the capacity to think for themselves.

Today, liberal arts academics and practicing managers too often view one another with disdain or suspicion. The gap between the "real world" and the "ivory tower" is in many respects an artifice. Professors do not simply train their replacements; they also help students develop broadly applicable skills, such as critical thinking, use of evidence in constructing an argument, and effective written and oral communication. Most business professionals recognize that college graduates are often weak in such areas because of the schools' emphasis on vocational-specific training. This is part of the drive behind the joint ventures between business schools and traditional liberal arts colleges.

Yet the divide still exists. Academics believe that management is a subject beneath them; managers feel that academics are out of touch with the real world. Part of this divide has to do with the heart of Drucker's vision of management as a liberal art: the concept of values. Academics view for-profit activities as "tainted," as violating the sanctity of the space of scholarly freedom; for most scholars, involving commerce necessarily corrupts the independent nature of academic inquiry. For the management world, money is part and parcel of daily life; it is the lifeblood of existence. It is valued for its ability to provide for an organization's continued existence as well as its role in paying employees, suppliers, and investors. Achievement of management as a liberal art, and reconciliation between the two interests, requires a reconciliation of *values*. Can the world of work and profits concern itself with such lofty ideals as character, integrity, and truth? It is our only hope that it do so in order to redeem management as a practice.

That is why Drucker focused on values rather than skills, tactics, or disciplines. If management is to be a moral force, governing institutions that give people meaning and status in a world defined by inconsistency and tension, it must be driven by values. Drucker believed that the liberal arts are the keepers of morality and values; to make management a moral force requires making management a liberal art. Although he never made an overt connection between the two, Drucker's idea of management as a liberal art unites the liberal arts ideal of instilling moral character and the management goal of producing effective leaders. Liberal arts managers have a thorough understanding of the nature of human existence, develop people in their organizations while curtailing the potential for abuse of power, and understand the larger role their organizations play in society. Driven by a sense of morality and an obligation to a greater good, liberal arts–oriented managers recognize that, while human beings are by nature imperfect, their organizations must strive to create a hopeful, if not a "bearable," society.

The origins of management as a liberal art are complex and intellectual. Implementing management as a liberal art requires not only an understanding of that intellectual background but also a strong sense of the spirit the liberal arts ideal. Drawing on the disciplines of history, economics, or philosophy can enable managers to make decisions that take into account the nature of human beings, the role of power in organizations, and external factors that cause discontinuities, as well as lead in challenging situations. Management as a liberal art also allows organizations to consider the source of their values and how they will uphold and live by those values that executives believe to be most important. If nothing else, this new approach requires managers to be more thoughtful about the impact their decisions and actions have on their coworkers, customers, competitors, suppliers, and society as a whole.

Our society begs for a new approach to management. It is not only the business community that is plagued by mismanagement; unfortunately, the problem is apparent in virtually all types of organizations. In June 2010, the National Collegiate Athletic Association (NCAA) penalized the University of Southern California for a variety of violations, most of which involved improper financial benefits given to football star Reggie Bush. The penalties were substantial, including the loss of scholarships and a two-year ban on college bowl participation (Beacham, 2010). Greed and lack of consideration for human beings exists not just in the corporate sector but even in our institutions of higher learning. However, as Drucker has shown, management as a liberal art can apply to any organization regardless of activity or status. We cannot hope to achieve anything close to an ideal society. But we certainly can strive for something attainable: a society in which work has meaning, leadership has integrity, management recognizes that its role is ultimately about human dignity and development, and organizations acknowledge their obligation to the greater good of the commonwealth. With management as a liberal art, we have a chance of achieving Drucker's vision of a tolerable society.

NOTES

Introduction

1. The October 2009 recall expanded on an earlier September 2007 recall related to floor mats and accelerator pedal entrapment.

Chapter 1

1. Dartmouth College's Daniel Webster Project in Ancient and Modern Studies indicates that its purpose is to bring "ancient and modern perspectives to bear on issues of permanent moral and political purpose." The 2009 inaugural lecturer was Professor Anthony Kronman, author of *Education's End: Why Our Colleges and Universities Have Given Up on the Meaning of Life* (The Daniel Webster Project Web site).

2. Jack Beatty states that Drucker found God in Kierkegaard's writing: "Where did He come from? Drucker found Him in a book by Søren Kierkegaard" (Beatty, 1998). See Beatty, *The World According to Peter Drucker,* p. 98.

3. "Law does not come into being and does not work, because I want it, but because I want it, it has validity for me. While authoritative working is a property of the law, validity is a property of moral law" (Drucker, 1932, p. 57). *Die Rechtfertigung des Völkerrechts aus dem Staatswillen. Eine logisch-kritische Untersuchung der Selbstverpflichtungs-und Vereinbarungslehre,* Berlin: Verlag von Franz Vahlen, p. 57. Translated from German to English by Timo Meynhardt in his unpublished paper "The Practical Wisdom of Peter Drucker: Its Roots in the Christian Tradition," 2009.

4. Berthold Freyberg, one of Drucker's oldest friends, has also argued for the importance of Stahl on Drucker's work, including the spiritual and irrational component: "What impressed Drucker was Stahl's belief that power must submit to responsibility. This is not a rational process: the acceptance of power as being governed by responsibility touches the roots of our spiritual existence, that is, our faith. . . . It manifests itself in an attitude of involved freedom in all our actions which, if applied to economics, is bound to 'ethicize the economy,' as Walter Rathenau termed it. This consciousness of involvement is fundamental for Drucker and can be traced in his writings wherever exertion of power is concerned" (Freyberg, 1970, pp. 20–21).

Chapter 2

1. There are several sources on the history of liberal arts education. See, for example, Kimball, 1986, and Axelrod, 2002.
2. Kimball refers to these opposing camps as the "philosophers" (Plato) and the "orators" (Cicero and Isocrates).
3. For example, in 2005, the University of Connecticut began requiring its students to take a specific number of courses in each of four content areas: Arts and Humanities, Social Sciences, Science and Technology, and Multiculturalism and Diversity (see http://services.clas.uconn.edu/gened.html). The University of Illinois at Chicago updated its general education curriculum for incoming freshmen in 2007, stating that the new course of study was intended to prepare students for a world in which they would need to "think independently; understand and critically evaluate information; analyze and evaluate arguments; develop and present cogent written and oral arguments; explore one's own culture and history as well as those of others; understand, interpret, and evaluate the arts; and think critically about how individuals influence and are influenced by political, economic, cultural, and family institutions." See http://www.uic.edu/depts/oaa/gened/purpose.html.
4. By the 1950s, undergraduate degrees in business were common. Khurana states that "by 1930, most large state-university systems offered a bachelor's or master's degree in business" (Khurana, 2007, p. 137).
5. This trend continued throughout the twentieth century, according to the U.S. Census Bureau. At the end of the twentieth century approxi-

mately 60 percent of the workforce were in occupations that were classified as professional ("Employment, White Collar," 2008).

Chapter 3

1. Lord Griffiths of Fforestfach dealt with this subject in a 1999 lecture at Said Business School, University of Oxford (Lord Griffiths of Fforestfach, 2005).
2. Augustine does differentiate between immoral voluntary actions and those driven by "brute desires" or irrational forces. In other words, he recognized that there are times when human beings are not truly in charge of their actions, and thus not exercising free will (MacDonald, 2003).
3. Leibniz changed the spelling of his name; his family name was spelled Leubnitz or Liebnutz (Antognazza, 2009).
4. Drucker borrows from Leibniz and Voltaire in the title of his 1982 novel *The Last of All Possible Worlds* (Drucker, 1982).
5. For more on Bonaventure's life and times, see Cullen, 2005, pages 3–22.

Chapter 4

1. Federalism is one of the many concepts that may be embodied in constitutionalism. Constitutionalism also embodies the need for and use of checks and balances in an organization as described by Drucker.
2. We use the term "corporate federalism" to describe the application of federalist principles to the governance of corporations. This should not be confused with the definition of corporate federalism that reflects federal regulation of corporate activities.
3. A thorough discussion of the origins of popular sovereignty is contained in Bailyn (1967, pp. 198–229).
4. Edmund Burke, like the American Federalists, believed that the common good should take precedence over factions in the framing of democratic constitutions. His brilliant guide to political theory is found in his book *Reflections on the Revolution in France* (1790), published after the U.S. Constitution was ratified. The U.S. Constitution was patterned after the British Constitution, and Burke became the chief expositor and champion of the British Constitution. David Hume in his *Idea of a Perfect Commonwealth* (1752) argued for a distribution of powers

between the central government and subunit governments; his influence on the Federalists was profound.

5. We are especially indebted to Charles Handy for these additional principles of corporate federalism. He describes them in detail in his article,
"Balancing Corporate Power: A New Federalist Paper" (Handy, 1993).

6. Subsidiarity is often mistakenly connected with constitutional federalism, but is rather a distinctive product of Catholic social thought and
not associated with the framers of the Constitution. See Carey, 2004,
and Grasso, Bradley, and Hunt, 1995.

Chapter 5

1. Attributed to fourteenth-century German priest Saint Ivo, who taught his
parishioners holiness by example (Gumbley, 1971, p. 46).

2. ServiceMaster was acquired by the private equity firm of Clayton,
Dubilier and Rice in March 2007, thus ending the company's history
as a public firm. The ServiceMaster Management System described in
this section evolved and changed over time from its incorporation in
1947 to its sale in 2007.

3. The implementation of the ServiceMaster model, which was based on
Drucker's vision, was limited to those employees who were managed
directly by company executives and did not fully extend to the company's franchise operations.

4. ServiceMaster admitted that it often fell short of its objectives. Request-
ing forgiveness is a necessity in organizational life. But lack of quality in
ServiceMaster's Terminix operations caused the company trouble and
embarrassment. *Fortune Magazine* reports that the company "admits
ripping off customers in Kentucky and polluting a stream in Pennsylvania" (Gunther, 2001). Pollard, then chairman of ServiceMaster, argued
that "[lapses from saintly standards] are inevitable in a company with
75,000 employees and another 175,000 'associates' [franchisees] who
are supervised by ServiceMaster" (Gunther, 2001). Pollard, in the same
article, contended, "There is no management-control system that can
manage those people to always do the right thing" (Gunther, 2001).
This is especially true in a company that uses franchisees so extensively.

5. This is consistent with the definition of authority provided by Barnard
(1938, 1968, p. 163): "Authority is the character of communication
(order) in a formal organization by virtue of which is accepted by the

contributor or 'member' of the organization as governing the action he contributes; that is, as governing or determining what he does or is not to do so far as the organization is concerned."

6. This trend established by the Berger Institute seems to have continued unabated (National Women's Law Center, 2008, p. 2).

7. This account is adapted from Pollard (1996), p. 113. The main training facility was in Downers Grove and has been moved to the new corporate headquarters of the company in Tennessee.

8. Specifically, the Securities and Exchange Commission charged Goldman and an employee, Fabrice Tourre, with securities fraud in a civil suit relating to a mortgage transaction, known as Abacus-207-AC1, a deal the government said was designed to fail. The SEC alleged that Goldman duped its clients by failing to disclose hedge fund Paulson and Company. It not only helped select the mortgages included in the deal but also bet against the transaction (Pulliam and Perez, 2010). The allegation against Goldman has been resolved as noted on page 8.

9. These principles, and a detailed explanation of how each one facilitated the implementation of one or more of the four objectives, are found in Maciariello, 2002, pages 36–49. A summary explanation of each principle is provided in this section.

10. For examples, see Murphy, 1998.

11. See, especially, their summary of the relationships between providing outstanding customer value and profitability on page 224.

12. Many articles may be cited to demonstrate the incidents where the question of God is raised in business. For example, see Swartz (2006).

13. This example is derived from two sources: a number of personal conversations from 2002 to 2004 between Michael Joseph and Joseph Maciariello, and the monograph *To Honor God* (Max De Pree Center for Leadership, 2004).

Chapter 6

1. This conversation (World Vision, 2002, p ii) is the only time known to the authors that Peter Drucker equated leadership with his previous definitions of effectiveness, used widely in his writings on management. It is, however, consistent with his discomfort with the use of the term *management*; he preferred to use *executive*, as reported by T. George Harris. He states, "And, while we're on the subject of words, I am not

comfortable with the word *manager* any more, because it implies sub-ordinates. I find myself using *executive* more, because it implies respon-sibility for an area, not necessarily dominion over people. . . . In the traditional organization—the organization of the last 100 years—the skeleton or internal structure, was a combination of rank and power. In the emerging organization, it has to be mutual understanding and responsibility" (Harris, 1993, p. 122).

2. See, for example, a description of McClellan's treatment of President Abraham Lincoln, his commander-in-chief, as noted by Doris Kearns Goodwin in *Team of Rivals*: "Observers noted with consternation that McClellan [when Lincoln visited him] often kept Lincoln waiting in the downstairs room, 'together with other mortals'" (p. 379).

3. Says Theodore Hesburgh: "The very essence of leadership is that you have to have vision. You can't blow an uncertain trumpet" (Hesburgh, n.d.).

4. Rather than accepting responsibility for his actions and for the actions of those under his command during the Civil War, General George McClellan was well known for trying to shift blame. "At the first whiff of censure, McClellan shifted blame onto any other shoulder but his own—onto Scott's failure to muster necessary resources, onto the incompetence of the cabinet, 'some of the greatest geese . . . I have ever seen—enough to tax the patience of Job.' He considered Seward 'a meddling, officious, incompetent little puppy,' Welles 'weaker than the most garrulous old woman,' and Bates 'an old fool'" (Goodwin, 2005, p. 380). Similarly, when McClellan lost the battle at Chickahominy to General Lee, he complained bitterly against Secretary of War Stanton for depriving him of sufficient troops to win the battle. Abraham Lin-coln came to the defense of Stanton at a Union rally in Washington on August 6, 1862, by describing the secretary as *"a brave and able man"* who did all he could to support McClellan. "If anyone was respon-sible for withholding troops," said Lincoln, it was himself (McPherson, 2008b, p. 102). Lincoln thus accepted responsibility for the failures of both McClellan and Stanton.

5. In an interview with Warren Bennis on leadership, Drucker asked Ben-nis, "How did . . . [leaders] develop their capacities to take charge?" Learning adaptive behaviors is one of the answers Bennis cites from his survey of 90 leaders, 60 from the private sector and 30 from the social sector. The Bennis interview is the first of a series of interviews

conducted by Peter F. Drucker and Fred Harmon in what became *The Nonprofit Drucker* (Drucker and Harmon, 1989).

6. See McPherson's discussion of the tightrope Lincoln walked in arriving at the Emancipation Proclamation in "Lincoln as Commander in Chief" (2008).

7. After massive Union losses at the Battle of Shiloh in 1862, Lincoln defended Grant despite rumors that Grant had been drinking during the battle. Grant biographer Josiah Bunting reports that "inevitably Grant's critics had taken up the rumor that he had been drinking and that he was unfit for command. 'I can't spare this man; he fights,' Lincoln said" (Bunting, 2004, p. 41).

8. Donald deems Hooker's plan "a hopelessly wrongheaded one" (Donald, 1995, p. 438).

Chapter 7

1. See Ernest Samuels' biography of Henry Adams in three volumes: *The Young Henry Adams* (1948), *Henry Adams: The Middle Years* (1959), and *Henry Adams: The Major Phase* (1964).

2. For a discussion of Drucker's relationship with Polanyi and their associated intellectual influences, see Immerwahr (2009).

3. It is interesting to trace the development of Drucker's thought on the relationship of management as the discipline that uses all knowledge and then feeds back this knowledge to other disciplines all for the purpose of action. We see then that the practice of social ecology is equivalent to the practice of management as a liberal art. "Its [management] subject matter is a process. It starts out with a purpose of accomplishment. . . . And the end product of the knowledge we are trying to gain is value decisions affecting individual and society. . . . The discipline we need cannot be a technical discipline—though it will have many technical areas. . . . It must be truly humanist: of human beings united in common vision and comon values and working for a common goal, yet acting individually. It must focus information, knowledge, judgment, values, understanding and expectations onto decision, action, performance and results. It must deal with men as thinking, doing, feeling and appraising beings, and must therefore pull together intellectual, emotional, esthetic and ethical knowledge. . . . The discipline of managing must be both fed from all

fields of knowledge dealing with man's experience and, in turn, feed new knowledge back to all of them" (Drucker, 1959, pp. 90–91).

4. This is the title of the cover story article authored by Peter Drucker and published in the *Futurist* on November 1, 1998 (Drucker, 1998).

5. Additional information can be found at 800-CEO-READ (2004). Information is repeated, in Drucker 1993c, on the back cover.

6. Drucker first wrote about knowledge work in his *Landmarks of Tomorrow* (1959); see especially page 122.

7. Although Peter Drucker was the first to write about knowledge work and the knowledge worker, in 1958, Fritz Machlup estimated the importance of the content of knowledge work in the economy of the United States. Machlup's book *The Production and Distribution of Knowledge* (1962) was published three years after Drucker's first writings on the subject. Machlup's book contains detailed empirical evidence of the movement of the U.S. economy toward knowledge products and services, thus supporting Drucker's claims. Machlup estimated that 29 percent of the U.S. gross national product was devoted to knowledge products and services in 1958.

8. For example, on page 29: "Productive work in today's society and economy is work that applies vision, knowledge and concepts—work that is based on the mind rather than on the hand." Chapter 5 of the book is titled "The Educated Society," and on page 120 Drucker states the case for the emergence of knowledge work and of the knowledge society: "The man who works exclusively or primarily with his hands is the one who is increasingly unproductive. Productive work in today's society and economy is work that applies vision, knowledge and concepts— work that is based on the mind rather than on the hand." But, Drucker's actual study of the emergence of the knowledge worker preceded the publication of *Landmarks of Tomorrow* in 1959 by at least a decade. He projected into the future what he saw occurring in education after World War II. As a result of the passage of the GI Bill of Rights, officially known as the Servicemen's Readjustment Act of 1944, all returning servicemen were entitled to a paid college education, producing an explosion in the college-educated population.

9. As noted elsewhere in this chapter, the topic is also discussed in three earlier Drucker books, *The Age of Discontinuity* (Drucker, 1969), *The*

Effective Executive (Drucker, 1966/1967), and *Post-Capitalist Society* (Drucker, 1993d).

10. Peter Drucker's two novels are *The Last of All Possible Worlds* (Harper-Collins, New York, 1982) and *The Temptation to Do Good* (HarperCollins, New York, 1984).

11. This concept of the "second half" of life and using it to move from "success to significance" is developed at length by Bob Buford in his book *Halftime: Moving from Success to Significance* (2009).

12. Clearly, megachurches are more diverse in their demographics than Drucker's knowledge workers. But, Drucker consulted with pastors for two decades who did target this growing segment of the population. For example, Rick Warren defined the target demographic of Saddleback Community Church in terms of "Saddleback Sam" and "Saddleback Samantha": "Saddleback Sam is the typical unchurched man who lives in our area. His age is late thirties or early forties. He has a college degree and may have an advanced degree. (The Saddleback Valley has one of the highest household education levels in America.) He is married to Saddleback Samantha, and they have two kids, Steve and Sally" (Warren, 1995, p. 169).

13. In 1988, Peter Drucker, in conjunction with Bob Buford of the *Leadership Network* in Dallas, Texas, produced a set of 25 one-hour audio cassettes titled *Leadership and Management in the Non-profit Institution*, that are now available in a five-volume set of CDs from The Drucker Institute, Claremont Graduate University, Claremont, CA, www.DRUCKERinstitute.com.

14. As noted on the General Motors Web site: "Founded in 1911 and named after famous race car driver Louis Chevrolet, Chevrolet is one of GM's four core brands. Last year, Chevrolet accounted for 44 percent of GM's global sales and registered a 21 percent increase in sales from the previous year" (General Motors, 2010). On November 17, 2010, GM raised over $20 billion in the biggest initial public offering in U.S. history, which will reduce the federal government's stake in the firm (Baldwin and Kim, 2010).

Chapter 8

1. Production of the two-seat Thunderbird ranged from 16,000 in 1955 to approximately 21,000 for 1957, numbers that were break-even at best

(Bellm, n.d.). In contrast, more than 67,000 of the four-seat Thunderbird were sold in 1959, and approximately 93,000 were sold in 1960
(Severson, 2008).

2. Peter Drucker learned early in life that one makes rapid progress by
focusing on areas of strengths—what one can do, not what one cannot.
He described how he learned this from his fourth-grade teacher, Miss
Elsa, in his book *Adventures of a Bystander* (1978, pp. 62–63). And then
in his autobiography, *My Personal History*, he repeated approximately
the same story but then extrapolated these lessons to his work as a management consultant: "As a management consultant, I've long advised
clients to focus on 'what people *can do*, not on what they *can't do*,' and
also on management by objectives (MBO). In these fields, I think Miss
Elsa was a pioneer far ahead of me, actually helping me form the foundation of what I do" (Drucker, 2009, pp. 48–49).

3. In a number of conversations with Joseph Maciariello during the sum-
mer of 2009, two prominent education scholars at Ohio State Uni-
versity, Kenneth Wilson and Constance Barsky, identified "Reading
Recovery as an example of an unexpected success" falling within
Drucker's category of unexpected success as a source of innovation.
Kenneth Wilson is coauthor with Bennett Daviss of the book *Redesign-
ing Education* (1996); he is also the winner of the 1982 Nobel Prize in
Physics.

4. The term "baby boom" is defined by the U.S. Census Bureau as "a
period of relatively high fertility after World War II, commonly considered as the period from 1946 to 1964. People born during this period
are often referred to as baby boomers. The term "baby bust" is defined
by the U.S. Census Bureau as "the period of declining fertility following
the baby boom from 1965 to 1976" (Hobbs, Frank, and Nicole Stoops,
2000, p. B2).

5. There are different projections for the year in which the Social Security
trust fund will no longer be able to meet its obligations. The Congressional Budget Office, for example, estimates that the fund will
be exhausted in 2049 (www.cbo.gov/ftpdocs/96xx/doc9649/Main
Text.3.1.shtml). The reason for differences in projections is that entities
use different assumptions about tax laws, income levels, composition of
income, and other factors.

6. Drucker mentions Fayol as one of the early writers in the preface of his book *The Practice of Management*. And he notes, "Fayol's language is outdated, but his insights into the work of management and its organization are still fresh and original" (Drucker, 1954, p. vii).

7. Drucker in *The Practice of Management* (1954, p. 27) laments the absence of a description as to "what management is supposed to do." In footnote 1 on the same page he makes an exception for Joel Dean: "Though Dean is concerned mainly with the adaptation of the economist's theoretical concepts and tools to business management, the book, especially its earlier, general parts, is required reading for any manager."

8 Drucker's article on the irrigation city, "The First Technological Revolution and Lessons," was also delivered as his presidential address to the Society for the History of Technology in 1965.

SOURCES

Preface

Drucker, Peter F. (1954), *The Practice of Management*, Harper and Row, New York.

Introduction

Boselovic, Len (2010, April 7), "Massey CEO Blankenship Can Evoke Strong Emotions," *Pittsburgh Post-Gazette*, www.post-gazette.com/pg/10097/1048360-28.stm, accessed June 9, 2010.

"BP Confirms Successful Completion of Well Kill Operations in Gulf of Mexico," (2010, September 19) http://www.bp.com/genericarticle.do?categoryId=2012968&contentId=7065079, accessed December 6, 2010.

Buford, Bob (1993), interview with Peter F. Drucker, August 10, 1993.

Bunkley, Nick, and Michelle Maynard (2010, January 29), "With Recall Expanding, Toyota Gives an Apology," *New York Times*, www.nytimes.com/2010/01/30/business/30toyota.html, accessed June 10, 2010.

Carney, John (2010, February 15), "Goldman Sachs Shorted Greek Debt After It Arranged Those Shady Swaps," http://www.businessinsider.com/goldman-sachs-shorted-greek-debt-after-it-arranged-those-shady-swaps-2010-2#ixzz17N4cOzt9, accessed December 6, 2010.

CBS News.com (2010, May 25), "Toyota 'Unintended Acceleration' Has Killed 89," *CBS News.com*, www.cbsnews.com/stories/2010/05/25/business/main6518794.shtml, accessed June 9, 2010.

"Coal Boss Don Blankenship Cast as Cavalier About Worker Safety in Lawsuits" (2010, April 8), *ABC News.com*, http://abcnews.go.com/Blotter/mine-owner-don-blankenship-cast-cavalier-worker-safety/story?id=10314692&page=2, accessed June 10, 2010.

Cruz, Nicole Santa, and Julie Cart (2010, May 26), "Oil Cleanup Workers Report Illness," *Los Angeles Times*, http://articles.latimes.com/2010/may/26/nation/la-na-oil-workers-sick-20100526, accessed June 10, 2010.

Drucker, Peter F. (1932), *Die Rechtfertigung des Völkerrechts aus dem Staatswillen. Eine logisch-kritische Untersuchung der Selbstverpflichtungs- und Vereinbarungslehre*, Verlag von Franz Vahlen, Berlin.

Drucker, Peter F. (1959/1996), *Landmarks of Tomorrow*, Harper and Brothers, New York. Republished in 1996 with a new introduction, Transaction Publishers, New Brunswick, NJ.

Drucker, Peter F. (1988, Fall), "Teaching the Work of Management," *New Management*, Vol. 6, No. 2, pp. 2–5.

Drucker, Peter F. (1993), *The Ecological Vision: Reflections on the American Condition*, Transaction Publishers, New Brunswick, NJ.

Drucker, Peter F. (1994, November–December), "Political Correctness and American Academe," *Society*, Vol. 32, No. 1, pp. 58–63.

Drucker, Peter F., (2008), *Management*, rev. ed., with Joseph A. Maciariello, HarperCollins, New York.

Fogel, Robert, W. (2000), *The Fourth Great Awakening and the Future of Egalitarianism*, University of Chicago Press, Chicago.

Greider, William (2004), *The Soul of Capitalism: Opening Paths to a Moral Economy*, Simon and Schuster, New York.

Hamburger, Tom, and Andrew Zajac (2010, April 7), "Massey Energy's Safety Record Questioned after Mine Explosion," *Los Angeles Times*, http://mobile.latimes.com/inf/infomo?view=page1&feed:a=latimes_1min&feed:c=nationnews&feed:i=53140937&nopaging=1, accessed June 9, 2010.

Khurana, Rakesh (2007), *From Higher Aims to Hired Hands: The Social Transformation of Business Schools and the Unfulfilled Promise of Management as a Profession*, Princeton University Press, Princeton, NJ.

Maher, Kris and Gina Chon (2010, December 4/5), "Massey CEO Will Retire, Making Sale More Likely," *Wall Street Journal*.

Morris, Jim, and M. B. Pell (2010, May 16), "Renegade Refiner: OSHA Says BP Has 'Systemic Safety Problem,'" The Center for Public Integrity, www.publicintegrity.org/articles/entry/2085/, accessed June 9, 2010.

MSNBC.com, "Toyota: Recalls May Not Solve All Problems" (2010, February 23), *MSNBC.com*, www.msnbc.msn.com/id/35536620/ns/businessus _business/, accessed June 9, 2010.

Mulkern, Anne C., and Patrick Reis (2010, April 9), "After W. Va. Mine Deaths, How Much Political Trouble Is Coal Industry In?" *New York Times*, www.nytimes.com/gwire/2010/04/09/09greenwire-after-wva-mine -deaths-how-much-political-troub-43969.html, accessed June 10, 2010.

Pepitone, Julianne (2010, July 16), "Goldman settles with SEC for $550 million," CNNMoney.com, http://money.cnn.com/2010/07/15/companies/SEC _goldman/index.htm, accessed November 19, 2010.

Power, Stephen (2010, May 25), "BP Cites Crucial 'Mistake,'" *Wall Street Journal.* http://online.wsj.com/article/SB10001424052748704026204575265701607603066.html?mod=WSJ_hpp_LEFTTopStories, accessed June 10, 2010.

Rhee, Joseph (2009, November 25), "Toyota Recall Fails to Address 'Root Cause' of Many Sudden Acceleration Cases, Safety Expert Says," *ABC News.com*, http://abcnews.go.com/Blotter/RunawayToyotas/toyota -recall-fails-address-sudden-acceleration-cases-expert/story?id=9173621, accessed June 9, 2010.

Tasini, Jonathan (2009), *The Audacity of Greed: Free Markets, Corporate Thieves and the Looting of America,* Ig Publishing, New York.

U.S. Department of Transportation (2010, April 5), "Secretary LaHood Announces DOT Is Seeking Maximum Civil Penalty from Toyota," news release, www.dot.gov/affairs/2010/dot5910.htm, accessed June 10, 2010.

Wallis, Jim (2010), *Rediscovering Values: On Wall Street, Main Street, and Your Street,* Howard Books.

Wuthnow, Robert (1994), *God and Mammon in America*, Free Press, New York.

Chapter 1

Augustine, Saint (1467/1984), *City of God*, translated by Henry Bettenson, 1972, introduction by John O'Meara, 1984, Penguin, New York.

Beatty, Jack (1998), *The World According to Peter Drucker*, The Free Press, New York.

Berle, Adolf A., and Gardiner C. Means (1932), *The Modern Corporation and Private Property*, Harcourt, Brace and World, New York. Reprinted in 1991 by Transaction Publishers, New Brunswick, NJ.

Buford, Bob (1991, June 15), "Interview with Peter F. Drucker," transcript of audiotape 1, Leadership Network, Dallas, TX.

Burke, Edmund (1790, 2005), *Reflections on the Revolution in France*, Digireads.com Publishing, Stilwell, KS.

Daniel Webster Project Web site, "Inaugural Janus Lecture," Dartmouth University, www.dartmouth.edu/~websterprogram/, accessed August 17, 2009.

Drucker, Peter F. (1932). *Die Rechtfertigung des Völkerrechts aus dem Staatswillen. Eine logisch-kritische Untersuchung der Selbstverpflichtungs- und Vereinbarungslehre*, Verlag von Franz Vahlen, Berlin. Translated from German to English by Timo Meynhardt in his unpublished paper "The Practical Wisdom of Peter Drucker: Its Roots in the Christian Tradition," 2009.

Drucker, Peter, F. (1933/2002), "Friedrich Julius Stahl: His Conservative Theory of the State," *Society*, pp. 46–57. Originally published in 1933 as *Frieddrich Julius Stahl: Konservative Staats-Theorie und Geschichtliche Entwicklung*, J.C.B. Mohr, Tübingen, DE.

Drucker, Peter F. (1939/1969), *The End of Economic Man*, John Day Company, New York. Republished in 1969, with a new preface, by Harper and Row, New York.

Drucker, Peter F. (1942), *The Future of Industrial Man*, John Day Company, New York.

Drucker, Peter F. (1942b), "The Freedom of Industrial Man," *The Virginia Quarterly Review*, Vol. 18, No. 4, pp. 481–499.

Drucker, Peter F. (1946/1993c), *The Concept of the Corporation*, John Day Company, New York. Republished in 1993 with a new introduction, and including 1983 epilogue, Transaction Publishers, New Brunswick, NJ.

Drucker, Peter F. (1949), "The Unfashionable Kierkegaard," *Sewanee Review*, Vol. 57, pp. 587–602.

Drucker, Peter F. (1950), *The New Society*, Harper and Row, New York.

Drucker, Peter F. (1954), *The Practice of Management*, Harper and Row, New York.

Drucker, Peter F. (1966), *The Effective Executive*, Harper and Row, New York.

Drucker, Peter F. (1966b, May), "The Romantic Generation," *Harper's Magazine*, pp. 12–22.

Drucker, Peter F. (1973, 1974), *Management: Tasks, Responsibilities, Practices*, Harper and Row, New York.

Drucker, Peter F. (1978), *Adventures of a Bystander*, Harper and Row, New York.

Drucker, Peter F. (1980), "Toward the Next Economics," *The Public Interest*, special issue, pp. 4–18.

Drucker, Peter F. (1981), *Towards the Next Economic and Other Essays*, Harper and Row, New York.

Drucker, Peter F. (1983, May 23), "Schumpeter and Keynes," *Forbes*, pp. 124–128.

Drucker, Peter F. (1985), *Innovation and Entrepreneurship*, HarperCollins, New York.

Drucker, Peter F. (1987, Summer), "The Poverty of Economic Theory," *New Management*, pp. 40–42.

Drucker, Peter F. (1988), "Teaching the Work of Management," *New Management*, Vol. 6, No. 2, pp. 2–5.

Drucker, Peter F. (1989/2004), *The New Realities*, Harper and Row, New York. Republished in 2004 with a new introduction, Transaction Publishers, New Brunswick, NJ.

Drucker, Peter F. (1990), "Why *My Years with General Motors* Is Must Reading: New Introduction," in A. P. Sloan, ed., *My Years with General Motors*, Doubleday, New York, pp. v–xii.

Drucker, Peter F. (1992), "Reflections of a Social Ecologist," *Society,* Vol. 29, No. 4, pp. 57–64. Reprinted as an afterword in *Ecological Vision* (1993), Transaction Publishers, New Brunswick, NJ, pp. 441–457.

Drucker, Peter F. (1993), *The Ecological Vision,* Transaction Publishers, New Brunswick, NJ.

Drucker, Peter F. (1998, October 5), "Management's New Paradigms" *Forbes,* pp. 152–176.

Drucker, Peter F. (2003), *A Functioning Society*, Transaction Publishers, New Brunswick, NJ.

Drucker, Peter F. (2008), *Management*, rev. ed., with Joseph A. Maciariello, HarperCollins, New York.

Edwards, David Cooper (1999), *Existentialism: A Reconstruction,* Blackwell, Oxford, UK.

Freyberg, Bertold (1970), "The Genesis of Drucker's Thought," in Tony H. Bonaparte and John E. Flaherty, eds., *Peter Drucker: Contributions to Business Enterprise*, New York University Press, New York, pp. 17–22.

Gabor, A. (2000), *The Capitalist Philosophers: The Geniuses of Modern Business —Their Lives, Times, and Ideas*, Times Books, New York.

Humboldt, Wilhelm von (1903–1920), *Wilhelm von Humboldt's Gesammelte Schriften*, trans. David Sorkin, 15 vols, Berlin, 1903–1920.

Kierkegaard, Søren (1849/1989), *The Sickness Unto Death*, trans. Alastair Hannay, 1989, Times Books, New York.

Kierkegaard, Søren (1994), *Fear and Trembling*, trans. Walter Lowrie, Everyman's Library, Alfred A. Knopf, New York.

Lock, F. P. (2006), *Edmund Burke: 1784–1797*, Oxford University Press, New York.

Lowith, Karl (1964), *From Hegel to Nietzsche: The Revolution in Nineteenth-Century Thought*, trans. David E. Green, Holt, Rinehart and Winston, New York.

"Management Guru Peter Drucker" (2004), radio interview from *On Point*, WBUR for National Public Radio, Boston, MA, available at www .onpointradio.org/shows/2005/08/20050802_a_main.asp, accessed June 1, 2008.

Raymond, Diane Barsoun, ed. (1991), *Existentialism and the Philosophical Tradition*, Prentice-Hall, Englewood Cliffs, NJ.

Schumpeter, Joseph A. (1934/1982), *The Theory of Economic Development*, President and Fellows of Harvard College, Cambridge, MA. Republished in 1982, with a new introduction by John Elliot, Transaction Publishers, New Brunswick, NJ.

Schumpeter, Joseph A. (1942), *Capitalism, Socialism, and Democracy*, Harper and Row, New York.

Sheehan, James J. (1970), *German History, 1770–1866* (Oxford History of Modern Europe), Oxford University Press, New York.

Sloan, Alfred P. (1963), *My Years with General Motors*, Doubleday, New York.

Stahl, Friedrich J. (2007), *Principles of Law*, trans. Reuben Alvarado, Woodbridge Publishing, Aalten, NL.

Stahl, Friedrich J. (2007b), *Private Law*, trans. Reuben Alvarado, Woodbridge Publishing, Aalten, NL.

Sweet, Paul R. (1980), *Wilhelm Von Humboldt: A Biography*, Ohio State University Press, Columbus.

Tarrant, John J. (1976), *Drucker: The Man Who Invented the Corporate Society*, Cahners, Boston.

Chapter 2

"Act for Liberty to Erect a Collegiate School" (1701, October 9), in Franklin Bowditch Dexter, ed., *Documentary History of Yale University*, Yale University Press, New Haven, CT.

Axelrod, Paul (2002), *Values in Conflict: The University, the Marketplace, and the Trials of Liberal Education*, McGill-Queen's University Press, Montreal and Kingston, CA.

Berle, Adolph, and Gardiner Means (1933), *The Modern Corporation and Private Property*, Macmillan, New York.

Bloom, Alan (1988), *The Closing of the American Mind*, Simon and Schuster, New York.

Bok, Derek (1987), *The President's Report 1986–87*, Harvard University Press, Cambridge, MA, pp. 1–37.

Chandler, Alfred (1977), *The Visible Hand: The Managerial Revolution in American Business,* Harvard Belknap, Cambridge, MA.

Chrucky, Andrew (2003), "The Aim of Liberal Education," September 1. www.ditext.com/chrucky/aim.html, accessed May 8, 2010.

Churchill, John (2006, April 10), "Liberal Arts, Deliberation, and Democracy," address to Phi Beta Kappa Society, Duke University, http://staging .pbk.org/infoview/pbk_infoview.aspx?id=69, accessed May 8, 2010.

Cotton, John (1956), "Christian Calling," in Perry Miller, ed., *The American Puritans: Their Prose and Poetry*, Columbia University Press, New York, pp. 172–182.

Cross, Timothy P. (1995), "An Inner Life of Sufficient Richness," Chapter 2 in *An Oasis of Order: The Core Curriculum at Columbia University*, Columbia College, New York, Office of the Dean. www.college.columbia .edu/core/oasis/history2.php, accessed May 17, 2010.

Drucker, Peter F. (1954), *The Practice of Management,* Harper and Row, New York.

Drucker, Peter F. (1998), *Peter Drucker on the Profession of Management*, edited with an Introduction by Nan Stone, Harvard Business School Publishing, Boston MA.

"Employment, White Collar" (n.d.), in *International Encyclopedia of the Social Sciences*, William A. Darity, ed., from *Encyclopedia.com*, www.encyclo pedia.com/doc/1G2-3045300713.html, accessed March 2, 2010.

Gordon, Robert Aaron, and James Edwin Howell (1959), *Higher Education for Business,* Columbia University Press, New York.

Harris, T. George (1993, May–June), "The Post-Capitalist Executive: An Interview with Peter F. Drucker," *Harvard Business Review*, Vol. 71, No. 3, pp. 114–122.

Hayes, Robert, and William J. Abernathy (1980), "Managing Our Way to Economic Decline," *Harvard Business Review*, Vol. 58, No. 4, pp. 67–77.

Holland, Kelley (2009, March 15), "Is It Time to Retrain B-Schools?" *New York Times.com*, www.nytimes.com/2009/03/15/business/15school.html?_r=1&em, accessed March 18, 2009.

Jefferson, Thomas (1818, August 4), "Report of the Commissioners for the University of Virginia," in Merrill D. Peterson (1984), *Thomas Jefferson: Writings*, Library of America, New York, pp. 459–460.

Kagan, Talia (2010, March 1), "Joint MBA Program Will Start Next Year," *Brown Daily Herald*, www.browndailyherald.com/joint-mba-program-will-start-next-year-1.2175188, accessed March 2, 2010.

Kennedy, David M. (2009, Summer), "What the New Deal Did," *Political Science Quarterly*, Vol. 124, No. 2, pp. 251–268.

Khurana, Rakesh (2007), *From Higher Aims to Hired Hands: The Social Transformation of American Business Schools and the Unfulfilled Promise of Management as a Profession*, Princeton University Press, Princeton, NJ.

Kimball, Bruce A. (1986), *Orators and Philosophers: A History of the Idea of Liberal Education*, Teachers College Press, New York.

Mankiewicz, Josh (2009, February 8), "Corporate Breed: Greed and Excess Is Off the Charts," *Dateline NBC*, www.msnbc.msn.com/id/29061759/, accessed August 15, 2009.

McLean, Bethany, and Peter Elkind (2003), *The Smartest Guys in the Room: The Amazing Rise and Scandalous Fall of Enron*, Penguin, New York.

Mills, C. Wright (1951), *White Collar: The American Middle Class*, Oxford University Press, New York.

Mintzberg, Henry (1973/1980), *The Nature of Managerial Work*, Prentice-Hall, Englewood Cliffs, NJ.

PBS.org (n.d.), "The 'Crisis of Confidence' Speech," *American Experience*, www.pbs.org/wgbh/amex/carter/filmmore/ps_crisis.html, accessed August 14, 2009.

Pierson, Frank (1959), *The Education of American Businessmen: A Study of University-College Programs in Business Administration*, McGraw-Hill, New York.

Readings, Bill (1996), *The University in Ruins*, Harvard University Press, Cambridge, MA.

Ringer, Fritz (1969), *The Decline of the German Mandarins: The German Academic Community, 1890–1933,* Harvard University Press, Cambridge, MA.

Sellers, Charles (1991), *The Market Revolution,* Oxford University Press, New York.

Solomon, Benjamin (1954, October), "The Growth of the White-Collar Workforce," *Journal of Business,* Vol. 27, No. 4, pp. 268–275.

Sorkin, David, (1983, Jan.-March), Wilhelm von Humboldt: The Theory and Practice of Self-Formation (Bildung), 1791–1810," *Journal of the History of Ideas,* Vol. 44, No. 1, pp. 55–73.

Stancil, Wilburn (2003), "The Goals of a Liberal Education," in Wilburn Stancil, ed., *A Student's Guide to the Liberal Arts,* Rockhurst University Press, Kansas City, MO, pp. 250–254.

Stewart, Matthew (2009), *The Management Myth: Debunking Modern Business Philosophy,* W.W. Norton, New York.

Whyte, William (1956), *The Organization Man,* Simon & Schuster, New York.

Wiebe, Robert (1967), *The Search for Order: 1877–1920,* Hill and Wang, New York.

Wood, Gordon (1998), *The Creation of the American Republic: 1776–1787,* University of North Carolina Press, Chapel Hill.

Chapter 3

"About Business Ethics," *Business Ethics,* New Mountain Media LLC, New York. Launched in 1987 as a quarterly magazine, *Business Ethics* was converted to an online publication in 2007. http://business-ethics.com/about/, accessed December 11, 2010.

Antognazza, Maria Rosa (2009), *Leibniz: An Intellectual Biography,* Cambridge University Press, New York.

Arenas, Daniel (2006), "Problematizing and Enlarging the Notion of Humanistic Education," in Pasquale Gagliardi and Barbara Czarniawska, eds., *Management Education and Humanities,* Edward Elgar Publishing, Cheltenham, UK, pp. 113–134.

Augspurger, Michael (2004), *An Economy of Abundant Beauty: Fortune Magazine and Depression America,* Cornell University Press, Ithaca, NY.

Bonaparte, Tony H. (1970), "The Philosophical Framework of Peter F. Drucker," in Tony H. Bonaparte and John E. Flaherty, eds., *Peter*

Drucker: Contributions to Business Enterprise, New York University Press, New York, pp. 23–34.

Brint, Steven, Mark Riddle, Lori Turk-Bicakci, and Charles S. Levy (2005, March–April), "From the Liberal to the Practical Arts in American Colleges and Universities: Organizational Analysis and Curricular Change," *The Journal of Higher Education*, Vol. 76, No. 2, pp. 151–180.

Buford, Bob (1991, June 15), "The Life Development Model," *Transcripts of Drucker-Buford Dialogue*, unpublished, Claremont, CA, p. 5.

Carr, David, and Jan Steutel, eds. (1999), *Virtue Ethics and Moral Education*, Routledge, London.

Chace, William M. (2009, Autumn), "The Decline of the English Department: How It Happened and What Could Be Done to Reverse It," *The American Scholar*, pp. 32–42.

Chevalier, Jacques (1928), *Henri Bergson,* Macmillan, New York.

Cook, Edward J. and Allen F. Chapman (1970), "Drucker, Holism, and Smuts," in Tony H. Bonaparte and John E. Flaherty, eds., *Peter Drucker: Contributions to Business Enterprise*, New York University Press, Stony Brook, NY, pp. 56–64.

Cullen, Christopher (2005), *Bonaventure,* Oxford University Press, New York.

Czarniawska, Barbara, and Carl Rhodes (2006), "Strong Plots: Popular Culture in Management Practice and Theory," in Pasquale Gagliardi and Barbara Czarniawska, eds., *Management Education and Humanities*, Edward Elgar Publishing, Cheltenham, UK, pp. 195–218.

Davis, Clark (2000), *Company Men: White-Collar Life and Corporate Cultures in Los Angeles, 1892–1941*, Johns Hopkins University Press, Baltimore, MD.

Drucker, Peter F. (1942), *The Future of Industrial Man,* John Day, New York. Reprinted in 1995, with a new introduction, Transaction Publishers, New Brunswick, NJ.

Drucker, Peter F. (1950), *The New Society,* Harper and Row, New York.

Drucker, Peter F. (1954), *The Practice of Management,* Harper and Row, New York.

Drucker, Peter F. (1959), *Landmarks of Tomorrow*, Harper and Row, New York. Reprinted in 1996, with a new introduction, Transaction Publishers, New Brunswick, NJ.

Drucker, Peter F. (1969), *The Age of Discontinuity*, Harper and Row, New York. Reprinted in 1992, with new introduction, Transaction Publishers, New Brunswick, NJ.

Drucker, Peter. F (1973, 1974), *Management: Tasks, Responsibilities, Practices*, Harper and Row, New York.

Drucker, Peter F. (1982), *The Last of All Possible Worlds*, HarperCollins, New York.

Drucker, Peter F. (1985, Winter), "You on Me," *New Management*, Vol. 2, No. 1, pp. 28–32.

Drucker, Peter F. (1988, Fall), "Teaching the Work of Management," *New Management*, Vol. 6, No. 2, pp. 2–5.

Drucker, Peter F. (1993), *The Post-Capitalist Society*, HarperCollins, New York.

Drucker, Peter F. (2003), *A Functioning Society*, Transaction Publishers, New Brunswick, NJ.

Drucker, Peter F (2008), *Management*, rev. ed., with Joseph A. Maciariello, HarperCollins, New York.

Fox, Richard Wrightman (1985), *Reinhold Niebuhr: A Biography*, Pantheon Books, New York.

Gracia, Jorge J. E., and Timothy B. Noone, eds. (2003), *A Companion to Philosophy in the Middle Ages*, Blackwell Publishing, Malden, MA.

Griffiths, Brian (2009), "The Role of the Business Corporation as a Moral Community," in Donald Holt, ed., *The Heart of a Business Ethic*, University Press of America, Lanham, MD, pp, 123–135.

Hendry, John (2006), "Management Education and the Humanities: The Challenge of Post-bureaucracy," in Pasquale Gagliardi and Barbara Czarniawska, eds., *Management Education and Humanities*, Edward Elgar, Cheltenham, UK, pp. 21–44.

Hooper, Kenneth, and William Hooper (2007), *The Puritan Gift: Triumph, Collapse and Revival of an American Dream*, I. B. Tauris and Company, London.

Immerwahr, Daniel (2009, July), "Polanyi in the United States: Peter Drucker, Karl Polanyi, and the Mid-century Critique of Economic Society," *Journal of the History of Ideas*, Vol. 70, No. 3, pp. 445–466.

Ingham, Kenneth (1986), *Jan Christian Smuts: The Conscience of a South African*, Weidenfeld and Nicolson, London.

Johnson, Elmer W. (2005), "Corporate Soulcraft in the Age of Brutal Markets," in Donald Holt, ed., *The Heart of a Business Ethic*, University Press of America, Lanham, MD, pp. 59–77.

Khurana, Rakesh (2007), *From Higher Aims to Hired Hands: The Social Transformation of American Business Schools and the Unfulfilled Promise of Management as a Profession*, Princeton University Press, Princeton, NJ.

Kot, Greg (2009, April 22), "Why the Grateful Dead Live On," *Chicago Tribune*, http://leisureblogs.chicagotribune.com/turn_it_up/2009/04/why-the-grateful-dead-live-on-.html, accessed March 3, 2010.

Leibniz, Gottfried W. (1985), *Theodicy: Essays on the Goodness of God, the Freedom of Man and the Origin of Evil*, Open Court Publishing, Peru, IL. Originally published in 1710.

Linkletter, Karen (2004), *Drucker Redux: Management as Intellectual and Philosophical Product*, unpublished Ph.D. dissertation, Claremont Graduate University, Claremont, CA.

Lord Griffiths of Fforestfach, "The Role of the Business Corporation as a Moral Community" (2005), in Donald D. Holt, ed., *The Heart of a Business Ethic*, University Press of America, Lanham, MD, pp. 123–135.

Lowe, Victor (1962), *Understanding Whitehead*, Johns Hopkins University Press, Baltimore, MD.

MacDonald, Scott (2003), "Augustine," in Jorge J. E. Gracia and Timothy B. Noone, eds., *A Companion to Philosophy in the Middle Ages*, Blackwell Publishing, Malden, MA, pp. 154–171.

MacIntyre, Alasdair (1981, 1984, 2007), *After Virtue*, University of Notre Dame Press, South Bend, IN.

Niebuhr, Reinhold (1932/2001), *Moral Man and Immoral Society*, Charles Scribner's Sons, reprinted in 2001, with new introduction by Langdon B. Gilkey, Westminster John Knox Press, Louisville, KY.

Niebuhr, Reinhold (1944), *The Children of Light and the Children of Darkness*, Scribner's, New York.

Palazzo, Bettina (2002, December), "U.S.–American and German Business Ethics: An Intercultural Comparison," *Journal of Business Ethics*, Vol. 41, No. 3, pp. 195–216.

Peskin, Lawrence (2003). *Manufacturing Revolution: The Intellectual Origins of Early American Industry*, Johns Hopkins University Press, Baltimore, MD.

Rafter, Michelle V. (2004, September 20), "Liberal Arts Grads Get the Business," *Workforce Management*, Vol. 83, No. 9, pp. 1–2.

Rescher, Nicholas (2000), *Process Philosophy: A Survey of Basic Issues*, University of Pittsburgh Press, Pittsburgh.

Schmitt, Richard B. (2002, November 4), "Companies Add Ethics Training: Will It Work?" *The Wall Street Journal*, B1.

Smith, Adam, (1976/1994), *Wealth of Nations*, edited with an introduction and notes by Edwin Cannan, The Modern Library, Random House, New York.

Smuts, Jan Christian (1893), "Law a Liberal Study," *Christ's College Magazine*.

Sorum, Christina Elliott (2005), "The Problem of Mission: A Brief Survey of the Changing Mission of the Liberal Arts," *Liberal Arts Colleges in American Higher Education: Challenges and Opportunities.* American Council of Learned Societies, ACLS Occasional Paper No. 59, pp. 26–39.

Tarrant, John (1966), *The Man Who Invented the Corporate Society,* Warner Books, New York.

Trachtenberg, Alan (1982), *The Incorporation of America: Culture and Society in the Gilded Age,* Hill and Wang, New York.

Voltaire, Francois (2005), *Candide,* translated by Theo Cuffe, 2005, Penguin, New York.

World Economic Forum (2009), *The World Economic Forum A Partner in Shaping History: The First 40 Years 1971–2010,* http://www.weforum.org/pdf/40years.pdf, accessed December 11, 2010.

Chapter 4

Bailyn, Bernard (1967), *The Ideological Origins of the American Revolution,* Belknap Press, Cambridge, MA.

Beatty, Jack (1998), *The World According to Peter Drucker,* Free Press, New York.

Booz Allen Hamilton, "CEO Succession 2005: The Crest of the Wave," *Strategy + Business,* Summer 2006, Issue 43. www.strategy-business.com/article/06210?gko=6e014, accessed October 8, 2009.

Burgess, Michael (2006), *Comparative Federalism: Theory and Practice,* Routledge, New York.

Carey, George W. (2004, Winter/Spring), "Conservatism, Centralization, and Constitutional Federalism," *Modern Age,* pp. 48–59.

Chandler, Alfred D., Jr. (1962), *Strategy and Structure: Chapters in the History of American Industrial Enterprise,* MIT Press, Cambridge, MA.

de Kluyver, Cornelius (2009), "Drucker on Corporate Governance," Chapter 5 in Craig L. Pearce, Joseph A. Maciariello, and Hideki Yamawaki (2010), *The Drucker Difference,* McGraw-Hill, New York, pp. 61–78.

Drucker, Peter F. (1939), *The End of Economic Man,* John Day, New York.

Drucker, Peter F. (1942), *The Future of Industrial Man,* John Day, New York.

Drucker, Peter F. (1942b), "The Freedom of Industrial Man," *The Virginia Quarterly Review,* Vol. 18, No. 4, pp. 481–499.

Drucker, Peter F. (1946), *Concept of the Corporation,* John Day Company, New York.

Drucker, Peter F. (1949), "The Unfashionable Kierkegaard," *Sewanee Review,* Vol. 57, pp. 587–602.

Drucker, Peter F. (1950), *The New Society*, Harper and Row, New York.

Drucker, Peter F. (1954), *The Practice of Management*, Harper and Row, New York.

Drucker, Peter F. (1966), *The Effective Executive*, Harper and Row, New York.

Drucker, Peter F. (1973), *Management: Tasks, Responsibilities, Practices*, Harper and Row, New York.

Drucker, Peter F. (1981, Spring), "What Is 'Business Ethics'?" *The Public Interest*, No. 63, pp. 18–36.

Drucker, Peter F. (1981b), *Towards the Next Economics and Other Essays*, Harper and Row, New York.

Drucker, Peter F. (1985, Winter), "You on Me," *New Management*, Vol. 2, No. 1, pp. 28–32.

Drucker, Peter F. (1985b), *Innovation and Entrepreneurship*, HarperCollins, New York.

Drucker, Peter F. (1988), "Teaching the Work of Management," *New Management*, Vol. 6, No. 2, pp. 2–5.

Drucker, Peter F. (1989), *The New Realities*, Harper and Row, New York.

Drucker, Peter F. (1993), *Post-Capitalist Society*, HarperCollins, New York.

Drucker, Peter F. (2008), *Management*, rev. ed., with Joseph A. Maciariello, HarperCollins, New York.

Drucker, Peter F., and Peter Paschek, eds. (2004), *Kardinaltugenden effektiver Führung* (Cardinal virtues and effective leadership), Redline Wirtschaft, Frankfurt, DE.

Elazar, Daniel J. (2001), "The United States and the European Union: Models for Their Epochs," in Kalypso Nicolaidis and Robert Howse, eds., *The Federal Vision: Legitimacy and Levels of Governance in the United States and the European Union*, Oxford University Press, New York, pp. 31–53.

Elkins, Stanley, and Eric McKitrick (1993), *The Age of Federalism*, Oxford University Press, New York.

General Electric Co. (1954), *Professional Management in General Electric*, Vol. 3: *The Work of a Professional Manager*, General Electric Co., New York, quoted in Ronald G. Greenwood (1981), "Management by Objectives: As Developed by Peter Drucker, Assisted by Harold Smiddy," *Academy of Management Review*, Vol. 6, No. 2, pp. 225–230.

Grasso, Kenneth L., Gerard V. Bradley, and Robert B. Hunt, eds. (1995), *Catholicism, Liberalism, and Communitarianism*, Rowman and Littlefield, Lanham, MD.

Hamilton, Alexander, James Madison, and John Jay (1961), *The Federalist Papers,* New American Library, New York. Original work published 1788.

Handy, Charles (1993, Summer), "Balancing Corporate Power: A New Federalist Paper," *The McKinsey Quarterly,* No. 3, pp. 159–182. Reprinted from "Balancing Corporate Power: A New Federalist Paper" (1992, November–December), *Harvard Business Review,* Vol. 70, No. 6, pp. 59–67.

Hofstadter, Richard (1970), *The Idea of a Party System: The Rise of Legitimate Opposition in the United States: 1780–1840,* University of California Press, Berkeley.

Kanter, Rosabeth M. (1985, Winter), "Drucker: The Unsolved Puzzle," *New Management,* Vol. 2, No. 1, pp. 10–13.

Linkletter, Karen E., and Joseph A. Maciariello (2009), "Genealogy of a Social Ecologist," *Journal of Management History,* Vol. 15, No. 4, pp. 334–356.

Manz, Charles C., and Henry P. Simms, Jr. (1993), *Business without Bosses: How Self-Managing Teams Are Building High-Performing Companies,* Wiley, New York.

Maslow, Abraham H. (1998), *Maslow on Management,* with Deborah C. Stephens and Gary Heil, Wiley, New York.

Millstein, Ira M., Holly J. Gregory, and Rebecca C. Grapsas (2006, March), "Six Priorities for Boards in 2006," *Law and Governance,* Vol. 10, No. 3, pp. 17–19.

O'Toole, James, and Warren Bennis (1992, Summer), "Our Federalist Future: The Leadership Imperative," *California Management Review,* Vol. 34, No. 4, pp. 73–90.

Paschek, Peter (2007, June 20), "How to Avoid Another Wasted Century," Global Drucker Forum, Claremont, CA.

Pearce, Craig, L., and Henry, P. Simms (2002), "Vertical versus Shared Leadership as Predictors of the Effectiveness of Change Management Teams: An Examination of Aversive, Directive, Transactional, Transformational, and Empowering Leader Behaviors," *Group Dynamics: Theory, Research, and Practice,* Vol. 6, No. 2, pp. 171–197.

Sloan, Alfred P. (1963, 1990), *My Years with General Motors,* Doubleday, New York.

Washington, George (1786, August 15), letter to John Jay, in John H. Rhodehamer, ed. (1997), *George Washington: Writings,* Library of America, New York.

Wood, Gordon S. (1969), *The Creation of the American Republic: 1776–1787,* University of North Carolina Press, Chapel Hill.

Wood, Gordon S. (2006), *Revolutionary Characters: What Made the Founders Different,* Penguin, New York.

Chapter 5

Bailyn, Bernard (1967), *The Ideological Origins of the American Revolution,* Harvard University Press, Cambridge, MA.

Barnard, Chester I. (1938/1968), *The Functions of the Executive,* Harvard University Press, Cambridge, MA.

Berger Institute for Work, Family, and Children (2004, Spring), "Work-Family Interactions," Vol. 4, Claremont McKenna College, Claremont, CA.

Buford, Bob (1993, August 10), *Transcript of Peter F. Drucker and Bob Buford Dialogue,* unpublished, Claremont, CA, p. 7.

Dacor (n.d.), "Our Company Value," Dacor.com, www.dacor.com/About-Us/Our-Company-Value.aspx, accessed February 11, 2010.

Dinerstein, Judy (2006, September), "The Guilt-Free Record of George Soros," transcript of interview on *60 Minutes,* December 20, 1998, *Soros Monitor,* www.sorosmonitor.com/absolutenm/templates/news.aspx?articleid=33&zoneid=1, accessed June 19, 2010.

Drucker, Peter F. (1942), *The Future of Industrial Man,* John Day, New York. Reprinted with a new introduction by Transaction Publishers, New Brunswick, NJ.

Drucker, Peter F. (1942b, Autumn), "The Freedom of Industrial Man," *The Virginia Quarterly Review,* Vol. 18, No. 4, pp. 481–499.

Drucker, Peter F. (1946), *Concept of the Corporation,* John Day, New York.

Drucker, Peter F. (1949), "The Unfashionable Kierkegaard," *Sewanee Review,* Vol. 57, pp. 587–602; reprinted in *Ecological Vision* (1993), Transaction Publishers, New Brunswick, NJ, pp. 427–439.

Drucker, Peter F. (1954), *The Practice of Management,* Harper and Row, New York.

Drucker, Peter F. (1966), *The Effective Executive,* Harper and Row, New York.

Drucker, Peter F. (1974), *Management: Tasks, Responsibilities, Practices,* Harper and Row, New York.

Drucker, Peter F. (1981, Spring), "What Is Business Ethics?" *The Public Interest,* Issue No. 3, pp. 18–36.

Drucker, Peter F. (1989), *Service Work and Service Workers, 1989 Annual Report,* ServiceMaster Corp., Downers Grove, IL.

Drucker, Peter F. (1990), *Managing the Non-Profit Organization*, HarperCollins Publishers, 1990.

Drucker, Peter F. (1992/1993), "Reflections of a Social Ecologist," *Society*, Vol. 29, No. 4, pp. 57–64. Reprinted with an afterword in *Ecological Vision* (1993), Transaction Publishers, New Brunswick, NJ, pp. 441–457.

Drucker, Peter F. (1994, September–October), "The Theory of the Business," *Harvard Business Review*, Vol. 72, No. 5, pp. 95–104.

Drucker, Peter F. (1999), "The Change Leader," Chapter 3 in *Management Challenges for the 21st Century*, HarperCollins, New York, pp. 72–93

Drucker, Peter F. (2002, February), "They're Not Employees, They're People," *Harvard Business Review*, Vol. 80, No. 2, pp. 70–77.

Drucker, Peter F. (2008), *Management*, rev. ed., with Joseph A. Maciariello, HarperCollins, New York.

Greenleaf, Robert K. (1977), *Servant Leadership*, Paulist Press, New York.

Gumbley, Walter (1971), *Parish Priests among the Saints: Canonized or Beatified Parish Priests,* Books for Libraries Press, Freeport, NY.

Gunther, Marc (2001, July 9), "God and Business," *Fortune Magazine*, pp. 58–80.

Heskett, James L., W. Earl Sasser, Jr., and Leonard A. Schlesinger (1997), *The Service Profit Chain*, Free Press, New York.

Isidore, Chris (2005, March 7), "Boeing CEO Out in Sex Scandal: Embattled Aircraft Maker Ousts Stonecipher After He Admits Relationship with Female Executive," *CNN/Money.com*, http://money.cnn.com/2005/03/07/news/fortune500/boeing_ceo/index.htm, accessed June 19, 2010.

Kanter, Rosabeth, M. (1985, Winter), "Drucker: The Unsolved Puzzle," *New Management*, Vol. 2, No. 1, pp. 10–13.

Maciariello, Joseph A. (2000), *Lasting Value: Lessons from a Century of Agility at Lincoln Electric,* Wiley, Inc., New York.

Maciariello, Joseph A. (2002), *Work and Human Nature: Leadership and Management Practices at ServiceMaster and the Drucker Tradition*, Max De Pree Center for Leadership, Pasadena, CA.

Max De Pree Center for Leadership (2004), *To Honor God: Dacor's Pursuit of Corporate Virtue,* with the Work Research Foundation, Max De Pree Center for Leadership, Pasadena, CA.

Murphy, Patrick E. (1998), *Eighty Exemplary Ethics Statements*, University of Notre Dame Press, South Bend, IN.

National Women's Law Center, http://www.nwlc.org/pdf/WorkingMothers March2008.pdf/WorkingMothersMarch2008.pdf, accessed December 17, 2010.

Nicholi, Dr. Armand M., Jr. (2002), *The Question of God: C. S. Lewis and Sigmund Freud Debate God, Love, Sex, and the Meaning of Life*, Free Press, New York.

Pollard, C. William (1996), personal communication with Joseph Maciariello.

Pollard, C. William (1996b), *The Soul of the Firm*, HarperCollins, New York.

Pollard, C. William (2006), *Serving Two Masters?* HarperCollins, New York.

Pulliam, Susan, and Evan Perez (2010, April 30), "Criminal Probe Looks into Goldman Trading," *Wall Street Journal*, http://online.wsj.com/article/SB1 0001424052748703572504575214652998348876.html, accessed May 4, 2010.

Rush, Benjamin (1787/1993), "Benjamin Rush Speaks Against a Bill of Rights," in Bernard Bailyn, ed., *The Debate on the Constitution: Part One,* Library of America, New York, pp. 816–817.

ServiceMaster Co. (1994), *Annual Report 1993–1994*, Downers Grove, IL.

ServiceMaster Co. (2001), *Annual Report 2000–2001*, Downers Grove, IL.

Solzhenitsyn, Alexander I. (1978, June 8), "A World Split Apart," text of commencement address at Harvard University, www.columbia.edu/cu/augustine/arch/solzhenitsyn/harvard1978.html, accessed February 15, 2010.

Swartz, Mark C. (2006, June), "God as a Managerial Stakeholder?" *Journal of Business Ethics*, Vol. 66, Nos. 2/3, pp. 291–306.

Wade, Marion E. (1966), *The Lord Is My Counsel*, with Glenn D. Kittler, Prentice-Hall, Englewood Cliffs, NJ. This book is available from Wheaton College at www.wheaton.edu/wadecenter/welcome/LordismyCounsel _Web.pdf. accessed April 10, 2010.

Chapter 6

"Abraham Lincoln as Commander in Chief" (2008, October 27), a conversation with James M. McPherson, Professor of History Emeritus, Princeton University, *Conversation with History* series, Harry Kreisler, host, Institute of International Studies, University of California, Berkeley, YouTube, www .youtube.com/watch?v=KnyWoq9qndU, accessed January 15–17, 2009.

Alcoholics Anonymous (1976), *Alcoholics Anonymous*, 3rd ed., Alcoholics Anonymous World Services, New York.

Barnard, Chester I. (1938/1968), *The Functions of an Executive*, Harvard University Press, Cambridge, MA. Originally published in 1938.

Basler, Roy P., ed. (1953), *Collected Works of Abraham Lincoln*, Rutgers University Press, New Brunswick, NJ.

Bass, Bernard M. and Riggio, Ronald E. (2006), *Transformational Leadership*, Lawrence Erlbaum Associates, Mahwah, NJ.

Bennett, Lerone (2000), *Forced into Glory: Abraham Lincoln's White Dream*, Johnson Publishing, Chicago.

Bennis, Warren G., and Burt Nanus (1985), *Leaders: The Strategies for Taking Charge*, Harper and Row, New York.

Berry, Stephen (2007), *House of Abraham: Lincoln and the Todds, a Family Divided by War*, Houghton Mifflin, New York.

Blight, David W. (2008), "The Theft of Lincoln in Scholarship, Politics, and Public Memory," in Eric Foner, ed., *Our Lincoln: New Perspectives on Lincoln and His World*, W.W. Norton, New York, pp. 269–282.

Bunting, Josiah (2004), *Ulysses S. Grant*, Henry Holt, New York.

Burns, John MacGregor (1978), *Leadership*, Harper and Row, New York.

Carwardine, Richard (2003, 2006), *Lincoln: A Life of Purpose and Power*, Alfred A. Knopf, New York.

Carwardine, Richard (2008), "Lincoln's Religion," in Eric Foner, ed., *Our Lincoln: New Perspectives on Lincoln and His World*, W.W. Norton, New York, pp. 223–248.

Cloud, Henry (2006), *Integrity*, HarperCollins, New York.

Collins, Jim (2001), *Good to Great*, HarperCollins, New York.

Dirck, Brian R. (2009), *Lincoln the Lawyer*, University of Illinois Press, Chicago.

Donald, David Herbert (1995), *Lincoln*, Simon and Schuster, New York.

Douglass, Frederick (1876, April 14), "Oration in Memory of Abraham Lincoln," Ashbrook Center for Public Affairs at Ashland University, www.ashbrook.org/library/19/douglass/lincolnoration.html, accessed January 27, 2011.

Drucker, Peter F. (1946), *Concept of the Corporation*, John Day, New York. Reprinted in 1983, with a new introduction, by Transaction Publishers, New Brunswick, NJ.

Drucker, Peter F. (1950/1993), *The New Society*, Harper and Brothers, New York. Reprinted, with a new introduction, by Transaction Publishers, 1993, New Brunswick, NJ.

Drucker, Peter F. (1954), *The Practice of Management*, Harper and Row, New York.

Drucker, Peter F. (1967), *The Effective Executive*, Harper and Row Publisher, New York.

Drucker, Peter F. (1973, 1974), *Management: Tasks, Responsibilities, Practices*, Harper and Row, New York.

Drucker, Peter F. (1990), *Managing the Non-profit Organization*, Harper-Collins, New York.

Drucker, Peter F., revised and updated by J.A. Maciariello (2008), *Management*, HarperCollins, New York.

Drucker, Peter F., and Fred Harmon (1989), *The Nonprofit Drucker*, Audio Tapes, Leadership Network, Dallas.

Drucker-Buford Dialogue (Buford, 1998, 2 February), *Transcript of Dialogue*, unpublished, Claremont, CA.

Foner, Eric, ed. (2008), *Our Lincoln: New Perspectives on Lincoln and His World*, W.W. Norton, New York.

Frederickson, George M. (2008), *Big Enough to Be Inconsistent*, Harvard University Press, Cambridge, MA.

Gienapp, William E. (2002), *Abraham Lincoln and Civil War America: A Biography* Oxford University Press, New York.

Goodwin, Doris Kearns (2005), *Team of Rivals: The Political Genius of Abraham Lincoln*, Simon and Schuster, New York.

"Great Leadership Quotes" (n.d.), 1000 Advices, www.1000advices.com/guru/leadership_quotes.html, accessed July 1, 2009.

Greenleaf, Robert K. (1970), *The Servant as Leader*, Greenleaf Center for Servant Leadership, Westfield, IN.

Greenleaf, Robert K. (1977), *Servant Leadership: A Journey into the Nature of Legitimate Power and Greatness*, Paulist Press, Mahwah, NJ.

Guelzo, Allen C. (2009, September), "The Not-So-Grand Review: Abraham Lincoln in *The Journal of American History*," *The Journal of American History*, Vol. 96, No. 2, pp. 400–416.

HarpWeek, "Finding Precedent: The Impeachment of Andrew Johnson," www.impeach-andrewjohnson.com/11BiographiesKeyIndividuals/William HSeward.htm, accessed July 15, 2009.

Harris, T. George (1993, May–June), "The Post-Capitalist Executive: An Interview with Peter F. Drucker," *Harvard Business Review*, Vol. 71, Issue 3, pp. 115–122.

Hattaway, Herman, Archer Jones, and Jerry A. Vanderlinde (1991), *How the North Won*, University of Illinois Press, Champaign, IL.

Hesburgh, Theodore (n.d.), "Theodore Hesburgh Quotes," ThinkExist.com, http://thinkexist.com/quotes/theodore_hesburgh/, accessed July 10, 2009.

Johnson and Johnson (n.d.), "Our Credo Values," JNJ.com, www.jnj.com/connect/about-jnj/jnj-credo/, accessed January 19, 2008.

Karlgaard, Rich (2004, November 19), "Peter Drucker on Leadership," Forbes.com, www.forbes.com/2004/11/19/cz_rk_1119drucker.html, accessed December 20, 2010.

Lewin, Kurt (1947), "Frontiers in Group Dynamics," *Human Relations*, 1 (1), pp. 5–41.

Lincoln, Abraham (1854, April 1), "Fragment on Slavery," in Roy P. Basler, ed. (1953), *Collected Works of Abraham Lincoln*, Rutgers University Press, New Brunswick, NJ, Vol. 2, p. 222.

Lincoln, Abraham (1858, July 10), "Speech at Chicago, Illinois," in Roy P. Basler, ed. (1953), *Collected Works of Abraham Lincoln*, Rutgers University Press, New Brunswick, NJ, Vol. 2, pp. 485–502.

Lincoln, Abraham (1860, December 8), "Letter to William H. Seward," in Roy P. Basler, ed. (1953), *Collected Works of Abraham Lincoln*, Rutgers University Press, New Brunswick, NJ, Vol. 4, p. 149.

Lincoln, Abraham (1861, September 22), "Letter to Orville H. Browning," in Roy P. Basler, ed. (1953), *Collected Works of Abraham Lincoln*, Rutgers University Press, New Brunswick, NJ, Vol. 4, pp. 531–533.

Lincoln, Abraham (1862, September 24), "Proclamation Suspending the Writ of Habeas Corpus," in Roy P. Basler, ed. (1953), *Collected Works of Abraham Lincoln*, Rutgers University Press, New Brunswick, NJ, Vol. 8, p. 437.

Lipman-Blumen, Jean (2006), *The Allure of Toxic Leaders*, Oxford University Press, New York.

Maciariello, Joseph (1996), personal communication with C. W. Pollard, chairman of ServiceMaster.

Maciariello, Joseph (2000), *Lasting Value: Lessons from a Century of Agility at Lincoln Electric*, John Wiley and Sons, New York.

Marvel, William (2008), *Lincoln's Darkest Year: The War in 1862*, Houghton Mifflin, New York.

Maslow, Abraham Harold (1954), *Motivation and Personality*, Harper, New York.

Maslow, Abraham Harold (1998), *Maslow on Management*, John Wiley and Sons, New York.

Mayo, Elton (1946/2003), *The Human Problems of an Industrial Civilization*, 2nd ed., Harvard University Press, Cambridge, MA; reprinted in 2003 by Routledge, Oxford, UK.

McGregor, Douglas (1960), *The Human Side of Enterprise*, McGraw-Hill, New York, 1960.

McPherson, James, M. (2008), "A. Lincoln, Commander in Chief," in Eric Foner, ed., *Our Lincoln: New Perspectives on Lincoln and His World*, W.W. Norton, New York, pp. 16–36.

McPherson, James M. (2008b), *Tried by War: Abraham Lincoln as Commander in Chief,* Penguin, New York.

Miller, Nicola, et al (2009), "Interchange: The Global Lincoln," (2009, September), *The Journal of American History*, Vol. 96, No. 2, pp. 462–499.

Miller, William Lee (2002), *Lincoln's Virtues: An Ethical Biography*, Knopf, New York.

Moreton, Bethany (2009), *To Serve God and Wal-Mart: The Making of Christian Free Enterprise,* Harvard University Press, Cambridge, MA.

Ohio History Central, "Salmon P. Chase," http://www.ohiohistorycentral .org/entry.php?rec=92, accessed December 20, 2010.

Ouchi, William G. (1982), *Theory Z,* Avon Books, a HarperCollins imprint, New York.

Pollard, C. William (1996), *The Soul of the Firm*, HarperCollins, New York.

Roethlisberger, Fritz J. and W. J. Dickson, (1939), *Management and the Worker.* Harvard University Press, Cambridge, MA.

Ross, Dorothy (2009, September), "Lincoln and the Ethics of Emancipation: Universalism, Nationalism, Exceptionalism," *The Journal of American History*, Vol. 96, No. 2, pp. 379–399.

Sidhu, Navjot Singh (n.d.), BrainyQuote.com, www.brainyquote.com/ quotes/keywords/ship.html, accessed July 11, 2009.

Sproul, R. C. (1991), *In Search of Significance*, Regal Books, Ventura, CA.

Steiner, Mark E. (2006), *An Honest Calling: The Law Practice of Abraham Lincoln*, Northern Illinois University Press, DeKalb, IL.

Striner, Richard (2006), *Father Abraham: Lincoln's Relentless Struggle to End Slavery*, Oxford University Press, New York.

Thomas, Benjamin P. (1952/2008), *Abraham Lincoln: A Biography*, Knopf, New York.

Tolstoy, Leo (1909, February 7), "Interview: Tolstoy on Lincoln," *The World*, New York.

Tolstoy, Leo (1991), *Childhood, Boyhood and Youth*, translated and with an introduction by Rosemary Edmonds, 1964, Penguin Books, New York. First published in 1852.

Tripp, C. A. (2005), *The Intimate World of Abraham Lincoln*, Lewis Gannett, ed., Basic Books, New York.

White, Ronald C., Jr. (2009), *A. Lincoln: A Biography*, Random House, New York.

World Vision, "Leadership Means to Get the Right Things Done" (2002, February 5), *Executive Summary: A Conversation with Peter Drucker on Leadership and Organizational Development*, Monrovia, CA, p. i.

Chapter 7

800-CEO-READ (2004, December 16), Drucker Bibliography, http://800ceoread.com/blog/archives/005381.html, accessed January 18, 2008.

Adams, Henry (1889), *History of the United States of America, 1801–1817*, Charles Scribner's Sons, New York.

Adams, Henry (1906/2009), *The Education of Henry Adams*, Wilder Publications, Blacksburg, VA. Originally published privately in 1906.

Anderson, Brian C. (2001, Spring), "Bertrand de Jouvenel's Melancholy Liberalism," *Public Interest*, No. 143, pp. 87–104.

Baldwin, Clare, and Soyoung Kim (2010, November 17), "GM IPO Raises $20.1 Billion," reuters.com, http://www.reuters.com/article/2010/11/17/us-gm-ipo-idUSTRE6AB43H20101117, accessed January 26, 2011.

Bonaparte, Tony H., and John E. Flaherty, eds. (1970), *Peter Drucker: Contributions to Business Enterprise,* New York University Press, New York.

Brogan, Hugh (1977, December), "America and Walter Bagehot," *Journal of American Studies*, Vol. 11, No. 3, pp. 335–356.

Buford, Bob (2009), *Halftime: Moving from Success to Significance*, rev. ed., Zondervan, Grand Rapids, MI.

"Butterfly Effect" (n.d.), Fortune City.com, www.fortunecity.com/emachines/e11/86/beffect.html, accessed January 18, 2009.

Commager, Henry Steele (1950), *The American Mind: An Interpretation of American Thought and Character Since the 1880s*, Yale University Press, New Haven, CT.

Commons, John (1919), *Industrial Goodwill*, McGraw-Hill, New York

Dorfman, Joseph (1934), *Thorstein Veblen and His America*, Harvard University Press, Cambridge, MA.

Drucker, Peter F. (1933), "Friedrich Julius Stahl: A Conservative Theory of the State and Historical Development," J. C. B. Mohr, Tübingen, DE. Translated into English and published in *Society*, July–August 2002. The essay is available online at www.peterdrucker.at/frmset_en_texts.html, accessed April 16, 2008.

Drucker, Peter F. (1942, Autumn), "The Freedom of Industrial Man," *The Virginia Quarterly Review*, Vol. 18, No. 4, pp. 481–499.

Drucker, Peter F. (1942b), *The Future of Industrial Man*, John Day, New York.

Drucker, Peter F. (1946), *The Concept of the Corporation*, John Day, New York.

Drucker, Peter F. (1950), *The New Society*, Harper and Brothers, New York, NY.

Drucker, Peter F. (1952, May), "The Myth of American Uniformity," *Harper's Magazine*, Vol. 204, No. 1224, pp. 70–77.

Drucker, Peter F. (1954), *The Practice of Management*, Harper and Row, New York.

Drucker, Peter F. (1959), *Landmarks of Tomorrow*, Harper and Row, New York.

Drucker, Peter F. (1964), *Managing for Results*, Harper and Row, New York.

Drucker, Peter F. (1967), *The Effective Executive*, Harper and Row, New York.

Drucker, Peter F. (1969), *The Age of Discontinuity*, Harper and Row, New York.

Drucker, Peter F. (1978), *Adventures of a Bystander*, Harper and Row, New York.

Drucker, Peter F. (1979), "A View of Japan through Japanese Art," *Songs of the Brush: Japanese Paintings from the Sanso Collection*, John M. Rosenfield and Henry Trubner, eds., Seattle Art Museum, Seattle. Reprinted in 1993 in *The Ecological Vision*, Transaction Publishers, New Brunswick, NJ, pp. 363–380.

Drucker, Peter F. (1989), *The New Realities*, Harper and Row, New York.

Drucker, Peter F. (1990), *Managing the Non-profit Organization*, HarperCollins, New York.

Drucker, Peter F. (1992), *The Age of Discontinuity*, with a new introduction by Transaction Publishers, New Brunswick, NJ.

Drucker, Peter F. (1992b),"Reflections of a Social Ecologist," *Society*, Vol. 29, No. 4, pp. 57–64. Reprinted as "Afterword," *The Ecological Vision*, Transaction Publishers, New Brunswick, NJ, 1993, pp. 441–457.

Drucker, Peter F. (1993), *The Concept of the Corporation*, Transaction Publishers, New Brunswick, NJ.

Drucker, Peter F. (1993b), *Ecological Vision*, Transaction Publishers, New Brunswick, NJ.

Drucker, Peter F. (1993c), *The New Society*, Transaction Publishers, New Brunswick, NJ.

Drucker, Peter F. (1993d), *Post-capitalist Society*, HarperCollins, New York.

Drucker, Peter F (1995, April 17), letter to Dr. Jim O'Toole, Aspen Institute, from the Peter F. Drucker Institute, Claremont, CA.

Drucker, Peter F. (1995b), "Mary Parker Follett: Prophet of Management," Introduction to Pauline Graham, ed. (1995), *Mary Parker Follett: Prophet of Management*, Harvard Business School Press, Boston, pp. 1–9.

Drucker, Peter F. (1997), *Adventures of a Bystander*, republished by John Wiley and Sons, New York.

Drucker, Peter F. (1998, November 1), "The Future That Has Already Happened," in *The Futurist*, Vol. 32, No. 8, p. 16, distributed digitally by Amazon.com, http://www.amazon.com/happened-economic-underpopulation-developed-countries/dp/B00098CINA, accessed December 22, 2010.

Drucker, Peter F. (1999), *Management Challenges in the 21st Century*, HarperCollins, New York.

Drucker, Peter F. (2001, November 3), "The Next Society," *The Economist*, Vol. 356, pp. 3–20.

Drucker, Peter F. (2002), "Knowledge Worker Productivity," Drucker Internet Module 8105, Corpedia Education.

Drucker, Peter F. (2002b), *Managing in the Next Society*, St. Martin's, New York.

Drucker, Peter F. (2003), *A Functioning Society*, Transaction Publishers, New Brunswick, NJ.

Drucker, Peter F., and Joseph A. Maciariello (2006), *The Effective Executive in Action*, HarperCollins, New York.

Drucker, Peter F. (2008), *Management*, rev. ed., with Joseph A. Maciariello, HarperCollins, New York.

Follett, Mary Parker (1896), *The Speaker of the House of Representatives*, Longmans, Green and Company, New York. http://books.google.com/books?id=YqY9AAAAYAAJ&printsec=frontcover&dq=the+speaker+of+the+house+of+representatives+mary+parker+follett&source=bl&ots=zVdwnWTLyJ&sig=2FPkrtf9JC9rmr9dDrUpg68nRMY&hl=en&ei=VTwSTYiuDYGqsAOK8qG4Ag&sa=X&oi=book_result&ct=result&resnum=1&ved=0CBcQ6AEwAA#v=onepage&q&f=false, accessed December 22, 2010.

Follett, Mary Parker (1918), *The New State: Group Organization the Solution of Popular Government*, Longmans, Green and Company, New York.

Follett, Mary Parker (1920), "The Unity of the Social Process," adapted from Follett, Mary Parker (1918/1920), *The New State: Group Organization the Solution of Popular Government*, Longmans, Green and Company, New York, in Pauline Graham, ed. (1995), *Mary Parker Follett: Prophet of Management*, Harvard Business School Press, Boston, pp. 247–263.

Follett, Mary Parker (1925, January), "Power," in Pauline Graham, ed. (1995), *Mary Parker Follett: Prophet of Management*, Harvard Business School Press, Boston, pp. 97–119.

Follett, Mary Parker (1925b, November), "How Must Business Management Develop in Order to Become a Profession?" in Pauline Graham, ed. (1995), *Mary Parker Follett: Prophet of Management*, Harvard Business School Press, Boston, pp. 267–281.

Frisby, David (1992), *Simmel and Since: Essays on Georg Simmel's Social Theory*, Routledge, New York.

Gabor, Andrea (2000), *The Capitalist Philosophers*, Times Business Books, New York.

General Motors (2010, May 24), "GM to Bring Chevrolet to Korea," GM.com, http://media.gm.com/content/media/us/en/news/news _detail.globalnews.html/content/Pages/news/global/en/2010/0428 _korea, accessed May 24, 2010.

Gilbreth Network (n.d.), http://gilbrethnetwork.tripod.com/bio.html, accessed July 20, 2009.

Graham, Pauline, ed. (1995), *Mary Parker Follett: Prophet of Management*, Harvard Business School Press, Boston.

Graham, Pauline, ed. (1995) "Mary Parker Follett (1868–1933): A Pioneering Life," in *Mary Parker Follett: Prophet of Management*, Harvard Business School Press, Boston, pp. 11–32.

Harrison, J. F. C. (1969), *Quest for the New Moral World: Robert Owen and the Owenites in Britain and America*, Simon and Schuster, New York.

Higgins, George, G. (1993c), endorsement on back cover, *The New Society* by Peter F. Drucker, Transaction Publishers, New Brunswick, NJ.

Immerwahr, Daniel (2009, July), "Polanyi in the United States: Peter Drucker, Karl Polanyi, and the Mid-century Critique of Economic Society," *Journal of the History of Ideas*, Vol. 70, No. 3, pp. 445–466.

Irvine, William (1970), *Walter Bagehot*, Archon Books, New York.

Isidore, Chris (2009, June 2), "GM Bankruptcy: End of an Era," *CNNMoney .com*, http://money.cnn.com/2009/06/01/news/companies/gm _bankruptcy/, accessed June 23, 2009.

Jouvenel, Bertrand (1967), *The Art of Conjecture*, trans. Nikita Lary, Basic Books, New York.

Leadership Network (2005, November 14), "Drucker's Impact on Leadership Network," *Leadership Network Advance*, www.pursuantgroup.com/ leadnet/advance/nov05o.htm, accessed April 30, 2010.

Levitt, Theodore (1970), "The Living Legacy of Peter Drucker," in Tony H. Bonaparte and John E. Flaherty, eds., *Peter Drucker: Contributions to Business Enterprise*, New York University Press, New York, pp. 5–16.

"Life Development Model" (1991, June 15), transcripts of the Drucker-Buford Dialogue, Claremont, CA.

Lowney, Chris (2003), *Heroic Leadership: Best Practices from a 450-Year-Old Company That Changed the World*, Loyola Press, Chicago.

Lyndall Fownes Urwick Archive (n.d.), PowerGen Library of the Henley Management College, www.cf.ac.uk/carbs/econ/boyns/schedule.pdf, accessed August 2, 2009.

Machlup, Fritz (1962), *The Production and Distribution of Knowledge*, Princeton University Press, Princeton, NJ.

Maciariello, Joseph (2000), *Lasting Value: Lessons from a Century of Agility at Lincoln Electric*, John Wiley and Sons, New York.

Maciariello, Joseph A. (2006), "Peter F. Drucker on Mission-Driven Leadership and Management in the Social Sector: Interviews and Postscript," *Journal of Management, Spirituality and Religion, A Special Double Issue: Values and Virtues in Organizations*, Vol. 3, Nos. 1 and 2, 2006, pp. 177–183.

Mary Parker Follett Foundation Web site (n.d.), www.follettfoundation.org/ mpf.htm, accessed July 31, 2009.

Merriam-Webster.com (n.d.), "Human Ecology," www.merriam-webster.com/ dictionary/human+ecology.

Morton, A. L. (1963), *The Life and Ideas of Robert Owen*, Monthly Review Press, New York.

Polanyi, Karl (1944), *The Great Transformation*, Beacon Press, Boston.

Rathe, Alex W., ed. (1961), *Gantt on Management: Guidelines for Today's Executives*, American Management Association and the American Association of Mechanical Engineers, New York. Originally published as

Alford, L. P. (1934), *Henry Laurence Gantt: Leader in Industry,* Harper and Brothers, New York.

Reisman, David (1953), *Thorstein Veblen,* Charles Scribner's Sons, New York.

Saddleback Church (n.d.), http://www.saddlebackresources.com/en-US/Pastors/Pastors.htm, accessed December 22, 2010.

Taylor, Frederick (1911), *The Principles of Scientific Management,* Harper and Brothers, New York.

Thumma, Scott, Dave Travis, and Warren Bird (2005), *Megachurches Today 2005: Summary of Research Findings,* http://hirr.hartsem.edu/mega church/megastoday2005_summaryreport.html, accessed July 9, 2008.

Thumma, Scott, and Dave Travis (2007), *Beyond Megachurch Myths: What We Can Learn from America's Largest Churches,* Jossey-Bass, San Francisco.

Thumma, Scott, Dave Travis, and Warren Bird (2007b), *Innovation 2007,* Leadership Network, Dallas.

Tocqueville, Alexis de (1959), *Journey to America,* edited by J. P. Mayer, translated by George Lawrence, Faber and Faber, London. Based on Tocqueville, Alexis de, and Tocqueville, Marie (Motley) Clérel de, M. Lévy Frères, Paris.

Tocqueville, Alexis de (1984), *Democracy in America,* edited by Richard C. Heffner, New American Library, Penguin Books, New York. Originally published as *De la démocratie en Amérique* in two volumes, Vol. 1, 1835, Vol. 2, 1840, by Charles Gosselin, Paris.

Toennies, Ferdinand (2002), *Community and Society,* David & Charles, Devon, UK. published in 1887 in German as *Gemeinschaft und Gesellschaft,* edited and translated by Charles P. Loomis, 1957, Michigan State University Press, East Lansing, MI.

Tonn, Joan C. (2003), *Mary P. Follett: Creating Democracy, Transforming Management,* Yale University Press, New Haven, CT.

Urwick, Lyndall F. (1943), *The Elements of Administration,* Harper and Brothers, New York.

Veblen, Thorstein Bunde (1899), *The Theory of the Leisure Class,* The Mac-Millan Company, London, republished in 2007 Cosimo, Inc., New York.

Veblen, Thorstein Bunde (1904), *The Theory of Business Enterprise,* Charles Scribner's Sons, New York. Republished in 1978 by Transaction Publishers, New Brunswick, NJ.

Warren, Rick (1995), *The Purpose-Driven Church,* Zondervan, Grand Rapids MI.

Chapter 8

Associated Press (2007, August 24), "More U.S. Women Dying in Childbirth," MSNBC, www.msnbc.msn.com/id/20427256/, accessed May 8, 2010.

Auto Editors of Consumer Guide (n.d.), "1960 Edsel," How Stuff Works .com, http://auto.howstuffworks.com/1960-edsel4.htm, accessed April 25, 2010.

Bellm, David (n.d.), "The 1955–1957 Thunderbird," Rewind of the Fifties, www.loti.com/fifties_cars/The_1955-57_Ford_Thunderbird.htm, accessed April 25, 2010.

California Public Employees' Retirement System (CalPERS) (n.d.), "Corporate Governance: Investing with a Corporate Governance Framework," www .calpers-governance.org/, accessed May 12, 2010.

The Conference Board (2006, September 2), "U.S. Institutional Investors Boost Ownership of U.S. Corporations to New Highs," press release, www.conference-board.org/utilities/pressdetail.cfm?press_id=3466, accessed May 10, 2010.

The Congressional Budget Office (n.d.), "Updated Long-Term Projections for Social Security," www.cbo.gov/ftpdocs/96xx/doc9649/Main Text.3.1.shtml, accessed July 23, 2008.

Crandall, Robert W. (2002, January 8), *The Futility of Steel Trade Protection,* Criterion, www.criterioneconomics.com/documents/crandall_report .pdf, accessed January 18, 2009.

Dean, Joel (1951), *Managerial Economics,* Prentice-Hall, New York.

Department of Homeland Security (n.d.), "National Infrastructure Protection Plan: Postal and Shipping Sector," www.dhs.gov/xlibrary/assets/ nipp_snapshot_postal.pdf, accessed April 29, 2010.

Drucker, Peter F. (1954), *The Practice of Management,* Harper and Row, New York.

Drucker, Peter F. (1959), *Landmarks of Tomorrow,* Harper and Row. Reprinted, with a new introduction, by Transaction Publishers, New Brunswick, NJ.

Drucker, Peter F. (1959–1960, Winter), "Work and Tools," *Technology and Culture,* Vol. 1, No. 1, pp. 28–37.

Drucker, Peter F. (1966, Spring), "The First Technological Revolution and Its Lessons," *Technology and Culture*, Vol. 7, No. 2, pp. 143–151.

Drucker, Peter F. (1973, 1974), *Management: Tasks, Responsibilities, Practices*, Harper and Row, New York.

Drucker, Peter F. (1976), *The Unseen Revolution*, Harper and Row, New York. Reprinted in 1996, with a new introduction, as *The Pension Fund Revolution* by Transaction Publishers, New Brunswick, NJ.

Drucker, Peter F. (1978), *Adventures of a Bystander*, John Wiley and Sons, New York.

Drucker, Peter F. (1985), *Innovation and Entrepreneurship*, HarperCollins, New York.

Drucker, Peter F. (1992b), "Reflections of a Social Ecologist," *Society*, Vol. 29, No. 4, pp. 57–64. Reprinted, with an afterword, in *Ecological Vision* (1993), Transaction Publishers, New Brunswick, NJ, pp. 441–457.

Drucker, Peter F. (1993), *Ecological Vision*, Transaction Publishers, New Brunswick, NJ.

Drucker, Peter F. (1996), *The Pension Fund Revolution*, Transaction Publishers, New Brunswick, NJ. Originally published in 1976 as *The Unseen Revolution* by Harper and Row, New York.

Drucker, Peter F. (2001, November 1), "The Next Society," *The Economist*, Print Edition.

Drucker, Peter F. (2008), *Management*, rev. ed., with Joseph A. Maciariello, HarperCollins, New York.

Drucker, Peter F. (2009), *My Personal History*, interviewer and translator Yo Makino, Nihon Keizai Shimbun, Tokyo, JP.

Drucker, Peter F., and Joseph A. Maciariello (2009b), *Management Cases*, rev. ed., HarperCollins, New York.

Fayol, Henri (1930), *Industrial and General Administration*, trans. John Adair, Coubrough, Sir I. Pitman and Sons, London.

Himmelstein, David U., Elizabeth Warren, Deborah Thorne, Steffie Woolhandler (2005), "MarketWatch: Illness and Injury As Contributors to Bankruptcy," *Health Affairs*, No. (2005), February 2, 2005, http://content.healthaffairs.org/content/suppl/2005/01/28/hlthaff.w5.63.DC1, accessed December 23, 2010.

Hobbs, Frank, and Nicole Stoops (2002), *Demographic Trends in the 20th Century*, U.S. Census Bureau, Census 2000 Special Reports, Series

CENSR-4, U.S. Government Printing Office, Washington, DC, www
.census.gov/prod/2002pubs/censr-4.pdf , accessed July 23, 2008.

Humphreys, Jeffrey M. (2009, 3d Q.), *The Multicultural Economy 2009*, Vol. 69, No. 3, The University of Georgia, Athens, GA.

Maciariello, Joseph A. (2000), *Lasting Value: Lessons from a Century of Agility at Lincoln Electric*, John Wiley and Sons, New York, p. 153.

"Motor Trend Car of the Year Complete Winners List," (n.d.), *Motor Trend*, www.motortrend.com/oftheyear/car/car_of_the_year_winners/index .html, accessed May 4, 2010.

Mumford, Lewis (1961), *The City in History: Its Origins, Its Transformations, and Its Prospects*, Harcourt, San Diego.

National Center for Health Statistics (2007), *Health, United States, With Chartbook on Trends in the Health of Americans* http://www.cdc.gov/ nchs/data/hus/hus07.pdf, accessed on December 23, 2010.

"Post-it Notes" (n.d.), The Great Idea Finder, www.ideafinder.com/history/ inventions/postit.htm, accessed June 25, 2009.

Reading Recovery Council of North America (2000), *Reading Recovery in North America: An Illustrated History*, Reading Recovery Council of North America, Columbus, OH, p. 8, www.eric.ed.gov/ERICDocs/data/ ericdocs2sql/content_storage_01/0000019b/80/16/06/64.pdf, accessed September 15, 2009.

Severson, Aaron (2008, July 17), "Glamour Is a Rocky Road: The Four-Seat Ford Thunderbird," Ate Up with Motor, http://ateupwithmotor.com/ luxury-and-personal-luxury-cars/103-glamour-is-a-rocky-road-the-four -seat-ford-thunderbird.html, accessed April 25, 2010.

Story, Louise, Landon Thomas, Jr., and Nelson O. Schwartz (2010, February 13), "Wall Street Helped to Mask Debt Fueling Europe's Crisis," *New York Times*, p. A1, www.nytimes.com/2010/02/14/business/global/ 14debt.html, accessed May 8, 2010.

Swartz, Stanley L. (n.d.), "California Early Literacy Learning and Reading Recovery: Two Innovative Programs for Teaching Children to Read and Write," www.stanswartz.com/cell_rr.htm, accessed May 8, 2010.

Taccone, Tony (2007, December 18), "Global Steel Demand Poised to Grow Along with GDP," Nerds of Steel, www.nerdsofsteel.com/2007/12/18/ global-steel-demand-poised-to-grow-along-with-gdp, accessed April 26, 2010.

Tafoya, Sonya (2004, December 6), "Shades of Belonging: Latinos and Racial Identity," Pew Hispanic Center, Washington, DC, http://pew hispanic.org/reports/report.php?ReportID=35, accessed May 8, 2010.

Tros, Daniel (2010, April 29), "The Euro Can Survive a Greek Default; Greece's Economy Would Collapse but the Contagion Is Containable," *Wall Street Journal*, pp. A1 and A12.

U.S. Census Bureau, Census 2000 Special Reports, Series CENSR-4 (2002), *Demographic Trends in the 20th Century*, U.S. Government Printing Office, Washington, DC, p. B-2, www.census.gov/prod/2002pubs/censr-4.pdf, accessed July 23, 2008.

Wilson, Kenneth, and Bennett Davis (1996), *Redesigning Education,* Teachers College Press, New York.

Conclusion

Beacham, Greg (2010, June 11), "USC Hit Hard By NCAA Sanctions," *ABC News.com*, http://abcnews.go.com/Sports/wireStory?id=10873199, accessed June 11,.2010.

INDEX